That
Woman

Also by Anne Sebba

Samplers: Five Centuries of a Gentle Craft
Enid Bagnold: A Life
Laura Ashley: A Life By Design
Battling for News: Women Reporters from the Risorgimento to
Tiananmen Square
Mother Teresa: Beyond the Image
The Exiled Collector: William Bankes and the Making of an English
Country House
Jennie Churchill: Winston's American Mother

That Woman

The Life of Wallis Simpson, Duchess of Windsor

ANNE SEBBA

St. Martin's Griffin ☙ New York

THAT WOMAN. Copyright © 2011 by Anne Sebba.
All rights reserved. Printed in the United States of America. For information, address
St. Martin's Press, 175 Fifth Avenue, New York, N.Y. 10010.

www.stmartins.com

The Library of Congress has cataloged the hardcover edition as follows:

Sebba, Anne.
   That woman : the life of Wallis Simpson, Duchess of Windsor / Anne Sebba.—1st U.S. ed.
      p. cm.
Includes bibliographical references and index.
   ISBN 978-1-250-00296-9 (hardcover)
   ISBN 978-1-4299-6245-2 (e-book)
   1. Windsor, Wallis Warfield, Duchess of, 1896–1986.   2. Windsor, Edward, Duke
of, 1894–1972—Marriage.   3. Nobility—Great Britain—Biography.   4. Marriages of
royalty and nobility—Great Britain—History—20th century.   I. Title.
   DA581.W5 S43 2012
   941.084092—dc23

2012450027

ISBN 978-1-250-02218-9 (trade paperback)

First published in Great Britain by Weidenfeld & Nicolson,
Orion Publishing Group Ltd, an Hachette UK Company

First St. Martin's Griffin Edition: February 2013

12   11   10   9   8

For Mark . . . Your turn again at last.

Acknowledgements

No one who researches the life of Wallis Simpson can go far without looking at letters between Wallis and Edward, many of which have been edited by Michael Bloch. My first debt is to him for this sterling work which has been an invaluable guide over the last years in my quest to understand Wallis and for allowing me to quote from these. For help with understanding the British political situation in 1936, especially with respect to Stanley Baldwin, I owe an immeasurable debt of gratitude to Professor Philip Williamson, Head of History at Durham University, who has not only given up valuable time to talk through some of the issues and discuss current historical interpretations with me but has also located photocopies of documents far beyond any reasonable expectation of a biographer. I have relished our (for me) all too brief conversations and thank him most warmly for sharing his scholarship with me. I want to thank Aharon Solomons, the son of Ernest Simpson and Mary Kirk, who not only opened up his home in Mexico most generously to me, but set me on a new path to seeing Wallis Simpson and her second husband in a different light. He I thank most warmly for some unforgettable conversations and I also thank Maria-Teresa (MT) Solomons for showing me some letters and photographs. I especially want to thank Pascale Lepeu, Curator of the Cartier Collection, for a wonderfully enjoyable day seeing the Collection and Michele Aliaga at the Cartier Archive for generously making available so many wonderful Cartier images, some of which magnificently enhance this edition. My thanks also go to Erika Bard, who has once again provided me not only with original thoughts about and psychological insights into the behaviour of my subjects but has also given me suggestions for further examination.

There are others whom I would like to thank publicly for enormous generosity and concern for historical accuracy but who have requested anonymity. They know who they are.

I have consulted a number of libraries and archives in the hunt for new material and would particularly like to thank the Master, Fellows and Scholars of Churchill College, Cambridge and the staff of the Churchill Archives Centre especially its Director, Allen Packwood, Natalie Adams, Andrew Riley, Sophie Bridges and Katharine Thomson for their unfailing help and cooperation, especially in trying to ferret out unpublished material, newly released documents or helping me locate those due for reclassification through Freedom of Information requests while I was writing this book. For permission to quote from the Spears Papers, housed at Churchill College, I thank Patrick Aylmer and for permission to quote from the Lascelles Papers also held at Churchill College I thank the Hon. Caroline Erskine.

I also owe a debt to the staff at the National Archives in Kew who made my work more pleasant in innumerable ways and would like especially to mention Mark Dunton who, seeing my dismay at the prospect of consulting endless files on microfilm – so dispiriting for all researchers – encouraged me to seek permission for original documents to be brought up from the vaults including the evocative, leather-bound Cabinet Office minutes and Conclusions to Cabinet Meetings. Seeing the originals in this way adds enormously to any author's 'feel' for the period and an understanding of the drama of events as they unfolded.

The London Library is, as ever, a most wonderful resource and again, its staff have found books that eluded me or books kept on special reserve, as did also the helpful team at the British Library. My days at the Bodleian always seemed to be accompanied by freezing weather and snow, especially testing as the collection was being moved from its permanent home to a temporary building demanding permanently open doors. But here too I encountered warmth from helpful librarians, especially Colin Harris, Helen Langley and Rebecca Wall. At Balliol College, which owns copyright for some of the Monckton Papers, my thanks go to Anna Sander. I must also mention the Highland Park Historical Society, in particular Jean Sogin and Julia Marshall, while Dorothy Hordubay, Joan Jermakian and Judy Smith are just three among the thoughtful and kind staff at Oldfields School, Baltimore, where Gentleness and Courtesy are still the rule. At the Maryland District Historical Society, Marc Thomas has been most helpful. Lambeth Palace Archives have been a delight to discover and my thanks go to the efficient and helpful staff there too. Thanks to the Radcliffe-Schlesinger library for permission to quote from the Hollingsworth-Kirk family archive and to the Osbert Sitwell estate for permission to quote the poem Rat Week. My thanks to Miss Pamela Clark at the Royal Archives for permission to quote from a letter and memorandum from King George VI. In New York I was privileged to meet Kirk Hollingsworth, nephew of Mary Kirk, who cast his mind back many years on my account, went to great trouble to ferret out unpublished material for me (Notes for Lady Donaldson) and grant me permission to publish that for which he owned copyright while pointing out that some comments ascribed to Wallis in these notes were Buckie's memory of what Wallis wrote but that he believed her memory was usually accurate. I have made strenuous attempts to contact all other copyright holders and if there are any I have inadvertently missed I will rectify this in any subsequent editions.

Many others have contributed to my understanding of this complex woman whose story is set against a critical period of world history or have helped me in other ways with my work. I should like to thank Diana Hutchins Angulo, Vicki Anstey, Andrew Barber, Damian Barr, Philp Baty, Francis Beckett, Chris Beetles, Jeremy Bigwood, Xandra Bingley, Marcus Binney, William Boyd, Piers Brendon, Victoria Buresch, Julia Cook, Stephen Cretney, The Lord Crathorne, Guiseppe D'Anna, Andrew Davies, Spencer Doddington, John Entwistle, Jonathan Fenby, Susan Fox, Mark Gaulding, Sir Martin Gilbert, Laura Gillott, Vicky Ginther, Tim Godfray, Veronica Franklin Gould, Vanessa Hall Smith, Fred Hauptfuhrer, Nicholas Haslam, Angela Holdsworth, Dr Christopher Inglefield, Tess Johnston, Hans Jorgensen, Hector Kerr-Smiley, Dixie de Koning, Lee Langley, the late Walter Lees, Jonathan Leiserach, Richard and Midge

Levy, Mary S Lovell, Andrew Lownie, Paul Masai, Neil McKenna, Linda Mortimer, David Metcalfe, Shelagh Montague Brown, Charlotte Mosley, Margan Mulvihill, Pamela Norris, Dr Iain Oswald, John Carleton Paget, Lady Camilla Jessel Panufnik, Della Pascoe, Martin Pick, Michina Ponzone-Pope, Lucy Popescu, David Prest, David Pryce Jones, Jane Ridley, Susan Ronald, Dr Domenico de Sceglie, David Seidler, Harriet Sergeant, William Shawcross, Polly Schomberg, Brian Smouha, Rory Sutherland, Professor Miles Taylor, John Toler, Rose Tremain, Bernard Wasserstein, Esther Weiner, Alison Weir, Kenneth Wolfe, Lindy Woodhead, Philip Ziegler.

A special mention must go to the Ritz hotel, Wallis's favourite haunt and the setting for many important unrecorded conversations in this story. Here I am indebted to Stephen Boxall and Amber Aldred for allowing us to film in their wonderful rooms and of course my thanks to John Stoddart for several terrific photos at the Ritz.

As ever, I owe gratitude to my dynamic agent, Clare Alexander, who always understood what a rewarding project I would find immersing myself in this examination of a woman and period in history. Her colleagues, especially Leah Middleton, Lesley Thorne and Cassie Metcalfe-Slovo, have all looked after me with concern and interest. Simon Berthon, too, has been excited by this story from the outset and immediately recognised the significance of the new material which was both heartening and stimulating. I have benefited enormously from discussions with him about *That Woman* over the past years and months. Peter James, my copy editor, deserves a special thank you for his unrivalled clarity of vision and for nobly giving up his weekends for *That Woman*. I am fortunate that once again Douglas Matthews has been prepared to offer his matchless indexing skills, and I thank him for this. At Weidenfeld & Nicolson, Alan Samson, Martha Ashby and Elizabeth Allen have displayed equal amounts of enthusiasm, inspiration and dedication, which have made working on the final stages of *That Woman* the sort of pleasure and delight which have made me the envy of my colleagues.

At the risk of embarrassing my family I must thank them all publicly for assistance of many kinds, especially technical. My children – Adam, Amy and Imogen – all have full lives and there have been times when my absence for research has been less than helpful. But above all heartfelt thanks to my husband, Mark Sebba, who, in addition to constant emotional support, has given me the key to open many doors into the world of fashion which Wallis would have relished.

In spite of freely acknowledging all the help I have received from those named above, any errors in the following pages are of course my own.

Contents

List of Illustrations

Severn Teackle Wallis (Author's own)
House at Blue Ridge (International News Photo/Corbis)
Wallis and Alice Montague (Getty Images)
Solomon Davies Warfield (State Archives of Florida)
Alice Montague alone (Corbis)
Wallis leaving Oldfields (Oldfields School, Baltimore)
House on Biddle Street (Getty Images)
Wallis wearing monocle (Oldfields School, Baltimore)
Earl Winfield Spencer Jr. (US Naval History and Heritage Command)
Wallis as a debutante (International News Photo/Corbis)
Wallis as Win's bride (Getty Images)
Mrs Wallis Spencer and Lt Alberto Da Zara (Diana Hutchins Angulo)
Wallis in the blue tiara (Cartier Archives)
Three generations of royalty (Corbis)
The young Prince of Wales (Corbis)
Mr and Mrs Ernest Spencer at court (Private collection)
Wallis and Edward on the *Nahlin* cruise (Corbis)
Wallis looking pensive (Getty Images)
Bracelet of crosses (Cartier Archives/Louis Tirilly)
Married at last (Corbis)
Wallis, Edward and Hitler (Getty)
Mary Kirk (International News Photo/Corbis)
Duke, Duchess and Fruity Metcalfe (Getty)
Wallis making up packages for the troops (Getty)
Duke and Duchess on their way to the Bahamas (Corbis)
Wallis in Red Cross uniform (Getty)

Wallis and Eleanor Roosevelt (Associated Press)
Duke with Queen Mary (Corbis)
The new Mr and Mrs Ernest Simpson (Private collection)
One of Ernest's personal favourites (Private collection)
The house in the Bois-de-Boulogne (Getty)
Reception in Miami by Jack Levine (Hirshhorn Musuem & Sculpture
    Garden, Smithsonian Institute, gift of Joseph J. Hirshhorn, 1966)
Wallis taking charge (both Corbis)
Duke, Duchess and Ben Hogan (courtesy of the Greenbrier Hotel)
Duke and Duchess dancing (courtesy of the Greenbrier Hotel)
A selection of Wallis's Cartier jewels and original sketches (Cartier
    Archives)
Duchess at the New Lido Revue (Getty)
Duchess and Aileen Plunkett (Getty)
Wallis at Queen Mary centenary commemoration (Corbis)
Frail Duke leaving a London clinic (Corbis)
Duke's funeral, 5 June 1972 (Corbis)
Duchess looking haggard (Getty)
Duchess's funeral, 30 April 1986 (Getty)

That
Woman

Preface

In 1973 I was invited to spend a weekend as the guest of a minor Austrian aristocrat at a magnificent castle just outside Vienna – Schloss Enzesfeld.

The name was resonant but I was twenty-one and unprepared for how deeply the emotional history of the castle would seep into me. I was greeted on arrival by an array of liveried servants who, over the next three days, provided for my every demand, as well as several I could never have anticipated. Dinner was elaborately – and terrifyingly – formal, served in a baronial dining hall for a handful of guests, who included the ageing German actor Kurt Jürgens. The waiters stood stiffly in the corners of the room as I played with my *foie gras*. The rest of the meal passed in a haze. Then I was led along a cold stone passageway to my bedroom, a ten-minute walk away. The next morning the man who had invited me, my own small-scale Princeling, drove me around the estate and gave me a detailed history. I had entered an unknown and hitherto unknowable world. Although I had just started working as a journalist for Reuters, this was not a story for the wires. I could not find words to write about what I had seen and was experiencing. I lacked both the context and the emotional maturity. But I knew instinctively that I was playing with fire, how smoothly such luxury – and we are talking here about Hermès scarves not Cartier jewels – could permeate the pores of my life. I have thought about those three days many times since and never once regretted my decision not to see my Prince Charming again.

Less than forty years before, this castle had been the refuge for a former British monarch, henceforth known as the Duke of Windsor, immediately after his abdication from the British throne. Eugène de Rothschild and his wife Kitty had offered it to him as he waited, bored and with mounting nervous tension, for the woman he loved to become his wife.

He had left his country plunged into a deep constitutional crisis. No one knew what the outcome would be as Europe bristled with threats of war. Yet his concern, as he paced the corridors of the castle at Enzesfeld, was to fill his bedroom with dozens of photographs of this woman. He telephoned her several times a day, at considerable expense, to the château in France where she was similarly imprisoned. Phone lines were primitive, so they had to shout at each other, and many people were close enough to be listening, as well as some who were paid to listen in. Lawyers insisted they must not meet or the divorce might be jeopardized. He passed the hours knitting a sweater for his love. She, in turn, sent him dozens of letters lamenting the situation in which she found herself and longing for the time when she had the protection of his name. This was, unquestionably, not a scenario she had foreseen. Christmas came and went and the Duke, the increasingly heavy bags under his eyes telling the world that he was hardly sleeping, morosely attended church in the village of Enzesfeld. When his hostess, Kitty de Rothschild, left the castle the Duke failed even to say goodbye. He was still without the woman he had told the world he loved, the woman for whom he had given up a kingdom, the woman who still had two living husbands, the woman for whom he had sent himself into this hellish exile.

Forty years later the scenery of the castle remains as sharply engraved in my brain as ever. Those who know only one thing about British history in the 1930s know about the king who abdicated because he could not continue without the help and support of 'the woman I love'. Yet many people cannot imagine who such a woman could be, one who could exert such a powerful magnetic force on a man groomed from birth to do his duty as head not just of Britain but of a great empire that stretched from India to Canada and Australia – the Dominions, as they were then known.

Because they cannot imagine such a woman they have invented an image of her, a process which began in 1936 and which gathered pace in the ensuing half-century. In the pages that follow I want to examine whether that picture is still valid in the twenty-first century. I want to let her own voice speak wherever possible, however 'rasping', as her detractors insist it was. It may not always be a sympathetic voice but it will, I hope, help readers understand what it was in her background or make-up that caused her to act or speak as she did. I hope to humanize rather than demonize the woman known as Wallis Simpson, to see her within her own social, historical and geographical context. Very simply, I want to start by understanding what sort of woman she was and then look at the crisis in which she was embroiled.

Money is often an important part of this story, but in the text I have always quoted the actual, contemporary amounts. As a very rough guide these figures can be multiplied by fifty to give an idea of the value today.

1

Becoming Wallis

'She has the Warfield look'

Choosing your own name is the supreme act of self-creation. Wallis, the androgynous and unusual name she insisted on for herself, is a bold statement of identity. 'Wallis' is saying not only this is who I am but you will know no one else like me. Take me on my own terms. It was a credo she lived by.

From the start this woman fashioned herself as something strong, intriguing, distinctive. In taking such a name she was constructing an identity, giving herself from a young age freedom that women of her era could not take for granted. She was displaying a contempt for tradition and the ordinary which would be so crucial to her destiny. Having chosen her own name she had to work hard to live up to it, to create a strong relationship with it. Although her surname changed many times, this name was one of the few constants in her life. 'Hi, I'm Wallis,' she would say when she entered a room.

The name her parents chose for her was 'Bessiewallis', to honour both her mother's beloved sister Bessie and her grandfather's illustrious friend Severn Teackle Wallis, an author and legislator and, in Baltimore, an important man. The latter had been imprisoned for a time during the Civil War, along with Wallis's grandfather, for supporting a call for secession from the Union, but was later appointed provost at the University of Maryland. Her own father, too, bore this man's name. His statue stands today at one end of Mount Vernon Square, the city's main plaza, overshadowed though it is by the imposing 178-foot-high monument of George Washington in the centre, the first erected in the first President's honour. But she soon jettisoned 'Bessie', describing it as a name fit only for cows.

'Wallis', however, was a man's name for a woman who could hold her own with men.

Wallis was never a woman's woman. She wanted to be something out of the ordinary for a woman. She was funny, clever, smart – in both the English and American uses of the term. She wanted to pit her wits not against other women but against men in a man's world. With her sharp understanding of appearances, she always knew the importance of a name. Of course she had seen her mother change from 'Alys' to 'Alice'. But that was subtle, gentle, barely noticeable. Choosing Wallis in her youth was as much part of her armour as the carefully selected designer clothes and decor of her middle years. When inviting friends to her third wedding, her husband-to-be, the ex-King, a man with even more names to accommodate, suddenly started referring to her as 'Mrs Warfield'. This was a name she had never owned, nor could claim any right to. She encouraged it to shield the man she had dragged along in her wake.

Defining herself by her name was one of the first acts of a young girl intent on controlling a cold and often unfriendly world. Whenever Wallis succeeded, she felt most at peace. But for much of her life she was dependent on the charity of others and this led to long bouts of unhappiness to which she responded in a variety of ways.

There is no birth certificate for Wallis. It was not a legal require-ment at the time to have one in Pennsylvania, where she was born amid some secrecy and scandal probably on 19 June 1896. Nor was there a newspaper announcement of her birth. The place where she was born, however, is not in doubt: a small wooden building known as Square Cottage at the back of the Monterey Inn in the summer resort of Blue Ridge Summit. The Blue Ridge Summit community, at the top of the South Mountain at Monterey Pass, was in its heyday as a fashionable spa and holiday area at the beginning of the twentieth century, after the introduction of the railroad in 1872. Blue Ridge Summit strays into four counties – two on the Pennsylvania side of the line and two on the Maryland side – and straddles the historic Mason–Dixon line, significantly giving Wallis aspects of both the

South and North of the United States in her make-up. This was something she was to make much of later.

Her parents had gone there ostensibly to escape the heat of a Baltimore summer and in the hope of improving her father's health, but also because they were in flight from disapproving families. In her memoirs, Wallis is vague about the marriage of her parents, the consumptive Teackle Wallis Warfield and the spirited if flighty Alice Montague, a marriage neither family wanted.

'Without taking their families into their confidence, they slipped away and were married, according to one story in a church in Washington, according to another in a church in Baltimore,' Wallis wrote sixty years later. She would have us believe that Teackle and Alice were married in June 1895 when both were twenty-six years old. But, more likely, the marriage had been solemnized just seven months before her birth, on 19 November 1895, as a monograph on the Church of St Michael and All Angels in Baltimore states. According to this account, Dr C. Ernest Smith, the Rector, was called upon to officiate at a quiet marriage which attracted little attention at the time. 'On that day Teackle Wallis Warfield took as his bride Miss Alice M. Montague, a communicant of the parish. The ceremony took place not in the main church itself but in the rectory at 1929 St Paul Street in the presence of several friends.'

This version makes it seem that the marriage was arranged as soon as Alice realized she was pregnant, that the first and only child of the union was most probably conceived out of wedlock and that neither family attended. Perhaps, more significantly, it also indicates there was never a time in Wallis's life when she did not have to harbour secrets.

Wallis, with an attempt at insouciance, wrote later in her own account of how she once asked her mother for the date and time of her birth 'and she answered impatiently that she had been far too busy at the time to consult the calendar let alone the clock'. But the child may also have arrived prematurely, as the family doctor was not available and the twenty-two-year-old, newly qualified Dr Lewis Miles Allen received an emergency call from the Monterey Inn and delivered the baby in Alice's hotel bedroom.

The Warfields and the Montagues, although both shared impeccable Southern credentials and both were supporters of the Confederacy during the Civil War, did not get on. Both came from ancient and respected stock and traced their arrival in America to the seventeenth century. There is a much trumpeted mention of the Warfields in the Domesday Book and one of Wallis's ancestors, Pagan de Warfield, is said to have accompanied William the Conqueror from France and fought in the Battle of Hastings. The Montagues, similarly, hailed from an old English aristocratic family that arrived in America in 1621 when one Peter Montague left Buckinghamshire and settled on land in Virginia granted him by King Charles I. Wallis always felt proud of her ancestry and had reason to. 'For those who are prepared to accept that there can be class distinctions of any kind in the United States,' wrote the social commentator Alastair Forbes in the mid-1970s, 'she can be said to come from a far higher stratum than say Princess Grace of Monaco, Jacqueline Bouvier or the Jerome or Vanderbilt ladies of the nineteenth century. By present English standards of birth she might rank rather below two recent royal duchesses and rather above two others.' But the Montagues, whatever their past prosperity as landowners, were no longer prosperous. They were much livelier than the politically and commercially active Warfields, whom they considered to be nouveau. They believed that their beautiful and vivacious Alice could have held out for a much better match than marriage to Teackle Wallis. The solemn Warfield clan in their turn not only looked down on the Montagues, they worried that Teackle Wallis would never be strong enough to support a wife and therefore should not seek one.

T. Wallis, as he styled himself, was the youngest of four brothers (the first, Daniel, had died young) and two daughters born to Henry Mactier Warfield and his wife Anna Emory. The Emorys were physicians and, like so many upper-class Marylanders, slave owners whose sympathies were Southern. Dr Emory joined the Confederate army as a surgeon and was stationed in Richmond, Virginia until the end of the war. The eldest surviving son, Solomon Davies Warfield, was a successful and prominent banker, president of the Continental Trust company (the premier investment company in Baltimore in that era), and a millionaire bachelor who kept an apartment on New York's Fifth Avenue where he was said to entertain his mistresses. The second son, Richard Emory Warfield, lived in Philadelphia and was thriving in the insurance business, while the fourth, Henry Warfield, had a farm at Timonium in Baltimore County.

Teackle was always frail but at eighteen, when he fell ill with consumption (tuberculosis), it was decided that, instead of sending him to recuperate at a sanatorium or in a more favourable climate, he should work as a lowly clerk in his uncle's Continental Trust in Baltimore, an environment not chosen to assuage his illness but which the family presumably hoped would draw attention away from such embarrassing debility. Little was known in the nineteenth century about cures for or reasons for contracting consumption, although its bacterial cause was eventually isolated in 1882. There was no definitive treatment for the disease until the mid-twentieth century. At the time of Wallis's birth, it was not only widespread but considered shameful, partly since it was thought to be a disease of poverty. Death was the likely outcome for at least 80 per cent of patients. Usually, after a horrific period of night sweats, chills and paroxysmal coughing, the disease spread to other organs of the body, leading to the wasting away which gave the disease its name. It was not surprising therefore that Teackle Wallis, a charmingly sensitive but melancholy consumptive, should have appeared a disastrous prospect for the Montague parents – William, who worked in insurance, and his wife, Mary Anne. Indeed medical advice at the time, which must surely have been offered by the Warfield doctor, was to avoid cohabiting with women for fear of spreading the disease. Those around TB patients were exposed to danger with each breath, as the bacillus is spread by droplet infection, mainly by coughing and sneezing, and inhaled droplets lodge in and infect the lungs.

Yet something powerfully attractive about T. Wallis Warfield must have appealed to the courageous and headstrong young Alice Montague. According to their only daughter, the deep-set staring eyes suggested a handsome poet, but they may instead have been indicative of the far-gone ravages of his disease. By the end of the summer of 1896, Teackle was a deeply sick and weak man. But he decided to move his family back to the centre of Baltimore and installed them in a residential hotel, the Brexton,[1] where he hoped if the worst happened they might be able to fend for themselves. This red-brick building containing eight small apartments was the only home Wallis ever shared with her father and mother.

As a frail, wheelchair invalid Teackle was allowed one photograph with his child. He died five months after her birth on 15 November 1896. According to family lore his last words were 'I'm afraid, Alice, she has the Warfield look. Let us hope that in spirit she'll be like you.' Her penetrating blue eyes, always said to be her best feature, came from her mother, and perhaps her spirit did too. From her father she inherited dark hair but no capital and an embedded fear of insecurity.

Baltimore at the time of Wallis's childhood was one of the fastest-growing, most economically vibrant cities in the United States. From the beginning of the nineteenth century, northern Baltimore attracted many wealthy families who lived in substantial three- or even four-storey houses that were being built around Mount Vernon when this was still a relatively rural fashionable residential district. As a port city, located on the northern Chesapeake Bay, Baltimore was well positioned to make a rapid recovery from the physical and economic damage inflicted by the Civil War, embarking during the reconstruction era on the period of its greatest prosperity. The city, attractive to both immigrants and investors between the 1880s and 1914, was home to large and complex populations of Italian, Polish, German, Irish and Chinese immigrants, as well as many thousands of East European Jews fleeing pogroms, political turmoil and poverty. Most Jews settled in East Baltimore, especially the Lombard Street area, and remained economically marginalized for at least one generation. Here, among

---

1 In 2009 this newly restored building reopened, trading on its connections with Wallis Warfield but refurbished in a splendid style which she would not have recognized.

the dozens of chicken coops with live chickens on the street, the aroma of pickling spices and the noise of clanking buckets, Yiddish greetings and kosher butchers, the Warfields and Montagues would have been most unlikely to venture.

But living in a city where at least one-third of the residents are foreign born reinforces notions of separation, especially among those who see themselves as poor relations, which Wallis and her mother clearly were. In addition during Wallis's childhood, forty or so years after the abolition of slavery, racial segregation was still practised in Baltimore, as it was in many Southern American cities. So deciding where young Wallis Warfield would live and would go to school was a matter of deep concern to her wider family.

Within a few weeks Anna Emory Warfield, the sixty-year-old matriarch of the family, invited her daughter-in-law and grand-daughter to live with her at 34 East Preston Street, a large and solid four-storey brownstone in the centre of the old part of the city, near the Monument. This staid and peaceful house of adults became home for the next four or five years. Wallis recognized later what a disturbing influence she must have been there. Her grandmother, whom she loved, took her shopping every Saturday to Richmond Market, 'as exciting as a trip to the moon'. Going to market was an important outing for the rich matrons of Baltimore. They dressed up for it and wore white gloves – after all they would not be touching anything. The servants who walked a discreet distance behind them carried out the purchasing.

Her grandmother – 'a solitary figure in a vast, awesomely darkened room, rocking evenly to and fro . . . and so erect that her back never seemed to touch the chair' – was, as Wallis recalled, in mourning and wore black dresses with high collars and a tiny white linen cap on which were stitched three small bows of black ribbon. ' "Bessiewallis," my grandmother would say severely, "how will you ever grow up to be a lady unless you learn to keep your back straight?" Or "Bessie-wallis, can't you be still for just a minute?" '

But her uncle Sol, a more terrifying presence for the young and not so young child, lived there too. Solomon Davies Warfield, the financier and politician whose hopes to become mayor of Baltimore were not realized, had to make do with the locally prestigious but lesser position as postmaster. He funded Wallis's childhood but in a cruelly controlling manner, the lessons of which cannot have been lost on this young girl given that she took the trouble to report his behaviour in her memoirs. Every month he deposited a sum of money in his sister-in-law's account at his bank. 'The trouble was that the amount was almost never the same. One month it might be quite enough to take care of the important bills, the next month barely enough to cover the rent.'

Uncle Sol's bedroom was at the back of the third floor with a private bath. Alice had a room on the same floor at the front, and connecting with it was a small room for Wallis. The arrangement was awkward for Alice and her daughter, who had to use her grandmother's bathroom on the floor below. But the idyll, if idyll it was, did not last. 'A subtly disturbing situation seems to have helped precipitate the separation,' Wallis wrote. She speculates that her uncle fell in love with her mother. 'She was young and attractive, living under the same roof, and she and uncle Sol were inevitably thrown much together.' At all events he must have made overtures that either Alice or old Mrs Warfield considered inappropriate.

So the pair returned to the Brexton residential hotel. There followed a deeply unhappy period for Wallis of meals alone with her mother 'and rather forlorn afternoon excursions to the house on Preston Street about which had so suddenly descended a mysterious and disturbing barrier'. Funds were now sometimes so low that her mother sold embroidery at the local Women's Exchange shop. But her mother's newly widowed sister, Aunt Bessie Merryman, then stepped in and invited the pair to live with her. Her own husband, Uncle Buck, had also died young and, childless herself, it suited her to have company. Wallis grew to love Aunt Bessie as a mother. Yet, although the sisters got on, Alice was determined to make one last stab at independence. She moved into the Preston Apartment House, a less than sumptuous set of rooms in the shadow of her Warfield family, and this time tried to make money inviting the other tenants in the block to become paying dinner guests. It was a disastrous experiment in every way. The prime sirloin steak, soft-shell crabs and elaborate pastries were never costed, but the damage this venture did to the reputation of mother and daughter, now branded as boarding-house keepers, was incalculable. These years of struggle and insecurity, when 'mother had the café and was forever working herself to death to give me things', were implanted so deeply in Wallis's psyche that she never entirely shed her worry and fear of what might lie around the corner. Once again it was her aunt Bessie who came to the rescue by insisting on disbanding the dubious operation.

Wallis went to her first school while living with Aunt Bessie. It was called Miss O'Donnell's after its founder, Miss Ada O'Donnell. Next, aged ten, she attended Arundell Girls School on nearby St Paul Street, neither the most exclusive nor the most expensive educational establishment, but a place of calm routine for girls of good backgrounds. There she would have learned, as every Baltimore school girl learned, the story of Elizabeth (Betsy) Patterson, a local girl from a wealthy family who married her prince but was not allowed to remain married to him. On a visit to America in 1803, Jérôme Bonaparte, brother of Napoleon Bonaparte, met and married Betsy. But Jérôme was a minor and his brother refused to recognize the marriage. When Jérôme returned to France in 1805, his wife was forbidden to land and went first to England, where her son, Jerome Napoleon Bonaparte, known as 'Bo', was born. In 1806 Napoleon issued a state decree of annulment to end his brother's marriage, and Betsy was given a large annual pension but, rather than return to 'what I hated most on earth – my Baltimore obscurity', she lived unhappily in exile in Paris for the rest of her life. Wallis never referred to the story in her memoirs.

Wallis had to take her monthly school reports to Uncle Sol for inspection – a further reminder that her dependence on his charity was not to be taken for granted. However, he did oblige with her next important request – that she be allowed to go to Oldfields for her final two years of education, the most expensive school in Maryland. Oldfields, just beyond the Gunpowder River in Glencoe County, was founded in 1867 in the hills beyond Timonium where Wallis had already spent many happy summers with her Warfield cousins. Although she had been parcelled out to all her cousins at various times, Pot Spring, the home of her uncle Emory and her aunt Betty Warfield, not far from Oldfields, was a favourite summer refuge. The school's 200-acre site was beautiful and today remains largely undeveloped countryside. For many years, a handsome coach and horses took students back and forth from Glencoe station, past the *ante bellum* white clapboard mansions and large plantation houses which had once housed hundreds of slaves.

The legendary co-principal of Oldfields was Anna McCulloh, called Miss Nan by all the pupils, a woman not unlike Grandmother Warfield who rigidly upheld her notion of the correct way to behave. Wallis had become a keen and athletic basketball player in her teens, encouraged by a young teacher, Charlotte Noland, who offered afternoon basketball session three times a week in a rented Baltimore garage. Miss Noland was, for the young Wallis, an ideal woman, 'a mixture of gay, deft teasing and a drill sergeant's sternness ... cultivated of manner, a marvellous horsewoman and a dashing figure in every setting'. Miss Noland's sister, Rosalie Noland, also taught at Oldfields, which was noted for its sporting and equestrian facilities, and Wallis, like Charlotte Noland, was a skilled horsewoman not afraid to tackle jumps nor to challenge others with whom she was riding. At Oldfields, basketball was deeply competitive, the girls keen to go out before breakfast to practise. Yet in these sports, as in everything else at the school, the competitive spirit was to some extent reined in by the simple expedient of dividing the girls into two teams, one named 'Gentleness' and the other 'Courtesy'. 'Gentleness and Courtesy' was the first rule in the Oldfields handbook, as the sign on the door of each child's room proclaimed. Wallis represented 'Gentleness', who flourished a white banner with green lettering; 'Courtesy' had a green banner with white lettering. In addition to sport and etiquette, acting and drama was encouraged and in one surviving photograph Wallis is dressed as a New Jersey mosquito, alongside a classmate impersonating Governor Woodrow Wilson, echoing a hot political issue of the day.[2]

---

2 In 1912, Governor Woodrow Wilson signed the country's first mosquito-control law which declared malaria a reportable disease.

The school fostered an aura of old-fashioned calm anchored by a set of old-fashioned rules. These rules were concerned with how to stand as well as how to behave. There was a Bible-reading group, and the school imposed an honour system on the sixty or so girls whereby each was meant to report her own misdeeds, such as talking or visiting each other's rooms after lights out or communicating by letter with a boy.

Wallis is said to have misbehaved by smoking, which was seriously frowned upon, and by jumping from a balcony to meet a boy. Such misdeeds are not recorded in the school annals and it just may be that rumours arose through what she later became. However, at the time she was clearly audacious, a daredevil ringleader never afraid to set the pace, a tomboy. She had at least one boyfriend by the time she went to Oldfields. He was Carter Osburn, son of a Baltimore bank president, who later gave an account that may have been the source of the rumours. His father owned a car which he was allowed to borrow. 'At a certain point in the road I'd stop, she spotted it. She'd slip out. I don't know yet how she managed it but as far as I know she never got caught; she not only got out [of Oldfields] but she also got back in without being observed. She was very independent in spirit, adhering to the conventions only for what they were worth and not for their own sake. Those dates were all the more exciting for being forbidden.' At the same time Wallis was writing to another boy telling him she hoped to go into town from time to time but how lovely it would be if he could come and visit. This was striking behaviour for a refined young lady with aspirations to enter society in the early part of the twentieth century. For a teenager at an elite establishment like Oldfields it was shocking. Some parents at the time believed that there was something extraordinary about Wallis Warfield and that her influence was malign.

By contrast, another student of that era described a rather more typical day as one that involved:

Getting up as late as possible ... starting our dressing modestly under both nighties and kimonos. Then we dashed out of our rooms to wash, crowds of us all trying to use the basins ... invariably the water stopped running completely whereupon we banged loudly on the pipes to notify the bold souls who had descended to the first floor and were getting all the water that they must stop. Then back to our rooms where we continued dressing still under cover of the kimonos.

Such rampant modesty is hardly a surprise in a girls' boarding school of the time. But the desire to be thin is more surprising and Miss Nan thought it dangerously unnecessary. She told the girls she knew they were taking doses of cod-liver oil in order to lose weight and ordered all those who had some in their possession to turn it over immediately to the infirmary. (This is according to a book Wallis later accused her best friend of having written under a pseudonym.)

Going to Oldfields in 1912 was especially important for Wallis. In the first place her mother had recently remarried and now lived part of the time in Atlanta. Alice Warfield's second husband was John Freeman Rasin, the wealthy but somewhat indolent son of the Democratic Party leader of Baltimore. The thirty-seven-year-old Rasin, who had not been married before, was already suffering from a variety of alcohol-induced ailments. Although he delivered financial security at last to mother and daughter, he could never replace the lost father figure that Wallis permanently mourned. And for a girl who had hitherto been the centre of a small adult world – her mother, grandmother and aunt – to find that someone else had replaced her in her mother's affections was a bitter blow. Aunt Bessie, always a more suitable figure as far as Baltimore society was concerned, now became her closest adviser.

Secondly, Oldfields was where her best friend Mary Kirk, a girl she had just met at Burrland, an exclusive summer camp near Middleburg, Virginia, was already a pupil. Mary's parents, Edith and Henry Child Kirk, were well born if not exactly rich, with a house full of servants. Samuel Kirk and Son were the oldest silversmiths in the United States, established in 1817, descendants of English silversmiths in Derbyshire and also of Sir Francis Child, Lord Mayor of London, who in 1669 founded the Child Banking House. The firm was known for its ornate repoussé silverware and a set of its heavily embossed flatware was, by the late nineteenth century, to be found in most well-to-do Baltimore families. Kirk and Son dominated the competition and set the style for decoration on fine silver throughout the nation.

Mary was the extremely pretty middle daughter, born the same year as Wallis and sandwiched in between an elder sister Edith Buckner, always known as 'Buckie', and a younger, Anne, born in 1901. The girls' grandfather had paid a release fee in order not to have to fight during the Civil War. This was a not uncommon practice but according to Anne, 'all my life I have been ashamed of this act of my grandfather's ... I am sure that our social status was greatly reduced by my grandfather's act which might be construed as bribery or (even worse in those days) cowardice.'

Mary and Wallis, just a few months apart in age, became close friends immediately. Buckie, being three years older, took a more measured view of her sister's new friend and remembered her as 'the amusing, vivacious girl who so often made us laugh and was always on tiptoe for any gaiety that might be forthcoming. She had a special talent for describing a person or an incident with a twist or a wisecrack that almost invariably made it entertaining.' She added, 'Both girls were boy-crazy, and both were far more interested in clothes than in school. Also, each girl had discovered at teenage parties that she had only to enter a room to be instantly surrounded by boys in droves.' Wallis, aged fifteen, was already aware of her magnetic power to attract boys and her first real beau was Lloyd Tabb, a boy she had met at summer camp who drove an exciting red Lagonda sports car. For him, she forced herself to be interested in football and he never forgot the effect. Her ability to make others feel how talented they were was a technique she honed over the years. Helpfully, Lloyd was always accompanied by his slightly older brother, Prosser Tabb, which meant that Wallis and Mary could go out on double dates, a practice that may have been intended to calm the adults and that set a pattern for the future.

The Kirk parents, far from being calmed, were from the first wary of this intense new friendship. Wallis was in and out of the

Kirk house as if she were a member of the family, as even the extended Kirk family could not fail to notice. She took to telephoning her new friend constantly – the telephone still something of a novelty and using it regularly a daring activity for a teenager. Wallis used it so recklessly that, as Anne recalled, her parents would mutter whenever she called that her motives were suspect. Mary's family clearly saw Wallis as an instigator of trouble, even if they could not quite pinpoint what sort of trouble. 'Sometimes when "old black John" announced to "Miss Mary" that "Miss Wallis" was on the phone he would grin and steal a sympathetic look at the frustrated expressions on the faces of our parents,' wrote Anne. Father would then say in a helpless kind of way to Mary, 'Won't you tell John to tell her that we are eating dinner?' John, a loyal servant in the Kirk family for generations – so loyal that he did not live with the Kirk household but walked twelve miles a day to arrive in time to serve breakfast – did what he could to pacify Miss Wallis and the Kirk parents. But the calls usually went ahead and the Kirk dinner hour was deprived of its serenity. 'As my parents discussed the problems of Wallis Warfield it always seemed that you (Mary) were in the midst of some plot with Wallis. She was a problem and no fun for anyone except YOU!'

Wallis had undertaken a campaign of persuasion begging her uncle Sol to pay for her to go to Oldfields. In doing so she was already making a clear choice without necessarily understanding the consequences: she would depend for the rest of her life on a man for security rather than pursuing a career for herself that would earn her money. She said later that she did not give a moment's thought to further education 'as not a single girl from my class at Oldfields went to college'. That was not exactly true. Oldfields did prepare some girls for careers and for limited independence and from its earliest days prided itself on its curriculum almost as much as on the social standing of its pupils. Miss Nan's school was one of the first to offer a high school degree to women. Nor is it exactly true to say that no one in her social circle went to college. Both Mary Kirk's sisters did: Anne to the Peabody Conservatory, graduating with a teacher's certificate in piano, Buckie to the prestigious Bryn Mawr, afterwards becoming an art editor and published writer who worked all her life as well as bringing up a family.

But Uncle Sol may have needed little persuasion. The Warfield clan no doubt hoped that a spell at this prestigious boarding school, which attracted daughters of wealthy industrialists as well as those descended from a select group of early Dutch settlers such as Julia Douw, daughter of John Douw, Mayor of Annapolis, Maryland at the time, might quell some of the young girl's more rebellious and dangerous attributes. Julia became a friend of Wallis and, like her, was to marry a naval officer. But Wallis's best friend remained Mary Kirk. Mary and Wallis were room mates 'and at school we swore eternal friendship ... in contrast to the usual boarding school loyalties ours did indeed continue'. That is Wallis's later version for public consumption. Mary, in private, was to have a dramatically different story to tell. What is not in doubt is that the two teenage girls did everything together, especially gossiping – everyone commented on that. Buckie recalled that even then the girls' main topic of conversation was 'the absorbing subject of marriage. On this score I remember very well a remark that Wallis made a number of times, even I think at our family dinner table – it was memorable because so unconventional. She would announce that the man she married would have to have lots of money – the kind of thing that "nice girls" did not say.'

In the spring of 1914, Mary and Wallis graduated from Oldfields following a traditional May Day ceremony which included a maypole dance on the vast Oldfields lawns presided over by a May queen – a role filled that year by their friend, Renée du Pont, heiress of the famous chemical family whose wealth, principally derived from the manufacture of gunpowder, had expanded dramatically during the Civil War years.

When Wallis signed the Oldfields leavers' book she wrote auspiciously 'All is Love' against her name. The remark jumps off the page. Other girls scribbled: 'It's the little things that count,' 'Three cheers for Oldfields,' or similarly prosaic pronouncements. But, whatever they wrote, the graduation class of 1914 was largely oblivious to the looming war in Europe, preferring to concentrate on matters closer to home: their high hopes for an exciting future with a hand-some man.

Mary and Wallis both became debutantes, an essential prerequisite in the hunt for a suitable husband from the right social background. But by December 1914, when they made their official debut into Baltimore high society at the first Monday German – the name for the coming-out balls given by the exclusive Bachelors' Cotillion Club – the war in Europe was impossible to ignore. Baltimore's debutantes that year were asked to sign a public pledge that they would abstain for the duration of the war from 'rivalry in elegance in respective [sic] social functions'. Such a pledge almost suited Wallis since by this time she and her mother were living together once again in somewhat straitened circumstances in a small apartment near Preston Street following the sudden death in 1913 of Alice's husband John Rasin. He and Alice had been married for just five years. Released from school to attend the funeral, Wallis was pained to see her mother reduced to 'a dark shadow': 'enveloped in a black crepe veil that fell to her knees she looked so tiny and pathetic that my heart broke'. Now it meant looking once more to her Warfield relations if she was to be launched with any style at all and, although Uncle Sol pressed $20 into her hand – two crumpled ten-dollar bills, as she graphically recounted – for a dress, many of her clothes were made by her mother or by a local seamstress called Ellen according to Wallis's own designs.

'If you don't go to the Cotillion, you're nothing. And if you do, it's so boring,' Wallis said later. 'The thing about Maryland is . . . they're the biggest snobs in the world. They never went anywhere outside of Maryland.' Yet go to the Cotillion she must, and she had to follow the rules; wearing white was *de rigueur*. But the dramatic style chosen by Wallis was a copy of a dress she had spotted being worn by the popular Broadway star Irene Castle – white satin covered with a loose chiffon knee-length tunic which respectably veiled her shoulders and ended in a band of pearly embroidery. It was made by Ellen and in between the endless rounds of debutante lunches, teas and chitchat, Wallis and her mother made several visits by street car to Ellen for fittings. For her escort at the ball she safely chose a cousin. Henry

Warfield, aged twenty-seven, came to collect her in her uncle Sol's Pierce Arrow, lent for the occasion, and presented her with a magnificent bouquet of American beauty roses; and after an evening being whirled around by a variety of partners she was officially 'out'. But where exactly was 'out'?

If she wanted her own party, customarily given for a debutante by her father, Uncle Sol would have to fund that. She asked. He refused, citing the war in Europe as an excuse. He told Wallis he had no spare money to spend on frivolities and that every dollar he could spare had to go to help the British and the French in their struggle against the Germans.

Devastated, she accepted whatever invitations came her way, wore whatever corsages were sent her and made a splash wherever she could, for example being the only one in the room on one occasion wearing a blue dress. Wallis, never classically pretty but always well dressed and charming, was widely agreed to be one of the most popular debutantes of the season. But the inevitable anticlimax around the end of the year was made worse in her case by the death of her Warfield grandmother, which demanded a period of serious mourning just when Wallis intended serious party-going. So, when an invitation arrived from one of her mother's cousins, the beautiful Corinne Mustin, suggesting that Wallis come and stay with her in Pensacola, Florida, Wallis seized on the suggestion. Corinne and her sister, Lelia Montague Barnett, the latter married to the general commanding the US Marine Corps at Wakefield in Virginia, had both extended frequent invitations at critical times to Wallis to come and stay. Lelia had even hosted a debutante party for Wallis in Washington. Wallis felt warmly towards them both and vividly remembered Corinne's wedding to the then thirty-three-year-old pioneer air pilot Henry Mustin in 1907 as one of the most glamorous events of her childhood. Now the Mustins had three children of their own and Henry, a captain in the US Navy, had recently been appointed commandant of the new Pensacola Air Station. There were family conclaves to decide if Wallis could accept or if her acceptance would be perceived as typical Montague gaiety in the face of Warfield mourning. Eventually it was agreed she could go on the grounds that she needed to see more of the world than Baltimore. After all, everyone knew the place was swarming with virile young aviators.

She arrived, aged nineteen, in April 1916 and within twenty-four hours had written to her mother: 'I have just met the world's most fascinating aviator.' The day after her arrival cousin Corinne had organized a lunch with three fellow officers. Wallis got on well with Corinne, who always referred to her younger cousin as 'Skinny' – a nickname she liked. Later she suspected that Corinne, herself married to a strong and silent older man, may have deliberately selected these men for her:

> Shortly before noon, as Corinne and I were sitting on the porch, I saw Henry Mustin rounding the corner deep in conversation with a young officer and followed closely by two more ... they were tanned and lean. But as they drew closer my eyes came to rest on the officer directly behind Henry Mustin. He was laughing yet there was a suggestion of inner force and vitality that struck me instantly.

Lieutenant Earl Winfield Spencer Jr at twenty-seven was eight years older than Wallis. He had film-star good looks set off by a close-cropped moustache and had already spent six years in the navy after graduating from Annapolis. Wallis was instantly smitten. She wrote that over lunch the gold stripes on his shoulder-boards, glimpsed out of the corner of her eye, 'acted like a magnet and drew me back to him. Above all, I gained an impression of resolution and courage. I felt here was a man you could rely on in a tight place.'

Previously Wallis had dated boys, but now she was in the company of men. Win Spencer was strong, confident, virile – and experienced. He suggested they meet the next day. By the end of that day Wallis was hopelessly in love. Until Pensacola, Wallis had never seen an aeroplane – the art of flying was so new that the navy had only one air station, the one at Pensacola – so everything she discovered that spring was exciting and new. And there were only a handful of pilots. Win Spencer was the twentieth naval pilot to win his wings. According to a limerick in the US naval academy yearbook:

> *On the stage, as a maid with a curl*
> *A perfect entrancer is Earl*
> *With a voice like Caruse*
> *It's clearly no use*
> *To try to beat him with a girl*

Other epithets applied to him in the yearbook included 'fiery and able' and 'a merry devil'.

Win and Wallis started seeing each other at every opportunity. He tried to teach her to play golf – one of life's games at which she never succeeded. But with Win, she always pretended that at least she enjoyed the attempt. She was blind to the bitter streak in him, the jealous and brooding quality deeply embedded in his nature, let alone the cynicism that she came to know painfully well later. But on the day he asked her to marry him, within weeks of their meeting, she replied that of course she loved him and wanted to marry him but would have to ask her family. He countered: 'I never expected you to say yes right away ... but don't keep me waiting too long.' Such a response indicates a man already weary of the games lovers play, telling Wallis he has seen it all before and not to bother with such sham. She promised to let him know in the summer – a decent interval – when he came to Baltimore for his final leave. But he knew that her answer was never in doubt. The next stage was meeting the parents.

Earl Winfield Spencer Sr was a successful and, by the time his son met Wallis, socially prominent Chicago stockbroker. Until 1905 when the Spencers moved to the exclusive suburb of Highland Park, Chicago, the family had lived in Evanston, Illinois. In August 1916, when Wallis went to visit them just before her marriage, they were living in a large clapboard house with a veranda and front lawn at Wade Street. The family was moderately religious and in 1906–8 Spencer Sr had served as a vestryman of Trinity Episcopal Church in Highland Park, where his wife undertook various charitable commitments. They had six children – four boys and two girls – all of whom were by 1916 in active service. Two daughters, Gladys and Ethel, had trained for Red Cross work and Gladys went to serve at a hospital in Paris. When America entered the war Mrs Spencer was quoted in a local newspaper as saying: 'I believe I am the happiest woman in the world. I could not be happier unless I might have a few more to offer for the cause of the nation.'

On 19 September, five months after Wallis and Win had met, Mrs John Freeman Rasin announced the engagement of her only daughter Wallis to Lieutenant Spencer. He might not have offered the sort of marriage to old money and ancient lineage to which the Warfields aspired, but catching a naval lieutenant was the height of excitement for many an Oldfields girl. Wallis had not only caught a handsome one but at just twenty she was one of the first of her group to be married. This was an important race for her to win. Mary Kirk, unattached and sad to see her best friend leave Baltimore, generously hosted a tea with her mother in honour of Wallis at the Baltimore Country Club. She agreed to be one of Wallis's bridesmaids.

The wedding took place on a cold autumn day, 8 November 1916, against a highly charged political background. It was the day after the US presidential election which had been fuelled by constant discussion about the war in Europe that had been raging for the last two years. Britain and France were deeply embroiled, suffering heavy casualties, but, while public sentiment in the United States leaned towards showing sympathy with the Allied forces, most American voters wanted to avoid active involvement in the war, preferring to continue a policy of neutrality. Hence Woodrow Wilson was returned to the White House on the campaign slogan 'He kept us out of war'.

The ceremony which saw Wallis marrying into a heavily involved military family, where sacrifice and duty were top priorities, took place at Christ Protestant Episcopal Church in Baltimore, the local church on St Paul Street which she had attended for so many Sunday services with her grandmother. The ushers were all naval officers and flyers in uniform. The *Baltimore Sun* described the evening wedding as 'one of the most important of the season ... performed in front of a large assemblage of guests'. The church was decorated with palms and white chrysanthemums while lighted tapers and annunciation lilies decorated the altar. The bride entered the church on the arm of her uncle Sol, who gave her away. She had designed her own gown of white panne velvet (an unusual fabric for a wedding dress at the time) made with a court train and a pointed bodice elaborately embroidered with pearls. The skirt tumbled over a petticoat of old family lace and her veil of tulle was edged with lace arranged coronet fashion with sprays of orange blossoms. She carried a bouquet of white orchids and lilies of the valley.

But with US involvement in the war felt to be imminent, the mood at the wedding was slightly sombre and there followed only a small reception for the two families and members of the wedding party held at the Stafford Hotel. The *Baltimore Sun* commented: 'since being presented to society two seasons ago the bride has been a great favourite and has spent much time in Washington with her aunt, Mrs D. B. Merryman, and her cousin Mrs George Barnett, wife of Major General Barnett USMC'.

The Spencer family had arrived from Chicago earlier in the week. Win's younger brother, Dumaresq Spencer, was best man and his sister Ethel one of the bridesmaids. Wallis was always a man's woman and was never close to her sisters-in-law let alone to her new mother-in-law. She was not looking for intimate friendships with her new family, in fact was slightly stunned by them, and considered her place at the centre of the family she already had quite enough.

Win had just two weeks' leave, so the honeymoon was spent partly at the Greenbrier Hotel in White Sulphur Springs, West Virginia and partly in New York. Win never wrote about his marriage to Wallis – he found the way his subsequent life was made public as the ex-husband especially painful – so we only have Wallis's account. She describes how on their first night he revealed what she had failed to notice in the previous few months, 'that the bottle was seldom far from my husband's thoughts or his hand'. Win fell into a rage as soon as he saw the hotel notices declaring that alcoholic beverages could not be bought on the premises as West Virginia was a dry state. Although nationwide prohibition was not yet enforced, the issue was already deeply controversial. Various progressive groups believed that a total ban on the sale of alcohol would improve society, as did many women's groups and Southerners. There was a frequently quoted joke told about the Southern pro-prohibitionists: 'The South is dry and will vote dry. That is, everybody sober enough to stagger to the polls.'

So when Win revealed a bottle of gin packed between the shirts in his suitcase it was clear he had known there was likely to be difficulty in finding enough alcohol to fuel his needs over the coming days. Wallis, having grown up in a household which had strong convictions about the evils of alcohol, was shocked. She must have noticed during the previous few months that drinking was a habit of many men in the navy. But, in her hurry to marry, she was blind to the consequences. Only half jokingly, Win accused her of being a prude – and quite possibly the tone of their marriage was set. But Win had a redeeming sense of humour and after two weeks they moved back into government accommodation at Pensacola where Lieutenant Spencer was an instructor at the Aviation School.

Wallis spent her days painting the inside of the small bungalow white, putting up chintz curtains and enjoying the luxury of having a cook and a maid while she embarked on the ritual of socializing with navy wives. The cook was a fortunate addition to the household since Wallis knew nothing about the important art of cooking but, recognizing the need to please her husband in all ways, set about learning to master it. Cooking was easier than learning to play golf and perhaps easier than having sex at this stage in her life. And so Wallis began to develop her talents as a hostess, deciding that some of the top naval brass needed to be entertained.

Four months later, in April 1917, the US joined the war and the couple moved for a short time to Boston, where Spencer was in command of the Naval Aviation School at Squantum, Massachusetts, training other men to go overseas or undertake dangerous missions. While Win brooded over what he perceived as a demotion, perhaps even punishment for his heavy drinking, Wallis had taken to playing poker. Both were gambling with their futures.

2
Understanding Wallis

'I am naturally gay and flirtatious'

There is a deeply revealing line in Wallis Simpson's autobiography where she states her 'private judgment that when I was being good I generally had a bad time and when I was being bad the opposite was true'. She had an appalling time for much of the eight years that followed her marriage in 1916 and, on balance, it is probably fair to conclude that she was trying her best in these years to be good.

From the first weeks back at the base at Pensacola she saw how superficially she had known Win Spencer before plunging into marriage with him and she learned to look upon the raucous Saturday-night parties full of drinking, dancing and carousing into the small hours as 'a kind of thanksgiving that another week was safely past'. That was hardly the language of young love, albeit written some years afterwards. But in 1916 she knew as little about life as she did about her new husband. In order to make sense of Wallis it is important to understand the horror of her marriage to Spencer. While they were courting they grabbed every opportunity to be alone. But Corinne, *in loco parentis*, had to make an attempt at chaperoning, so there had been few opportunities for them to be alone and talk about their hopes and ambitions for a life together, let alone about their feelings for each other. When they did manage to grab a quiet few minutes somewhere deserted, Win would immediately seize Wallis and kiss her passionately. But, according to Wallis, that was all; 'spooning or petting' was impossible, however much either might have wished even for that. Ever keen to push the boundaries, she knew while she was being watched that she had to put the brakes on or be labelled 'fast'. She admitted later that she was ignorant of the facts of life when she married. Cousin Lelia once remarked to her only a little in jest, 'you know perfectly well you just married him out of curiosity'. Oldfields may have taught her the difference between an oyster fork and a lemon fork or the easiest way to do up an arm-length, seven-button glove. But these were skills of little use to her in the bedroom with Win. All her schoolfriends remember Wallis as exceptionally flirtatious from a very young age – not just charming in a typically Southern way but teasingly and unusually enticing. The Kirks, who knew her best, were profoundly concerned by her influence on their daughter.

There is now evidence to indicate there may have been sound medical and psychological reasons for Wallis behaving in this way which were not understood at the time and certainly would never have been discussed. She may have been born with what is currently labelled a Disorder of Sexual Development (DSD) or intersexuality, a term which embraces a wide range of conditions. Some are so subtle that even today doctors delivering babies with ambiguous genitals cannot be immediately certain if they are holding a boy or a girl. Since one baby in 15,000 is born with some degree of DSD – which amounts to approximately 4,000 in the UK and 400,000 globally per annum – the problem can no longer be considered rare. This does not mean that Wallis was a man, in fact the reverse, and she was certainly not a freak. Wallis herself, if she were born with some degree of DSD – and there is no medical proof that this is an accurate assessment of her case – would not have known that anything was wrong, at least for many years, and even then might have been given confused information unless she had cause to undergo an operation. Yet the diagnosis is more than wild conjecture because there is strong circumstantial and psychosexual evidence that Wallis fits into this category. Michael Bloch, Wallis's biographer, who lived and worked in her house in Paris for years while his subject lay largely comatose, came to believe after discussing her case with doctors that she may have suffered from Androgen Insensitivity Syndrome, or AIS, which is at the milder end of the spectrum. He reached this view based on extensive personal knowledge.

Patients with AIS are born genetically male as they have the XY chromosome and produce testosterone. Because the body's receptors in this case are insensitive to testosterone the individual develops outwardly as a woman, although at puberty the testosterone build-up may result in strong muscles giving her athletic prowess, long legs or large hands. Such a child to all purposes appears female and only later can it be discovered that their karyotype is XY if a DNA test is carried out, and that of course was not an option during Wallis's childhood. The first clue for Wallis that something might be different would have been at puberty if she did not have periods. But even this might not have seemed unusual, nor would it have been an easy subject for discussion given the frequent absences of her mother at this time in her life.

Another possibility is that she was born a pseudo-hermaphrodite, the term itself only coined in 1886, ten years before Wallis was born, indicating how little was known and understood about that condition. At the end of the nineteenth century there would have been very little discussion around such a risqué subject, even in medical circles, least of all with the parents of the newborn baby. A patient with pseudo-hermaphroditism has the internal reproductive organs of one sex while exhibiting the opposite in their external genitalia so a man has female characteristics which may include small breasts and a woman some form of male genitalia that are possibly barely noticeable, as well as usually a shallow vagina, but no uterus, cervix or ovaries (though this is variable). Full hermaphroditism, a term now considered offensive, where individuals carry both types of gonad, is extremely rare. For the Victorians, already confused by the Woman Question, the term used to convey the challenge to traditional notions of a woman's place, merely trying to grapple with such a concept was deeply disconcerting. 'So much of what is repulsive attaches to our ideas of the condition of an hermaphrodite that we experience a reluctance even to use the word,' wrote one doctor, Jonathan Hutchinson, in the year of Wallis's birth. Hermaphroditism challenged notions of what defined a woman or a man and the whole social order depended on these clear definitions. A person who could not be defined was a dangerously disruptive presence. For whatever reason, Wallis was certainly that.

Without a full ultrasound or scan the condition could not possibly have been detected at birth. Young Dr Lewis Allen, fresh out of medical school, who came to deliver the baby in Blue Ridge Summit, might have noticed that the baby had slightly strange-looking genitalia: the most common description is of slightly larger labia than usual or slightly enlarged clitoris resembling a small penis; in some cases the child would have testicles which do not descend (today they would be removed since they could pose a serious medical risk later in life). But in 1896 there was no question that such a child would have been brought up as female; there was no available means of checking chromosomal abnormality. What usually happened in such cases is that the doctor would have done his best to reassure the parents that although the baby might appear unusual, they should not worry. 'She'll grow out of it,' he would have told them, or 'Everything will be normal in a few years.' And indeed before puberty such individuals would easily pass as normal pre-pubescent females. After puberty there might be a noticeable drift towards the external features of a male including bone structure, muscle development and voice change, but even these features might be easily missed and obvious signs such as facial hair are usually prevented by the condition's inability to convert the testosterone.

James Pope-Hennessy, visiting the Windsors in 1958 in the course of writing the official biography of Queen Mary, commented in his journal that Wallis was 'one of the very oddest women I have ever seen. She is, to look at, phenomenal. She is flat and angular and could have been designed for a medieval playing card … I should be tempted to classify her as an American woman *par excellence* … were it not for the suspicion that she is not a woman at all.' It was not just her physical characteristics that came under scrutiny. In 1936 Nancy Dugdale, wife of Prime Minister Stanley Baldwin's Parliamentary Private Secretary, Tommy Dugdale, sent a letter written by Wallis to a well-known German graphologist, Gusti Oesterreicher. Mrs Dugdale insisted the analysis had been done in complete ignorance of the writer's identity and that Oesterreicher did not speak English. Oesterreicher's report concluded that the author of the letter was:

A woman with a strong male inclination in the sense of activity, vitality and initiative. She *MUST* dominate, she *MUST* have authority, and without sufficient scope for her powers can become disagreeable. In a narrow circle without big tasks to perform and the possibility for expansion her temperament would be impatient, irritable ... but not without some instincts of nobility and generosity. She is ruled by contradictory impulses ... In the physical sense of the word sadistic, cold, overbearing, vain.

According Dr Christopher Inglefield, a plastic surgeon specializing in gender surgery, Wallis's known physical and behavioural characteristics clearly fit the stereotype. He explains:

The problem for these individuals is how do you confirm that you are female if your biological responses are not like other girls? How do you come to terms with this strange situation? Often these individuals don't understand what or who they are so, for a female lacking female organs, being boy mad is one typical response, another is to get married as quickly as possible, thereby telling your peers you are a normal female.

Marriage, according to Dr Inglefield, is thus seen as a reaffirmation of being female.

Not only is early marriage often the norm but so is the urge to dress in the most feminizing way because of the need to fit into society. Dressing is just one way of behaving in an ultra-feminine way. Another is sexual behaviour. There is a strong need to do everything in the most feminine way possible. 'Look at me, I'm a woman,' Wallis is saying. 'I'm not the prettiest thing you've ever seen but I am so elegant. I'm the epitome of womanhood.' The clothes and the sex are all of a piece.

Thus a deeply significant characteristic for women with some form of DSD is the realization that one of the most powerful ways to reaffirm their womanhood is the ability to give men intense sexual pleasure. Giving intense pleasure can easily lead to manipulating men in order to please them. Vaginal intercourse is often possible, even where the vagina is shallow, but so, of course, are other activities, including oral sex.

Dr Inglefield, through advising patients who seek his advice on corrective surgery, is experienced in assessing a number of factors, including facial and bodily characteristics, to determine if an individual is predisposed to survive as one sex or the other. Wallis, he believes, had an angular, almost square-jawed and masculine-shaped face which indicates a lack of oestrogen. Looking at photographs of Wallis alongside her girlfriends gives an especially good comparison. 'Oestrogen is very softening. You can see it clearly next to the very rounded face of Mary Kirk. Today a course of oestrogen therapy can transform facial features. Had it been available in Wallis's day it would have dramatically changed her appearance.'

So there are clues in the behaviour, bone structure and build, as well as in the facial shape. When cousin Corinne shouted out for 'Skinny' to come here or go there she was acknowledging, without knowing it, that lack of ovaries affects body shape and breast development. Several successful models with an impossibly lean, rangy look are known to be women born with Disorders of Sexual Development. Keeping slim, which became a lifelong mantra for Wallis, was always of critical importance in avoiding a masculine, solid appearance with no waistline. It was something she appears to have understood intuitively. Once she was in the public eye, controlling her weight with rigid discipline was a matter of survival.

The ultimate confirmation for Wallis of being totally female would be to get pregnant, which is not possible without a uterus. Yet, extraordinarily, this is a subject she never broaches while telling the story of her life. Almost all childless women writing reminiscences, especially those who are married, born a century or so ago when birth control was not readily available, manage in some way or other to refer to their deep longing for a child with which they were not blessed. Or else to insist that a choice was made not to bring children into the world for whatever reason. Wallis's decision not to cover this subject, even if she had to lie about gynaecological adventures or miscarriages, is striking. On the last page of her book, almost as an afterthought, she writes starkly of a 'continuing regret. I have never known the joy of having children of my own.' Yet the assumption must be that, for an ordinary couple marrying in the early part of the twentieth century where the wife had neither career nor desire for one, starting a family would have been the expectation, especially in the Spencer family. So when, after several months, Wallis did not become pregnant it is quite possible that she consulted a doctor and underwent an examination. At that point the doctor might have been suspicious if he could not see a cervix. But even that could have been confusing and, since there was so little scientific knowledge available about what to do in cases of infertility, the embarrassed doctor might not have known what to advise his young patient other than to hope. Contemporary advice in such cases included old wives' tales such as the importance of drinking the first morning milk of a particular type of cow. Given the unhappy state of her marriage, Wallis may not have been very concerned. But, just as likely, her inability to conceive or difficulties the couple may have encountered having intercourse could have been a contributory factor in the dis-integration of her first marriage. Ralph Martin, one of Wallis's earliest biographers writing about her in 1974, claimed that Alice Montague had said on her deathbed that her daughter could never have children. If that is the case, and if it was something Wallis always knew, she may have steeled herself very early on to the idea of being childless. At all events, she seems by her twenties to have resigned herself rather easily to the idea that she could not have children and, with similar ease, taken the next best algorithm for her life – the discovery that she could use her sexuality to get the status she was denied as a child without risking an unwanted pregnancy, a serious problem for sexually active women at the time.

Discovering that she was in some way different yet unable to discuss, explore or acknowledge this humiliating stigma with anyone would have turned Wallis into a strong personality if she were to survive. Most of those with gender identity issues who survive emo-tionally undamaged do so because they have a robust belief that they are unusual or special; indeed this belief is centuries old, because the condition itself is hardly new. In Wallis's case a typical result would have been a determination to make herself the most perfect being by over-compensating for the unspoken, humiliating part of her.

'It's not only a way of over-compensating. It is also a way of managing the sense of inadequacy which would otherwise have been there. If a woman knows that she possesses a secret which makes her a unique person she can live with this by believing that she has something which makes her stand out against the rest. It is like having a special gift,' explains consultant psychiatrist Dr Domenico di Ceglie. How she used this gift was to become clear in the years ahead.

But for the first twenty years of her life Wallis would also have had to come to terms with the demands of secrecy. The consequences of secrecy where developing sexuality is concerned are often that the sexuality and the secrecy can be merged, which means that to perform certain activities in a semi-secret way becomes more exciting. And this explains why the risk and excitement element of relationships was attractive to Wallis. Once this is understood, Wallis's insight into her own condition 'that when I was being good I generally had a bad time and when I was being bad the opposite was true', suddenly becomes powerfully clear.

Win seems to have done a good job at Squantum. The couple lived in a hotel and Wallis did not complain of being lonely but filled her day as best she could, largely wandering the streets of Boston and watching court cases. But then, in October 1918, he was moved again. To his bitter disappointment, according to Wallis, instead of being sent overseas in an active fighting role he was ordered to San Diego to set up a new flyers' base. But setting up the nation's first naval airbase on North Island, a short commute from the Coronado Peninsula, was not only a mammoth task, it was one which commanded enormous respect from those who served under him, as letters from junior officers to their parents indicate.

Again, Wallis did not find it difficult to spend the day sunbathing and planning meals. For shopping and cooking her *Fannie Farmer Cookbook* came to her aid; for the cleaning and other chores a Japanese houseboy helped. It was the sort of leisurely lifestyle she had always wanted. The newlyweds entertained frequently, sometimes important naval people, top brass, until the small hours – Wallis, master of the wisecrack, laughing till it hurt. Win, according to

Wallis, was furious about his posting, a fury made worse in January 1918 when he learned that his twenty-one-year-old younger brother, Dumaresq, Yale graduate and golden boy of the family, had been killed in action while fighting with the Lafayette Escadrille, an air force squadron composed largely of American volunteer pilots in France. Not only that, his even younger brother, Frederick, aged seventeen, had just been awarded the Croix de Guerre, likewise on the Western Front. That news, together with his mother's response – 'I would that I had another son to send to take his place' – all fuelled Win's anger at his inactivity and his longing to prove himself. Wallis may have lacked the maturity to tackle Win's demons – if indeed anyone could have. And Win may have had a violent temper. Mary Kirk, in spite of what happened later, always told her family that she believed Spencer had been brutal, a cad. In addition, his three subsequent wives all cited in their divorce petitions his irritability and irascibility, cruelty and abusive behaviour. But an accurate description of any marriage, especially a disintegrating one, is something only those inside it can give. At the time of their marriage, Win was one of an elite band of naval aviators, young, fit, handsome and at the peak of his powers. No doubt like many fellow naval officers at the time he was often drunk and smoked a lot. But what provoked his anger and violence is not clear, and Wallis's account was written more than thirty years later with a particular agenda.

The marriage, shaky from the start, dramatically deteriorated after little more than a year together. In San Diego Wallis flirted, behaviour which she realized ignited Win's jealousy and led to further alcohol and violence. 'I am naturally gay and flirtatious,' she wrote. 'I was brought up to believe that one should be as entertaining as one can at a party.' She also had a low boredom threshold and now seriously questioned whether a service life, constantly on the move and involving 'brief sojourns in rented bungalows or tasteless government housing, endlessly repeated associations with the same people conditioned to the same interests', was for her. It is true that he was constantly on the move, sometimes staying in one place for only a matter of weeks and sometimes having to put up in a hotel while a suitable small cottage was found. But the archives indicate that Wallis, unlike other navy wives, did not always follow her husband from one base to another. Almost every document that lists her addresses at this time has her at a different address from him. She is listed either as at the Washington-based Riggs Bank or as at an address in Maryland. In addition, although none of their homes was grand, it is not entirely fair to describe them as tasteless government housing. Their first home in San Diego – two furnished rooms in the fashionable Palomar Apartments – was, as Wallis herself admitted, so delightful that she did not see how she and Win could fail to be happy there.

But Wallis's life at this time was, she says, 'a harrowing experience'. She tells of repeatedly being locked up in a room while he went out 'often for hours on end' and of being the subject of Win's 'running barrage of subtle innuendoes and veiled insults. Outsiders were not supposed to understand these clever thrusts but I certainly did.' It's not hard to imagine that these innuendoes and insults might well have been taunts about the unsatisfactory nature of their sex life. According to the American author Donald Spoto, in his 1995 book *Dynasty*, Wallis told her closest male friend Herman Rogers, who was to give her away on her marriage to the Duke of Windsor in 1937, that she had 'never had sexual intercourse with either of her first two husbands nor had she ever allowed anyone else to touch her below what she called her personal Mason–Dixon line', more usually the border between the Southern and Northern parts of the United States.

Wallis tried hard to widen her circle of friends – what else was there to do? – while living in Coronado and was photographed with, among others, John Barrymore and Charlie Chaplin. One of the major events during her time there was a ball at the Hotel del Coronado on 7 April 1920 in honour of the then Prince of Wales as he stopped off during a major tour en route to Australia on HMS *Renown*. For years the romantic story flourished that it was here that Wallis met the Prince for the first time.

Win Spencer, by then Lieutenant Commander Spencer, was later quoted as saying of the evening of the ball: 'Practically all navy officers stationed here were present with their wives. We all went down the receiving line. My former wife [Wallis] was with me most of the

evening. Of course I'm not quite sure but she may have been introduced to him. As I recall she slipped away for a few minutes and may
have been received by the Prince ...'

The legend that Wallis and Edward first met in a hotel ballroom
in San Diego not only grew but was embellished in subsequent years.
Not surprisingly the hotel itself still today fosters the idea, displaying
prominently a portrait of the Duke and Duchess as well as featuring
a small alcove for parties called the Duchess's private dining room.
According to another story: 'Mrs Spencer was wearing a red evening
gown that night and stood out so much from the rest of the women
that the Prince asked to be presented to her.'

But the reality is more interesting. According to a short newspaper
article of 31 March 1920 in the *San Diego Union* devoted to social
activity in the community, Mrs Winfield Spencer left that afternoon
for Los Angeles, 'taking the *Lark* tonight for Monterey, where she
will be the house guest for the weekend at the Del Monte Lodge of
Mrs Jane Selby Hayne of San Francisco. Mrs Spencer goes north to
attend the polo games.' Two weeks later, in an issue of the same
journal dated Sunday 18 April 1920, there appeared the following:
'Mrs E. Winfield Spencer returned to Hotel del Coronado Tuesday
evening [13 April 1920] after several weeks' visit with Mrs Jane Selby
Hayne at Del Monte.'

Other articles in the *San Francisco Chronicle* for the two weeks
in question confirm her presence with Mrs Selby Hayne and report
that the two women 'spent much time on the Del Monte Polo field
practising with ball and mallet'. In other words, Wallis was not in
Coronado at the time of the ball. Instead, she was staying with the
prominent San Francisco socialite, skilled horsewoman, ardent polo
aficionado and, perhaps most significantly, newly divorced Mrs
Selby Hayne. Jane Selby Hayne had been visiting Coronado in
March 1920, so quite possibly Wallis met her just a month previously
and jumped at the chance to cement the new friendship. In her
memoirs Wallis stated emphatically that she did not, 'as popular
story has it', meet the Prince of Wales when he visited that April.
But nor does she say why she did not, nor where she was. She
writes evasively that when their marriage was breaking up in

earnest many invitations came to them both, including one for 'polo at Del Monte'. She does not elaborate. Yet had she been in Coronado she would hardly have refused an opportunity to meet the Prince. Most likely it did not suit her story to reveal that she was the one on the move in the young marriage, the one who had gone looking for fun elsewhere and missed the one big social event of her time at Coronado.

Meanwhile the Prince wrote to his then girlfriend that the dinner dance at the Coronado Hotel was 'most bloody awful ... I've never hated a party as much as I did this evening's ... I'm near unto cwying [sic].'

Wallis insists that her first husband's drinking was aggravated by lack of promotion or by being passed over when he had the chance to serve in a combat zone. Maybe. But the jobs he was given were not insignificant ones and clearly required a man of forceful personality and talent. Just as likely, if Wallis went north alone and had an exciting time, it was in fact his wife's behaviour that provoked Spencer, who had plenty of evidence already of how easily his wife could have a good time. Spencer's sister Ethel, one of Wallis's bridesmaids, who probably knew her brother as well as anyone, described her former sister-in-law thus: 'I'd call her just a typical southern belle. She could no more keep from flirting than from breathing. She could come into a room full of women and you wouldn't pay any attention to her but the minute a man came in she would sparkle and turn on the charm. Win was frightfully jealous so that caused them a great deal of unhappiness.'

So if, as Wallis alleged, Spencer now drank more and shouted more, if he frequently abused her verbally and physically, went out alone after tying her to the bed or subjected her to bizarre rituals such as forcing her to witness the destruction of her family photographs, perhaps there was a part of her that had, wittingly or not, encouraged him, even enjoyed it? A woman who knew Wallis in those days remarked on 'her beautiful dark sapphire blue eyes, full of sparkle and nice mischief. Her laugh was contagious, like a tonic ...' She was after all reverting to type – the type that needed constant con-firmation of her attractiveness to all men, the type who was born with ambivalent sexuality. It was part of her insecurity which would never leave her.

Later that year Wallis's mother Alice Rasin came to stay. The visit gave the warring couple a month's respite as both behaved impeccably in front of her. At the end of the year Win was given a temporary job back in Pensacola and it was agreed that they should live separately for a while, with Wallis staying behind, alone in Coronado for a whole winter. But early in 1921 he was assigned a new and important position with the navy's Bureau of Aeronautics in Washington. This time both welcomed the change of location and they decided to move there together, living in a service apartment in a hotel called the Brighton. Wallis recounts: 'But as so often happens since nothing was right at the office, nothing was right at home. Whatever I did was wrong in Win's eyes and in this unhappy situation he did what was so easy for him, he took to the bottle.'

Through the thin walls of the hotel everyone knew about their shouting matches. 'Brought up as I had been in families ruled by a code of considerate conduct I could not bear any public indelicacy.' Wallis says that Win was being transformed 'from a brilliant officer into a mixed-up neurotic'.

Then, one Sunday afternoon, he locked her in the bathroom of their apartment.

> For hours I heard no sound from beyond the door. Whether Win had gone out or whether he was still in the apartment playing a practical joke I could not tell. I tried to unscrew the lock with a nail file . . . As the afternoon wore on and evening came I was seized with panic at the thought that Win might mean to keep me a prisoner all night. I wanted desperately to call for help but held myself in check.

Eventually Wallis heard the sound of a key turn in the lock but was too scared to try it herself and venture out. She finally plucked up enough courage to do so and, seeing him asleep in the marital bed, slept the night on the sofa. By morning she had decided she had to leave him. More than that, she decided she had to divorce him, and she knew that in her family divorce was a matter for deep shame.

She discussed it first with her mother, who warned her that she would be making a terrible mistake if she went ahead. Aunt Bessie was similarly appalled by the idea of Wallis being the first Montague to be divorced. 'Unthinkable,' she told her niece. As a divorced woman she would be entering the wilderness. She would be a woman who had failed as a wife. These two were partly concerned for Wallis but also aware of the realities in the 1920s. In order to have something to live on she would have to square it with Uncle Sol and he, when she paid him a visit in Baltimore the next day, predictably thundered: 'I won't let you bring this disgrace upon us.' She would be the first Warfield to be divorced. But then he softened slightly and admitted that, never having been married himself, perhaps he was not the best person to pronounce. But he was not going to support her and urged her to return to Win and try again.

This she did for two more weeks. But she could stand it no longer. When she finally told Win she was leaving he was, she says, essentially a gentleman. Wallis now moved in with her mother, and in June 1921 gave her address to the US naval board as Earl Court, Baltimore – her mother's apartment. But life was tough for Alice, working as a paid hostess at the Chevy Chase Country Club. In February 1922 Win was posted to the Far East as commander of a gunboat stationed in Hong Kong. There was no question of Wallis accompanying him. It was easier for unhappy naval wives like Wallis to keep up appearances of still being married while living alone. Wallis was twenty-five, and she now discovered freedom. Win's regular cheques for $225 a month were all she had to live on.

3

Wallis in Wonderland

'Too good for a woman'

Nineteen-twenties Washington was a most exciting place to be. In 1921 the country had a new president, the Republican Warren G. Harding, and political talk was everywhere. There was also discussion of his controversial private life, including his marriage to a divorcée five years older than him and his extramarital affairs. Harding was to serve for just two scandal-ridden years and his administration was generally considered a disaster. Wallis loved the political buzz as well as the gossip but, desperate to lead an independent life, found living with her mother unbearably constricting. Alice always waited up for her to come home, even if it was 2 a.m., and as one who had suffered from unpleasantly wagging tongues herself, disapproved of her being out after midnight with a man who was not her husband.

'Hazardous' is the word Wallis herself used about life for a single woman in 1920s Washington surrounded by so many surplus men. Single women needed a code of behaviour and she believed she had just such a personal rule, 'which was never to allow myself to drift into light affairs of the moment ... I was determined to wait until I was sure I had found a deep love that would engage both my mind and my emotions.' But her mother took a different view about what constituted a suitable code and did not hesitate to tell Wallis. Not surprisingly, as soon as she could, Wallis moved out and, in the autumn of 1922, went to stay in the Georgetown house of a naval friend whose husband was also in the Far East. Living with Admiral's daughter Dorothy McNamee gave Wallis social standing and enabled her to move effortlessly into a diplomatic and political circle where she honed her natural talent for making friends in high places, and remembering them. Her cousin Corinne Mustin – now a widow after her husband Henry died suddenly in 1923 – was also in Washington at this time opening another door for her into naval circles. In addition to Corinne, she had a small coterie of women friends, including Marianna Sands, from San Diego, and Ethel Noyes, daughter of the president of the Associated Press, both separated from their husbands and with whom she often went to embassy parties and weekend picnics.

Wallis, finding herself in what she described as a 'special paradise' for a woman on her own, among so many unattached, attractive and cultured men, was an eager learner. This exposure to an international network of men in high-powered jobs taught her some basic rules for a woman who wished to engage in conversations with the opposite sex in the early part of the century. She made sure she was always well informed about world affairs in general and about the individual person in particular; then she listened and flattered. This was a skill Wallis was determined to master if she was to move up the social scale.

A favourite event was a weekly meeting of a group known as the Soixante Gourmets. Each of the sixty young men in this exclusive club brought a female companion to lunch at the Hotel Hamilton and it was here that Wallis was introduced to the most stimulating group of men she was ever to meet. They included the witty and opinionated journalist Willmott (Bill) Lewis of *The Times*, who was to marry her friend Ethel Noyes; Prince Gelasio Caetani, the Italian Ambassador, fierce nationalist and First World War veteran, a brilliant and handsome man who planted the seeds of Wallis's interest in the Italian political scene.

She may have written off her marriage with Win, but she insisted she still believed in marriage and was keen to marry again:

> In my mind I had the picture of the sort of man I wanted. Ideally he would be a young man who was making his mark in business, diplomacy or one of the professions. He would like and understand people and above all appreciate me. I wanted someone who would make me a part of his life and whom I could help in his career.

I wanted a man who would draw me into the full circle of his existence in all its aspects.

The description, although written by Wallis years after her marriage to the ex-King, is probably a fair account of what she hoped, indeed was working, to achieve at this time, while still in her twenties. Apparently she met several men in this enticing milieu who measured up to her ideal, but only one of them 'stirred her heart'. She described him as a young diplomat of great promise attached to the Embassy of a Latin American country, 'both teacher and model in the art of living . . . in many respects, the most fascinating man I have ever met with principles of steel and a spirit that bubbled like champagne'. Her use of 'ever' can hardly have been an accident.

Don Felipe Espil, at thirty-five, was eight years older than Wallis and a man of experience of women and the world. He was slim, dark and tall and spoke with an attractively marked South American accent. A qualified lawyer, his interests were extraordinarily wide ranging and included music, economics, bridge, baseball, golf and riding, at all of which he excelled. Many a Washington matron hoped to catch him for her daughter. When he met Wallis he was first secretary at the Argentine Embassy, but no one was in any doubt of his ambition to be ambassador, a position that would require considerable funds. He indulged in a brief relationship with Wallis, which caused some scandal in Washington, presumably because she was considered unsuitable, and it may have been this affair in particular that Alice Rasin so objected to. Espil clearly enjoyed Wallis's company – for a while – and perhaps especially while he thought she was safely married. But she, as she confided in friends, was passionately in love with him and was prepared to do anything to keep him, including converting to Catholicism if necessary. Then he fell in love with Courtney Louise Letts, one of the quartet of Chicago debutantes known as the Big Four who attended parties, played tennis together and were legendary for their beauty, money and magnetism. All had multiple relationships, at least two of which provided the inspiration for F. Scott Fitzgerald's characters in *The Great Gatsby*. Letts was wealthy, beautiful and, as the daughter of a

US senator, socially desirable. Although younger than Wallis, she too had already been once married – to the well-connected Wellesley H. Stillwell. But she divorced him in 1924 and married and divorced a second time before eventually marrying Espil in 1933, by which time he had finally been promoted to ambassador to the US. Wallis, the mere wife of a naval lieutenant, with neither money nor social standing, could not compete.

Wallis, furious to learn that Espil was involved with another woman, could do nothing but absorb for herself the mores of the time and the place. She was a novice engaging with a world of deep hypocrisy and it took her some time to learn the rules of this circle. Some got away with scandalous adultery followed by divorce and went on to live a new life with a new partner. Others paid a heavy price. When Polly Peabody met Harry Crosby in 1920 and within two weeks tried to divorce her husband, Richard J. Peabody, who had become a dangerous alcoholic, blue-blooded Boston society was scandalized. Both Crosby and Peabody were wealthy sons of socially prominent Boston families and both were victims and veterans of the recent war. Crosby married Polly in 1922 but, shortly afterwards, he had a passionate affair with Constance Coolidge, the Comtesse de Jumilhac, who later became a close friend of Wallis for a time. In 1929 Crosby committed suicide with his latest young lover, Josephine Rotch, after taking a mixture of drink and drugs.

Espil's rejection of her for a better-connected rival was publicly humiliating. Wallis, unusually, had lost control of the situation, which represented a crushing defeat. Washington was suddenly cold and unwelcoming. So when Corinne suggested a trip to Paris she jumped at the idea. Ethel Noyes, also getting a divorce at this time, was in Paris just before her marriage to Bill Lewis. The cousins sailed to Europe in January 1924, Wallis half hoping that she might find a divorce easier and cheaper in Paris, or even that Espil might pursue her. He never did and she discovered that a divorce would cost her several thousand dollars, money her uncle Sol had once again declined to provide. Deeply hurt by Espil and, aged twenty-eight, increasingly uncertain of the future, she responded warmly when Win wrote to invite her to forget the past and join him in China. It felt like there was nothing to lose. She would be tougher in future, never lose control. Win sent instructions for her to join a naval transport at Norfolk, Virginia, and then sail on to China at government expense.

Wallis travelled with a cargo of navy wives on the USS *Chaumont*, arriving in Hong Kong in September 1924 after a six-week voyage. Travelling to China at that time was not only prohibitively expensive for most people, it was also exotic and an opportunity to see something of the world – which she realized had become a necessity, having had a taste of it from the talk of others in the hothouse diplomatic circles of Washington. She badly wanted the marriage to work this time and, for a short while, it did. Win, on the dock to meet her, was looking tanned, clear-eyed and physically fit. He took her back to his navy-supplied apartment in Kowloon on the Chinese mainland and told her that he had stopped drinking from the day he had heard she was coming.

This second honeymoon was, however, short lived. Again, there is only Wallis's account of the final breakdown. She recounts how Win, after two weeks, returned to his old pattern of drinking and erratic behaviour leading to abuse and violence. There is good reason to believe her. Her frame of mind was such that she would have tried hard to keep the marriage together at this point in her life if she could have, and, revealingly, she admits that perhaps there was something about the two of them together that set off this vicious cycle. When she asked Win if she was responsible for lighting the fire of his anger, he apparently responded that he could not explain what happened but 'something lets go, like the cables of a plane'. In the days before therapy it may be unfair to blame Wallis for a lack of sympathy, as some biographers have done. But, even assuming Win and Wallis did not encounter a physical difficulty in their relationship which unleashed his fury and determination to punish her, it is clear that Wallis was not interested in trying to understand his problems nor in encouraging him to seek help. This may have been because she knew she was the one who needed it more.

There followed another short period of calm for Wallis to reflect as Win, undertaking river patrol duties, was sent away. Wallis set off to join him in Canton, but as soon as she arrived there she came down with a high temperature. She described it as a kidney infection and said that while she was ill he was solicitous. Drinking the polluted water was renowned for causing illness. But it is also possible that the infection was the result of Win kicking her in the stomach and assaulting her, as one biographer claims he was told by a friend of Wallis in her latter years, which would explain his unusual contrition subsequently. His anger presumably derived from jealousy, fed by his accusations, later recounted by Wallis herself, that she had 'carried on' with officers aboard the *Chaumont* and flirted with men in Hong Kong during his absence. He now started opening her letters to find evidence of this.

Wallis described what happened next: 'To his already formidable repertory of taunts and humiliations he now added some oriental variations. I gathered that during our long absence he had spent a considerable amount of his time ashore in the local sing-song houses. In any event, he now insisted on my accompanying him to his favourite haunts where he would ostentatiously make a fuss over the girls.' It may seem strange that Wallis chose to refer to such activities at all in her memoirs. But, from her perspective, it was vital to prove that her first husband was the betrayer and abuser, even if she was the one who walked out of the marriage – a factor of critical importance at a time when all she was hoping for was special permission to be presented at Court. It's a paragraph that has given rise to much insidious comment and blighted any subsequent serious discussion of Wallis's life in China, what she later called 'her lotus year'. The sing-song houses were places of entertainment where clients were usually entertained with erotic songs and some music and dancing as a prelude to sex. If she admitted to frequenting such places, which usually offered opium and gambling as well and were only slightly more respectable than ordinary brothels, as a threesome, perhaps she also visited brothels without Win and perhaps she learned from Chinese prostitutes some ancient oriental techniques for pleasuring men – it is an impossible scenario to verify or disprove. But what is clear is that a woman with Wallis's energy and gusto for life travelling alone in the orient at this time was inevitably going to be a target for gossip.

At all events, when Wallis took the decision to tell Win that their attempt at a reunion had failed and that she was leaving him for good, he put up no resistance. He quietly offered to resume his monthly payments to her. But instead of going directly home to the US, where she would have to admit to friends and family this new failure in her private life, she went first to Shanghai, perhaps, as she maintained, because someone had told her there was an American court there where it might be possible to get a divorce. Or perhaps she was simply not ready to return and, having come all this way, decided it would be a shame to leave without seeing such an exciting place. However, while still in Washington she had been given letters of introduction to single men living there, so it was clearly always a backstop on her personal horizon, a place to visit if things did not work out with Win.

Nineteen-twenties Shanghai was a legend: a free city, sometimes described as a freak city, where new arrivals required neither visa nor passport to enter, so it was home to myriad adventurers, gangsters and foreign traders. This diverse society with a criminal underbelly and overt sexual frisson included American conmen, White Russian tarts, Japanese jazz players, Korean tram conductors and many others on the make or fleeing repressive systems, not least some Jews and Chinese revolutionaries. She might as well seize the chance to sample what was often described as 'a narrow layer of heaven on a thick slice of hell' without being watched by any Warfields, Washington hostesses or other tutting Baltimore matrons. Win saw her off on a steamer to Shanghai, and they were to meet only once again.

There were several navy wives on the boat and Wallis was pleased to find Mary Sadler, already a Washington acquaintance and wife of the now Admiral F. H. Sadler, commanding officer of the USS *Saratoga*. As the pair sailed up the Huangpu River into the Soochow Creek to the accompaniment of foghorns booming on the river and the rattle of a tram on the nearby Nanking Road she would have been struck by signs illuminated by gas lamps, electric lights not yet having been installed in the city, adding to its air of mystery and half-lit gloom or decadence. Passing the often dilapidated junks anchored four deep, she would have smelled the unique mixture of sewage, seaweed and sulphurous steam that permeated the city, a reminder of its origins as a muddy swamp.

All China in 1924 was in a febrile state after the collapse of the ruling dynasties in 1911 while various warlords fought for control. Many of these power struggles were centred on Shanghai, where in 1921 the Communist Party of China was founded. Shanghai was one of the major treaty ports awarded to the British in 1842 following the Opium War, with leases which were now causing increasing resentment among the restive Chinese. The British and the American settlements had joined to form the International Settlement, run by the Shanghai Municipal Council but ruled by a British police force and judiciary. The French opted out and instead maintained their own French Concession, located to the south of the International Settlement and largely governed by French laws. It was here, in the Rue Molière, that Sun Yat-sen, the Chinese revolutionary and political leader largely responsible for the overthrow of the last imperial dynasty, chose to live. Many of the White Russians who had fled the Bolsheviks made their homes close by. There was also a Chinese-administered part of the city where the largely impoverished native populations were subject to Chinese law overseen by the so-called Mixed Courts in the Settlement and this left many of them at the mercy of the warlords.

From the end of the nineteenth century, the treaties forced the opening up of all of China but especially Shanghai and other ports to Western culture and influence through trade. By the early twentieth century, the city was poised to reap the rewards of having avoided any involvement in the First World War and swiftly became a booming economic centre, the commercial hub of East Asia attracting banks from all over the world as well as economic migrants and many shady types. It was a fashionable centre of prosperity with British emporia where staples such as marmalade could be found and French boutiques with high-fashion clothes and accessories. The city was also the centre of national and international opium smuggling during the 1920s. The notorious Green Gang became a major influence in the

International Settlement with the Commissioner of the Shanghai Municipal Police reporting that corruption associated with the trade had affected a large proportion of his force. An extensive crackdown in 1925 simply displaced the focus of the trade to the neighbouring French Concession.

Prostitution flourished in Shanghai as nowhere else. In 1920 the Municipal Council calculated that there were more than 70,000 prostitutes in the foreign concession, among them 8,000 White Russians. By 1930, Shanghai had more prostitutes – or 'flowers' – per capita than any other city in the world, and they had a defined hierarchy listed in guidebooks. At the top, able to command most money, were male opera singers, then first-class courtesans followed by ordinary courtesans, prostitutes in tea houses, street walkers, prostitutes in opium dens, prostitutes in nail sheds, who offered sex standing up, and prostitutes at wharves, sometimes called Saltwater Sisters, who as their name suggests catered to sailors and were on the bottom rung. There were, as in any city, special streets including the enticingly named Love Lane with both tea houses and sing-song establishments; and there were courtyard bordellos, which offered not only sex but places for Chinese men to socialize, and to smoke opium, gamble or play mah-jong, and permanently moored or cruising 'flower boats' which could be hired for the whole evening. In other words there were few tastes that were not catered to.

Later, when Wallis became involved with the Prince of Wales, rumours arose that a 'China Dossier' had been compiled by Prime Minister Stanley Baldwin on orders from Queen Mary detailing her lewd or undercover activities. But such a dossier has never been identified, even though spies abounded in Shanghai's International Settlement and even though the Special Branch there apparently kept files on all important people in the city. Britain's National Archives in Kew have several leather-bound marbled volumes from the country's various consular posts in China indicating that the British government was very worried about the increasing anti-British resentment which burst forth during strike-related riots in the summer of 1924 and which it feared could be exploited by Bolshevik propagandists and spread to the whole of China. The Secret Intelligence

Service (SIS) received reports in August 1924 that Soviet consuls in Shanghai were openly supplying funds to Chinese students in the guise of relief.

Another file headed 'Bad Hats or Sundry Suspects' contains some extraordinary material, including notes about Irish missionary priests shown to be members of Sinn Fein, arms smugglers, Bolshevik agitators and petty criminals, with or without a limp, who tried to get new passports and new identities. Gerve Baronet, wife of an Italian politician, comes under attack in a note headed 'Peking Gossip', while the maverick former member of the British House of Commons turned Buddhist monk Trebitsch Lincoln was being watched by Harry Steptoe, the SIS representative in Shanghai and Peking. But even at such a time of feverish activity and suspicion there is no mention of an American woman called Mrs Spencer acting in any unusual way.

Nonetheless, in spite of numerous attempts, the worst that can be pinned on Wallis is a rumour that she appeared in a series of naughty postcards, posing in nothing more than a lifebuoy. There is even a whole book written about the story. But although serious authors insist that these images exist and Harriet Sergeant, author of a scholarly tome on Shanghai, writes of having interviewed a responsible ex-policeman who had seen them – 'a former member of the International Settlement's Special Branch told me that he had confiscated a number as pornographic material' – no one today can provide the postcards themselves.

The Astor House Hotel, something of a rabbit warren comprising at least four different buildings, but a favourite haunt of most naval wives and celebrities stopping off in Shanghai, is where Wallis and Mary Sadler appear to have stayed. Its faded grandeur still evident today, the Astor House Hotel was close by the Garden Bridge and a short walk from the main street, the Bund. The Bund was home to the grand banks, trading companies and newspaper offices, their magnificent neo-classical edifices graced with marble entrance halls on one side and overlooking the river with its constantly loading and unloading cargo ships and wharves on the other. Number 3 The Bund was the most exclusive place of all: the British, male-only

Shanghai Club with its famous Long Bar. The Bund was also where the Palace Hotel was to be found. Wallis wrote that she stayed here, and she may have done on other occasions when she visited Shanghai; there are a number of discrepancies and ellipses in her account of her year in China.

Wallis wasted little time in contacting the Englishman to whom she had been given an introduction. 'His name does not matter. I came to know him as "Robbie"', she wrote, insisting rather bizarrely that she got in touch only at the urging of a woman she did not know in the next-door hotel room. She describes him as young, handsome, beautifully dressed with an attractive voice. For as soon as she sent him an introductory note he responded, first with a basket of exotic fruit and then with a telephone call inviting her to join him for a cocktail in the bar later that afternoon. Wallis, wearing a single red camellia, was clearly an attractive prospect as the drink turned into dinner, which proved 'even more pleasant'.

Who was this man and why was Wallis so coy about naming him? Others have named him as Harold Robinson, a British diplomat, but there was no British diplomat of that name in the city. He was probably Harold Graham Fector Robinson, a British architect born in Hampstead in north London who went (or was sent) to Shanghai as a young man, returning to the UK briefly around 1910 to qualify for election as an associate of the Royal Institute of British Architects (RIBA). According to Kelly's Street Directory for 1924 Shanghai, Harold Robinson had a residence at 27 Great Western Road, a good address in the west end of town, close to the Kadoorie Marble Hall mansion. There is neither wife nor children listed for that address. As Wallis remarked, Robbie lived in a large house with his (male) business partner, 'where they entertained the more amusing members of the foreign colony then predominantly British'. Robbie knew everyone in Shanghai, and he swiftly drew Wallis into the sort of world she thrived on – garden parties and race meetings at the Shanghai Race Club, which was at the centre of all social life. In the 1930s, when the clubhouse was rebuilt, he was the architect responsible for the rebuilding the 66-acre racecourse, where polo and bowling also took place. Yet Wallis described continuing the warm friendship with him as 'purposeless', even though she clearly relished his company.

Robbie also escorted Wallis to dinners at the Majestic Hotel on Bubbling Well Road where:

> in a bower of flowers one danced in a sunken courtyard by the light of coloured lanterns. It was here in the company of Robbie that I first heard Vincent Youmans' *Tea for Two* and the combination of that melody, the moonlight, the perfume of jasmine, not to mention the Shangri-la illusion of the courtyard, made me feel that I had really entered the Celestial Kingdom. No doubt about it, life in Shanghai in 1924 was good, very good and in fact almost too good for a woman under a dangerous illusion of quasi-independence.

Wallis, like any woman of her class, could not be expected to know about the desperate conditions of poor factory workers or rickshaw pullers sleeping in alleyways or sampans. But she was clearly oblivious to the deep political unrest and frequent dangerous skirmishes in the city. The Shanghai Wallis is referring to in 1924 was one of dinner parties and tea dances – although according to one commentator more whisky than tea was often drunk at both – as well as boutiques selling fine silks, jade and choice pieces of chinoiserie. Several luxury hotels employed top American jazz bands to entertain the hundreds of couples who twirled around the magnificent sprung floors. But her account is interesting because, although she refers to being in the city in 1924, she obviously returned at least once more the following year as there exists a Shanghai Race Club complimentary member's badge in the name of Mrs Spencer for the spring 1925 meeting.

Robbie tried to help her with a divorce by introducing her to a lawyer in Shanghai, but this attempt too was abandoned once she discovered the cost. Instead she decided, rather than return to the US and her disapproving mother, that she would visit Peking. As she was not yet thirty, there was an element of now or never about it for her. In 1925 there was no direct rail link between the two cities, so getting to the capital involved a journey of at least a thousand miles, taking a coastal steamer to Tientsin and then transferring by train, the famous 'blue express'. The warlords were renowned for stopping trains in remote places, boarding them and arousing fear and havoc among the passengers. Wallis, having persuaded Mary Sadler to travel with her, was warned when she arrived at Tientsin that trains were experiencing daily raids. Both women were firmly advised by the American Consul not to proceed to Peking, and Mary Sadler, taken ill at this point, returned to Shanghai. Yet Wallis insisted on her right to proceed. 'Having come so far, I did not propose to be stopped by a mere Civil War and accordingly informed the Consul that I was sure my husband would have no objections to my going on and there could be no question of the government being held responsible for me.'

Wallis disobeyed the Consul's advice and continued on what became a thirty-eight-hour train journey, interrupted by brigands with rifles boarding the train several times. But although they looked menacing, nothing disastrous happened to her and she arrived in Peking several hours late to be met on the platform by Colonel Louis Little, the officer commanding the US Legation Guard at Peking and a man she had known slightly in Washington through Corinne. The Consul, snubbed by Wallis, had wired forward about this brazen American subject. Wallis's ability to use to her advantage contacts she barely knew was an art form enabling her to leap around the world. The Colonel forgave her and helped her on her way to the Grand Hôtel de Pékin, located close to the US Legation and just across the road from the old Imperial City and Palace.

Staying here was a luxury which for the two weeks she had in mind would have used up all of Win's $225-a-month allowance. But one evening, escorted by a man she had met once or twice in Paris through Corinne, a minor diplomat called Gerry Green who had invited her to a dance at the hotel, Wallis spotted yet another friend on the other side of the ballroom. Katherine Bigelow was a stunningly beautiful friend from Coronado days whose first husband had been killed early on in the First World War and who was now married to an American would-be writer and dilettante, Herman Rogers. Pleased to see an old friend, Katherine introduced Wallis to Herman: 'an unusually attractive man with a lean handsome face, brown wavy hair and the bearing and look of an athlete'.

Herman, who came from a wealthy family in New York, had been a rower at Yale. He met Katherine in 1918 in France as a soldier on a train passing through a station where she was working as a Red Cross nurse. After they married they travelled the world searching for a beautiful place to make their home that would also inspire Herman to write. They were currently in Peking living in an old courtyard house in a *hutong*, or narrow alleyway, in the Tartar City close to the Hataman Gate. They invited Wallis to lunch the next day and 'insisted that I leave the hotel and come to stay with them'.

Wallis admits she did not resist when they pressed her to stay. They had created a delightful home with a leisurely lifestyle and offered to put an amah (maid) and a rickshaw boy at her personal disposal. Motor cars were rare in Peking but servants came cheap – about $15 a month. Wallis wanted to pay but had only her allowance from Win on which to live, plus a small amount from a legacy left by her grandmother. In the event her skill at poker, learned at Pensacola, carried her through. The first time she played with Herman and Katherine Rogers she won $225 – the same as her monthly allowance. Gambling came naturally and thus began 'without conscious plan or foreknowledge what was beyond doubt the most delightful, the most carefree, the most lyric interval of my youth – the nearest thing I imagine to a lotus eater's dream that a young woman brought up the "right" way could ever expect to know'. She wrote an 'ecstatic' letter to her friend Mary Kirk at this time about her life in China 'entirely devoted to a lyrical list of the servants that she Wallis was now able to afford from the number one boy down through the whole long roll'.

If Washington was hazardous, Shanghai dangerous and illusory, Peking was exotic, sexually liberating and pulsing with life, yet all from the security of living with a respectable couple, Herman and Katherine Rogers. Life for a foreigner in that walled city enclave, especially in the legation quarter, where bachelors outnumbered women by about ten to one, was magical. It was, she said later, 'an ideal place for a woman with time on her hands and a secret sorrow in her heart' – the sorrow more for Espil than for Win. Almost everything about the charm of Peking captivated Wallis, including the noisy street vendors and camel trains. But the language she never mastered, having decided early on that the effort was too great. Herman and Katherine had a Chinese scholar in a long black gown who came to instruct them every day before lunch. Wallis joined in briefly but gave up; it wasn't that she lacked the ability had she applied herself, but she did not need the skill badly enough. 'I'm tone deaf and Chinese has different tones on different levels and they all have different meanings,' she explained. She had the same inability to appreciate music. She preferred riding, swimming in the big new pool at the American Legation, polo and dinner dances every night until the small hours.

Word of Wallis and her doings had spread rapidly long before her train actually reached Shanghai. Even her arrival in Peking was immediately the subject of gossip and scandal among the foreign and Chinese communities alike. There was always a story worth repeating about 'the lively Mrs Spencer', and her visit was the source of seemingly endless tales according to long-time Peking resident Diana Hutchins Angulo, whose parents were close friends of Herman and Katherine Rogers. The families spent weekends together in the temples of the Western Hills (Rogers rented his own temple), enjoyed outings to the racecourse together at Pao Ma Chang, and explored the many palaces, temples and monuments of the city.

Herman and Katherine entertained constantly at their courtyard house, with a regular stream of international diplomats passing through, boosting the native coterie of artists and writers. Wallis was often the life and soul of the party. One of those who now fell for Wallis was the Italian naval attaché (later Admiral), Alberto Da Zara, a thirty-five-year-old diplomat, not as handsome as Espil but with a similar gallant charm and perfect manners, love of poetry, command of many languages and broad knowledge, as well as a talent for riding. Based in Peking, he ran military missions along the Yangtze River. Writing of the season of 1924–5 and the acres of newsprint devoted to horseracing, beautiful women and other sporting passions in Peking, he said that Wallis Spencer was one of the most enthusiastic racegoers. In his memoirs he talks carefully about their relationship but rhapsodizes about her looks, how 'her best features were her eyes and her hair worn off the face and the way her classic hairstyle suited the beauty of her forehead'. He then devotes the rest of the paragraph to the exquisite nature of her blue eyes, into which he evidently spent hours staring.

Others remember the affair rather differently. 'Mrs Spencer was infamous for arousing bouts of passion among adoring males,' recalls Diana Angulo, who knew Wallis, Robbie and her Italian admirer not only then but later. 'Through the years I think men found her witty, and that special ability of giving them her full attention, quite an art! I think men were more generous and complimentary than women.' Angula adds: 'Lt Alberto Da Zara, an excellent horseman with a keen and practised eye for charming women, fell under her spell.' Decades later when he returned to China aboard his flagship *Montecucolli* as Admiral Da Zara there was a splendid photo in his quarters of Wallis in Court dress inscribed 'To you'. Wallis herself admits that he bequeathed to her some poetry that he had written.

The inscription is worth pausing over, indicating as it does how adept Wallis was at making a man feel he was the only one in the world. There was therefore no need for further identification; he was the only one. In another photograph from a private family collection of Wallis with Lieutenant Da Zara she is not, as others might be, looking at the camera but is focusing entirely on her man. However, as Diana Angulo, whose family knew many Italian old-school diplomats in China, explains: 'in that league Italians tended to marry into the old aristocratic families'.

There had been other men friends during the Lotus Year including one described as a 'dashing British Military Officer', and she also met at this time, probably through Da Zara, the glamorous and wealthy young Italian aristocrat Count Galeazzo Ciano, playboy son of a First World War hero. Ciano was already a Fascist sympathizer having taken part in the 1922 march on Rome. Diana Angulo recalls: 'From Italian friends I often heard that Ciano was very taken by her.' But the Count was twenty-one at the time, seven years younger than Wallis, a newly qualified law graduate embarking on a diplomatic career which took him to Rio de Janeiro, the Holy See and Peking in the space of one year, 1925. Later, Count Ciano became Mussolini's son-in-law with a well-deserved reputation for ruthlessness and promiscuity and was executed by an anti-Fascist firing squad in 1944. In 1930, newly married to the nineteen-year-old Edda Mussolini, he came to serve as Italian consul in Shanghai. A casual acquaintance with Wallis five years earlier in China was thus embellished to create a story that they had had an affair which resulted in an unwanted pregnancy and botched abortion.

But none of her friendships blossomed into likely marriage and, as she was about to turn thirty, she knew it was time to face reality – what she calls the unfinished business of her marriage to Win – and either get a divorce and find another man to marry, or look for a job, a prospect she did not relish.

Wallis writes of a Peking summer and winter and spring, of an inner voice suddenly speaking to her quite severely telling her that she was deluding herself if she stayed any longer. In fact she had returned to Shanghai in the spring of 1925, possibly because she recognized that she was becoming too close to Herman, in many ways her ideal man. Sometimes, in the late afternoon, he would take her walking along the broad parapet of the great wall around the city. She had had many hours to brood about what she should do and, with renewed confidence that she could still attract men, decided it was time to find a ship that would carry her across the Pacific, to take her home to America and to the future that she now had to face.

4
Wallis on the Lookout

'I can't go on wandering for the rest of my life'

Wallis sailed from Japan to Seattle in early September 1925, but while en route across the Pacific fell ill with 'an obscure internal ailment'. She recalled that the ship's doctor 'struggled valiantly with a very puzzling case' and then had her transferred to hospital as soon as the ship docked in Seattle. There followed an operation, which she described as not long but 'one more thing I had to go through alone in a strange city'. If ever a woman sounded in need of a husband this was she.

The mention of an internal ailment has made critics of Wallis – and some biographers – rush to insist upon a bungled abortion in China being the cause. But if this were the case she would be unlikely to refer to it in this way. Perhaps the ailment was something else, a complication resulting from having internal male sex organs, which is a common problem for DSD sufferers – such an obscure complaint that Wallis might have concluded it was something she would never need to explain, and she was anyway often in pain from what she called 'stomach attacks'. But in the narrative of her life which Wallis was intent on shaping – that of a lone woman struggling to live a good and decent life after her husband had abused her – facing an operation alone on her way to fight for a divorce is an integral part of the story.

In fact she contacted Win after the operation because she had to travel by train across the continent, from west coast to east, while she was still feeling very weak. He was on leave with his family in Chicago and boarded the train there to accompany her on the final leg to Washington. Wallis then went to stay with her mother who, aged fifty-six, had now remarried: her third husband was Charles Gordon Allen, a Washington civil servant. Alice had been unlucky in love and her attempts to make ends meet had often caused embarrassment to her daughter, but she never lost her sense of humour. Photographed sitting on the knee of her new husband she signed the picture: 'Alice on her last lap'. But Wallis was less keen than ever to stay with her mother and new stepfather, so, as soon as she had recuperated, she set out to get a divorce and make a new life. In the international diplomatic circles in which she moved this seemed to be what women did when things didn't work out, not only a common occurrence but far removed from the shameful state that her family insisted it was. She soon found the advice she had been looking for. In Virginia she could obtain a divorce for a total cost of $300 (a not insignificant sum) on grounds of desertion if she could prove three years' separation from her husband. There was also a residency requirement of one year, which was no great hardship. She knew Virginia well, having spent many happy summers there with cousins and at camp. Aubrey Weaver, the young lawyer to whom she had been recommended, was a family friend of the Mustins and he suggested she stay in a small town called Warrenton in Fauquier County, where he knew of an inexpensive but comfortable hotel. It was a horsy place where almost everyone rode or hunted even if they did not own a horse, and the Warrenton Gold Cup Race for Gentlemen Jockeys was a major local event. During the week Wallis could go for walks and read – an activity that held little appeal for her either then or subsequently. Among books she subsequently claimed to have read in that year of waiting, 1927, were the novels of Somerset Maugham, John Galsworthy and Sinclair Lewis, some poetry and one book of philosophy.

She described her time there as the most tranquil she had ever known. 'I simply rusticated and when I wasn't rusticating I vegetated with equal satisfaction.'

So it was from Room 212 of the Warren Green Hotel, a room with a view of the Fauquier National Bank, with 'faded flower wallpaper, a high brass bed, battered night table, imitation mahogany bureau ... a classic example of what my mother used to call inferior decorating', that Wallis set out to rebuild her life. She would have to share a bathroom, but that did not bother her. The other guests were mostly travelling salesmen, but that, too, did not concern her as she had many connections and wasted little time in rediscovering them. There were schoolfriends from Arundell and Oldfields days, mostly married now, and even an old boyfriend, Lloyd Tabb, whom she had dated after meeting him at Burrland summer camp, who was not yet married. But her most loyal escort was Hugh Armistead Spilman, a childhood friend from Baltimore who had served in France during the First World War and now worked at the bank in the main square. He was happy to take Wallis dancing or to dinner parties, but, even though he professed keenness, there was no question of marriage. Wallis made it clear that this time she was going to marry money.

The divorce required a letter from Win stating that he no longer wanted to live with her and had deserted her. Wallis asked him to backdate this statement to June 1924 so that the divorce could, she hoped, be granted in June 1927, exactly three years later. Wallis in her deposition stated that she had not lived with Win for four years, omitting any mention of having seen him in China.

While waiting for the decree she needed little persuasion when invited by her aunt Bessie, who had never remarried and was fond of Wallis's company, to travel with her to Europe. It infringed the Virginia residency requirement somewhat to be sailing for months around the Mediterranean, but she was prepared to risk that in order to sightsee in Naples, Palermo and along the Dalmatian coast, as well as in Monte Carlo, Nice and Avignon. Wallis was in Paris alone, Bessie having returned home, when she received a cable from her mother telling her that Uncle Sol had died. She arranged to sail home immediately, believing that, as her uncle's favourite niece, she stood to inherit a considerable fortune. There had been talk of him leaving $5 million – no wonder she had not been in any hurry to tie herself down with another man. However, two months before his death, Solomon Warfield had apparently changed his will, angry with Wallis for going ahead with a shameful divorce against his advice. She was well aware of his views but not that he would behave in such a vindictive manner. He now left most of his money to establish a home for aged and indigent gentlewomen as a memorial to his mother, Anna Emory Warfield. Insultingly, he stipulated that a room be set aside for Wallis in the home if she ever needed it. He also made a bequest:

> If my niece Bessiewallis Spencer, wife of Winfield Spencer, shall survive me I give to the Continental Trust Company the sum of $15,000 in trust to collect and receive the income arising therefrom and to pay over the income to my niece in quarterly instalments so long as she shall live and not remarry.

Wallis was not just angry about Uncle Sol's will, she was, Mary Kirk told her sister Buckie, furious. It showed a cruelly controlling hand from the grave and Wallis contested it, charging that her uncle was mentally incompetent and emotionally disturbed at the time he made the will. On appeal, the court was to impose a slightly more favourable settlement, and a few months later Wallis received about $37,500 worth of US shares from the executors who were concerned that other War-fields were threatening to challenge the will. But for the moment her lawyer advised her to return to Warrenton to maintain her residency requirement if she wanted her divorce to go through smoothly. On 6 December 1927 Judge George Latham Fletcher considered her request and, four days later, granted her a divorce decree.

Wallis was now a free woman but uncertain what to do next or where to go. One of the attractions of Warrenton for her had been its good rail connections, enabling her to see her mother and friends in New York or Washington at weekends. As soon as she returned from China she had renewed the friendship with her old schoolfriend Mary Kirk, now married to Jacques Raffray, a glamorous Frenchman. Jacques Achille Louis Raffray, always known as Jackie, was a First World War veteran who had come to America to train US troops to fight in France. At first the Kirk parents had not been in favour of this moneyless marriage but gave way in the face of Mary's evident passion for such a charming, unusual and attractive man. Raffray came from a much travelled and adventurous family: his parents had once made a dangerous crossing of the Abyssinian desert. But shortly after Jacques' birth his mother had died, and he grew up in Rome where his father, a scientist, lived.

Having stayed for some weeks during March 1926 with Mary and

Jackie in their elegant New York apartment overlooking Washington Square, Wallis took to escaping Warrenton for shorter weekend shopping trips in New York. She spent Christmas that year with the Raffrays, waiting out her divorce. The two young women had remained in regular mail contact for the last few years and had plenty to tell each other. Mary, who tried to earn a living by managing a small boutique, no doubt welcomed a chance to tell her old schoolfriend about the difficulties she was encountering in her marriage to Jacques, having suffered three miscarriages. The Kirk family believed that these were most likely caused by Jacques' syphilis. He soon began drinking heavily and Mary felt powerless to stop him.

Mary's sister Buckie also saw a lot of Wallis during the two years after her return from China because she too was living in New York. She remembers the first time she introduced her new husband, the artist Will (or Bill) Hollingsworth, to Wallis. 'En route I warned him not to fall for her and he was vastly amused ... I elaborated. Any attention [she gave him] would only be her automatic reaction to any attractive man. I suspected that now her fling at romance had failed she would revert to her intention to marry for money.' Wallis was included in many Kirk family lunches and dinners at this time, often with others present as well.

> Whatever the company, one topic of conversation emerged; how, once she got her divorce, Wallis would support herself. Although this often became hilarious, as Wallis described her deficiencies for every job suggested, Bill and I grew a bit tired of talk we were both convinced was no more than talk – what Wallis wanted was not a job but a husband well provided with money.

Wallis did make some half-hearted attempts at finding work. Her mother suggested a secretarial course, but this foundered on her distaste for the typewriter. Working as a shopgirl was beneath her dignity. She tried to write an essay about spring hats for a competition in a fashion magazine but one polite rejection letter instantly convinced her that journalism was not her métier either. Her next foray into the job market was trying to persuade Morgan and Elisabeth Schiller, friends who lived in Pittsburgh and owned a company manufacturing tubular steel scaffolding for construction, that she would make a brilliant saleswoman. What appealed to Wallis was the idea of 'doing something different, something out of the ordinary for a woman, a job in which I could pit my wits not against other women but against men in a man's world'. She went to Pittsburgh for three weeks, staying with her friends in an attempt to understand all about tubular steel. But, when she realized that the job required quick-fire mathematical calculations, she gave up on that idea too, recognizing that this was never going to be where her future lay. Now a free woman but without Win's allowance to support her, she had to decide urgently. She could not live on friends' charity for ever.

Some months earlier, at the Raffrays', she had met friends of theirs called Ernest and Dorothea Simpson, or as Wallis wrote in her memoir, Mr and Mrs Ernest Simpson, never mentioning his wife by name. She was the former Dorothea Parsons Dechert, descended from generations of lawyers and politicians, with one great-grandfather who was a senator and another who was Chief Justice Theophilus Parsons of Massachusetts. The couple, married in 1923, lived in style on the Upper East Side and had one child together, a daughter called Audrey; there was another daughter, Cynthia, from a previous marriage of Dorothea's. At first Wallis met the Simpsons only on her visits to New York at the Raffrays'. But then Mary invited Ernest alone to make up a fourth at bridge and soon Ernest fell prey to Wallis's magnetism. Although still married, and a father, he started taking Wallis to art galleries and museums in the city, as well as to lunches and dinners. It was not long before he had asked Wallis if she would marry him as soon as they were both free. Wallis, naturally, always insisted that the four-year Simpson marriage was on the rocks long before she met Ernest. But Dorothea, who was unwell at the time and in hospital, said later: 'From the moment I met her I never liked her at all. I've never been around anybody like that ... she moved in and helped herself to my house and my clothes and, finally, to everything.' The dislike was mutual, soon to be compounded for Wallis by increasing resentment of Ernest's regular payments to his ex-wife and their daughter Audrey which she felt they could ill afford.

Wallis was now thirty and desperate to find stability and a comfortable lifestyle. Ernest was not quite in the Espil or even the Da Zara league of dashing diplomats. But he had a certain world outlook that appealed, was well read and intensely knowledgeable about the classics, art and antiques among a wide range of other things. Wallis liked that in a man, perhaps aware of her own intellectual short-comings. He was not bad looking either and, she believed, was moderately well off thanks to his family shipping company. Perhaps the key attraction lay in the fact that she could move to London with him and make a fresh start in a city where she was not known.

Ernest Aldrich Simpson was born in New York in 1897, one year after Wallis. His parents, the former Charlotte Gaines and Ernest Louis Simpson, had been married for more than twenty years at the time of his birth and already had a daughter, Maud, two decades older. A mere generation before, the Simpsons had been an observant Jewish family called Solomon who lived in Plymouth, in south-west England. Leon Solomon, the patriarch and Ernest's grandfather, came to London in his twenties from Warsaw, where he was born around 1840. But within a few years he had married a Penzance-born Jewish girl, Rose Joseph, and quickly became the prosperous head of a family of twelve children. In the 1861 census Leon listed a butler, footman, coachman, coachman's wife, groom and young professor of Hebrew studies in his household. He described himself as a 'capitalist'. They were well-known worshippers at the Western Synagogue where, it was noted, he had not only bequeathed a magnificent torah mantle but in 1863, 'unsolicited', had enlarged the gallery and redecorated the entire synagogue at his own expense. In 1841 there were only about two or three hundred Jews in Plymouth and Exeter, while the total population of Jews overall in England was fewer than 40,000. Plymouth was a popular destination for those, economic migrants in today's parlance, who had family and business connections in the area, as the Solomons clearly did; one Solomon Solomons was recorded as living there in 1769. Many Jews who chose to live in the south-west corner of England traded in and around the docks, shipping goods around the world. The Solomons had strong connections with other parts of the family in Hamburg which endured until the 1940s, when the Hamburg Solomons were all killed by the Nazis.

Ernest Louis, the seventh child of Leon, was a man determined to make his way in life. Like his father he left home before he was twenty, the only child of the family it appears to have left at this young age, and in 1873 went to America, changing his name to Simpson and becoming a naturalized US citizen shortly afterwards. He set up the shipping and brokerage firm Simpson and Spence in 1880, which still exists today as Simpson, Spence and Young. Within three years of his arrival in America, Ernest Louis, aged twenty-two, married Charlotte Gaines, the well-connected daughter of a New York lawyer who was just nineteen. After Maud's birth, Ernest Louis devoted all his time and energy to building up a flourishing business and, by all accounts, the marriage quickly soured. But in 1897, more than twenty years after they were married, a son was born, called 'Ernest' after his father and 'Aldrich' after Charlotte's mother. Ernest Louis was by this time constantly travelling and often took a young French lady, Leah Métral, known as 'Midget' (or, by Wallis, as 'the French Hussy'), as his very public mistress. Charlotte Simpson, not surprisingly increasingly aggrieved, was expected to put up with it.

Ernest Aldrich was always made aware of his dual British–American heritage and, aged twenty-one, was allowed to choose where he wanted to live. Perhaps because of tension in the New York home or perhaps because his sister, married with children, lived in Britain, Ernest decided while still at Harvard to leave for England without graduating and do his patriotic duty. It was a courageous decision in 1917 before the United States was involved in the First World War, to join the Coldstream Guards as a second lieutenant and fight if one did not have to. In the event, he remained in England training and was not sent to the trenches. But young Ernest was always living in the shadow of his steely and difficult father – a small man with a huge ego and ambition – and perhaps decided that this would be a way of proving his worth. At all events he survived the war unscathed and found friendships made in those months a source of strength in the coming years. He elected to become not just a British subject but as British as he could possibly be, obliterating any suggestion of foreignness let alone Jewishness. He wore his Guards tie most days.

According to his only son, being British and all the supposed traditional values that went with that became young Ernest's code of behaviour from now on. Stiff upper lip may be a cliché but, underneath the neat moustache, Ernest's lip was rigid. Belief in the monarchy, not spending more than you earn, behaving at all times like a gentleman, were inalienable principles for Ernest. 'A gentleman never offended a lady unintentionally' was a mantra for life that he ensured his own son grew up with. Having Jewish blood was an attribute never mentioned at a time when several clubs he wished to join would not have had Jews as members. Mixing with Jews was not something Ernest Simpson would have done and dinner-table conversation was, according to his son reminiscing about the 1950s, even casually anti-Semitic. What attracted Wallis to Ernest was probably his dependability, the air of security and breeding that he radiated. He was good looking and in love with her. She would not have known about his Jewish background at this point, if ever – he never once mentioned it to his son, who discovered only after his father's death.[3] But in any case Wallis in 1928 would have had only the haziest notion of what it meant to be Jewish. She had grown up avoiding Baltimore's poor immigrant Jewish community, and she had not been part of Shanghai's rich Jewish merchant scene which included Sassoons, Ezras, Kadoories and Hardoons, although she may have heard tales of their fabulous wealth. Ernest may even have been the first Jew she had known. When she wrote in her memoirs, without intentional irony, that Ernest had always yearned 'to follow the ways of his father's people' she certainly did not have in mind that he longed to meet any Solomon cousins in the West Country.

However, Wallis probably was well aware of the society marriage that his sister Maud had made to Peter Smiley in 1905. Peter Kerr-Smiley became a prominent Member of Parliament for North Antrim from 1910 to 1922 and ardent supporter of Sir Edward Carson with his 'Keep Ulster British' campaign. Family lore recounts that the name 'Kerr' was formally added to 'Smiley' at Maud's insistence when she belatedly discovered that, as a younger son, her future husband would not inherit a title from her father-in-law, Sir Hugh

---

3 See p. 243.

Houston Smiley, created a baronet two years previously. She settled for a double-barrelled surname as consolation, taking 'Kerr' from her Scottish mother-in-law, Elizabeth Anne Kerr. The family was both well connected and prosperous as Sir Hugh had made a fortune in the Irish linen industry and his wife's family owned a large sewing-thread business in Paisley, enabling them to create a fine home, Drumalis House in Larne, County Antrim, which reflected their wealth and position in society. But Drumalis passed to Sir John Smiley, Peter's elder brother, and was never home for the Kerr-Smileys. They lived mostly in London, in a large house in Belgrave Square, which became Maud's home after she separated from her husband. It was from here that Maud, a tiny, birdlike woman, dazzled as she carried on her various charitable works among the viscounts and countesses who became her friends and which was to give Wallis a basis for her launch into society.

In the spring of 1928 Wallis went once more to stay with her friends Herman and Katherine Rogers, now living in the South of France, to think about her future. They gave her time and space to decide, as she explained to her mother from London in July:

> that the best and wisest thing for me to do is to marry Ernest. I am very fond of him and he is *kind*, which will be a contrast ... I can't go on wandering for the rest of my life and I really feel so tired of fighting the world all alone and with no money. Also, 32 doesn't seem so young when you see all the really fresh youthful faces one has to compete against. So I shall just settle down to a fairly comfortable old age ... I hope this hasn't upset you darling – but I should think you would feel happier knowing somebody was looking after me.

In May, five months after her divorce, Wallis had told Ernest, then living in London, that she was ready to marry him. She sailed to London later that month and based herself in a small flat in St James's Street until they married and could look for a house together. They decided to have a registry-office wedding as soon as it could be arranged.

21st July 1928 was a sunny summer's day and, wearing a

yellow dress and blue coat that she had fortuitously just had made in Paris, Wallis was collected by Ernest's chauffeur, Hughes, and driven to Chelsea Register Office. The other witnesses were Ernest's father and nephew, Maud Kerr-Smiley's son. Wallis described the setting as 'a gloomy Victorian pile more appropriate for a trial than the culmination of a romance. The ceremony – "a cold little job" as Ernest later called it, was over in a flash.' But then, as she wrote to her mother, who was ill and unable to make the journey across the Atlantic, 'the second time round doesn't seem so important'.

After a champagne toast in the Grosvenor Hotel, 'a rambling soot-stained structure at Victoria Station', where Ernest senior was staying – as ever without his wife – the new Mr and Mrs Simpson, with Hughes at the wheel, set off for Paris and Spain in a yellow Lagonda touring car that Ernest had bought for the honeymoon. Ernest spoke fluent French and, with his vast knowledge of art and architecture, acted, according to Wallis, as 'a *Baedeker*, a *Guide Michelin* and an encyclopaedia all wrapped up in a retiring and modest manner'. For the moment, this was all she wanted from life and it was blissful. 'I felt a security that I had never really experienced since early childhood,' she wrote.

On their return, Maud, now in her fifties, set about helping to launch her new American sister-in-law. With her help, the Simpsons found a house to rent temporarily in the West End of London while they looked for a home of their own; 12 Upper Berkeley Street was available while its owner, Lady Chesham, was separated from her husband. It came with a small battery of servants and defective plumbing. Maud also gave luncheon parties – according to Barbara Cartland, then a young society hostess and fledgling novelist, the best in London – to introduce Wallis to her circle and teach her some of the niceties of British etiquette. Cartland, meeting Wallis when she first arrived, considered her not only 'badly dressed but aggressively American. She also told us rather vulgar stories and I was shocked to the core.' But Maud and Ernest were never close – the twenty-year gap was only one difference among many. And since Wallis was determined that the only way she would make a mark in

British society was by standing out she was never prepared to conform in the way Maud had in mind for her.

Maud's life revolved around fundraising for a number of good causes and launching her twenty-one-year-old daughter Elizabeth into society as a debutante. If Wallis could be relied upon to be amusing, she would be useful. The winter of 1928–9 was bitterly cold and foggy. Wallis, initially with few friends, was homesick and sometimes lonely, and considered London gloomy, grey and unfriendly. 'It evoked in me a bone-deep dislike. There was about the city a pervading indifference, a remoteness and withdrawal that seemed alien to the human spirit.' In her memoirs she explains her behaviour as something she had learned in the interests of her first husband:

> I had been shaped in the circle of naval officers and their wives, where a woman learned to manoeuvre furiously for her husband's promotion and where an American woman of my generation judged it important to be a little different or in any case interesting, and was prepared to pit her ideas spiritedly against those of the male . . . English women, though formidably powerful in their own sphere, were still accepting the status of a second sex.

But at least, in these first few months, she found Ernest's company pleasant. Weekdays she spent shopping in the morning, keen to visit the butcher, baker and fishmonger in person in order to poke and prod and ensure she was given the right cuts of meat and portions of equal sizes – the latter was then considered an unusual request for hostesses who tended to serve a roast or stew and leave quantities, as well as presentation, to chance. But, for Wallis, attention to detail was always part of her desire to control her environment as far as she could. It was also necessary as a way of passing the time after Ernest left home at 9 a.m. when, as she admitted, 'the day sometimes stretched vacantly before me' until he returned, which was never before seven in the evening. Sometimes she met people for lunch or went to the hairdresser and continued with her old habit of reading the newspapers to make sure she was *au fait* with the latest news. Revealingly, she explained how she would scour the Court Circular, which monitored royal activities, but what a superficial picture that gave her of the country she had come to live in and the people she was to live among. For Ernest, hoping to be as successful as his father, the business was his existence. But he would happily spend evenings quietly at home reading, or admiring his fine collection of first editions. At weekends he would plan careful visits to old churches and other buildings in London or else to country towns famed for their ancient castles and cathedrals. At first Wallis was intrigued by everything Ernest had to impart. But this quickly palled. Parties were what she lived for, and without those she became bored.

Their routine was interrupted in the spring of 1929 by a trip to the United States to visit Wallis's mother Alice, now bedridden with a cancerous tumour behind her eye which affected her spirit as much as her eyesight. She rallied sufficiently to meet her new son-in-law, but a few months later Wallis was summoned back across the Atlantic. This time Mary Raffray was there to greet her old friend when the ship docked in New York. Alice was in a coma by the time her daughter arrived and died on 2 November 1929. There was no money to pass on, her savings having been all but wiped out in the Wall Street Crash that year. Wallis felt her mother's poverty as a deep, personal injustice, and part of the ambition which consumed her for the rest of her life was predicated on a determination to avenge this cruelty.

Back in London Wallis now threw all her energies into decorating the flat they had found in a smart new block a stone's throw from the rented house. George Street was nowhere near as fashionable as Belgravia, but Wallis had decided that it was better than Kensington, 'where all the aunts in England live' and it had a smart 'Ambassador double-two-one-five' telephone number. By moving in to 5 Bryanston Court Wallis, although well within childbearing years, was acknowledging that she and Ernest were not intending to produce a family of their own, nor does there ever seem to have been any discussion of inviting Ernest's young daughter Audrey to stay. The apartment had a large and spacious drawing room and an elegant dining room with a spectacular mirror-top table large enough to seat fourteen, but it was hardly child friendly. In addition to the master bedroom with a large 'pink plush' bed, and a pale pink chaise longue, there was a small guest bedroom, 'with an almost perfectly round bed of antique white, upholstered in oyster white satin, and [topped with] pink linen sheets and many pillows', as well as a dressing room cum study for Ernest and two bathrooms. The staff of four – the precious cook, Mrs Ralph, a parlourmaid, a housemaid and a personal maid called Mary Burke, who was to prove most loyal – lived off site.

But planning the decor gave Wallis another activity. She described creating this home as 'giving expression to her feminine interests' and it is clear that the rooms for which she alone was responsible were ultra-feminine, pink and frilly. Where Syrie Maugham, wife of the novelist Somerset Maugham, whose dramatic white style was all the rage by 1928, helped advise, the look was more sophisticated. It was Maugham's idea to have high-backed dining chairs upholstered in white leather and to set tall vases on the table filled with flame-coloured flowers. The drawing room was to be pale chartreuse with cream and beige furnishings, which would show off Wallis's Chinese elephants and other precious pieces of chinoiserie. Once a week she and Ernest set aside a whole evening to go over the household accounts together. All Wallis's purchases, from frocks to fish, from partridges to peonies, were listed for Ernest to scrutinize one by one. Wallis recognized that life in England was extraordinarily cheap by American standards and in addition she now had a little trickle of capital from the unravelling of her uncle's will. They may have lived slightly beyond their means but Ernest, meticulously, paid all the bills and the couple were given extra funding by old Mr Simpson, who lived mostly in London at this time. In return, the least Wallis could do was to submit dutifully to a regular Sunday-evening dinner with this 'tiny, dwarf-like figure with an unusually intelligent face, a goatee and piercing eyes that seemed to go right through one'. She came to despise him for not being more generous towards her and Ernest and she worried, having learned once how fickle old men could be when it came to wills, that he might leave all his capital to Midget.

Ernest had few friends of his own, but Bryanston Court was five minutes from the home of his closest companion, Bernard Rickatson-Hatt, whom he had met during his time in the Brigade of Guards. Rickatson-Hatt had seen action in France and had been badly gassed, which left him permanently nervous. He remained in the army however until 1925 when he joined Reuters News Agency and was soon promoted to the role of editor in chief. He too was newly married to an American woman, Frances née Sharpe, whom he had met while working for Reuters in New York, and they too were childless, enduring a deeply unhappy and fraught marriage. He had read classics at Oxford and, like Ernest, was an enthusiastic bibliophile with a fine collection of Greek and Latin books. Rickatson-Hatt was easy to mock with his monocle, bowler hat and small pug dog, usually carried under his arm. Some evenings he and Ernest read aloud to each other in Latin, but both were far too constrained to discuss their marital problems with each other. For such men in the 1930s to have discussed personal matters of this nature is unimaginable, but each may have had his suspicions about the other having to put up with a disappointing marriage. The details of Rickatson-Hatt's eventually emerged before a divorce court judge in 1939, and it is fair to say that his staunch support and his determination to help his friend in the years ahead owed more than a little to the unfulfilled and deviant nature of his own marital arrangements.

As for Wallis, now she had somewhere to entertain she set about collecting an interesting array of guests, inevitably with a strong American nucleus. Those whom she invited for dinner were drawn almost entirely from her carefully nurtured contacts. Chief among these was Benjamin Thaw, newly appointed First Secretary of the US Embassy, married to Consuelo, one of the trio of glamorous Morgan sisters who had exotic Spanish looks and lots of money. Wallis had known Benjamin's brother, Bill, at Coronado where he had been a beau of Katherine Bigelow before she married Herman Rogers. She also knew of, though she had not met, Consuelo's twin sisters Thelma Furness and Gloria Vanderbilt, both celebrated society beauties. Thelma was currently the much gossiped-about lover of the Prince of Wales and Wallis knew that the pair sometimes met at the Thaws' home.

Among regulars at her table there was also Wallis's favourite cousin Corinne, now married to Lieutenant Commander George Murray assigned as assistant naval attaché at the Embassy, Major Martin

'Mike' Scanlon, 'a dashing bachelor who gave gay cocktail and dinner parties' at his house, the former Ethel Noyes now Lady Lewis and her husband Sir Bill (Willmott), Vincent Massey, the Oxford-educated and immensely wealthy Canadian diplomat and his pretty film-actress wife Alice and many others passing through, as well as an occasional sprinkling of British friends for form's sake.

Wallis quickly established a reputation as a successful and unusual hostess. Her food, her conversation, her decor and her circle were all considered original and of note. Her parties were small but the attention to detail was second to none and the food and wines were lavish. She exaggerated her Americanness with a smattering of Southern recipes, food no one else prepared, and by her ability to mix cocktails – 'a trifling but widely appreciated knack'. With her cocktails – or KTs as she called them – she served sausages, but not on skewers, followed perhaps by caviar with vodka, soup with sherry, and fish with white wine, as well as champagne and brandy. 'Wallis' parties have so much pep no one ever wants to leave,' commented one guest.

In 1931 Mr and Mrs Kirk, Mary's parents, came to Europe and, while they were in London, Wallis proudly invited them to see her new home. She told Edith Kirk that she loved living in England, 'though there is one thing that bothers me a little. I don't know a single Englishwoman well enough to go to the bathroom with her.' Mrs Kirk thought the words sounded vulgar, implying that Wallis wanted to go to the powder room in order to confide some interesting remark or incident about a tall handsome man she might have been dancing with. They knew Wallis well enough to see that she was constantly on the lookout for excitement and interesting people to spice up her life. They could not fail to be impressed at seeing how the poor girl from Baltimore with one broken marriage behind her had succeeded in swiftly making a place for herself in London society thanks to her second marriage to a dull but worthy shipbroker. It was after this visit that Wallis wrote to Mary encouraging her to come and stay, learning from her parents of further unhappiness in her schoolfriend's marriage.

Wallis on the Sidelines

'I suppose I'll have to take the fatal plunge one of these days'

Ever since her arrival in London, Wallis admitted to her aunt, 'I've had my mind made up' to meet the Prince of Wales. She accomplished this feat fairly effortlessly in 1931 through her friendship with Thelma Furness, 'the Prince's girl', and considered the achievement a relief. If she had further aspirations they were to be accorded more respect among her friends and to receive more glamorous invitations to fashionable parties as a result. Prince Edward, now thirty-seven years old, with his still boyish good looks and radiant charm, was adored by millions around the world who did not know him at all. Wallis herself knew much about his activities thanks to gossip and to the Court Circular newspaper announcements, but she knew little about the man himself other than what Thelma let slip.

Edward Albert Christian George Andrew Patrick David was born on 23 June 1894 at White Lodge in Richmond Park, the home of his maternal grandparents, the Duke and Duchess of Teck. He was the first child born to the future King George V and Queen Mary, although his parents were still Duke and Duchess of York at the time of his birth. Through his great-grandmother, Queen Victoria, he was related to most of the crowned heads in Europe. After he had been educated by tutors at home and then at Osborne Naval College, it was decided in 1912 that he would benefit from a more academic life, and Magdalen College, Oxford was selected for him, as were his putative friends there. But, as his official biographer, Philip Ziegler, observed: 'It cannot be said that Oxford widened his cultural horizons.' Yet the young Prince was not without attributes, as was noted by Lord Esher, who had been consulted by Queen Mary about the education and upbringing of the Prince and took long walks with him at Balmoral: 'His memory is excellent and his vocabulary unusual and, above all things, he thinks his own thoughts.' But he found university life, and indeed much of his official life, 'very dull', and he never acquired a habit of reading or of disciplining those thoughts; moreover, his spelling was a disaster. Always chafing against restrictive authority, he left Oxford without graduating.

On the outbreak of war in August 1914, aged twenty, he was allowed to join the Grenadier Guards despite being a mere five feet seven inches tall instead of the regulation six foot, but was then kept as far away from danger as possible. As he grew into adulthood he was full of resentment against his parents and advisers over a range of issues. His father, by now King George V, was a shy disciplinarian unable to communicate with any of his children, all of whom were frightened of him, even as adults. He had a terrible temper and, when he was not venting his fury at them, was making fun of them. Even his most loyal staff, such as his Assistant Private Secretary Alexander Hardinge, were moved to comment upon the mystery of why this essentially kind man 'was such a brute to his children'. His mother, perhaps kinder than history has portrayed her, was also motivated by duty above all and found it hard to display the affection she felt for all her children but especially for her sweet-faced firstborn. Neither parent believed that keeping up with modern trends was important, so many of the arguments they had with David, as Prince Edward was known to the family, were over trivialities such as trouser turn-ups, jazz, cocktails and painted fingernails or the telephone, an innovation which Queen Mary never used.

The Prince's determination to get to the front line and be allowed to serve with his regiment whatever the dangers became a major source of friction. He bitterly reproached himself for leading such a comfortable life when his fellow officers were suffering and dying. 'I do hate being a prince and not allowed to fight!!' he told Godfrey Thomas, a former diplomat who became his equerry and later his private secretary. In a courageous attempt to share the appalling risk and hardship faced by other soldiers, he appealed to Lord Kitchener, Secretary of State for War, to allow him to go to the front, reminding him that as he had four brothers who could take his place it would not matter if he were killed. But Kitchener responded that the real fear was not that he might be killed but that he might be captured and held prisoner.

As Philip Ziegler has suggested: 'The ferocious battering to which he subjected his body, with a regime of endless walks and runs, a minimum of food and sleep, must have been in part a mortification of the flesh to assuage this conviction of his inadequacy.' One of the specific tasks assigned to Godfrey Thomas when he first joined the Prince's staff was to try to get him to eat more and exercise less. Even dancing, when part of an official function and with a girl he detested, could be endured only if he looked upon it as strenuous exercise. This sometimes came as rather a shock for the girl involved. Although deliberate self-starvation was hardly new, by the 1880s eating disorders were slowly being recognized as a disease, mostly affecting women and girls, and the label 'anorexia nervosa' was introduced in 1873 by Queen Victoria's personal physician, Sir William Gull.[4] Staving off puberty is often cited as a factor in female anorexia, but trying to remain eternally childlike is common to both sexes. In the Prince's case, although the symptoms were recognized, no one in royal circles would have dared look into the causes. Thomas became a loyal friend who remained in the Prince's service until the abdication, 'never hesitating to point out or tell me of any failings he may think I am guilty of', according to the Prince. But nor was he ever strong enough to overrule his master.

Edward's letters and diary entries in the 1920s are so full of dismal self-disparagement that sometimes they appear close to childish whining at not being given what he wanted, at others they resemble a deeply worrying *cri de coeur* from a depressed adolescent. One day he wrote, 'I could not face ... any company. I wanted to be alone in my misery!! I feel quite ready to commit suicide and would if I didn't think it unfair on Papa.' But his desire to be of use was genuine and

---

4 That year, Gull published his paper 'Anorexia Nervosa (Apepsia Hysterica, Anorexia Hysterica)', in which he described two cases of young women he had treated for severe weight loss and two others treated by other physicians.

his brief taste of the war in France in 1915, though he had been kept away from shells and behind the front lines, had left him desperately thirsting to do more than inspect troops, visit hospitals and play the largely morale-boosting role that he had been assigned. He was shown the trenches and even allowed to spend a night in one, but was forbidden by his father to fight. One observer commented: 'his main desire appeared to be to get either killed or wounded'. His sense of frustration and shame at his own inadequacy are palpable, if exaggerated, and may have been aggravated by sexual deficiencies. Much as he apparently enjoyed sex, girlfriends openly referred to him as 'the little man'. But he may also have worried that he was sterile. Without tests, he is unlikely to have known whether this was the case but his heavy smoking and drinking were both habits now known to have a drastic effect on sperm count, and he would have had a strong suspicion if, at a time of ineffective contraception, none of his many dalliances with women resulted in a pregnancy. Many of his later ideas about pacifism as well as his deepest feelings of self-loathing can be traced to this time. The love of a good and sensible woman helped him through in 1918.

One evening while on leave in February that year, Edward was attending a party in Belgrave Square (hosted coincidentally by Maud Kerr-Smiley) when he was suddenly ushered into the cellar following an air-raid warning. There he met Mrs Dudley Ward, who had been out for the evening at a different party in the square but was invited in, with her escort for the evening, to take shelter when the siren went off. When the all-clear sounded, the Prince was introduced to Mrs Dudley Ward and the pair spent the rest of the evening together. The attraction was instant and a month later he was writing her very indiscreet letters – addressed to 'my Angel!!' – in which he expressed the hope that he had not said anything terrible, 'though how I long to angel!!'

Freda Dudley Ward was the pretty and petite twenty-eight-year-old daughter of a prosperous Nottingham businessman and his American wife. She had been married for the previous five years to a Liberal MP, William Dudley Ward, sixteen years her senior, with whom she had two daughters, Penelope and Angela. Freda was spirited and fun loving, popular in her own circle and always surrounded by a barrage of admirers. Her husband, known as Duddie, was vice chamberlain of the Royal Household and therefore often out late on public duties – the ideal *mari complaisant*. For the next sixteen years, even though both had other minor dalliances, Freda became the Prince's ever-supportive confidante and lover. The affair was all consuming for the Prince, but relatively discreet, at least to the wider public. At first the couple would meet in a variety of London houses which Freda would buy, decorate and then sell at a profit. But shortly after the war, when the Dudley Wards moved to a magnificent Georgian mansion at Sunbury on Thames, the Prince rented a little Georgian cottage just across the road and came to visit his lover through a side gate into the garden and across the tennis court to the house itself. This, he decided, was more proper than entering through the front door a house belonging to the husband of his mistress. The locals in Sunbury all knew when the Prince's landau arrived for the weekend – a good example of the hypocrisy he was to tell Baldwin later he refused to countenance and of the marital double standards which the Church and the country at large were struggling so hard to oppose.

Freda became something of an ideal, if unattainable, love for the heir to the throne. In pouring out his feelings to her he was discovering himself, a luxury his parents had not thought a necessary part of his education. 'How utterly sick of soldiering one is and anything to do with the Army,' he wrote to her shortly after the Armistice, 'but one can't help liking all the men and taking a huge interest in them ... And how one does sympathise with them and understand how hopelessly bored and fed up they are.' His passionate letters to Freda, sometimes three a day, expose a deeply troubled, insecure young man, uncertain of his future who thought his father, the King, was 'hopelessly out of touch and ignorant', his 'studied hostility to the United States ... a national disaster'. In 1920, when he undertook a seven-month tour of New Zealand and Australia, he revealed more of his inner turmoil:

Now I am going to write something that I know I ought not to really ... but *mon amour* I swear I'll never marry any other woman but you!!! Each day I long more and more to chuck in this job and be out of it and free for you, Sweetie. The more I think of it all, the more certain I am that really the day for kings and princes is past, monarchies are out of date, though I know it is a rotten thing for me to say and sounds Bolshevik.

It was a particularly jarring comment since the principal reason for sending Edward on such a world tour at this time was to show the world that the monarchies had survived in the wake of the overthrow of the Russian Tsar by the Bolshevik revolution.

Just before visiting Washington he told her: 'I'm like you, angel, want to die young & how marvellously divine if only WE could die together ... I'm just dippy to die with YOU even if we can't live together ...'. On many occasions he told her that without her love and support he would prefer to die. 'It's only you who keeps [me] alive and going ... I do get so terribly fed up with it and despondent sometimes and begin to feel like "resigning"!!'

His letters with their invented baby language, using words like *pleath* and *vewy* for 'please' and 'very' and referring to himself in the third person as 'your poor hard worked little boy', are those of an adolescent who has fallen obsessively in love with a more mature woman and convinced himself no one else in the world understands him. To Freda he expressed all the impossibilities of his future life as he saw them and, trusting heavily in her discretion, complained constantly of his difficulties with his 'tyrannical' father. 'He's really been the absolute limit snubbing me and finding fault sarcastically at every possible occasion ... he maddens me, beloved one and I often feel like turning Bolshy as it's so hopeless trying to work for him.' But however much balm she offered him, and however much he pressed – 'I just don't feel I can even exist let alone try to live much longer without you, my precious darling beloved little mummie!!' – she would not marry him, knowing the effect this would have on the royal family and the nation itself.

This dependence on others, frequently a mother figure, is just one aspect of a personality defect brilliantly identified by the psychologist Simon Baron Cohen. In the case of Edward, Prince of Wales, it may

A statue in Baltimore's Mount Vernon Square of the man after whom Wallis was named – lawyer, political reformer and friend of the family, Severn Teackle Wallis.

The house at Blue Ridge Summit, Pennsylvania, where Bessiewallis Warfield was born on 19 June 1896. She always believed she had inherited two conflicting strains: the Warfield toughness and practical ability, and the Montague gentleness and artistic sensibility.

Wallis aged six months with her mother, the spirited and beautiful Alice Montague Warfield, from then on a single parent responsible for Wallis's upbringing.

Uncle Solomon Davies Warfield, Wallis's paternal uncle, a wealthy bachelor on whom she depended for her education and who was to disappoint her when he left his fortune to set up a home in memory of his mother.

Wallis's mother, Alice Montague, was remarried twice more and her hard life helped fuel her daughter's ambition. 'Wouldn't mother have loved it all,' she wrote to her aunt of the exciting times when she first entered the Prince's circle.

A signed portrait of Wallis looking demure as she left Oldfields School ready to conquer the world.

The brief time Wallis spent at the house on Biddle Street – a three-storey brownstone in a fashionable district of Baltimore – was happy and free of financial worry.

Wallis wearing a monocle – one of her schoolgirl experiments with different styles while she was a pupil at Oldfields.

Earl Winfield Spencer Jr (*second from left*), a naval officer and pioneer aviator from Chicago in training at Florida shortly before he met Wallis.

Wallis as a debutante, short of money but never lacking style and said to have more beaux than any other debutante after she was introduced to Baltimore high society in December 1914.

Wallis, as Win's bride, on a cold day in November 1916. The *Baltimore Sun* described the evening wedding as 'one of the most important of the season'.

Mrs Wallis Spencer gazing intently at the Italian naval officer Lt Alberto Da Zara, one of many adoring males who fell for her charms in 1924 in Peking.

A young Wallis posing for a study for a blue Cartier tiara, 1937.

Jack Levine, the American satirical artist, painted *Reception in Miami* in 1948 in response to his disappointment at the way the Duke and Duchess were greeted by fawning admirers in Miami.

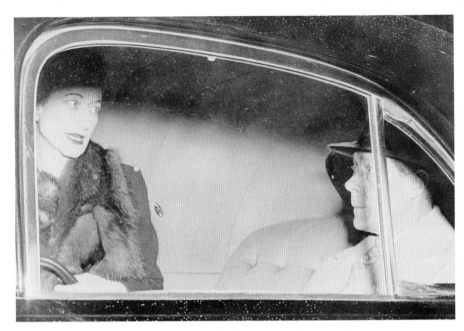

Wallis takes charge, telling the Duke what she thinks … and how his hair should look.

The Duke and Duchess in 1950 at their favourite spa hotel, the Greenbrier in West Virginia, awarding a prize to the legendary golfer Ben Hogan.

The Duke and Duchess dancing at the Greenbrier – an activity the Duchess enjoyed more than golf.

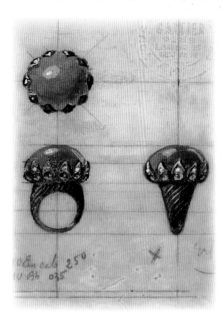

A selection of Cartier jewellery, including
the original sketches, especially made for
The Duchess of Windsor.

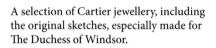

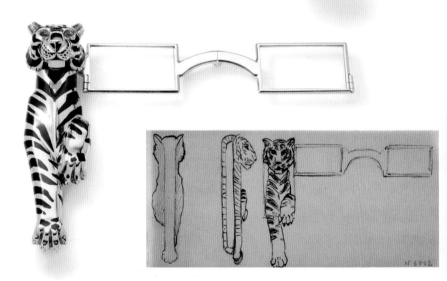

The Duchess at a gala opening of the New Lido Revue in Paris, December 1959, displaying a variety of jewellery including the articulated panther bracelet, made by Cartier with her in mind and sold in London for the second time in 2010.

A rare fashion faux pas – the Duchess chatting to Mrs Aileen Plunkett at a Paris party in 1966 where both women are in the same dress, a stripy shift by Givenchy.

Wallis looking elegant in a plain dark coat with white fur stole in London in 1967. This was a dedication ceremony for a statue to commemorate the centenary of the birth of her mother-in-law, Queen Mary.

The frail Duke, leaving the London Clinic in 1965 following an operation on his eye, flanked by nurses with the Duchess leading the way.

5 June 1972. The funeral of the Duke of Windsor at St George's Chapel, Windsor. Queen Elizabeth II is followed by the Duchess, veiled, and the Duke of Edinburgh.

The Duchess looking haggard, May 1980. She was already ill but survived another six painful and reclusive years.

30 April 1986. The Queen Mother (*top right*) watches as the coffin of the Duchess of Windsor is carried by Welsh Guards down the steps of St George's Chapel, Windsor, before being laid to rest next to the Duke at Frogmore.

not be possible to give it a name but his extremes of behaviour – including a refusal to eat adequately, violent exercise and obsessive concern about weight or the thinness of his legs, verging on anorexia, arranging his myriad clothes in serried rows, his unusual speech, social insensitivity and nervous tics such as constantly fiddling with his cuffs – are just some of the characteristics that come under the broad spectrum of autism or its sometimes less virulent cousin Asperger's Syndrome. Several of those who worked with him closely believed him in different ways to be 'mad', a word that could not be written about him while he was alive. Certainly Prime Minister Baldwin came to believe it to be the case. Alan 'Tommy' Lascelles, who had joined the Prince's staff in 1920 as assistant private secretary under Godfrey Thomas, and was himself severely critical of the Prince, nonetheless advised Nigel Nicolson, editing his father Harold Nicolson's diaries in the 1960s, to remove the word from the text while the ex-King was still alive. 'One must not print it,' he wrote, 'certainly not of anybody with so frightening a mental ancestry as poor Edward P [Edward, Prince of Wales styled himself "EP"].' Lascelles himself commented after a long conversation with the Prince in 1927 that he had been struck by 'the curious absence of belief in ordinary general ideas', what he called his 'ethical impotence'.

> I was always astonished by EP's total inability to comprehend such ideas ... words like 'decency' ' honesty' 'duty' ' dignity' and so on meant absolutely nothing to him. If one said to him 'But surely Sir, you can't do that,' he would reply in quite genuine bewilderment: 'But I don't know what you mean, Tommy. I know I can get away with it.'

Clive Wigram, George V's Private Secretary from 1931 to 1936, was also once heard emerging from a conversation with the Prince 'coming down the King's staircase at Buck. Pal. And exclaiming in his shrill staccato "He's mad – he's mad. We shall have to lock him up. We shall have to lock him up."' Perhaps the most crucial witness is Lord Dawson of Penn, the royal family's doctor, who was similarly 'convinced that EP's moral development ... had for some reason been arrested in his adolescence and that would account for this limitation. An outward symptom of such arrestation, D of P would say, was the absence of hair on the face ... EP only had to shave about once a week.'

From the first, the Prince's entourage was always worried about his unreliable behaviour on foreign tours. Within a decade this had become more and more irresponsible as he would be up all hours at nightclubs drinking and womanizing, not taking his official duties seriously and exhibiting a cavalier attitude to punctuality, much to the consternation of the local dignitaries. His refusal to eat adequately (while drinking and smoking more than adequately) often left him exhausted and without stamina to face the heavy schedule organized for him on tours, so that some of those travelling with him felt he was teetering dangerously on the edge of extreme depression.

For Lascelles the nadir came in 1928, one year after his long talk with the Prince, when George V was, it seemed, close to death while his son was away on a trip to Kenya. The government sent a telegram saying that the King was extremely ill and urgently requesting that the Prince return. When Lascelles showed him the telegram he joked about 'silly old Baldwin' and accused the Prime Minister of using the wire as an electoral dodge. He was not going home. 'I said "Sir, the King is dying and if that doesn't matter to you it certainly matters to us." The Prince of Wales shrugged and gave me a look and went on with his plans for seducing the wife of a colonial official, Mrs Barnes. He was very happy to tell me what he'd done the next morning.' The Prince did return sooner than intended, but, shortly afterwards, Lascelles resigned in disgust at the Prince's attitude; by way of explanation, he was to tell the above story many times. As Duff Hart-Davis, the editor of his diaries, remarked, perhaps Lascelles was the wrong person for the Prince of Wales. 'It could be said', Hart-Davis went on, 'that his moral outlook was too severe, his idea of duty too rigid, his code of conduct too unbending for him to be compatible with such a high-spirited employer. Yet it could equally be said that he was exactly the *right* person for the Prince and that someone of precisely his calibre, with his powerful intellect and high principles, was needed to shape the future King for his role.'

After his resignation from Edward's service, Lascelles took up another post abroad. But in 1935 he returned to royal service as assistant private secretary to the Prince's ailing father, George V, and thus was at the epicentre of the unfolding royal drama. In addition to his intimate knowledge of the protagonists, he was a cousin of Henry Lascelles, 6th Earl of Harewood, who married Mary, the Princess Royal, sister of the Prince of Wales and the future George VI, and therefore was also an insider who saw events coloured by the considerable distaste of the rest of the royal family. What was becoming clear was that the Prince's household, now based in London at York House, a wing of St James's Palace, was increasingly alienated from his father's Court at nearby Buckingham Palace. While it may be true that many of the courtiers reflected the snobbisms of a previous age, isolation from sources of good advice had taken the place of legitimate independence for an heir to the throne. The Prince resented what he called the old order and as Hector Bolitho, an early biographer of Edward VIII, wrote, 'conventional society did not amuse him ... In time the dwindling ranks of society resented the originality of his choice of friends. He seldom went to stay in great country houses, where he might have met and known his contemporaries and ... he was almost stubborn in his habit of turning his back upon the conventions of polite society.'

Those who spoke with an American accent had a much easier chance of amusing the Prince. He liked almost everything that he characterized as new and modern and much of it was American. His foreign tours (including the one to Australia, where he narrowly missed meeting Wallis in Coronado en route) had done much to introduce him to the wider world – or at least that part of it that was still called the Empire. His intensely English good looks – blond hair, wistful blue eyes and generous mouth, often with cigarette dangling – had ensured he was a pin-up figure for millions. As he said to Freda in some half-Americanese he had picked up on his travels, 'Princing' was much easier abroad. The ecstatic response he received wherever he went led to an easy belief that his views chimed with those of 'ordinary men and women' in a way that his father's did not. He did, however, have a genuine sympathy with those who faced unemployment and destitution so soon after offering their lives in the Great

War. 'One can't help seeing the work people's point of view,' he told his mother, Queen Mary, 'and in a way it's only human nature to get as much as one can out of one's employer.' But there's scant evidence that he had any notion of what to do about the situation. It was sincere but vague benevolence, the original triumph of style over substance.

He loathed ceremony of all kind and in 1922, when his sister Mary married Viscount Lascelles, wrote to his mother that he did not mind not being able to attend as 'I have an inordinate dislike for weddings ... I always feel so sorry for the couple concerned.' The following year his closest sibling, Bertie, the Duke of York, married Elizabeth Bowes Lyon, the vivacious and highly suitable twenty-three-year-old daughter of the Earl of Strathmore, a marriage which brought his parents much pleasure. Elizabeth had once harboured romantic feelings herself for the Prince of Wales and had initially been extremely reluctant to accept Bertie's proposal of marriage. True she came from impeccable stock, but there was one skeleton in her ancient cupboard: her great-grandmother Anne, possessing 'a flirtatious nature', divorced her dull husband and eloped with Lord Charles Cavendish-Bentinck and had his child. She was never again received in society.

But the marriages of Edward's siblings scarcely relieved the pressure on him to marry immediately. However much he might wish it away, his awareness of his duty to marry and produce an heir to continue the dynasty was ever lurking. As he told his close friend and travelling companion Lord Louis Mountbatten in 1924, 'I suppose I'll have to take the fatal plunge one of these days tho' I'll put it off as long as I can cos it'll destroy me.'

In 1932, in an unusually frank conversation with his father, the King asked him if he had ever considered marrying 'a suitable well born English girl'. The Prince answered that the only woman he had ever wanted to marry had been Freda Dudley Ward. But she was not available. As long as he remained in love with Freda he persuaded himself that his commitment to her prevented marriage. Yet even though he balked at marriage he longed for an emotionally and physically fulfilling relationship. His liaison with Thelma Furness never really promised this. The pair met at a provincial cattle show while he was still involved with Freda. The Prince, undertaking the sort of mindless royal task which he hated, was awarding rosettes to prize-winning cows.

Thelma, like Freda, was half American and bored in her marriage to a much older man. Thelma Morgan was first married, aged seventeen, to James Vail Converse, but was divorced three years later and in 1926 settled for a second marriage to Marmaduke, 1st Viscount Furness, nearly twenty years older than her. They had a son, Tony, born in 1929, but then led separate lives indulging in frequent affairs. Thelma was exquisitely pretty with dark hair and eyes inherited from her mixed Irish-American and Chilean ancestry, and was allowed plenty of money by her elderly husband, who was known as Duke. His immense wealth derived from the Furness Withy shipping company, founded by his grandfather, of which he was chairman.

Both Thelma and Freda pandered to the Prince's needs to be mothered and indulged his childish whims, especially his craving for teddy bears. One of the biggest, a giant topiary teddy bear at Sunbury, given by the Prince to Freda, is still there today for all who pass the river bank to admire. However, Thelma was much more of a hedonist than Freda and enjoyed encouraging rather than curbing the Prince's natural tendencies towards selfishness and self-indulgence. She admitted that her conversations with the Prince were 'mostly about trivialities'. According to Henry 'Chips' Channon, the well-connected, American-born diarist, it was Thelma Furness (although unnamed by him at the time) who was 'the woman who first "modernised" him and Americanized him, making him over-democratic, casual and a little common. Hers is the true blame for this drama.' From now on observers were often struck by his inimitable blend of cockney and American, which he mixed into his upper-class drawl.

Thelma swiftly moved into the Prince's life and into his new country home – Fort Belvedere – memorably described by Lady Diana Cooper as a child's idea of a fort 'missing only fifty red soldiers ... between the battlements to make it into a Walt Disney coloured symphony toy'. The eighteenth-century house, thirty miles outside

London in the grounds of Windsor Great Park and not far from Sunningdale, was originally constructed as a folly, before being converted into a royal hunting lodge and gradually extended until it had seven bedrooms. In 1929 the building became vacant once again and was given to Prince Edward by his father 'for those damn weekends, I suppose'. Thelma tinkered with various renovation schemes there and had one guest room done up in shocking pink, decorating the top of the bedposts with the Prince of Wales feathers – an exhibition of vulgarity that apparently the Prince found vastly amusing. He installed central heating and up-to-date bathrooms and often arrived in a private plane – all examples of what he had in mind by modernizing. The Fort became his favourite residence and retreat from reality. He remembered playing there as a child with his sister and brothers, some of his happiest moments. The Fort offered a chance to return to that lost world.

A year after they met, the Prince suggested that Thelma and her husband might like to join him and his party on a continuation of the African safari which he had been forced to leave hurriedly when his father was ill. Once his father seemed to have recovered he could see no reason not to return and was away from January until April 1930. In February Lord and Lady Furness met up with the Prince in Kenya. Thelma later wrote in purple prose how, after a day of lion hunting organized by the Governor, she and the Prince had a secret rendezvous:

> This was our Eden and we were alone in it. His arms about me were the only reality; his words of love my only bridge to life. Borne along on the mounting tide of his ardour I found myself swept from the accustomed mooring of caution. Each night I felt more completely possessed by our love, carried ever more swiftly into uncharted seas of feeling content to let the Prince chart the course heedless of where the voyage would end.

Wallis became a friend of Thelma through her connection with Benny and Consuelo Thaw. The women often met for lunch at the Ritz and in early January 1931 Consuelo invited the Simpsons to the Furness home at Melton Mowbray in Leicestershire in the heart of England's fox-hunting country for a Saturday to Monday. The Prince of Wales was to be there, as was Thelma, the hostess, but without her husband, who was away. Convention demanded that one married couple should also be there to act as chaperones, but Consuelo herself could not make it. Would Wallis and Ernest help out?

Wallis was extremely nervous, but accepted. For her, this promised an important step up the social ladder. For Ernest, who revered the monarchy, it was close to his pinnacle of achievement. For both, it was amusing to see Maud Kerr-Smiley provoked into jealousy, especially as she insisted on giving Wallis last-minute etiquette lessons. Wallis admitted that she spent an entire Friday on 'hair and nails etc' and on Saturday 10 January she, Ernest and Benny Thaw went up to Melton Mowbray by train. Wallis had a cold and could not prevent herself snuffling and coughing. But her poker-playing skills came in useful once again as they played for stakes that even she considered 'frighteningly high'. According to the Prince's later account, they discussed central heating or the lack of it in British houses. Wallis was to claim that she did not remember the conversation, only the Prince's 'very loud-checked tweeds . . . and utter naturalness'. But according to other versions of the occasion, she boldly told the Prince that she was disappointed in his predictable choice of topic of conversation: 'Every American woman is asked the same question. I had hoped for something more original from the Prince of Wales.' Thelma Furness insisted there had never been such a conversation and if so Wallis's brusque answer would have been 'not only bad taste but bad manners'. But by the time everyone was recalling in print their memories of this meeting, Wallis had shown herself to be a woman never afraid to adopt this sort of tone when speaking to the Prince in public. Others present maintain that she made little impression on the Prince that weekend, while Wallis herself wrote: 'the facts are as I shall now relate them . . . we met late in the fall of 1930 . . . I am sure I am right.' She dates the meeting according to the clothes she remembers wearing and is dismissive about the conversation. But in a letter dated 13 January 1931 it is clear that she wrote to Aunt Bessie about the weekend, saying 'what a treat it was to meet the Prince in such an informal way', though she later added, 'probably we will never hear or see any of them again'.

Wallis was certain about the date because she had just been to Paris in the autumn of 1930 and had indulged herself in what she called 'a little splurge' – buying a dress from each of the three or four leading couturiers. 'The prospect of having a few chic clothes from the great couturiers was more than I could resist.' Why? Any woman will immediately understand. She knew, given the circles in which she was moving in this 'frowzy dressed town', that an invitation to meet the Prince would come her way very soon and she was going to be prepared for it, in control of how she looked insofar as she could be. She was not buying couture clothes to hang in her wardrobe for quiet dinners with Ernest.

Although some weeks passed with no prospect of a second meeting because the Prince was travelling, Wallis was now busy arranging to have herself presented at Court that season. On 15 May Thelma again invited the Simpsons to a cocktail party she was giving for the Prince's return from a tour of South America. Wallis was excited about this 'as I would like to be given the once-over without the cold'. Also invited was Felipe Espil, the diplomat who had spurned Wallis eight years earlier. But any chagrin she might have felt over seeing him again was more than mitigated by the Prince, who when introduced to the Simpsons that evening, whispered to Thelma that he thought he recognized Wallis. Thelma reminded him of the weekend at Melton Mowbray and, as Wallis rose from her curtsey, he told her how much he had enjoyed that encounter.

By the time Mary Raffray arrived in London later that month Wallis, not yet thirty-five, was moving, if not exactly in the highest echelons of London society, then in those circles which had access to the Prince. When they last met, Wallis had crossed the Atlantic to say goodbye to her dying mother and was feeling lonely and friendless in London. Mary considered that the transformation in her friend's life, just over two years after making a new start in England, was extraordinary – a transformation that, as Ernest understood, would have been inconceivable had she been Mrs Solomon.[5] On the day of her arrival there was a lunch at the Thaws', so Wallis explained that she could not make it down to the docks to greet Mary after her long voyage but instructed her to take a train into London the minute she disembarked. From the station she was to go directly to the lunch before seeing Bryanston Court or changing her clothes. After lunch the women played bridge all afternoon – not what Mary wanted: she complained that she could play bridge any day in New York – then went to Ethel Lewis for a KT. When they returned from Ethel's that first night, Wallis and Mary changed into 'tea gown and pajamas' for dinner. 'Ernest of course always dresses and, except for such evenings at home, wears full dress designated here simply as "white tie" and we sat around and talked until 2 o'clock.'

The next day another American friend who had made a successful marriage to an Englishman, Minerva Dodge, called round early, inspected Mary's wardrobe and went with them for a lunch at the Ritz given by some Argentine diplomats for Lord and Lady Sackville, who were among Wallis's newest friends and owners of the historic Knole House in Kent. Lady Sackville was another American – the former actress Anne Meredith Bigelow. After lunch there was shopping and in the evening Wallis gave a dinner for twelve, which included Ethel and Bill, Corinne and Lieutenant Commander Murray and the Rickatson-Hatts plus Minerva 'and her pompous husband, John'. The next day was lunch with Gilbert Miller, a theatrical producer married to the fabulously rich New Yorker Kitty Bache, followed by a few hands of bridge.

Mary wrote excitedly to her mother about plans for the coming weeks, which included more dinners, more shopping and a visit to Knole. This was a thrill for Wallis because they had been invited to have tea there with Lord and Lady Sackville, a thrill for Ernest because the partly fifteenth-century house was steeped in history. On 3 June

---

5 For example, the Prince wrote to Freda Dudley Ward on 13 December 1918: 'I've got a major attached to me … & he seems alright though I think he's a Jew; anyhow he looks it!!' (Rupert Godfrey (ed.), *Letters from a Prince* (Warner Books 1999), p. 146).

there was the Derby, where they went in a jolly party with the US diplomat William Galbraith and his wife, and two days later 'Trooping of the Colours [sic]'.

> Wallis thinks I have a slim chance of meeting the Prince. She said if I had gotten there a week sooner I would have met him twice but we have nothing booked so far where he'd be apt to be [although] his girl, Lady Furness, is lunching here with us on Monday with Gloria Vanderbilt and Lady Milford Haven. Wallis is to be presented on June 10th. I wish I could see it but I will see her dress for it anyway.

Wallis insists that the idea for her presentation at Court came first from Maud. 'I was reluctant ... because I would have to buy special clothes for the occasion and I didn't feel justified in such an extravagance,' she claimed. Maud herself could not do the honours as she had just presented her own debutante daughter and, according to the rules, had to wait three years before a second presentation. But in any case she and Wallis were no longer on good terms. The rules demanded that divorcées could be presented only if they were the injured party, so Wallis had to send her Warrenton documentation to the Lord Chamberlain and hope it would be accepted. Another friend was found to do the actual presentation – Mildred Anderson, an American married to a London businessman – and although Wallis borrowed a dress, train, feathers and fan from Connie and Thelma, she could not resist buying for herself some impressive jewellery: a large aquamarine cross which dangled on a necklace ('imitations but effective') and white kid three-quarter-length gloves.

Ernest, in his full-dress uniform of the Coldstream Guards, was in his element as his wife waited in line in the magnificent Buckingham Palace ballroom in order to curtsey to the King and Queen on their red dais. Not a word was exchanged but Wallis had overheard the Prince of Wales mutter under his breath as she passed that something ought to be done about the lights 'as they make all the women look ghastly'. After the formalities there was more partying at Thelma's house and when the Prince complimented Wallis on her gown she snapped back, 'But Sir, I thought you said we all looked ghastly' –

the sort of repartee for which she soon became well known. She had quickly learned how the Prince responded to such directness, considering it American. It came naturally to Wallis and was not entirely a studied response. Understanding Wallis means understanding that in Baltimore the Warfields were aristocracy. Not for the last time, the Prince found himself apologizing to this audacious woman, telling her that he had had no idea his voice carried so far. Far from being offended, the Prince was amused and drove the Simpsons home in his own car that night, causing quite a stir at Bryanston Court. 'She always had a challenging line for the Prince,' recalled Mary Kirk in her diary. In the early days she used to say to him: 'You are just a heartbreak to any woman because you can never marry her.' She understood her prey and knew that the tease would bring a response.

A month later old Mr Simpson invited Wallis and Mary to go with him and Midget to Paris. Wallis by now had had her fill of having to entertain Mary, 'the house pest' as she called her, so she accepted. Wallis in any case was en route to Cannes for a five-week holiday without Ernest but with Consuelo Thaw and Nada Milford Haven, an exotic Russian married to Lord Mountbatten's brother, and a renowned lesbian. It was a holiday she could ill afford and she had to borrow from the bank 'as poor old E. can't help me'. But she concluded that it would be worth it to get to know such nice people. Two days after their arrival Mary had a terrifying accident. She was knocked down on the street by a taxi and rushed to the American hospital in Neuilly where her condition was said to be critical. Wallis telephoned Jackie Raffray, who rang Buckie in a state of near hysteria. The injuries were to her kidneys and it was feared one might have to be removed. Wallis promised that if Mary was still in danger the next day she would stay with her at the hospital. If she was out of danger, she had a lunch engagement with a friend.

The next morning Buckie telephoned the apartment where Wallis was staying for news. 'A perfectly familiar voice said without so much as a preliminary "hello", "Mary's out of danger, Buckie."' Midget had summoned a leading French surgeon who concluded that no operation was necessary and that with proper hospital care and treatment Mary would recover. Wallis had spent the night at Mary's bedside but, once it was clear she was going to live, continued with her plans to travel to the South of France. Mary made a slow recovery and the pains in her side were often excruciating. But, as she told her sister, she forced herself to get up and take a few steps every day to get over the pins and needles. Her health was permanently impaired, but she returned to New York to see if her marriage could be similarly patched up.

Wallis cut short her holiday in Cannes, perhaps because Ernest, who could not afford a holiday himself, was restless without her and perhaps because she did not like sharing a room with Nada, who seems to have found her attractive. Just as she was building a social circle leading upwards she was terrified of any scandal which might jeopardize this and was only too aware of the power of gossip. At all events she came back to a gloomy autumn in London beset with health and financial worries of her own. Ernest was so deeply concerned about their spending habits and the dark prospects for his business in the wake of the world recession and American stock-market collapse of 1929 that he decided they must give up the car and chauffeur, complaining that he was the one who always did the giving up.

In November Wallis had to go into hospital to have her tonsils removed. But a sparkle of promise came before Christmas when they again met the Prince at the Thaws' and persuaded him to dine with them at Bryanston Court in the new year.

6
Wallis in Control

'Keeping up with 2 men is making me move all the time'

Early in 1932, the Simpsons entertained the Prince of Wales for the first time to dinner at their flat in Bryanston Court. Many of Wallis's letters at this time reflect a typical concern about maids – they were not good enough, they wanted too much money or they disliked working in a flat – and a not so typical concern about not really being able to afford to give more than three big dinners a month. But this event put her staff on their mettle. For this, no expense was spared and her cook, Mrs Ralph, was beside herself with excitement. Wallis decided to serve a typical American dinner: black bean soup, grilled lobster, fried chicken Maryland and a cold raspberry soufflé. Since the Prince stayed until 4 a.m. and asked for one of her recipes Wallis concluded: 'Everything, I am happy to say, went very well.' Almost immediately came the longed-for invitation in response: to spend a weekend with him at the Fort.

Wallis described the Princely existence at the Fort as 'amazingly informal' compared with the stately routine at Knole, her only point of comparison. There were cocktails before dinner at which the Prince wore a kilt and the ladies – Connie and Thelma – their simplest evening dresses. They all retired to bed before midnight. Others described activities at the Fort rather differently. They were said to include 'orgies ... when Mrs Simpson did the "danse du ventre" and other un-English performances of an unsavoury nature'. In the morning the Simpsons found the Prince up and dressed before them; brandishing a fearsome-looking billhook, he was engaged in cutting back the tangle of undergrowth outside the Fort. The guests were expected to help. Neither Ernest nor Wallis was known for their gardening skills, but while Ernest, typically obliging, promised to join in and went upstairs to get a sweater, Wallis had a private tour of the grounds with the Prince. She was a fast learner where men were concerned and could easily see the intense pleasure that living there, planting flowering rhododendrons where there had once been weeds, creating a haven out of a wilderness, gave their host. She also understood that he was lonely. 'Perhaps I had been one of the first to penetrate the heart of his inner loneliness ... For a long time,' Wallis wrote in her memoirs, 'I would carry in my mind the odd and incongruous picture of a slight figure in plus fours loping up the slope of the Terrace swinging the billhook and whistling.' And at all times he was followed by the dogs, two Cairn terriers Cora and Jaggs, which Wallis, hitherto not a dog lover, tried unsuccessfully to fuss over.

The thank-you letter they sent was in the form of doggerel which she and Ernest composed together. Ernest, she convinced herself, had had a wonderful time, which on this occasion was no doubt the case. That he was as much appreciated by their host as she was – the two men were able to discuss history together until 'dates and circumstances were flying back and forth across the table like ping pong balls' – was less certain. Ernest, working harder than ever in the City, was starting to be exhausted by his wife's apparently insatiable need to go to and give parties. The shipping business had slumped dramatically after 1929, causing him serious concern as companies defaulted owing the family firm substantial sums. Maud, who also derived an income from SS&Y, insisted she was making economies, though 'no one seems able to say what', Wallis complained, deeply worried about how much longer they could hang on to their flat. She and Maud were now, in early 1932, barely on speaking terms.

In the midst of this difficult year the Simpsons' social life took what Wallis felt was 'a battering'. They entertained less – just one dinner a month – but nonetheless managed a short holiday to Tunis where Ernest's friend Georges Sebastian, a Romanian millionaire businessman with aristocratic connections, lived in a magnificent beachfront home that the architect Frank Lloyd Wright was to call the most beautiful house he had ever seen. When they pleaded poverty he paid for their travel there as well, a gesture they 'simply could not resist'. Aunt Bessie came to visit them in London in the summer, and in July the threesome set off on a tour of France and Austria. Later in the year there was another weekend plus a tea visit to the Fort, but Wallis, weighing just eight stone at this time, was still suffering recurring stomach trouble, which she believed was caused by an ulcer, so 'I am only allowed whiskey and plain water for the next six months,' she told Aunt Bessie.

But then, over the next year, the Simpsons started to be invited regularly to the Fort. This was partly Thelma's initiative as she feared she was losing her grip on the Prince's attentions and cast around to find amusing guests outside the normal circles to keep him happy, and partly the Prince's, who found he was indeed amused by Wallis with her sharp tongue and risqué repartee. There was one memorable weekend in January 1933 when Ernest was away. It was so cold that she and Thelma along with the Duke and Duchess of York all went skating on the frozen lake, the Prince having presented the two women with skates. Wallis recalled later that in the course of that year 'we found ourselves becoming permanent fixtures at the Fort weekends. The association imperceptibly but swiftly passed from an acquaintanceship to a friendship.' But it was not so much 'we' as she who had become a permanent fixture – a piece of recurrent misinformation in her otherwise revelatory memoirs.

Wallis told the Kirk family that she was making weekly visits to the Fort:

A friend of mine, Thelma Furness, is the Prince of Wales' girl and I chaperone her when she goes out to Fort Belvedere to stay with him. She comes by for me once a week in her car and we drive out to the Fort together. The first time she came I asked what those long poles were that were strapped to the side of the car but she just laughed and said I would find out later. It was after dinner that I found out. The three of us came into the sitting room for coffee. On either side of the fireplace, where a grand fire was blazing, stood a comfortable chair and beside each chair stood something that looked to me like an artist's easel. When I went closer and looked I found that each of these held a piece of canvas on which was an unfinished piece of embroidery. When we had finished our coffee Thelma and the Prince settled themselves down to work and I, sitting between them, was asked to read from a book Thelma handed me.

Wallis never took up needlepoint, taught to the princes by their mother, Queen Mary, but she now came to know the Prince's brother Prince George, who was often at the Fort, as well as the Duke and Duchess of York. The Prince of Wales was especially close to the Yorks during his five-year liaison with Thelma Furness, whom they liked very much.

Wallis and Ernest's lives, inevitably, also started to diverge now. Ernest's business, if it were to survive at a time of such reduced economic activity, required him to make frequent trips abroad. And in March, Wallis made a longed-for trip to the US, paid for by her generous aunt, whom Wallis promised she loved 'better than anyone in the world and [I] will always be on hand when you need me'. She had not been to the United States since her mother died, had friends and family she was desperate to see and wanted a break from money worries. Just as she sailed she received a bon-voyage radiogram signed 'Edward P.' wishing her a safe crossing and a speedy return to England. In her memoirs she wrote that she was sailing with Ernest and that the message was for them both. But, as her biographer Michael Bloch tactfully revealed, Wallis's memory was at fault here because she went alone. The message may have been the first intimation that she had more than piqued the Prince's interest and so may have foreshadowed the turmoil which was to follow. As such, the radiogram would have loomed large in her memory as a milestone. Nonetheless at this stage Wallis believed that it was evidence of nothing more than a mild interest, though perhaps something to make Thelma jealous, and that she had the situation well under control.

Wallis needed the trip for another reason too: to act as confirmation, as she approached her fortieth birthday, that she was still attractive to men. She viewed it as her swansong 'unless I can hang on to my figure' and thus take another trip in the next three years before hitting forty, an arbitrary date in many women's lives when they see their femininity come to an end with their childbearing years. Wallis, who had mastered the ability to flirt since Oldfields days, needed this more than most as she was without children to flaunt. She felt a deep emotional, not necessarily sexual, need to show that she was still alluring and believed that she had only three more years in which to do it. As ever, she was on the lookout for interesting diplomats, and in Washington particularly enjoyed the attentions of John Cooper Wiley, subsequently a highly regarded US ambassador.

She returned with her self-confidence restored and almost immediately the weekend visits to Sunningdale increased. It was her assurance, poise and buoyancy that the Prince admired, as he could not see the underlying insecurity. After her return Wallis wrote to her aunt that 'Thelma is still Princess of Wales' – an indication that the women had discussed the possibility that she soon might not be – and then joked that a collection of funny butter moulds she had found, which stamped animal patterns on to butter, were a great success. 'Thelma is so mad for them and I have refused her,' revealing that rivalry was already under way. On 19 June the Prince gave a birthday dinner for Wallis's thirty-seventh birthday at Quaglino's in London's Jermyn Street. Wallis was already thinking about clever ways to please him in response. A few days later, for his thirty-ninth birthday, she gave him a present which demonstrated how much time and ingenuity she was investing in this relationship. She had borrowed a royal spoon from Osborne, the butler at the Fort, in order to have his cipher engraved on a silver Bryant & May matchbox holder. She followed this up with a special 4 July American Independence Day dinner for him at Bryanston Court. But the shipping business had not picked up that much and since 'Pa S – the most selfish old pig –' had stopped their allowance and was keeping them on a tight rein, the Simpsons found entertaining at this level a huge strain. Wallis now tried seriously to rent out their apartment, which was costing them a hefty £600 per annum, a bill they found hard to meet.

The night of 31 December saw the Simpsons celebrating with the

Prince until 5 a.m. to see in the new year. And shortly afterwards, the situation changed dramatically when it was Thelma's turn to sail for the United States to see her family. In January 1934, Wallis and she had a farewell lunch at the Ritz, their regular meeting place. According to Wallis, Thelma said laughingly, 'I'm afraid the Prince is going to be lonely. Wallis, won't you look after him?' Thelma's version of events has Wallis initiating the conversation: 'Oh, Thelma the little man is going to be lonely.' Wallis confided to her aunt, 'I tried my best to cheer him up.'

Until now, Ernest was still tolerating everything that was happening, flattered that the heir to the throne called at his home sometimes as often as twice a week in the evenings for supper or a KT. Even if he objected, because the society gossip about his wife – 'that I am the latest', as she put it – was immediate once Thelma sailed, he did not relinquish his belief that one should at all times be deeply deferential to the future monarch. But, when these evenings went on until the small hours, and Ernest had brought work home he needed to do, 'he developed the art of tactfully excusing himself and retiring to his room with his papers'. Wallis was left to discuss plans for the Fort or the latest American jazz record or perhaps some project the Prince had in mind to promote British trade. She became adept at making him believe she was truly interested in his work but admitted privately, 'this man is exhausting'. When occasionally she and Ernest both went to the Fort at weekends, 'he increasingly singled me out as his partner during the dancing'.

To Aunt Bessie she was frank about the situation for the moment. 'I think I do amuse him. I'm the comedy relief and we like to dance together but I always have Ernest hanging around my neck so all is safe.' And even to herself she was still remarkably clear-eyed about the relationship. She liked the attention and the way other invitations now came flooding in from society hostesses as a result. But the Prince was very demanding, telephoning two or three times a day as soon as Thelma had departed, sometimes in the small hours of the night, as well as visiting the flat most days, and she missed seeing her other friends. She certainly did not want to risk losing Ernest, who not only offered her the best chance of the secure lifestyle she craved above all else but with whom she had a 'congenial', easy-going relationship. The need to 'keep Ernest in good humour' was critical. 'At the moment he's flattered with it all and lets me dine once a week with him *alone*,' she reported comfortingly to the increasingly worried Bessie Merryman. But for how much longer? 'It all takes a certain amount of tact handling another swansong before 40.'

For the moment she could genuinely reassure her husband with her belief that the attention was useful for them both, that the infatuation would not last, that soon the Prince would find another girl or return to one of his old flames. In the meantime she found juggling her life to keep two men happy as exciting as it was exhausting. 'Wouldn't mother have loved it all?' she wrote to Bessie. Sometimes she wondered if 'in any way I'll ever be able to reward her efforts? Or if my insatiable ambitions will land me back in such a flat as the one room on Conn Hill, the Woburn.' That building, where Wallis's mother briefly lodged in the 1920s, had been so grim she nicknamed it 'the Woebegone'. 'Only time will show.' Insecurity at the thought of losing everything, the deepest of all her many fears, was now corrosive; she was becoming mean and grasping in preparation for the day the clocks stopped.

But there was a more serious concern: how to manage until then? Wallis and Ernest simply could not keep up their lifestyle any longer. That summer Ernest had to forgo an outing to Ascot since he could afford neither the clothes nor the ticket, let alone the time. The Prince provided a single ticket for Wallis and invited her to stay at the Fort for the week, behaviour which appalled Bessie who sent her niece a stern warning.

Wallis still believed she was in control of the situation and promised her aunt that if Ernest raised any objection she would give the Prince up at once. She admitted that 'keeping up with 2 men is making me move all the time'. But the Prince was now giving Wallis presents of jewellery as well as money to buy clothes and many other luxuries. It was these she found so hard to turn her back on. Soon he arrived at the flat with another present, a Cairn puppy like his own, suggestively called Slipper but nicknamed Mr Loo. House-training her dogs was a talent Wallis never managed. Ernest, too, came in for occasional appeasement, including a gift of a bolt of brown and beige houndstooth tweed to be made up by the Prince's tailor into an overcoat, an exact replica of one the Prince himself wore and which Ernest had admired. This coat is still in the possession of the Kerr-Smiley family, giving rise to the family's jibe that Ernest was the man who sold his wife for a bolt of cloth. Another priceless gift, valued hugely by Ernest, was ensuring his smooth admittance into the Prince's own Masonic Lodge, presided over by Sir Maurice Jenks, a well-connected former lord mayor. At first Jenks had agreed but was then challenged by fellow Masons who said they would not accept a candidate on the recommendation of the wife's lover 'as it would produce a situation in which the fundamental law that no Mason may sleep with another Mason's wife would be broken. The P of W denied that there was anything between himself & Mrs S & gave a pledge to that effect as a Mason.' Ernest was duly admitted. According to Godfrey Thomas: 'The story now goes throughout the city that HRH has violated his Masonic oath, that ES wishes to be a Mason for business reasons and that HRH, to keep him quiet about Mrs S, was more or less blackmailed into sponsoring him.'

For Ernest this was the pinnacle of social achievement yet it came at a price he may not have realised he was paying at the time: losing Wallis. By May 1934 Wallis had not only replaced Thelma as the Prince's favourite, she was his only. Even at the height of the Prince's passion for Lady Furness, Freda Dudley Ward, by then divorced, was still on hand as the mother figure to whom he turned for comfort and advice. The advent of Wallis destroyed that. That month Freda's elder daughter, Penelope, had an operation for acute appendicitis with complications. Freda spent desperate days and nights by her daughter's bedside, registering only after the crisis had passed that she had not heard from the Prince for several weeks. She called York House, and the telephone operator whom she had known for years answered it with a choking sound, she later recalled. 'He didn't seem able to speak. I suddenly realised to my horror that he was crying. "Everyone seems to have gone mad around here," he said. The Prince had given orders that none of my phone calls be put through. I never heard from him again.' This was especially hurtful for Penelope and

Angela who had been close to the Prince since childhood and viewed him almost as a stepfather. They had given him the only taste of warm family life he was ever to know.

Thelma was similarly dismissed. She had returned from America in the spring but after one visit to the Fort – her last – knew instantly that something had happened between Wallis and the Prince to the detriment of her own relationship with him. He was not only avoiding her but going out of his way to be charming to Wallis, hanging on her every word even in front of Ernest, who was there too. The Prince and Wallis seemed to have little private jokes. For Thelma, the revelation came when the Prince picked up a lettuce leaf to eat in his fingers and Wallis slapped his hand, telling him he should use a knife and fork in future. 'I knew then that she had looked after him exceedingly well.' When he also refused to take Thelma's telephone calls, she decided to visit Wallis at Bryanston Court to ask if the Prince was keen on her now. 'This was a question I had expected,' Wallis wrote in her memoirs. '"Thelma," I said, "I think he likes me. He may be fond of me. But if you mean by keen that he is in love with me, the answer is definitely no."'

Wallis has generally been blamed for the summary dismissal of old friends such as Thelma and Freda on the assumption that she insisted he sever all ties. But her position was not so strong in early 1934. The cruel discarding of Freda and Thelma is however deeply revealing of the Prince's weak character; confronted with a situation he could not handle, he avoided it. It was not the last time he retreated into the safety of the Fort in such circumstances, unable to summon the moral courage required. In his youth the Prince's physical courage in wishing to fight in the trenches, to race in dangerous steeplechase events or to fly his own aircraft had been notable; some believed that Wallis's influence and her own myriad fears sapped his physical courage too. Once Thelma was off the scene, Wallis's hold on the Prince intensified. Many of the staff at the Fort loathed the new regime from the start as Wallis imposed her ideas on decoration, food and general routine there, causing hurt, annoyance and offence.

The Prince's personal entourage had more snobbish but no less negative grounds for complaint. 'His friends of his own selection are awful,' commented the Hon. John Aird, the Prince's equerry. 'One of the worst examples was there, a couple called Simson [sic], she is an American 150 per cent and HRH seems to like her a bit extra; he is a very unattractive and common Englishman ... they seem terrible at first and this feeling does not decrease as one sees them more often.' Aird did see them more often and detested them both, describing Ernest as 'full of general information like a Whitaker, while she pretends to have taste in decoration and food – maybe the *first*, but certainly not the second'.

That summer the Prince planned to take a house in Biarritz and Ernest was, yet again, fortuitously away on a business trip to the US. While 'regretting Ernest couldn't join the party', the Prince suggested inviting Wallis's disapproving aunt along to regularize the arrangement and hoping to win her over. It was the first time that Wallis and the Prince had been seen in public without Ernest, although the British press was still completely silent about the friendship. In addition to the Prince, Wallis and Mrs Merryman, the party consisted of Lieutenant Commander and Mrs Colin Buist, John Aird and a private secretary, Hugh Lloyd Thomas. From Biarritz they decided to go on a cruise on Lord Moyne's rather unsuitable vessel, the *Rosaura*, this time leaving Aunt Bessie behind. But they were joined by Herman and Katherine Rogers. The boat hit a storm in the Bay of Biscay and Wallis was terrified. Aird believed that she infected the Prince with her fears as 'he was really frightened and in my opinion is a coward at heart'. As the equerry responsible for organizing the trip, Aird was appalled by Wallis's behaviour. She complained to him that she was not being introduced to important and interesting English people in Biarritz, but he noted in his diary: 'I think she would complain more if she was ... I feel that she is not basically a bad sort of tough girl out to get what she can, but unless she is much cleverer than I think, she does not quite know how to work it so as to cash in best.' By the end of the holiday Aird was almost despairing of the Prince, who 'has lost all confidence in himself and follows W around like a dog'. He might have despaired even more had he seen the Prince put a velvet pouch from Cartier in her hand. It contained a small diamond and emerald charm, the first of many. Wallis herself later wrote coyly of the voyage: 'Perhaps it was during these evenings off the Spanish coast that we crossed the line that marks the indefinable boundary between friendship and love.'

Having seen the situation for herself, Aunt Bessie was more worried than ever, convinced that the Prince's undoubted infatuation would pass and that Wallis would end up with neither husband nor Prince. Wallis had tried to set her mind at rest by telling her that she would 'try and be clever enough to keep them both'. It was some help that Ernest was often away on business. But then she thought up a plan.

During her recent visit to America she had seen Mary Raffray only briefly. Her old friend was under intense strain nursing her mother Edith, who had cancer, and coping with her alcoholic husband. After Henry Kirk had died in 1933, the responsibility for looking after Edith fell to Mary, the childless sister. Mary and Jackie decided that they would move old Mrs Kirk to New York City with them where they both looked after her with great kindness and devotion in her final year. Mary decided that while her mother was alive there could be no question of divorce or separation. But when she died in 1934 Mary was exhausted. There was no reason for her to remain now watching Jackie destroy himself with drink, however much affection they still felt for each other. Thus Wallis's invitation to come over to London and stay at Bryanston Court arrived at a perfect moment. Wallis, remembering the outings they had made as a threesome three years back, and how Mary had listened, rapt, to her husband's historical disquisitions on old buildings, thought she had found the perfect diversion for Ernest while she continued to be entertained by the Prince. Mary accepted with alacrity.

But whatever line was crossed in the summer, the Prince now decided he wanted to go further and present Wallis to his parents at Buckingham Palace. In November there was to be a glittering reception to celebrate the forthcoming wedding of his younger brother Prince George, Duke of Kent to Princess Marina of Greece. Wallis had got to know George through her weekends at the Fort. But the King did not want to meet Mr and Mrs Simpson and deleted their names from the guest list. The Prince, persuading his parents that inviting the Simpsons was somehow good for Anglo-American relations, managed to reinstate them. And so Wallis, wearing jewels given to her by her royal lover and a tiara borrowed from Cartier, was presented to King George and Queen Mary. Ernest was repeatedly left unhappily standing alone at the edge of the room with no one to talk to. The King was outraged. 'That woman in my own house!' he shouted to his cousin, the Austro-Hungarian diplomat Count Albert Mensdorff-Pouilly-Dietrichstein, known to history as Mensdorff and an intimate of King George V as he had been of his father, Edward VII. Afterwards he gave orders that Mrs Simpson was not to be invited to any Silver Jubilee functions being planned for the following year nor to the Royal Enclosure at Ascot.

Wallis later characterized the meeting with the King of England – the only time she ever met either of her future husband's parents – as 'a few words of perfunctory greeting, an exchange of meaningless pleasantries'. About her husband's enforced appearance as a wallflower she made no comment. She had had a dress made for the occasion by Eva Lutyens, daughter of the architect, in violet lamé with a vivid green sash, which she believed was 'outstanding'. Others in the royal party found it brash, like its owner. Prince Christopher of Greece described in his memoirs how the Prince of Wales:

> laid a hand on my arm in his impulsive way.
> 'Christo, come with me. I want you to meet Mrs Simpson.'
> 'Who is she?'
> 'An American. She's wonderful.'
> The two words told me everything. It was as though he had said she is the only woman in the world.

The pressure from so insistent a lover was, already, almost more than Wallis could cope with. When the Prince went to Sandringham for Christmas with his family she viewed it as 'a lovely rest for us and especially me'. The moment he was back he started dreaming up ways to be with Wallis more and now suggested a skiing holiday in Austria. Wallis accepted without consulting Ernest and for the first time he was furious; they had a fierce row and Ernest, uncharacteristically, went out slamming the door. In her memoirs Wallis claimed that her husband did not join the skiing party because he had a business trip to

America and had hoped that this time his wife would accompany him. In fact, he remained forlornly at home, unable to watch the increasingly public love affair between his Prince and his wife any longer.

Wallis now realized that she was indeed pushing her husband over the limit and by playing this dangerous double game risked losing him. But she did not step back. Why? She was not in love with Edward himself but in love with the opulence, the lifestyle, the way doors opened for her, the way he made all her childish dreams come true. She was sure it was a fairy tale that would end, but while it lasted could not bring herself to end it herself. She believed Ernest still loved her enough to catch her when she fell – and for the moment he did. If there was a moment to call a halt this was it. But she could not. She wrote to Bessie about the lovely jewellery she had received so far, 'not many things but awfully nice stones', which Ernest had to pay to insure. By October, Lady Diana Cooper, invited to dine at Fort Belvedere, had observed that Wallis was 'glittering, and dripped in new jewels and clothes'. Wallis's jewellery was now a lively topic of conversation in London society, a spectacle so amazing that many, including the diarist Mrs Belloc Lowndes, assumed when she saw Wallis that same year that it must be costume jewellery. Those in the know put her right, as they 'screeched with laughter exclaiming that all the jewels were real, that the then Prince of Wales had given her fifty thousand pounds' worth at Christmas, following it up with sixty thousand pounds' worth of jewels a week later at the New Year'. This was a staggering amount.

Wallis hated skiing and the Duke himself hardly excelled. Dudley Forwood, later the Duke's equerry but then a young attaché at the British Legation in Vienna, who had been hauled out of post and was expected to accompany the Duke everywhere, recalled Wallis standing on the mountainside in Kitzbühel in unsuitable high-heeled shoes looking anxious. As the Duke descended the slopes Forwood heard him call out to her in his strange, half-cockney voice: 'Aren't I doing splendidly, Wallis?' Not many thought he was.

This almost month-long holiday in February 1935 – after Kitzbühel they went on to Vienna and Budapest – caused a definite turning point in other ways aside from the fact that Austria was an unstable country with a growing pro-Nazi party and that its leader, Chancellor Engelbert Dollfuss, had been assassinated the previous year. A hurt letter from Wallis to the Prince around this time – which she asked him to tear up – indicates just how precarious her position was or at least how precarious she thought it was, as well as pointing to a rare occasion when he did not do as she asked. Preserving smooth relations with Ernest mattered intensely to her and she reveals that she had had 'a long quiet talk with E last night and I felt very eanum [a private word between Wallis and Edward meaning small, weak or insignificant] at the end'. She berated the Prince for staying too long on his visits to their flat, demanding too much of her, constantly telephoning and thoughtlessly stepping on other people. 'Doesn't your love for me reach to the heights of wanting to make things a little easier for me?' She begged him for a little more consideration of her position with Ernest and told him she thought he had not grown up where love was concerned 'and perhaps it's only a boyish passion'. Still convinced that this was an infatuation that would pass, she told him that his 'behaviour last night made me realise how very alone I shall be some day – and because I love you I don't seem to have the strength to protect myself from your youthfulness'. If she was not deemed good enough for Felipe Espil when she was a decade younger, surely it was only a matter of time before the heir to the British throne treated her in the same way? Frozen with anxiety, she could not move. The Prince responded by giving her more gifts of money and jewellery, further sapping her resolve to walk away. It would not be out of character to imagine that Wallis was making a mental calculation of what she would need if she were to be abandoned by both men. Admiral Sir Lionel Halsey, Comptroller and Treasurer to the Prince since 1920 when he retired from the navy, was the Prince's closest adviser and, for a time, had the confidence of both King and Prince. He told the King in July 1935 that Mrs Simpson was already receiving 'a very handsome income' from the Prince. Aird put the figure at £6,000 per annum.

At the same time, several royal courtiers now started openly to voice their disquiet over Mrs Simpson. Halsey warned that the newspapers would not stay silent for much longer about the forty-one-year-old Prince's unsuitable attachment to a married woman. As Wallis recognized after her return from skiing, there was scarcely an evening when she was not with the Duke at the theatre, at an embassy reception or for dinner. She described Jubilee Year as a wave that was bearing her upwards, surging ever faster and higher. She told her aunt that she was invited everywhere in the hope that the Prince would follow in her wake. Society was madly gossiping, and the arch-gossiper Chips Channon noted astutely on 5 April, following a luncheon party he hosted to do a 'politesse' to Mrs Simpson: 'She is a jolly, plain, intelligent, quiet, unpretentious and unprepossessing little woman, but as I wrote to Paul of Yugoslavia today, she has already the air of a personage who walks into a room as though she almost expected to be curtsied to. At least, she wouldn't be too surprised. She has complete power over the Prince of Wales.'

But society was forming two camps. There were those, broadly speaking of ancient lineage, who stood squarely behind the King, found her unacceptable and did their best to avoid her if possible – the establishment. The Duchess of York had said openly she would no longer meet Mrs Simpson, which resulted in her group having to make a hasty retreat when 'that woman' walked in to the same party. Helen Hardinge (née Gascoyne-Cecil), a friend of the Yorks, explained that 'Of course, we did not seek her company, ourselves.' She and her husband Alexander (Alec) Hardinge, Assistant Private Secretary to the King, both came from families not of vast wealth but involved in public service as diplomats, colonial administrators or soldiers for generations, several of whom had given their lives in the service of their country. Alec had met Wallis only once by 1935 and Helen insisted that she and he were 'quite uncensorious', as servants of the King must be, even if the idea of a woman with two living husbands consorting with the heir to the throne was distasteful. They did their best not to confront Wallis but they had friends in society who, if they came across her, could not avoid her.

Helen wrote about one who, when introduced to Wallis at a party,

absolutely refused to shake hands with her.

'What did you do?' I asked her.

'Oh,' she replied, 'it was quite easy. I dropped my handbag just as she got to me so I had to stoop down to find it.'

Others, many of whom had American connections and money and were new to London – 'the Ritz Bar Set' as they were often called – felt differently. 'To them Mrs Simpson seemed to provide a heaven-sent opportunity to enter Royal society.'

At the end of May Channon noted a revealing scene in Lady Cunard's box at the opera. Emerald Cunard, the former American heiress Maud Burke, had married Sir Bache Cunard but lived separately from him and was widely known as a patron of the arts and mistress of Sir Thomas Beecham. 'I was interested to see', wrote Channon, 'what an extraordinary hold Mrs Simpson has over the Prince. In the interval she told him to hurry away as he would be late in joining the Queen at the LCC [London County Council] Ball – and she made him take a cigar out of his breast pocket. "It doesn't look very pretty," she said. He went, but was back in half an hour.'

Lord Wigram, a sixty-three-year-old former soldier and experienced courtier who had served his sovereign for two generations, decided it was time for action. Urged on by Halsey, he paid a special visit to the Prince after this holiday to convey how worried the King was about his private life. But he was merely the first of many to receive a princely rebuff. 'The Prince', he reported, 'said he was astonished that anyone could take offence about his personal friends. Mrs Simpson was a charming, cultivated woman.' This was more or less the attitude he took throughout the rest of his life. He believed that Wallis was a uniquely wonderful woman and that anyone who did not share those views, having met her, was blind to the facts. Wigram's shot across the bows had, as Godfrey Thomas, who was closer to the Prince, was well aware, been totally ineffective.

It was not only the King but the government which was now concerned about this unorthodox alliance. A surveillance report by Special Branch in June 1935 sent to the Commissioner of the Metropolitan Police indicated that the Simpsons' activities were already being monitored because it was believed that Wallis was not only juggling Ernest and the Prince of Wales but also seeing another man whose identity they had not yet ascertained. A week later, the man they suspected was revealed as Guy Marcus Trundle. Trundle, a vicar's son born in York and a well-known rake, was said to be a married man and a motorcar salesman employed by the Ford Motor Company. According to this report, 'Trundle is described as a very charming adventurer, very good looking, well bred and an excellent dancer ... He meets Mrs Simpson quite openly at informal social gatherings as a personal friend, but secret meetings are made by appointment when intimate relations take place. Trundle receives money from Mrs Simpson as well as expensive presents. He has admitted this.'

It's a curious story. Clearly detectives were now talking to those who knew the Simpsons, including their staff, in the hope of finding some indiscretions. While it is quite possible that Trundle met Wallis Simpson and that this led him to boast about 'intimate relations' – after all, he was known to boast that every woman he met fell for him – it is highly unlikely that they had any personal relationship. But it was also not out of character for Wallis to enjoy making men jealous. It was part of the flirtatious and promiscuous behaviour pattern which provided her with continual reassurance of her attract-iveness to men, and one meeting with a rogue such as Trundle would have been enough to inflame the Prince's ardour, had she chosen to tell him. The Special Branch reports are bald but, as Stephen Cretney makes clear in his account of the abdication crisis, 'whether they could have been sustained in legal proceedings is not clear'.

But there is another line in the report which states: 'Mrs Simpson has said that her husband is now suspicious of her association with other men as he thinks this will eventually cause trouble with POW.' If this is what she told Trundle, which he repeated, it gives further evidence that the man Wallis most wanted to keep was Ernest and that she was using the Prince of Wales for the time being, intending to revert to Ernest as soon as the shine faded. Ernest, according to the report, 'is bragging to the effect that he expects to get "high honours" before very long. He says that P.O.W will succeed his father at no distant date. He has mentioned that he expects, at least, to be created a Baron. He is very talkative when in drink.' The report was obviously circulated to a select few in the government as Sir Edward

Peacock, Receiver General to the Duchy of Cornwall, and responsible for the royal finances at many levels, later told Joseph Kennedy when he became US ambassador, that 'they all had evidence Wallie [sic] was having an affair with a young man and of course this embittered the Cabinet more than ever. Peacock is convinced', added Kennedy, 'they would have gladly taken an American for Queen but not Wallie.'

King George did manage one conversation about Wallis Simpson with his son at this time. The King insisted he could not invite his son's mistress to the forthcoming Court Ball. The Prince swore to his father that Mrs Simpson was not his mistress. The King relented and she was therefore invited. But although there are various reports of the Prince having always protested that he had not had sexual intercourse with Mrs Simpson before they married, this was of course open to dispute then as it is now. His servants and staff knew that one of the bedrooms at the Fort, previously a dressing room situated between Wallis's and the Prince's bedrooms, had now been allocated to her as an extra room allowing unimpeded access between the rooms. Courtiers *au fait* with the latest gossip were more horrified than ever, believing now that their future sovereign was a liar as well as an adulterer. Wigram wrote: 'Apart from actually seeing HRH and Mrs S in bed together they [the staff] had positive proof that HRH lived with her.' Aird joined in, giving details of how he had seen him emerge early one morning with his upper lip all red!! So that's that and no mistake.' Wigram's view was the one the King believed in the end – that his son had lied to him. The sovereign wrote in his diary on 6 November 1935 following the marriage of his third son Prince Henry, Duke of Gloucester to Alice, daughter of the Duke of Buccleuch: 'Now all the children are married except David.' A few weeks later he was heard to exclaim: 'I pray to God that my eldest son will never marry and have children and that nothing will come between Bertie and Lilibet [the pet name for Princess Elizabeth, the King's granddaughter] and the throne.'

The Prince had known it would be impossible to arrange for Wallis officially to see the Jubilee procession on 6 May, the actual anniversary of the King's accession which, that year, happened to fall on a glorious summer's day. Instead, he begged a favour of Helen Hardinge, as her apartment in St James's Palace overlooked the processional route to St Paul's Cathedral. Could she, he asked, find accommodation for 'one or two scullery maids' to watch as the windows of his own residence at York House did not overlook the processional route? Slightly puzzled as to why the Prince could not find space for his humble servants at a Buckingham Palace window, she nonetheless obliged. 'Some time after we returned home ... I learned the identity of the "one or two scullery maids". They were Mrs Simpson and one of her friends.' The Hardinges came to believe that the Prince had not deliberately played a trick on them. So consumed was he by his love affair with Wallis, he assumed that everyone else was too and that the identity of the scullery maids would have been obvious. A week later Wallis was, grudgingly, invited to the Jubilee Ball, where she 'felt the King's eyes rest searchingly on me. Something in his look made me feel that all this graciousness and pageantry were but the glittering tip of an iceberg ... filled with an icy menace for such as me.'

In spite of referring to the occasion as the 'Silly Jubilee', Wallis was happy to receive a pair of beautiful diamond clips as a Jubilee present from the Prince. Yet the real lessons of the Jubilee seem to have passed her by. In her bubble of worry about losing both husband and lover, she had failed to see just how deeply the British monarchy was loved and revered, not just in London but throughout the country and the wider Empire. When on Jubilee Day itself King George and Queen Mary appeared on the balcony of Buckingham Palace, some 100,000 people cheered enthusiastically, a scene repeated every night that week and which she could not fail to have been aware was happening. His Grace the Archbishop of Canterbury, Cosmo Gordon Lang, 'listened with evident satisfaction to the words which fell from royal lips', wrote his chaplain, Alan Don, in his diary that Jubilee night. No wonder. The Archbishop had written them. Men like Don and Lang were increasingly worried about how they would ever be able to write such speeches for King George's son to utter with conviction when the time came.

But there was a deeper meaning of service which the royal family embodied and which could not have been made clearer that week. 'A leading theme of statements about the monarchy [in 1935] was that although its political power had declined, its public significance had increased,' notes Baldwin's official biographer, Philip Williamson. Even renowned left-wingers like George Orwell had to admit they were impressed by 'the survival, or recrudescence, of an idea almost as old as history, the idea of the King and the common people being in some sort of alliance against the upper classes'. For the Jubilee was a brilliant opportunity to raise many thousands of pounds for a wide variety of charities, not just in England but all over the Empire, to launch Jubilee Appeals, usually with members of the royal family as patrons. Canada raised £250,000 for a Silver Jubilee Cancer Fund within weeks of the charity's launch. Wallis may have thought the celebrations silly but she must have known about King George V's Jubilee Trust, which quickly raised £1 million to 'promote the welfare of the younger generation', as the appeal was headed by the Prince of Wales. According to the historian Frank Prochaska:

> Few subjects bring out so well the differences between ourselves and our ancestors as the history of Christian charity. In an increasingly mobile and materialist world, in which culture has grown more national, indeed global, we no longer relate to the lost world of nineteenth-century parish life. Today, we can hardly imagine a voluntary society that boasted millions of religious associations providing essential services, in which the public rarely saw a government official apart from the post office clerk. Against the background of the welfare state and the collapse of church membership, the very idea of Christian social reform has a quaint, Victorian air about it.

Shortly after the celebrations ended in early June, Prime Minister Ramsay MacDonald resigned on grounds of ill health and was replaced by Stanley Baldwin. At the end of July, Wallis left for Cannes where the Prince had taken a villa. Unfortunately, as she wrote to her aunt, Ernest was not able to join them. All summer Wallis was writing to Bessie about how saintly Ernest was, running the business, looking after his deaf mother, irascible father and jealous sister. He even tried, vainly, to bring over his ten-year-old daughter Audrey to live in

London, perhaps to keep him company or perhaps thinking she might benefit from the royal connection his wife had forged. But his former wife refused. Wallis tried to reassure Bessie that no divorce was planned at all and that she, Ernest and the Prince had an understanding. She worried about Ernest endlessly, thought he looked extremely handsome at the Court Ball and described him as 'still the man of my dreams'. When Ernest made a ten-week business trip to the US that autumn she missed him and wrote to Bessie in early October just before his return: 'I shall be glad to see that angelic Ernest again.'

But by then the Prince had found he could barely stand a day without Wallis. His love letters to her were increasingly intense and, by now, unambiguous about his intention to marry her. At three o'clock one morning at the Fort he declared: 'I love you more and more every minute and NO difficulties or complications can possibly prevent our ultimate happiness ... am just going mad at the mere thought ... that you are alone there with Ernest. God bless WE for ever my Wallis. You know your David will love you and look after you so long as he has breath in this eanum body.'

Wallis Out of Control

*'I have of course been under a most awful strain with
Ernest and H.M.'*

In the years since 1935 Wallis Simpson has acquired the reputation of a seductress with legendary contractile vaginal talents. She had, according to one study, 'the ability to make a matchstick feel like a cigar'. Charles Higham, one of her early biographers, went into greater detail, describing an ancient Chinese skill at which she was apparently adept involving 'relaxation of the male partner through a prolonged and carefully modulated hot oil massage of the nipples, stomach, thighs and after a deliberately, almost cruelly protracted delay, the genitals'. When Thelma Furness was abandoned by the Prince, she made it her business to ensure that everyone in London knew that 'the little man' was so called for a reason; he was sexually inadequate and suffered from a common complaint among men at the time – premature ejaculation. Wallis, it was alleged, having spent so much time in Chinese bordellos, had learned special techniques to overcome this and give him the satisfaction he craved. But as the China Dossier, said to detail how she learned techniques variously called the Baltimore grip, Shanghai squeeze or China clinch, has never been found, the intimate pleasures Wallis gave the Prince must remain conjecture. That such breezy rumours landed on so much fertile ground reveals plenty but little that is about Wallis directly. The stories flowered so convincingly because they played on ignorance and fantasy, on the Western vision of the orient as a highly sexualized society coupled with the embarrassed repression and sexual taboos prevalent in most British homes at the time.

Every biographer of Wallis, as well as courtiers who knew her, in trying to explain the inexplicable – how could a middle-aged, not especially beautiful, rather masculine-looking woman have exerted such a powerful effect on a king that he gave up his throne in order to possess her? – produces a different theory. What most agree on is that Wallis was the bad girl, the wicked temptress, the *femme fatale* who, in teaching a repressed prince satisfying techniques in bed, nearly destroyed the monarchy. Just as Eve was responsible for man's original sin, these ideas tap into some deep and ancient fears of women's carnality. Wigram believed that Wallis was, effectively, a witch, while other scandalmongers, whisperers and tittle-tattlers blabbed that she must have hypnotized the Prince. Servants talked to chauffeurs about rowdy parties, and plenty of the rumours, embellished on the way, reached higher places, including Lambeth Palace, residence of the Archbishop of Canterbury. Another woman whose sexual allure proved irresistible to an English king, Henry VIII, was similarly accused of bewitching him. Those accusations were based partly on Anne Boleyn's alleged sixth fingernail and partly, some scholars argue, on the fact that when she miscarried in 1536 the apparently deformed foetus thus 'proved' that she was a witch, even though serious historians today insist that the foetus bore no abnormalities. After being found guilty of treason on the grounds that she had allegedly committed adultery, she was beheaded for her 'crime'.

But the difficulty with theories which insist that Wallis was a sexual predator is that they underplay the fact that Edward was a man of considerable sexual appetite and experience. As Prince of Wales he had sought out women for fornication in almost every corner of the globe and, apparently, had no difficulty in possessing them. But who is to know how satisfying these activities had ever been? Clearly this time something was different. Wallis's remark to Herman Rogers about her marital chastity was now backed up by the Prince's insistence that he and Wallis had never slept together before marriage and his threats to sue anyone who dared to write that Wallis had been his mistress. Wallis might well have taught him some adventurous new activity. What is not in doubt is that she was at the very least a woman of the world, unusually experienced for a well-brought-up young lady in the early twentieth century who liked to tell people about her 'tough, rough past life in China and cooking and doing housework for a loathed husband with the smell of your husband's bacon getting in your hair etc'. What she would have learned from her years as a naval wife married to Win Spencer as much as from life in China was that pleasure as well as pain can be derived from sex. And she probably knew about a variety of non-vaginal sexual techniques, including oral sex, which would not have been standard education for most English or American girls of the day.

The great ignorance in sexual matters in early twentieth-century middle- and working-class Britain is key to understanding the story of Wallis, why she was attacked so fiercely at the time, and why she has since become such a talisman for gay and lesbian minorities even though she herself was not lesbian. For many, her struggle is emblematic of a wider struggle for greater sexual freedom against the establishment's narrow interpretation of what was acceptable. In the 1930s, some who wanted information about sex resorted to pornography. A variety of erotic literature could be purchased then but only through expensive underground channels, so in practice it was available only to satisfy well-off men, probably those whose wives were shy, ignorant or both. The Rickatson-Hatt divorce, awarded in 1939 on grounds of genuine non-consummation after ten years of traumatic marriage, illustrates only too clearly and in painful detail the overpowering middle-class taboos involved in seeking help, medical or otherwise, to discuss sex. When Rickatson-Hatt died it was discovered that he had amassed a fine collection of erotic literature. But, although he had gone on to marry a second time and father a son, it did not help him in his marriage to an American wife, Frances, who evidently struggled to establish normal marital relations with her reserved husband. Neither of them felt able to talk, even in private, to their friends, Wallis and Ernest Simpson.

Of course there were books, by Marie Stopes and others, containing sexual information for the lay public as well as medical textbooks which, while describing the sex organs, omitted to detail what was done with them. But there was almost nothing for the general reader nor anything that looked at the psychology of sexual behaviour. One trainee gynaecologist who tried to remedy this state of affairs by writing a simple and straightforward guide had to do so under a pseudonym for fear that the medical hierarchy would prevent him getting a post in obstetrics and gynaecology. When he eventually found a publisher – the Wales Publishing Company – they insisted that any illustrations in the book were bound and sealed separately in a packet at the back of the book as these were, according to the preface, 'of interest only to the serious reader'. Even so the book, first published in 1939, was banned in some areas and burned publicly in Blackpool. *The Technique of Sex* by Anthony Havil (pseudonym of Dr Elliot Philipp) cost fourpence a copy, stayed in print for a remarkable fifty years and sold half a million copies in hardback alone, clearly satisfying a national demand.

But, since no one can know for certain what activities go on behind a closed door except those who are inside, all speculation about what exactly Wallis and her Prince did or did not do together must remain just that – speculation. Of the facts that are known, many of those who saw the Prince naked commented on his lack of bodily hair, implicitly questioning his virility. But, drawing the conclusion that Wallis, with her obvious dominating personality, was therefore able to satisfy both his repressed homosexuality and his yearning for a mother figure is, again, speculation, however likely it may seem. Much could be observed by watching them together in public and examples abound of Wallis bossing the Prince or humiliating him contemptuously, depending on the occasion or one's point of view. The young Alfred Shaughnessy, stepson of a courtier at the heart of the crisis, Sir Piers 'Joey' Legh, was so struck by her manly behaviour that he had to ask his mother 'who the bossy American woman was': she had 'got up at lunch and seized the carving knife from the Prince as he struggled with the roast chicken on the sideboard and told him to sit down saying in a grating voice: "I'll take care of that, Sir"'. When the weekend guests had departed from the Fort and only Wallis remained, the staff would notice how she would 'taunt and berate him until he was reduced to tears'. Lady Diana Cooper, one of the keenest observers of the Prince's demeaning devotion, noticed that once 'Wallis tore her nail and said "oh" and forgot about it, but he needs must disappear and arrive back in two minutes, panting, with two little emery-boards for her to file the offending nail'. The more Wallis was beset by fears of her future the more, it seemed, she found new ways to humiliate the Prince more brazenly. Philip Ziegler believes that Wallis provoked in him both 'slavish devotion' and 'profound sexual excitement. That such excitement may have had some kind of sadomasochistic trimmings is possible, even likely.'

Yet sexual magnetism was clearly not all that Wallis offered the Prince, even if it was at the root of their relationship. Edward may not have realized how deeply he needed someone like Wallis, nor she him, until they became entangled. If Wallis had grown up with an unexplained and unnamed Disorder of Sexual Development she would always have known there was something unusual about her that she could not talk about, something that was humiliating, and she may have discovered that she was more comfortable when projecting this on to someone else. Wallis could be remarkably self-aware on occasions and in letters as well as her memoirs often talks of the 'two sides' of her own personality in flat, straightforward terms such as 'good' and 'bad'. At the same time she now said of her husband, Ernest, that he is 'much too good for "the likes of me"'.

Psychologists may have an explanation for this behaviour: the ideal partner for her personality would be one who allowed her to appear as the perfect one, the other (him) as the inadequate one and the one who carried the flaw. This allowed for an aspect of herself, instead of being owned by her, to be projected on to someone else. This type of personality needs someone else to engage with closely so that the other person can be the receptacle of those parts of oneself that are despised. In this way an aspect of one is transferred to the other which makes both partners feel good and as a result each person develops a vital sense of closeness with the other.

To the outsider this phenomenon is observed by watching the transference process which is effected, however unconsciously, by giving the other person tasks and then criticizing them for the way they do them, thus making them feel at first inadequate but then eager to do better another time. Wallis excelled at this and the Prince responded by returning for more.

Outsiders were indeed aware that the Prince was in the grip of an abnormal obsession but were at a loss to explain it. He insisted it was love and in some ways it was. Walter Monckton, a barrister friend of

Edward's since Oxford days who acted as his trusted legal adviser in the months to follow, commented:

> It is a great mistake to assume that he was merely in love with her in the ordinary physical sense of the term. There was an intellectual companionship and there is no doubt that his lonely nature found in her a spiritual companionship ... He felt that he and Mrs Simpson were made for one another and there was no other honest way of meeting the situation than marrying her.

Winston Churchill MP, whose warnings in the 1930s of the need for Britain to rearm in the face of the Nazi threat made him suspect as a warmonger, was even more understanding and retained a roseate romantic view of the relationship longer than most. Churchill felt deeply that abdication should be avoided in the hope that the crisis would resolve itself. He believed that 'the Prince found in her qualities as necessary to his happiness as the air he breathed. Those who ... watched him closely noticed that many little tricks and fidgetings of nervousness fell away from him. He was a completed being instead of a sick and harassed soul.' Churchill wrote shortly after the abdication that:

> the King's love for Mrs Simpson was branded with the stigma of a guilty love ... no companionship could have appeared more natural, more free from impropriety or grossness ...
>
> The character and record of the lady upon whom the affection of Edward VIII became so fatally fixed is relevant only upon a lower plane to the constitutional and moral issues which have been raised. No one has been more victimised by gossip and scandal but gossip and scandal in themselves would not have been decisive. The only fact of which the Church could take notice was that she had divorced one husband and was in the process of divorcing another.

Lord Dawson of Penn, asked by the King for a medical opinion on his son's infatuation, believed that the Prince's age had something to do with his obsession. 'A *first* absorbing love coming after 40 is so apt to take possession. To have abandoned it would have spoilt life and work and therefore worth. To preserve it in marriage was impossible,' the doctor wrote. By the late autumn of 1935, the old King was, after years of poor health, seriously ill, suffering from bronchitis and a weak heart aggravated by heavy smoking. Worried about his eldest son he now predicted to his Prime Minister, Stanley Baldwin, 'After I am dead the boy will ruin himself in twelve months.'

The new year of 1936 started with exceptionally cold and snowy weather and on 16 January the Prince was out shooting in Windsor Great Park when he received a restrained message from his mother suggesting he might 'propose' himself for the weekend at Sandringham. He flew up immediately with his own pilot – flying was part of the Prince's glamour – and, as soon as he arrived, was shocked to find his father had only hours to live. He immediately wrote to Wallis, terrified that the new situation might change her feelings, imploring her to keep faith. 'You are all and everything I have in life and WE must hold each other so tight.' On 20 January at five minutes to midnight King George V died, his end hastened by an overdose of morphine and cocaine injected by the royal physician, Lord Dawson, to ensure that the death announcement was in time for the quality newspapers. The Queen's first act was to take her eldest son's hand and kiss it, offering fealty to the new King. He was embarrassed by such subservience and broke down, weeping hysterically and noisily with dread at what the future might hold as much as for the passing of his father. Wallis was at a charity gala in a London cinema with some friends, the Lawson Johnstons, when she heard the bulletin. 'I am so very sorry,' she told the new King, adding later, 'God bless you and above all make you strong where you have been weak.' Ernest, the next day, wrote 'as a devoted, loyal subject' offering 'the warmest sentiments that friendship can engender . . . in the ordeal through which you have passed'.

'I miss him dreadfully,' the Duchess of York wrote to Dawson. 'Unlike his own children I was never afraid of him, and in all the 12 years of having me as daughter-in-law he never spoke one unkind or abrupt word to me, and was always ready to listen and give advice on one's own silly little affairs.' Two days later the will was read to the family and the former Prince was shocked to discover that his father had left him a life interest in Balmoral and Sandringham, but no cash, because it was expected that he had considerable reserves from his Duchy of Cornwall estates – which, as it transpired later, he did, although he failed to admit it then. Alan Lascelles described how, with a face like thunder, he strode out of the room and immediately telephoned Mrs Simpson to tell her the bad news.

The next few days were a shock to many as the new King, believing he was on a mission to modernize the monarchy, constantly breached protocol. The first important ceremony was his own proclamation by Garter King of Arms at St James's Palace. Not only did Edward VIII arrange for Mrs Simpson to view the proceedings from a highly visible front window; he then, at the last minute, decided he wanted to stand next to her there and watch his accession being proclaimed. Chips Channon, like many of those in the know, was enthralled.

> Afterwards I saw a large black car (the King's) drive away, with the blinds pulled half down. The crowd bowed, thinking that it contained the Duchess of Kent, but I saw Mrs Simpson ...
>
> We are all riveted by the position of Mrs S. No man has ever been so in love as the present King but can she be another Mrs Fitzherbert?[6] If he drops her she will fall – fall – into the nothingness from whence she came.

A desire to gainsay this nothingness prompted Wallis to ask her aunt to have 'one of those family tree things' made up of the Warfields and the Montagues, reminding Bessie that in England Montague with an e meant the Jewish family – 'the swell spell it without an e!!' She did not specify why she wanted this genealogy but said she hoped her own family histories 'would stand up against these 1066 families here'. Meanwhile the Duchess of York spent the day of the proclamation travelling to Sandringham to be with the widowed Queen.

---

6 Maria Fitzherbert, a Catholic, had also been married twice, and twice widowed, by the time she met the Prince of Wales, later King George IV, in 1784. They were married secretly the following year, though the marriage was considered invalid. The King married again, Caroline of Brunswick, in 1795, but continued his relationship with Mrs Fitzherbert.

There were trivial aspects to the modernizing, too, all of which aroused comment. For example, Wallis liked the King to call a taxi for her at St James's Palace. Lady Carlisle, who saw him doing this, commented: 'anything more undignified than the King going past sentries to call a taxi is difficult to imagine'. And the same 'democratic' approach was introduced at the Fort where Wallis, acting as hostess, would say 'We don't dress for dinner.' This caused the women much embarrassment as often they had not brought the appropriate clothes. For example Lady Diana Cooper, arriving late for dinner, began gushing apologies whereupon Mrs Simpson said: 'Oh cut it out. David and I don't mind.'

Others were more deeply offended by her easy, proprietorial attitude. Lascelles told his wife, Joan, how the Wigrams had been invited to see a film show at Windsor:

> When it was over Mrs S said to Lady W (who has lived at Windsor for 20 years and knows everything in the castle as well as she knows her own drawing room) 'wouldn't you like me to show you the pictures in the long corridor' and when they left 'Goodbye, <u>we</u> were so glad you and Lord W were able to come.' That shows an incredible lack of elementary tact. Don't leave this about!

Lascelles concluded that this indicated that Wallis 'cannot really be a very clever woman'.

'Clever' was not the issue as far as hostesses such as Emerald Cunard, who had never been on good terms with the old regime, were concerned. Almost immediately the invitations turned from a trickle to a flood. In 1935 Lady Cunard had enjoyed what she believed to be a position of pre-eminence among those chasing after the Prince and his paramour. Partly hoping the Prince would become a patron of the opera so important to her lover, Sir Thomas Beecham, she had pursued Wallis from the first. Wallis responded, believing that some musical culture would be of benefit to the future monarch. But Edward always loathed opera and took every opportunity to escape into the corridor and smoke. Emerald genuinely liked her fellow American, describing 'little Mrs Simpson' as 'a woman of character who reads Balzac' – a questionable boast.

When the Prince and Mrs Simpson expressed a desire to see a play called *Storm over Patsy*, a light romantic comedy based on a German play by Bruno Frank which had just opened at the Theatre Royal Haymarket and which they, solipsistically, believed had echoes of their own story, it was Emerald who arranged for them to see an abridged version privately at her house to save them the embarrassment of going publicly.[7] She rashly told friends she hoped to be appointed mistress of the robes and preside over a court where poets, musicians and artists held sway, a remark which may have reached Queen Mary who always singled Lady Cunard out – not entirely justifiably – as having played a mischievous role by encouraging Wallis to believe she was accepted in society. 'I fear she has done David a great deal of harm as there is no doubt she was great friends with Mrs S and gave parties for her . . . several people have mentioned to me what harm she has done.'

Other hostesses, notably Lady Colefax and Lady Astor, vied with each other to entertain the woman they assumed would be queen, but older money invited her as well, including the Marlboroughs, Sackville Wests, Buccleuchs and Sutherlands. Noël Coward, exhausted by the chase, refused one of Emerald's invitations, telling her acidly: 'I am sick to *death* of having quiet suppers with the King *and* Mrs Simpson.'

From the first, the new Court caused deep consternation among the old guard. 'I think he will make a great King of a new era,' Wallis told her aunt, 'and I believe the country thinks the same.' The old regime, she believed, 'was a little behind the times . . . the late King was not sociable nor the Queen and I'm sure this one will entertain more at the Palace.' What the old guard objected to was not so much the new King's awkwardness or obstinacy – a monarch was entitled to that and after all George V had often not been easy. What they minded was the obstinacy devoid of any sense of duty or service. Men like Lascelles had been aware of the chasm since 1928, constantly hoping that Edward would mature. In fact the reverse now seemed

---

7 In 1937 this was adapted as *Storm in a Teacup*, a film starring Vivien Leigh and Rex Harrison, which acquired cult status as a minor British comedy classic.

to be the case. On 12 February there was tea with Lord and Lady Brownlow, where Chips Channon recorded 'Mrs Simpson [as being] very charming and gay and vivacious. She said she had not worn black stockings since she gave up the Can Can,' a remark some felt out of order so soon after the King's death, but which Channon considered was typical of her 'breezy humour, quick and American but not profound'. While some courtiers were optimistic that Wallis would have a positive effect on the King, encouraging him to take his job more seriously, and were therefore prepared to overlook her brashness, others quickly despaired. Philip Ziegler believes that by 1936 it was too late for anyone to effect any change, that by then Edward 'was corroded by idleness. He may have had a better brain than his brother, and a capacity to communicate and charisma ... but the charisma was wasted by the time he had met Wallis and the charm had become a dangerous attribute.'

'Wallis must not get too bossy,' wrote Diana Cooper, having heard her reprimand the King in front of his guests for wanting to have his papers and documents read to him instead of reading them himself. She told him he simply had to learn to master the points in them. 'She is right of course as he made haste to say. "Wallis is quite right. She always is. I shall learn it quite soon."' The King was used to having information fed to him and if, as Prince of Wales, he appeared well informed this was because he had been well briefed. Reading an entire book was so low on his list of priorities that in 1936, fitting out the hired yacht that was to take Wallis and him cruising for the summer, instructions were given for all the books to be removed from the yacht's library as they would not be needed. This is not a matter of intellectual snobbery; it meant in practice that he drained Wallis as his sole source of information and, when he needed to draw on his own emotional reserves, he was not supported by any books he had read. When Baldwin had to have serious discussions with Edward in November 1936 he felt the lack of reading acutely disadvantaged him. He described him as an 'abnormal being, half-child, half-genius ... it is almost as though two or three cells in his brain had remained entirely undeveloped while the rest of him is a mature man ... he is not a thinker. He takes his ideas from the daily press instead of thinking things out for himself. He never reads – except, of course, the papers. No serious reading: none at all . . .'

Of greater concern, however, to those around him was the way he now deferred to Wallis in everything, including matters of state. Within weeks of his accession he was no longer reading state papers at all but leaving the task entirely to Alec Hardinge, his despairing Private Secretary. Not only were the papers unread, much to Baldwin's horror they were apparently left lying around the Fort during his ever longer weekends, now often from Thursday to Tuesday. If scrutinized by anyone it was Wallis's eye that fell on them. When they were returned they were decorated by rings from wet glasses left on top of them. Despatch boxes were sometimes lost entirely. But it was not only at the Fort that work was neglected. Even in London, according to Alan Lascelles, the King shut himself up giggling with Mrs Simpson for hours on end while the royal footmen would say to the waiting secretaries 'The Lady is still there.' Hardinge fed Baldwin a tale of ever increasing dereliction of duty, resulting in the Prime Minister's decision to restrict the documents made available to the King to those requiring the royal signature.

Within weeks, as he felt the loneliness and boredom of his new job, his infatuation and desperate need for Wallis increased. Exhausted, frustrated and even angry, she escaped to Paris in the early spring with her divorced, redheaded friend Josephine 'Foxy' Gwynne. The trip was partly to stock up on her couture wardrobe; she was especially keen to buy from the Chicago-born Main Rousseau Bocher, known as Mainbocher, her latest favourite, whose haute-couture gowns were endorsed by an exclusive clientele that included Syrie Maugham, Diana Vreeland and many Hollywood stars. But another reason for the visit was that she hated the pressure on her, with the King constantly telephoning her, relying on her; she felt she was losing control of the situation and wanted to get Ernest back as her husband. As she admitted to her aunt, 'I have of course been under a most awful strain with Ernest and H.M.' What the King's mother called his 'violent infatuation', which she hoped would pass, had turned into an obsession so all consuming that he could concentrate on nothing more than how he could arrange to marry Wallis Simpson as quickly as possible. Wallis now felt trapped.

Nineteen-thirty-six was a critical year throughout Europe as dramatic events with enormous consequences unfurled with lightning speed and the rise of the far right was allowed to go unchecked. In Spain, a Popular Front government was elected in February but almost immediately came under pressure from strikes and violent uprisings, and by July the country was locked in a bloody civil war. France, too, had elected a socialist prime minister in February but the Popular Front of Léon Blum was weakened from constant and vicious attacks from both the extreme left and the extreme right. On 7 March German troops marched into the Rhineland, an action in direct contravention of the Treaty of Versailles which had laid out terms which the defeated Germany had accepted. It was Hitler's first illegal act in foreign relations since coming to power in 1933 and it threw the European allies, especially France and Britain, into confusion. Yet public opinion in Britain was strongly opposed to going to war with Germany over this. No politician wanted to unleash another great war in Europe.

However, it was now clear that Hitler had no qualms about repudiating treaties which he argued had been imposed on Germany by force. As Baldwin's Foreign Secretary Anthony Eden commented: 'We must be prepared for him to repudiate any treaty even if freely negotiated (a) when it becomes inconvenient; and (b) when Germany is sufficiently strong and the circumstances are otherwise favourable for doing so.' But although no one expected (or wanted) the King to be directly involved, the fact remains that during this year of unprecedented turbulence in Europe, the British sovereign was concentrating on one matter only: how to marry Wallis and make her his queen. His obsession impacted on his government.

One evening in early February, Ernest went to have dinner with the King at York House and decided to take with him his friend Bernard Rickatson-Hatt, by then editor in chief at Reuters. When Rickatson-Hatt got up to leave, Ernest pressed him to stay. He wanted his friend to hear what he felt he now had to state clearly to the King, 'that Wallis would have to choose between them and what did the

King mean to do about it? Did he intend to marry her? The King then rose from his chair and said: "Do you really think that I would be crowned without Wallis at my side?"' That evening, according to Rickatson-Hatt's version, the King and Ernest Simpson reached an accommodation whereby Ernest agreed to put an end to his marriage provided the King promised to look after Wallis.

Naturally, events could not rest there. According to a memorandum by Lord Davidson, Baldwin's close ally, written immediately after this:

> Simpson Mason asks to see Jenks Mason – the *Mari Complaisant* is now the sorrowing and devastated spouse. He tells Jenks that the King wants to marry Mrs S, (unbelievable) & that he – S – would like to leave England only that would make divorce easier – what he wants is his wife back. S suggests he should see the P.M. SB replies to this suggest [sic] with a flat negative. He is the King's chief adviser not Mr S's ... Clive Wigram, SB and I have a frank talk. I am quite convinced Blackmail sticks out at every stage. HM has already paid large sums to Mrs S and given valuable presents. I advocate most drastic steps (deportation) if it is true that S is an American but if he isn't the situation is very delicate. The Masonic move is very clever. The POW got S in on a lie – is now living in open breach of the Masonic Law of chastity because of the lie he first told. S and Mrs S, who is obviously a gold digger, have obviously got him on toast ... Mrs S is very close to [the German Ambassador Leopold von] Hoesch and has, if she likes to read them access to all Secret and Cabinet papers!!!!!

Realizing that Simpson, as a British subject, could not be deported, Sir Maurice Jenks managed to reassure the frightened Wigram that Ernest was an honourable man who wanted above all to avoid scandal. Couldn't Simpson be persuaded then to go back voluntarily to the United States and take his wife with him, Wigram urged Jenks? The story of the King's meeting with his nemesis was passed around a frightened inner circle of advisers, including Sir Maurice Gwyer, First Parliamentary Counsel to the Treasury, Sir Lionel Halsey, then a Council Member of the Duchy of Cornwall, and Walter Monckton. Monckton, while questioning whether indeed the King could have said what was attributed to him, predicted 'blackmail upon an extravagant basis'.

The Davidson memorandum not only lays bare deeply felt establishment concerns about Wallis becoming queen, but, more significantly, makes plain the twin fear some had of her passing on secrets to the Germans at a time of critical international tension. This fear never went away and was partly responsible for royal attitudes towards Wallis in the ensuing decades. Just eight years later the King's brother and successor George VI was to write in a private and confidential letter to his Prime Minister: 'I must tell you quite honestly that I do not trust the Duchess's [Wallis's] loyalty.' In 1936 the ambassadors of Nazi Germany and Fascist Italy were actively courting all the hostesses, as well as newspaper editors and politicians. Bernard Rickatson-Hatt's boss at Reuters, Sir Roderick Jones, had been meeting Joachim von Ribbentrop, the German former champagne salesman acting as Hitler's special envoy, socially since 1933. He described him as a man who, when he invited him to luncheon at his own home, 'held me there with a flow of argument and talk from which I could not very well escape without appearing discourteous'. The Archbishop of Canterbury, Cosmo Lang, arguably more aware of the Nazi reality than most through Germany's bishops informing him of Nazi policy, also lunched with Ribbentrop in the summer of 1935 and described him as 'most genial and friendly'.

Wallis herself met Ribbentrop at least twice at Lady Cunard's. This was Ribbentrop's job, to assess the degree of pro-Nazi feeling in British society, so naturally he made a point of socializing with the woman now being called the King's mistress. He may even have sent her regular bouquets after the dinners in the hope of currying favour, as Mary Raffray asserted later. According to the Kirk family version, when Ribbentrop was in London he called on Wallis daily, 'except when some engagement took him out of town and then, said Mary, flinging her arms wide to indicate size, he always sent Wallis a huge box of the most glorious flowers'. As Helen Hardinge noted in her diary, 'one of the factors in the situation was Mrs Simpson's partiality for Nazi Germans'. But there is no evidence of an affair with Rib-bentrop beyond Wallis's ever-ready preparedness to flirt – especially with diplomats – and society's love of gossiping. German diplomats in 1936 believed she would soon be very useful and she enjoyed having their attention. She was probably no more pro-Nazi than the pro-appeasement Foreign Secretary Lord Halifax and many of the Cabinet at the time. It is noteworthy that Baldwin himself never accused her of having German sympathies, either then or later. Yet, because many found her untrustworthy on other private matters, it was easy to assume that she was untrustworthy generally. The views of the King himself were more dangerously pro-German, although predominantly pacifist, and more easily bent out of shape; they were views Wallis doubtless absorbed as being easier than exercising her mind about such matters when her own security was paramount. Not only did the King have many German relations, he spoke German fluently and believed, like many, that a repeat of the carnage of the First World War had to be avoided above all else. Recently released German documents have now made clear that the Nazis were ready to exploit the King's sympathies if the opportunity arose and, although his friends wanted to believe that his deep patriotism would always win through, Wallis's over-arching influence was an unknown factor.

At the end of March 1936, Wallis returned from Paris 'in a state of collapse'. Her health was never robust and she often complained of suffering from 'the old nervous indigestion'. But this time her unhappiness stemmed as much from the King's almost suffocating need for her as from Ernest's increasing detachment. She was still convinced that her days with the King were numbered, especially now that the pressures on him to provide an heir were redoubled, and this need she knew she could never satisfy. 'In the back of my mind I had always known that the dream one day would have to end – somewhere sometime somehow. But I had characteristically refused to be dismayed by this prospect.' And she soon realized why Ernest was quite so pliant. On 24 March, Mary Raffray had arrived in London again. Even before she came Wallis was annoyed by the idea of having a houseguest. Once she arrived she had no time for Mary and thought the clothes she had brought with her were unsuitable other than for a nightclub. But she was still Wallis's most intimate friend, the one person in whom she could confide with utter frankness sure of a sympathetic and understanding listener. Or so she thought.

It rapidly became clear to Wallis that while Mary may have started by taking pity on Ernest, as well as genuinely enjoying his historical explanations as they toured ancient buildings, she had now fallen in love with him. Wallis felt deeply hurt by the new relationship between her husband and Mary but cannot have been surprised. It was a situation of her own contriving which she had believed she could control. Mary understood later that she had been manipulated, such as 'the night she tricked me into going to the opera and then at the last minute failed to appear because she told everyone Ernest's mistress was there ... She thought she could use me as a scapegoat and did,' wrote Mary, 'that Ernest would turn to me in his great unhappiness as he did. Even though she loathed and despised having me there, it served her purpose as then she could say that Ernest was having an affair with me and so she would have to get a divorce.'

'Mary's first letters to me', her sister Buckie recalled of 1936, 'were in sharp contrast to those I had had the previous year,' although she still wrote of occasional small dinners at York House and of weekends at the Fort. In one of these Mary described how the King had the entire house party, which included Ernest, driven over to Windsor Castle to see movies of the Grand National and how thrilled she felt at being able to walk casually around at least part of the castle, admiring some of the magnificent paintings. 'Wallis is in the very thick of things, received and toadied to by everyone,' Mary wrote.

Very soon, though, Wallis had had enough of her old schoolfriend. 'Within a few days I received a note from Mary on unfamiliar paper bearing the letterhead of a London hotel,' her sister recalled. 'It was brief and to the point. Yesterday, Mary wrote me, Wallis had accused her of having seduced Ernest. Mary had left the room where they were talking, gone to her own, thrown all her possessions into suitcases, phoned for a taxi and then walked out of Bryanston Court and Wallis' life forever.'

Wallis fed her aunt little of this drama, explaining only that she had gone to great lengths to amuse Mary. But, she added ominously, 'I am afraid.' She then wrote to her aunt with remarkable self-knowledge of how people of her age, nearly forty, must make their own lives. 'As I wasn't in a position to have it arranged for me by money or position and though I have had many hard times, disappointments etc I've managed not to go under as yet – and never having known security until I married Ernest, perhaps I don't get along well with it, knowing and understanding the thrill of its opposite much better – the old bromide, nothing ventured nothing gained.' Bessie Merryman decided that it was time to come over to England again and support her niece more actively, but she could not do so immediately.

On 2 April the Simpsons hosted a black-tie, black-waistcoat dinner in the King's honour at Bryanston Court where Ernest, bizarrely, made a grand entrance into the drawing room of his own home escorting his sovereign. Harold Nicolson, a guest that evening, found 'Mrs Simpson a perfectly harmless type of American but the whole setting is slightly second rate'. After this there was to be only one more occasion when Ernest accompanied his wife in public, but the society jokes about him did not abate. The Duchess of Devonshire suggested that while other staff were being sacked a job might be found for him such as '"Guardian of the Bedchamber" or "Master of the Mistress"'.

In May, the Prime Minister and his wife, Lucy, were invited to dine at York House, where the King still lived. Until recently Lucy Baldwin had been completely unaware of Mrs Simpson's existence – and her discovery was the cause of much mirth in smart London gatherings. But this was not her milieu. The Baldwins had been married for more than forty years and had six surviving children, and, although their roots were in the country, in Worcestershire, they were not part of the Tory landed gentry who spent weekends hunting and shooting. Lucy was first and foremost a homemaker, a formidable woman dedicated to a life of service. She was the founder of the Anaesthetics Appeal Fund, associated with a machine, which was named after her, for self-administration of oxygen analgesia in obstetrics, the aim of which was to address the high incidence of maternal mortality. She was involved in the Young Women's Christian Association and various other charitable bodies for women, especially those concerned with improving maternity care, after having herself suffered difficult pregnancies and lost her first child in a stillbirth. She was also a member of the White Heather Club, the first women's cricket club founded in Yorkshire in 1887, and she created a small theatre at Astley Hall in Worcestershire where her children with cousins and friends often put on small productions. It is hard to imagine which of these topics would have resulted in congenial conversation with Wallis Simpson.

The King had warned Wallis weeks beforehand that he wanted her at this dinner. 'He paused, and after a moment, with his most Prince Charming smile, added: "It's got to be done. Sooner or later my Prime Minister must meet my future wife."' Wallis, recounting this story, maintains that it was the first time he had proposed marriage. They planned the evening together and, on the surface, the dinner passed off uneventfully. The other guests included the Mountbattens, the Wigrams, Admiral of the Fleet Sir Ernle Chatfield and Lady Chatfield and the American aviator Charles Lindbergh and his wife, Anne. Baldwin had no prior knowledge of the significance of the occasion and, although surprised to see Mrs Simpson at one end of the table and Lady Cunard at the other, neither disliked Wallis nor took offence at his own wife's placement, which was on the King's right. In fact he was one of those who believed that 'Mrs Simpson's influence was not without its good side'. Neither was he out of touch with modern morals nor without sympathy for her predicament, having recently seen his own daughter go through a painful divorce. But others were more distressed, especially when the names of Mr and Mrs Ernest Simpson were announced in the Court Circular. Sir John (later Lord) Reith, a minister's son and strict Presbyterian who rose to become director general of the BBC, was deeply disapproving of 'the Simpson woman' and described the affair as 'too horrible and ... serious and sad beyond calculation'.

As Harold Nicolson had observed in calling the group surrounding Wallis and the new King second rate, and as the guest books from the Fort reveal, most of those invited to inform or stimulate the

King came from their existing small circle of friends in London (the Hunters, Prendergasts, Buists, Lawson-Johnstons), those who took a broad-minded view of divorce, with a sprinkling of courtiers and diplomats every now and again but a marked absence of artists, writers, politicians or statesmen or those who might have challenged them to think differently about a wide range of issues. Fred Bate, the British representative for America's National Broadcasting Company (NBC) who had lived in Britain for some twenty years, was an exception in that he was better informed than most of their friends. But he too was divorced, in 1929, and remarried. When Wallis and Edward were exposed to the world of culture it was often a disaster, never more so than on 10 June when Sibyl Colefax invited them as guests of honour and persuaded Artur Rubinstein to play after dinner, a rare honour granted by the Polish maestro. Several after-dinner guests swelled the numbers at this point, including Winston and Clementine Churchill, and there was a considerable hubbub about politics which Sibyl did her best to hush as Rubinstein was ready to play. After three Chopin pieces during which the King, seated on a stool close to the piano, had chatted intermittently, openly displaying his boredom, Rubinstein prepared himself for a fourth. But before he could do so the King got up and walked over to him saying, 'We enjoyed that very much, Mr Rubinstein,' which, as everyone knew, was a clear command to stop. Rubinstein made a barely audible reply, 'I am afraid that you do not like my playing, Your Majesty,' and, accompanied by Kenneth Clark, the influential Surveyor of the King's Pictures and director of the National Gallery, left the party angered by the humiliation. One of the guests was the Princesse de Polignac, the former sewing-machine heiress Winnaretta Singer and a noted musician herself, who said later how shocked she had been by the rudeness shown to Rubinstein. Such philistinism could never happen in Paris where she hosted musical salons, she declared.

Among the elite, everyone knew who Wallis Simpson was. But Alan Lascelles noticed how naively keen the King was that they should know her better. He wrote to his wife Joan of a meeting at which the King:

gave me an example of his ostrich-like mentality, which nearly made me burst out laughing. I was telling him about my hunting experiences in Maryland and he asked me searching questions about various places in that part of the world. I couldn't imagine why he was so excited about them when he said, 'I'm very interested in that country because rather a friend of mine, Mrs Simpson, Wallie Simpson, I don't think you know her? comes from down there.' It struck me as the most child-like simplicity; can he really think I've not heard of Mrs Simpson?

The King had often in his life revealed a lack of intellectual curiosity but, now with the petulance of a child who does not want to be told no, was going dangerously further by putting himself beyond the reach of anyone who might disagree with his chosen lifestyle. Even the judicious Walter Monckton was forced to remark, 'he was not well placed at Fort Belvedere to judge public opinion'. Among those whom he rarely saw in 1936 were his brother and sister-in-law, the Duke and Duchess of York. It was partly in order to remedy that situation that he suggested in the spring that he and Wallis should drive over from the Fort in his new American station wagon, the height of modernity, to visit the Yorks' nearby home, Royal Lodge; he wanted to show Bertie the car.

He took enormous pleasure driving there, Wallis recalled. The Yorks met the King at the door and they all had tea in the drawing room. Wallis, in a perfectly polished paragraph of her memoirs, describes how the Duchess's 'justly famous charm was highly evident'. The hour passed with innocuous conversation but left Wallis with 'a distinct impression that while the Duke of York was sold on the American station wagon the Duchess was not sold on David's other American interest'.

The antipathy between the two women may have had a deeper source, as Lady Mosley, the former Diana Mitford, who knew both women, believed. 'Probably the theory of their [the Windsors'] contemporaries that Cake [a Mitford nickname for the Queen Mother, derived from her confectionary fashion sense] was rather in love with him [the Duke] (as a girl) & took second best, may account for much.'

But there were more recent grievances too, such as the occasion when Wallis decided to entertain guests at the Fort with an impersonation of the Duchess, whom she thought not only dowdy but possessed of a 'goody-goodiness [that was] false and artificial'. The Duchess walked into the room while Wallis was in full flow and, 'from that moment of overhearing, the Duchess of York became her implacable enemy', according to Ella Hogg, wife of Brigadier Oliver Hogg, who was there at the time. Wallis maintained that the episode showed the Duchess had no sense of humour; the old courtiers thought it indicated that she had no idea how to behave with royalty.

Throughout May and June Wallis had more weekends at the Fort as well as buying sprees in Paris, while the King bought her more and more jewellery to go with the frocks and sent more declarations of eternal love couched in the private, infantile language they used for each other. In March a magnificent ruby and diamond bracelet from Van Cleef and Arpels had come with a note full of underlinings telling her that 'THEY say that THEY liked this bracelet and that THEY want you to wear it always in the evening . . . A boy loves a girl more and more and more.' Inscribed on the clasp are the date '27-iii-36' and the words 'Hold Tight', a reference perhaps to Wallis's sexual prowess as well as to the need to endure political difficulties.

Meanwhile Ernest bought a small flat for Mary near by at Albion Gate in Hyde Park and although Mary was 'homesick and lonely', as she told her sisters, she wanted to stay in London for the sake of Ernest. In early June the King had had another 'difficult' talk with Ernest and told Wallis that he 'must get after him now or he won't move'. But Ernest was still required to put in an appearance with his wife on occasions and the day she was writing this letter, 28 June, he was at Blenheim with her and the King and the Duke and Duchess of Marlborough. In her memoirs Wallis wrote that 'as best as I can recall' the last time she and Ernest 'were publicly together in David's company' was the dinner on 28 May for the Baldwins. 'Not long afterwards I told Ernest that I was starting divorce proceedings.' As Mary's letter shows this was not the case. Ernest had not quite yet given up on Wallis – nor on his love of visiting England's stately homes. But this particular occasion of togetherness was one she absolutely could not recall publicly.

Wallis was suffering from a serious and painful recurrence of her stomach trouble in the summer of 1936. X-rays, she told her aunt, had found 'a *healed* ulcer scar', but this could have been a healed scar from another internal operation. By the end of June she felt better as 'I have the sort of stomach that needs care and I have a diet which evidently agrees as I haven't had a pain for a month', she told her aunt. But the pain from the intensity of her marital situation was harder to assuage. In July, Ernest accepted the inevitable and booked in to the riverside Hotel de Paris at Bray on the night of 21 July with a female companion who gave her name as Buttercup Kennedy. In an interview with the King's Proctor in 1937 Ernest insisted that on his return he found a formal letter from Wallis suing for divorce which, he explained, meant not that she had been colluding in the proceedings but that she must have had him followed. He immediately moved out of Bryanston Court to live at the Guards Club in Piccadilly. In the letter Wallis wrote to Ernest she complained that 'instead of being on business, as you led me to believe, you have been staying at Bray with a lady. I am sure you realise this is conduct which I cannot possibly overlook and must insist you do not continue to live here with me.' Furthermore she was, she told him, instructing solicitors.

Having set her divorce in motion it was time once again to go on a summer holiday. The King was determined not to follow royal tradition and spend August in Scotland; neither Balmoral nor grouse shooting had much appeal for him. He planned at first to rent the American actress Maxine Elliott's villa on the French Riviera but was later advised against that by the Foreign Office because of the instability in the area caused by the Spanish Civil War. 'I really am very annoyed with the FO for having messed up my holiday in this stupid manner,' he wrote to his mother. According to John Aird, increasingly critical of Wallis's baneful influence, the King was about to offer Maxine Elliott £1,000 as compensation for the cancellation but 'then consulted Mrs Simpson and reduced the amount to £100'. Her fear – not irrational – that she would be cast aside without enough to live on and have to suffer as her mother had, was still not conquered.

Instead the King now decided to charter a yacht and after an inspection of Lady Yule's lavish vessel, the *Nahlin* – 'furnished rather like a Calais whore-shop', as Aird described the floating palace with its own swimming pool, gymnasium and dance floor – plans were nonetheless made for a cruise along the Dalmatian coast. Because Wallis would not fly, they went first to France, then took the Orient Express through Austria to Yugoslavia and on 10 August, with some of their party, boarded the yacht. The other guests included Godfrey Thomas, Aird, the Humphrey Butlers, Helen Fitzgerald, Duff and Lady Diana Cooper, the Earl of Sefton and Alan Lascelles. The latter commented: 'Outwardly as respectable as a boatload of archdeacons. But the fact remains that the two chief passengers [the King and the Earl] were cohabiting with other men's wives.'[8] Others joined for part of the trip, including Katherine and Herman Rogers – 'a very good sort of yank and intelligent and much the nicest man here', according to Lascelles.

Diana Cooper, daughter of a duchess, thought the three women on board were very common: 'goodness how common they are ... they each have a pair of those immense field glasses which they glued to their eyes all saying "I don't see any hotel. Do you think that's one?" For all the world as if they had just come off the Gobi desert after weeks of yak milk diet.' In Diana Cooper's hilarious account of the cruise nothing seemed to miss her eager eye or wicked sense of fun, from Wallis's voice rasping out wisecracks and the way she constantly referred to 'the King and myself', to her diet of whisky and water, her fear verging on panic when they all rode on donkeys up a hill or the way she could talk everyone's head off and how parties suited and stimulated her. She wrote: 'No sooner had we anchored than the king got nakidish [sic] into a row boat and went off to discover a sandy beach for Wallis. He asked her to go with him. She said it was too hot. She looked a figure of fun in a child's piquet [sic]

---

8 In 1941 Lord Sefton married Wallis's divorced friend, Josephine 'Foxy' Gwynne.

dress and ridiculous baby bonnet. Her face is an adult face "par excellence" and the silly bonnet' – she then drew a picture of it – 'really was grotesque.'

One day Cooper described how the young King came scrambling down the stairs 'naked but for two little straw sandals and two little grey flannel shorts and two little crosses on a gold chain around his neck, one of diamonds the other I haven't seen yet. It always turns the wrong way. I note that Wallis has duplicates on her wrist.' For some, a king wandering the streets with no shirt on was almost as shocking as travelling with his mistress, which was what everyone assumed Wallis to be. After a few days, Aird could not take it any longer and told him frankly that 'Much as I liked him as a man I could not despise him more as a King,' and threatened to go home.

The King may have been travelling under a well-worn incognito as the Duke of Lancaster but the yacht, accompanied everywhere by two destroyers, was hardly secret and pictures of him with Wallis were widely splashed across American and foreign newspapers. Amazingly, the story was still ignored in the self-censoring and obedient British press. The King was mobbed wherever the party landed by 'a yelling jostling crowd that does not leave him ... shouting cheerio and following [him]'; and when the King went rowing 'all the craft and canoes and top heavy tourist launches and the rubber necks glared at the decks of the *Nahlin* and never knew that this hot, tow-headed little nude in their midst was what they were looking for'. For Diana and her husband Duff the most annoying part of the trip was the way the yacht sailed past the beautiful sights at nighttime – the King not wishing Wallis to suffer from the heat too much – and so missed most of the antiquities. They had to visit temples and churches on their own.

Frances Donaldson, in her biography of the King, pinpoints an important moment on the cruise when the party visited the King's cousin King George of the Hellenes, who was accompanied by his beautiful English lady friend, Rosemary Brittain-Jones – 'Wallis' opposite number', as Diana Cooper rather charmingly called her. '"Why doesn't he marry her?" Mrs Simpson asked. Upon which one of the guests replied in astonished tones with a simple statement of fact: it was impossible for the King to marry a woman who was both a commoner and already married. This it seems put the King in one of his black moods but as so often he refused to face the implications and the pair continued their folie à deux.' But that evening ended badly for another reason, as Cooper saw with embarrassment. The King was constantly fussing over Wallis, proud of her, and once:

> went down on hands and knees to pull her dress from under her chair foot. She stared at him as one would a freak and said, 'Well, that's the *maust* extraordinary performance I ever saw in my life.' She then started on him for having been silent and rude to Mrs Jones at dinner. On and on she went until I began to think he had perhaps talked too long and too animatedly to Mrs Jones for her fancy. He got a little bit irritated and sad and when I left . . . I knew that it would not be dropped all night.

On balance, as they went past five capitals in thirty-six hours, Lascelles was pleasantly relieved by the King's behaviour. It was better than it had been on earlier royal tours, even though 'there may be many faults of temperament and character, and though, as I always knew, certain cells in his brain have never grown'. Writing to Joan he said: 'It is an immense relief to have recovered some confidence, after all these months of gloomy foreboding . . . Of course I don't pretend everything in the garden is lovely by any means . . . I was really rather worried to sit down in St James's Palace with an "abandon hope all ye who enter here" feeling. Now I shall have to convince some of my colleagues that things are not quite as black as they have been painting them to me all these months.' Lascelles's first impressions were that 'the lady is a v good influence. She has excellent manners and suggests doing the right thing at the right moment . . . anyhow it is an immense convenience having a permanency instead of a fresh one in every port as in old days.'

In the following months Mrs Simpson's place in the King's life threatened to take on rather more permanency than the Court was comfortable with.

8

Wallis in the Witness Box

'I've been pretty flattened out by the world in general'

When Wallis attended Ascot in June 1936 she had to go alone, without the King, who was still officially in mourning. But he sent the woman widely touted as his mistress in a royal carriage, causing consternation and fury in official circles. Ramsay MacDonald, the former Prime Minister, made a trenchant observation: had she been a widow there would have been no problem. 'The people of this country do not mind fornication, but they loathe adultery.'

Wallis has been caricatured both then and now as witch, whore or Nazi spy – some believing she combined elements of all three. Yet ultimately it was not any of these accusations which made the idea of her marrying the British sovereign so unacceptable to 'the people of this country'. Her unacceptability was, as MacDonald understood, because she was a woman with two living husbands who now appeared ready to make sacred promises to a third to love him for better or for worse and for all time. Lady Diana Cooper, the duchess's daughter, Harold Nicolson, married to a well-known lesbian, and Lord Sefton, an earl with a mistress, were all part of a privileged elite who took a broad-minded attitude to sex. But they were not remotely representative of ordinary people, especially those outside London and those who were regular churchgoers. Stanley Baldwin, the Prime Minister, on the other hand, was. 'If compared to a wireless, Mr Baldwin has his earth in the British soil and his aerial listening in to the British public,' wrote Nancy Dugdale, wife of his Parliamentary Private Secretary, Tom. Baldwin was a plain, undemonstrative Englishman, prosperous and in a way unambitious. He was a man whose jackets became shapeless from the large tobacco tin and pipe in his side pockets, who walked 'with a quick, long stride that suggested one accustomed to tramping much over ploughed fields with a gun under his arm and smoking a pipe with unremitting enjoyment'. The objection that 'ordinary people' had to Wallis was not that she was common, brash or American but the awkward fact that she already had two living husbands.

Divorce was a fiendishly hot issue in late 1930s Britain, for some a much greater and more tangible threat than anything happening in Europe, which felt remote. By coincidence there was a Bill (eventually the Matrimonial Causes Act 1937) currently before Parliament and just at the crucial Committee stage in the autumn of 1936. Divorce in England, first legalized in 1857, had changed little since then and was a two-stage process: first a decree nisi and then (but not automatically) a decree absolute six months later after a full investigation, if necessary, by a government official known as the King's Proctor, into the truth of the matters alleged in the petition. Although the number of divorces was increasing slowly, there were still in 1937 fewer than 5,000 a year – a figure that was to double by 1939 when the law changed, giving an indication of the frustration among many who felt trapped in broken marriages. Until 1937, divorce was a costly and complex business available to a wife only in cases of her husband's adultery. It was necessary to prove not only the guilt of the respondent but also the 'innocence' – in the sense of not being an adulterer – of the petitioner and to demonstrate that none of the other bars to divorce, such as the couple putting up an agreed story (that is, collusion), were operative. In effect this meant that it was easy for the rich to divorce by mutual consent if the husband was willing to provide his wife with the evidence by a procedure known as 'a hotel bill case'. What usually happened was that an impoverished young (female) stranger was hired for a free trip to an expensive seaside hotel where the couple were found in bed together as breakfast was brought in. So the double standards and hypocrisy involved in obtaining a divorce had engendered a widespread sense of moral shame, as the collusion and duplicity so often involved appeared just as scandalous as the adultery. The current Bill was sponsored by the MP A. P. Herbert, who in a novel entitled *Holy Deadlock* had pointed out the absurdity of a law where, if it could be proved that husband

and wife had *each* committed adultery, then neither could obtain a divorce. For most of law-abiding Britain this was an issue of the deepest significance; once divorce was made easier, the looming idea that, if you were married and saw someone you liked better you could simply ditch your current husband or wife and snatch a new one, was appalling. Women, most of whom did not have access to jobs or money at this time, had much to fear from family break-up. Not surprisingly, one of the most active bodies opposing any change in the divorce laws was the 500,000-strong Mothers' Union.

At the same time the way the law currently operated no longer reflected trends in society and the attractive new ideology promoting individualism and the pursuit of personal happiness. There were women as well as men who wanted wider grounds for divorce, to include desertion and cruelty, and who found the present law unacceptable on grounds of cost, which put it out of their reach. Among the fashionable London elite, divorce was no longer rare as many found ways to accommodate personal happiness. These ideas naturally filtered through to the King, but that did not mean they were available for him to enjoy. The King represented an ideal: he was meant to uphold the law not to condone subversion of it. Making acceptable the craving for personal happiness and individual development and freedom, which so shocked Queen Mary, is ironically perhaps one of the genuinely 'modern' achievements of King Edward VIII. As he wrote in his memoir, *A King's Story*:

> The taboo of no divorced person being received at court, which rightly or wrongly I regarded as barbarous and hypocritical, meant that an ever increasing number of otherwise worthy and blameless British men and women were forced to stand apart in a permanent state of obloquy and the sovereign and indeed the whole nation were deprived of the full services of many brilliant people. It had long been in my mind that, were I ever to succeed to the throne, I should strive to rectify this form of social tyranny.

In September 1936, Wallis returned from the cruise via Paris, where she stayed again at what had become her favourite hotel, the Meurice.

And there she caught up with her mail – which included a batch of American newspaper cuttings sent, calculatedly perhaps, by Aunt Bessie. The international press had not held back on pictures of the couple holidaying together, some of them revealing the often shirtless King, infatuation leaping out of his eyes as he looked at Wallis, she with her hand tellingly on his arm. This was an epiphany. In England she had been shielded from sensational (or indeed any) accounts of her affair, partly through the King cultivating a friendship with two of the major press barons, the Hon. Esmond Harmsworth and the Canadian Lord Beaverbrook, formerly Max Aitken, and also through the actions of Rickatson-Hatt, who, knowing more than almost anyone else on Fleet Street, nonetheless discarded basic journalistic instincts for the sake of honour, telling his staff that 'Mrs Simpson's name is not be mentioned in either the inward or outward services without reference [to him]'. The Press Association followed suit. Now, laid low by a cold and reading the lurid details of what was being said about her in her homeland, she made a belated attempt to recapture her earlier life and break with the King. She told him she really had to return to Ernest and the 'calm, congenial' life he offered, 'where it all runs smoothly and no nerve strain. True we are poor and unable to do the attractive amusing things in life which I must confess I do love and enjoy . . . I am sure you and I would only create disaster together.' Alone at the Fort, the King immediately telephoned and wrote and made clear he was never going to let her go. If she tried to leave him, according to Lascelles, he threatened to cut his throat. So frayed were his nerves at this time that, according to Helen Hardinge, he even slept with a loaded pistol under his pillow.

Ernest's mother also read the foreign press and was upset to see her son cast as the guilty party, allowing himself to be petitioned for divorce. 'You must rest assured that I have behaved in a correct manner,' he told her.

In fact I have been complimented on every side. The malicious gossips do not count, they, for the most part, let their tongues wag to entertain a women's luncheon party. Frankly I am in no way anxious to see the divorce upset. I don't see how I could ever live with W again. All the nice things are spoiled and I don't want to be tied for life to someone I cannot live with.

From now on there is a painful inexorability to Wallis's life. She was carried forward, more or less unwillingly, by the King's alternating threats, blandishments and jewels. She had been consulting lawyers since the summer after Charles Russell, the first firm she asked, declined to represent her for various reasons. John Theodore Goddard agreed. Goddard, the senior of five partners in the firm he had founded and one of the most experienced solicitors of his generation, was, according to Baldwin, 'a man of blameless reputation but extraordinary ingenuity ... a man whom every crook in London employs by reason of his cleverness; everybody who gets into a mess applies immediately to Goddard, who gets them out at once'.

But, as previously unpublished letters to Ernest reveal, Wallis regretted losing the earlier companionship – and even fun – she had once shared with her husband. 'I wake up in the night sometimes and I think I must be lying on that strange chaise longue and hear your footsteps coming down the passage of the flat and there you are with the Evening Standard under your arm! I can't believe that such a thing could have happened to two people who got along so well,' she wrote to him. Privately, they continued to poke fun at the King, referring to him as the child who never grew up, Peter Pan. Rickatson-Hatt later told Walter Monckton, based on what Ernest had confided to him, that Wallis had always reassured her husband that there was no harm in the liaison since it would not last for ever and that in the meantime she could look after herself. Wallis knew that, with less to play for, she behaved better with Ernest than with the King, and the security Ernest offered suddenly appeared as something to be cherished compared with the hate and loathing she increasingly had to face as the King's lover. But her divorce petition had now been set down for hearing at Ipswich Assizes on 27 October – Ipswich chosen in order to have the case heard quickly and, it was hoped, with less press coverage than a London case would attract. If it went through, and a decree nisi was granted six months later at the end of April, there would be just enough time for the King to have Wallis alongside him at the Coronation, whose date was already set for May 1937. She knew therefore that there was no way out of this difficult and lonely legal process, and it is hardly surprising that in her memoirs, written in 1956, she does not describe how she felt towards Ernest at this time nor how she perceived herself trapped by a situation that terrified her. Not only would this have been offensive to the ex-King, by then her husband, but it would have been admitting perjury and a collusive divorce procedure.

Churchill was one of the few politicians who, in early 1936, looked at the situation through a long historical lens and, at the beginning of the summer, expressed the view that Mrs Simpson was 'acceptable'. According to Helen Hardinge, he believed that 'in the ultimate analysis of the Monarchy, she simply did not count one way or the other ... moral and social considerations apart, he considered her presence to be irrelevant to King Edward's performance as Sovereign'. Broadly speaking, he was in great sympathy with the King's predicament, believing he should be allowed to follow the dictates of his heart. But at the same time he was pragmatic and opposed to the divorce, considering it 'most dangerous as it would give any minister of religion opportunity to say from the pulpit that an innocent man had allowed himself to be divorced on account of the King's intimacies with his wife ...' and advised against taking Wallis to stay at Balmoral on the grounds that it was 'a highly official place sacred to the memory of Queen Victoria and John Brown'.[9] When his views were reported back to Mrs Simpson she was not at all pleased 'and declared that I had shown myself against her', Churchill wrote.

But she went anyway, as the King begged her to do, and on 23 September, together with the loyal Herman and Katherine Rogers, took the train from London to Balmoral. It was a disastrous visit. Even – or perhaps especially – her innovation of triple-decker sandwiches was not well received by the kitchen staff. More seriously the King, to save Wallis from changing trains and waiting at railway platforms, as most visitors to Balmoral had to do, drove himself the

9 Queen Victoria's faithful servant, with whom she was rumoured to have had an affair.

sixty or so miles and met them at the railway station in Aberdeen in order to escort them in person to Balmoral. He wore his motoring goggles, believing these would conceal his identity, but of course he was easily recognized – except by one policeman who told him off for leaving his car in the wrong part of the station yard. As he had already refused to attend a dedication of the new Aberdeen Royal Infirmary that day on the shaky grounds that he was in mourning and so sent his brother instead – a strange excuse since he too was in mourning – the sight of him with Wallis on a motoring trip caused deep offence. His 'surprise' visit duly made the headlines of the *Aberdeen Evening Argus*. The Duke and Duchess of York, staying at nearby Brickhall, loaned to them by the King, were furious and felt they had been made to look foolish and complicit. They would have found a sympathetic listener on whom to vent their fury in their houseguest, Cosmo Gordon Lang, the seventy-one-year-old Archbishop of Canterbury who was no longer in good health. They had invited him to stay to make up for the fact that the new King had not invited him to Balmoral as in previous years and he found it 'a delightful visit. They were kindness itself ... Strange to think of the destiny which may be awaiting the little Elizabeth at present second from the throne.'

The Yorks nonetheless agreed to attend a dinner at Balmoral three days later, where further friction ensued. They arrived late but when Wallis stepped forward to greet them, smiling and extending her hand in a friendly way, the Duchess walked past Wallis and, according to author Michael Thornton, who has vividly reconstructed this scene based on personal information given in confidence by a descendant of one of those present on the night, said in a loud voice, 'I came to dine with the King.' As Churchill had feared, by inviting his mistress to preside in Queen Victoria's favourite house, sleeping in the bedroom where once she and Queen Mary had slept, the King had ensured not only the royal family but society was painfully divided. Philip Ziegler points out that the King 'could not forget how rudely his sister-in-law had treated the woman he loved'. Wallis after all had been asked to act as hostess and had offered a friendly greeting. In addition the King viewed the invitation to the Archbishop, an intensely close friend of his parents, as undermining his attempts to create informality and modernity at Balmoral.

William Shawcross, the Duchess of York's official biographer, by way of defence quotes Elizabeth's distraught letter to her mother-in-law written some days later. 'I feel that the whole difficulty is a certain person,' the Duchess wrote. 'I do not feel that I <u>can</u> make advances to her & ask her to our house, as I imagine would be liked, and this fact is bound to make relations a little difficult ... the whole situation is complicated and <u>horrible</u> and I feel so unhappy about it sometimes.'

Not long afterwards, the Duchess of York wrote a kind and gentle letter to 'Darling David' thanking him for lending them Brickhall. But from now on her sweetness was derided as cloying. The relationship between the two brothers as well as that between the two women was irreparably damaged. In Aberdeen itself someone daubed a wall with graffiti: 'Down with the American harlot.' Six weeks later the Balmoral debacle had become such an issue that a joke went the rounds stating that when Wallis took a taxi and asked for King's Cross, the driver answered: 'I'm sorry, lady.' Chips Channon believed the weekend was a turning point. 'Aberdeen will never forgive him,' he reported six weeks later.

On their return from Scotland the King, somewhat reluctantly as he considered it oppressive and gloomy, finally took up residence at Buckingham Palace. He disliked eating meals there so would escape lunch and manage with just an orange all day; this became a lifelong habit. He rented a house for Wallis in Regent's Park at 16 Cumberland Terrace, one of the fine Nash terrace houses topped with magnificent ionic statuary on the outer circle of the Park. But it was being redecorated and not yet ready. So, after a brief spell at Claridge's, in early October she took up residence in Felixstowe, as required in order to establish residency (just as it had been in Warrenton nine years earlier), before her case could be heard at the local court. Her friends George and Kitty Hunter gallantly came to keep her company in the depressingly faded rented house and the King ordered a Scotland Yard detective to guard against intruders. From there she wrote to Ernest, staying with some Kerr-Smiley cousins who had taken pity on him. It was Sunday evening, two days before the case was heard.

Wallis was feeling lower than she had for years. 'I really can't concentrate on ... anything at the moment my dear,' she told him, the only man she could still turn to.

> I have had so MUCH trouble and complications <u>with everyone</u>. Also I am terrified of the court etc – and the US press has done <u>untold harm</u> in every direction besides printing wicked lies – I feel small and licked by it all. I shall come back Wednesday afternoon but remain in seclusion as last time I went out I was followed everywhere by cameramen, so horrible I can't think what sort of mess ... I am leaving for. I am sorry about the club ghosts, I am sorry about Mary – I am sorry for myself. I am sorry for the King. I hate the U.S. press, I hate stuffy British minds and last but not least I don't understand myself, which is the cause of all the misery.
> Give me courage
> 2.15 Tuesday
> Love Wallis
> I am so lonely.

Although the British press was still heavily self-censored (with the exception of *Cavalcade*, a magazine unafraid of publishing pictures of Wallis and the King), American magazines were sold in Britain but with whole pages scissored out. It was easy enough for those with access to international news to read expansive accounts of the affair. The coverage was, Nancy Dugdale confided to her diary, 'vulgar in the extreme'. The American newspaper magnate William Randolph Hearst had weeks beforehand sent over one of his top reporters, Adela Rogers St Johns, who worked on the story for months interviewing anyone close to the couple. One enterprising reporter in New York had traced Ernest's first wife Dorothea, who issued a statement saying: 'If what the newspapers say of my former husband's present financial standing is true, Audrey and I wish he could find it possible to provide adequately for her education and maintenance...' Wallis decided that she now needed to have some society photographs taken, so she arranged to sit for the fashionable photographer Cecil Beaton.

If Wallis had any lingering doubts about how excited the American and international press was by her story, the arrival of hundreds of clamouring journalists at Ipswich dispelled them. Policemen outside the court smashed two press cameras with their truncheons as Wallis, wearing a simple and carefully chosen navy-blue double-breasted coat, with a matching skirt and navy-blue felt hat with veil, had to be hustled through the throng to enter the courtroom. Once inside she sat, immobile, in the barristers' well with a lawyer either side of her surrounded by seven policemen and four plainclothes detectives. The judge, described by *Time* magazine as 'the jovial, golfing Sir John Anthony Hawke, who was for five years attached to the present King in the capacity of Attorney General to the Prince of Wales', opened by asking why the case had come to Ipswich. After some hurried whispering and nodding he carried on.

Wallis was led through her questions by her assured barrister, Norman Birkett KC, and rarely had to say anything other than answer in the affirmative. Asked if, from the autumn of 1934 she had complained about her husband's indifference and the way he often went away for weekends alone, she answered, 'Yes, I did.'

But the essential piece of evidence – that Ernest Simpson had been served breakfast in bed at the Hotel de Paris with a woman who was not his wife – was not in doubt. Ernest, who did not defend the case and was thus spared taking the witness stand, had hoped that his companion could remain nameless, and indeed the first petition did not name her. But within a day of lodging his statement, having been told that the absence of any name might lead to worse problems as the press ferreted one out, he agreed to name the woman as Mrs Elizabeth Kennedy, known as Buttercup. She was almost certainly Mary Raffray, the name probably deriving from a hat she once wore, and the mild subterfuge is typical of Ernest trying to act the gentleman. He would have hated the idea of taking a paid stranger to bed for this purpose and yet equally he could not possibly allow Mary to be publicly named.[10]

It was all over in fourteen minutes and Birkett asked for a decree

---

10 Years later, inexplicably taking his only son to show him the hotel, Ernest still refused to divulge the identity of Buttercup Kennedy, who was probably the boy's mother.

nisi to be granted with costs. Hawke hesitated at first, apparently puzzled by the request, but concluded: 'I suppose I must in these unusual circumstances. So you have it with costs.'[11]

'King's Moll Reno'd in Wolsey's Home Town' was one of the less lurid headlines that appeared in the American press. 'Cutie Simpson cuts out bloodless British women in royal choice' was another. Others announced that the King, who as long as he remained on the throne was immune from investigation himself, was to 'Wed Wally' and some even gave a date for the forthcoming nuptials.

Wallis returned immediately to London and dined that night with the King. Only now did he tell her of the visit he had had one week previously from Prime Minister Baldwin. His deliberate shielding of this fact from her until after the hearing reveals his awareness of Wallis's nervous and volatile state. On 20 October Baldwin had been summoned from Downing Street 'and made aware of the King's firm intention of marrying Mrs Simpson. As can well be imagined,' wrote Nancy Dugdale, 'the shock was severe. This twice divorced woman of low birth with an intermittent career of coquetry behind her, whose first marriage was dissolved in America; whose second marriage took place in England where it is doubtful if her first divorce would be acknowledged as legal, whom the king now proposed should take Queen Mary's place.' Nancy Dugdale, of all those close to events, might have been expected to be sympathetic towards Wallis since she was divorced herself, following a painful and abusive first marriage. That even she so bitterly opposed the idea of Wallis Simpson marrying the King is indicative of the widespread reverence for the institution of the monarchy and of the views of most who met Wallis at this fraught time that she was 'a third class kind of woman ... but no heart' or 'a hard bitten bitch'.

---

11 Wallis, presumably funded by the King, later paid back these costs to Ernest under an agreement they had between them, according to Michael Bloch. This is further evidence of collusion. Wallis herself refers to some IOUs in a letter to Ernest (*Wallis and Edward: Letters 1931–37: The Intimate Correspondence of the Duke and Duchess of Windsor*, ed. Michael Bloch (Weidenfeld & Nicolson 1986), p. 206, and private archive).

In the autumn of 1936 Stanley Baldwin was sixty-nine, hard of hearing and, as he had told close colleagues, ready to retire. He had only recently returned to active politics after three months' rest following exhaustion and felt that his duty was to remain at the helm in a crisis, if at all possible. His private view of Wallis was relatively broad-minded; he 'wouldn't mind if she were a respectable whore . . . kept out of the public view'. But he did not relish the prospect of discussing with the King his personal life and had declined earlier suggestions from Palace officials and government ministers that he should do so. 'Poor Stan how he hated the idea,' his wife recorded in her diary. Nonetheless he understood the necessity of facing the King and so on 20 October he went to Fort Belvedere and did his duty. He urged the King, who was 'at his most courteous and nicest', to call off the divorce. Later, recounting the events of that day to the influential Australian High Commissioner, Stanley Bruce, Baldwin told how the the King had insisted that he could not possibly interfere in a private decision taken by Mrs Simpson which he had nothing to do with whatever. 'This statement, the PM said quite bluntly, was a lie.' 'Poor S', wrote Lucy immediately afterwards, 'asked for a whisky and soda in the middle of the confab for he felt the strain of it all intensely.' There are various accounts of this first meeting, which the Prime Minister kept secret 'except for 3 or 4 of his elder colleagues'. According to his niece Monica Baldwin, recounting the conversation as told to her by her uncle:

I said to him, was it absolutely necessary that he should <u>marry</u> her? In their peculiar circumstances certain things are sometimes permitted to Royalty which are not allowed to the ordinary man.

To this he replied immediately: 'Oh there's no question of that. I am going to marry her . . .'

Baldwin's suggestion to the King that he could keep Mrs Simpson as his lover, just not marry her, may not have been made on this occasion.[12] But it was certainly what he felt. He had even discussed it

---

12 Nancy Dugdale has a more circumspect version of Baldwin's suggestion to which the King is supposed to have responded, 'Mrs S is a lady' (Nancy Dugdale diary, Crathorne Papers).

with Archbishop Lang, who responded, not unreasonably, that this would be a difficult line for a man of the cloth to advocate. The King himself affected, somewhat disingenuously, to be shocked by the hypocrisy of the suggestion. But in fact the exchange reveals a deep-seated belief in the 1930s in the importance of maintaining public standards, just as it indicates the distance between private mores and public values, a distinction that was considered virtuous until the 1960s. Thus Violet Bonham-Carter, daughter of the former Prime Minister H. H. Asquith and an active Liberal politician herself in the 1930s, was echoing the views of many in 1936 Britain when she admitted to Churchill that the King faced 'a dilemma that many human beings have had to face and meet with less at stake. Many after all have died for this country not so long ago. The sacrifice now demanded falls far short of life.'

If the King's Proctor were to be involved in investigating that the decree had not been obtained by agreement or even by faked evidence, that the wife had not herself committed adultery and that there was no omission of material facts, it would be now, once the first stage of the divorce had been granted. Any private citizen could (on the payment of half-a-crown) intervene to 'show cause' why any decree nisi should not be made absolute. It was not long before Mr Francis Stephenson, an elderly gentleman described as a solicitor's clerk, did exactly that, writing to object on the grounds that he believed this was a collusive divorce and that the petitioner had committed adultery with King Edward VIII. And so Sir Thomas Barnes, the King's Proctor, had the unenviable responsibility of investigating whether or not Wallis Simpson was 'innocent'. If Barnes found that anything was suspicious, he could intervene to put the facts he had discovered before the court. The court then had the power to rescind the decree nisi, thus leaving Wallis in a permanent state of limbo, separated from one husband but not free to marry another. It was a ghastly prospect and Wallis had good reason to be terrified, for although only a tiny proportion of divorces overall were blocked at the second stage, the overwhelming majority of cases where there were proctorial interventions did indeed result in cancellation of the divorce. For example, in 1935 Barnes intervened in twenty-three cases, twenty-one of which were rescinded, and in 1936 he acted in twenty-six, leaving twenty-five individuals without their final decree.

Nearly seventy years after they were written, the public may today view the files of letters written to the King's Proctor preserved in the National Archives at Kew in south-west London and closed until 2003. Once I have been granted special permission to read them, just three at a time, I am placed in a closed invigilation room, locked behind double doors under supervision and with video cameras trained on me. The King's Proctor files contain such sensitive material, I am told, that they come into the same category as files on Jack the Ripper. But, as I puzzle over what I am reading, I realize that the sensitivity derives not from pornography, criminality or espionage. What it reveals is much more shocking, especially given the self-censorship of the British newspapers until December 1936. For even though the royal affair had been hidden from the general public, enough was known for Barnes to be deluged with angry letters. Reading these mostly well-argued and articulate letters from a range of social classes, from both men and women, shows clearly that there was a powerful belief that the law had been subverted so seriously that the entire legal structure had been brought into disrepute and threatened the continuance of the monarchy. As Elspeth Huxley, the author and journalist, wrote in an American newspaper: 'There is a letting down all over the world but one looks to England to preserve its highest standards.'

There was a furore that the King had not been named as co-respondent, that less than a week before the hearing he had stayed the night at Mrs Simpson's rented house in Felixstowe, that there was no discretion statement by the petitioner (a formal admission of her own adultery but asking the court to take this into sympathetic consideration and still grant a decree) and, if there had been, the case could not have been tried in Ipswich. There were letters calling Wallis a prostitute, a Yankee harlot and worse. None seems to have complained that Wallis's first divorce in the United States, on the grounds of desertion, would not be recognized by the Church of England and, if challenged, might have been rejected under English law where adultery was the only grounds for divorce. According to this argument, her marriage to Ernest would have been bigamous and invalid. But above all there was enormous public resentment, especially among women, arising out of the belief that Mrs Simpson was being allowed 'to get away with a divorce which would certainly not have escaped the attentions of your staff if the position of the Crown had not been indirectly involved'. Many complained that the decree smacked of one law for the rich and another for the poor. Others expressed a deep-seated view that Britain could not possibly have as queen a woman who should *prima facie* be in the dock at the Old Bailey for perjury and that if the King's Proctor did not intervene in this case he should intervene in none. Some wrote insisting they had names of servants who had evidence that the King had been seen leaving Mrs Simpson's house many mornings at 8 a.m.

While these investigations were under way, preparations for the Coronation were simultaneously if somewhat nervously proceeding with hoteliers and other British businessmen who had an interest in souvenirs of the event suddenly worried by the possibility that it might be postponed. Desperate for news of what was going on, many were making costly transatlantic telephone calls to have American newspapers read to them and London insurance brokers were suddenly swamped with an avalanche of anxious customers. Finally the market became so top heavy that brokers were unwilling to take at any price the risk of what Edward VIII might do. It was not only trade but numerous charities and voluntary organizations that regarded this prospect of the King being married to that woman most unsettling.

Hilda Runciman, wife of President of the Board of Trade Sir Walter Runciman, and a formidable Liberal politician in her own right, was another who kept a diary at this time. Hilda was deeply involved in issues of education, housing and welfare and, as a leading Methodist, had served as president of the Women's Free Church Council. She wrote in measured tones of her concerns: 'ever since Mrs Simpson's divorce in Ipswich we have felt really anxious about their future relations, because there seemed no adequate reason for the disadvantage of the divorce scandal unless marriage was intended'.

Walter, who 'as a member of the cabinet and a Christian feels his responsibility acutely', was having discussions with both Baldwin and Archbishop Lang about what all three perceived as the dangers for the monarchy if the King persisted in his plan to marry Mrs Simpson. Hilda wrote of a meeting on 15 November between her husband and Sir Frederick Maurice, one of the founders of the British Legion, of which he was now president, at which Maurice said frankly that his organization 'certainly would not tolerate W.S. as a Queen of England'. He then wrote to Runciman to make it completely clear that the British Legion 'could not stand the shock of the proposed marriage of the King and Wallis Simpson'.

The Church had been worried about the new King long before the accession. 'One trembles to think of the loneliness of his position. Things will inevitably be very different here,' Don recorded after the old King's funeral. That the new King did not attend church was a serious problem for the Archbishop, who admitted that 'the thought of my having to consecrate *him* as King weighed on me as a heavy burden. Indeed I considered whether I could bring myself to do so.' In association with the Coronation, the Church was also planning an evangelical campaign, 'A Recall to Religion', which would urge the people of Britain to rededicate themselves to serving God and country. This was not just a question of 'religion' narrowly interpreted. The King was meant to serve and sacrifice and help. Previous coronations and special thanksgiving services held in St Paul's Cathedral had been with kings who did attend church. The monarch had responsibilities to the Dominions and his or her regular church attendance was seen as a means of bringing people in, making them feel they were part of the British Empire. The throne was the vital link. Yet now there was fear that the new King would break that.

Even as those at Lambeth Palace were reading all the American newspapers, sickened by what they read and heard, most churchmen still believed that restraint and making no criticism was the best policy. 'And yet HM protests that Mrs S is not his mistress but he spends immense sums of money on her – is he quite normal?' Alan Don asked rhetorically. That was precisely the question worrying Lord Wigram as well. He believed that the King was not 'normal . . .

and might any day develop into a George III'. He thought it was necessary to pass a Regency Bill as soon as possible 'so that if necessary he could be certified'.

Westminster now buzzed with politicians clamouring to know what was going to happen. At the state opening on 3 November the King looked 'like a young, happy Prince Charming', serene and dignified, according to Chips Channon. But several people commented on his strange American accent – he said 'rowts' instead of 'roots' and ended with 'And Moy the blessing of Almoighty God rest upon your deliberoitions,' an affectation considered to be yet another unattractive result of Wallis's influence. Not unnaturally, Wallis wanted to watch the proceedings, 'and was in the Royal Gallery in the House of Lords yesterday ... in full view of everybody. She must be a brazen-faced woman to appear thus among the assembled aristocracy within a week of the divorce,' wrote Don, voicing widespread criticism of those who felt she should demonstrate contrition at the breaking of such a serious promise by staying quietly at home.

But it was not until 10 November – when (as Chips Channon recorded) the Labour MP John McGovern answered a question about the forthcoming Coronation by shouting, '"Why bother, in view of the gambling at Lloyd's that there will not be one?" There were roars of "Shame! Shame!" and he called out, "Yes ... Mrs Simpson"' – that her name was actually uttered publicly in the House of Commons. November was an agonizing time for Wallis as she could no longer fail to be aware of how much she was disliked, not just in royal circles but by the small but ever widening section of the public who knew about her. She had her defenders and flatterers who still wrote to her supportively, believing that she was good for the King – at least she had controlled his drinking, a merit even Queen Mary acknowledged. But they were few in number and dwindled as the crisis progressed. Perhaps she derived a shred of comfort from her old friend Herman Rogers, who wrote warmly to her: 'You are still my one living example of a perfectly wise and complete person.' And she had Aunt Bessie, who had now arrived in London to help.

Events moved swiftly after 13 November when the King opened a letter from Alexander Hardinge, written with the backing of senior

ministers, warning him that the British press would not keep its
silence about his relationship with Mrs Simpson for much longer
and that the effect would be 'calamitous'. Until now Mrs Simpson's
affair with the King had been a problem for Palace officials rather
than government ministers. That was no longer the case. Hardinge
warned that the government might have to resign, in which case the
King's private affairs would be the chief issue in any election. He
therefore recommended that the best course of action would be for
Mrs Simpson to go abroad without further delay, and 'I would *beg*
your majesty to give this proposal your earnest consideration before
the position has become irretrievable.'

The King was furious. He responded, typically, by ending all contact
with Hardinge, but without sacking him, and increasingly turned to
Walter Monckton, a lawyer he had known since university days, to act
as intermediary and adviser. The King had always had his way and until
now never allowed the idea to enter his consciousness that this time
would be any different. Instead, he summoned Baldwin, who the day
before had had a meeting at Chequers with Stanley Bruce, the influential Australian High Commissioner, at the latter's request. Bruce
passed on the views of his Prime Minister, Joseph Lyons, who, as a
devout Catholic, could not support the marriage of a divorced person,
that if there were any question of marriage with Mrs Simpson the
King would have to go as far as Australia was concerned. Now he told
Baldwin forcefully how offensive the King's behaviour was to ordinary
Australians, as reflected by an old Anzac soldier who had said 'it's a bit
thick, his taking that woman with him to Gallipoli'. This was a reference to a stopover the King made while cruising in the *Nahlin* a few
months earlier to enable him to visit the cemeteries and battlefields on
the peninsula where thousands of Australian and New Zealand soldiers had lost their lives in 1911.

Bruce came to believe that his conversation with Baldwin, who until
that time 'had not got the thing clearly in his own mind', had been
decisive. He maintained that he had warned him over lunch on 15
November of 'the alarming and devastating possibility that the King
should marry the woman ... the people of this country and the
Dominions would never accept the woman as Queen, quite possibly

the House of Commons would cancel the Civil List, the throne would be imperilled, the Empire would be endangered, the Government would resign and it would be impossible to get an alternative government.'

Baldwin put to the King the feelings of both Bruce and William Mackenzie King, the Canadian Prime Minister, that marriage to Wallis would break up the Empire, but the King responded by telling him: 'I want you to be the first to know that I have made up my mind and nothing will alter it. I have looked into it from all sides. I mean to abdicate and marry Mrs Simpson.' Baldwin was stunned. He simply could not imagine that the King would insist on marriage to this woman with such a high cost attached. And, in spite of the divorce, Wallis had continued to reiterate even to close friends that she was not intending to marry the King and that the action had been forced on her by her husband's adultery. It was a necessary answer in view of the law, but she also believed that marriage to the King would eventually be prevented by those more powerful than her. According to Lucy Baldwin, who made 'a faithful record' of the meeting as soon as her husband told her about it on his return:

> S. said he felt a streak of almost madness. The King simply could not understand & S. couldn't make him. The King was obsessed by a woman & that was the long & short of it ... she was the best friend he had ever had & he couldn't live without her. S. was so impressed by the want of sanity & clear vision in it all that he feared that really he might completely go 'off it' if at the moment he was more directly opposed & Mrs Simpson disappeared. On leaving, the King held Stanley's hand for a long time & there were almost tears in his eyes as he said good-bye.

Baldwin now had to see the Queen who, he said, 'came trotting across the room <u>exactly</u> like a puppy dog and before I had time to bow she took hold of my hand in both of hers and held it tight. "Well, Prime Minister," she said, "here's a pretty kettle of fish!"' And a few days later the King himself wrote to his mother telling her how relieved he was finally to have been able to share with her his 'wonderful secret. A dream which I have for so long been praying might one day come true. Now that Wallis will be free to marry me in April it only remains for me to decide the best action I take for our future happiness and for the good of all concerned.' Nancy Dugdale recorded that when the Queen remonstrated with the King, calling up the obvious arguments of duty and responsibility, his answer was: '"The only thing that matters is our happiness." After that there was no more possibility of understanding between two people whose point of view was so divergent.'

Baldwin was in constant contact with elder statesmen from the three main political parties, as well as with Canadian, Australian, New Zealand and Indian leaders appalled at the effect in the Dominions of the prospect of 'Queen Wallis'. He was only too aware of the seriousness of a possible government collapse in view of the fragile world situation. At the same time Parliamentary Counsel were now instructed to draw up an Abdication Bill and associated measures, while the King went about his business with renewed vigour looking for all the world like a confident young monarch full of new ideas. He surpassed himself when he toured the mining villages of South Wales for two cold and damp days in mid-November, meeting the unemployed and destitute, offering his famous words of comfort, 'Something must be done,' without having any clear idea of what. This former Prince of Wales, uttering greetings in Welsh when he could, was welcomed by more than 2,000 cheering people, including flag-waving children and the Dowlais Aged Comrades Choir, which gave a spirited rendering of God Save the King. There is no doubting his genuine sympathy for the poor as he travelled around the desperately depressed mining towns and villages walking among his loyal subjects. But when he left all he could offer was 'to think about what can be done'.

And while the politicians were scrabbling around for a way out of this crisis, Wallis was feeling 'really miserable', as she admitted to Sibyl Colefax, her most trusted confidante that autumn. To Sibyl she had admitted that 'Ernest and myself' living apart this winter had left her 'in a rather upset and confused state of mind'. She could not see friends 'until I can break the shell I have temporarily gone into'. The situation had plunged dramatically out of her control and she felt manipulated by politicians and caught up in the inexorability of the legal process. But those who urged her to abandon a situation that had become untenable 'do not understand that if I did so, the King would come after me regardless of anything. They would then get their scandal in a far worse form than they are getting it now.' In her memoirs Wallis blames 'the fundamental inability of a woman to go against the urgent wishes of the man she loves'. But the most likely reason for staying put was, as ever with Wallis, fear – in this case fear that the King would come after her and abandon everything. 'If the country won't approve our marrying, I'm ready to go,' he told her now. 'It was the first mention between us that he had ever entertained any thought of stepping down from the Throne,' she claimed in her memoirs, insisting that she had begged him now to let her go. 'I tried to convince him of the hopelessness of our position … to go on fighting the inevitable could only mean tragedy for him and catastrophe for me.'

Quite probably they had both failed to confront reality until this very last moment when it was foisted upon then. The death of George V had come too soon for any plans. Blinded by single-mindedness and solipsism, Edward was convinced that his popularity would allow him to marry whomever he wanted and Wallis was afloat on his buoyancy. But now, unnerved by the growing pile of threatening letters, exhausted by the King's demands and unhappy at being an object of hate blamed for the feared destruction of the British monarchy, she wanted to leave while she still had a shred of dignity. Yet again, though, she did not. She was almost paralysed by fear.

Matters changed slightly at the end of November. While the King was away in Wales, Esmond Harmsworth took Wallis to lunch at Claridge's in order to put to her the possibility of a morganatic marriage, whereby she would marry the King but, instead of becoming queen, would take another of his titles and become Duchess of Cornwall or Lancaster. This very unEnglish idea seemed briefly to offer a way out of the crisis and Wallis urged the idea on the King that weekend at the Fort with her aunt. Initially reluctant, the King soon espoused the idea enthusiastically. He agreed to discuss it with Baldwin, as legislation would be required not just in Britain but in the Dominions.

Baldwin, appalled that the suggestion had come from Harmsworth – 'a disgustingly conceited fellow' – was convinced that neither the House of Commons nor the British people would accept the idea, which in any event would require legislation that he did not think would be passed by Parliament. But, to avoid a confrontation, he agreed to meet the King again on 25 November. He sounded out opinion in advance and individually summoned the Labour Party leader Clement Attlee, Sir Archibald Sinclair, leader of Liberals, 'and the possible snake in the grass, Winston Churchill, whose very freedom from loyalties makes him a dark horse in a loose box', according to Nancy Dugdale, mixing her metaphors to imply that Churchill, whom she and others did not trust, could change sides whenever it suited. There was always a lurking fear of the country being split and Churchill being called upon to lead a King's party which accepted the marriage to Wallis. Just a few days beforehand Churchill had been arguing that the King should 'be allowed to marry his Cutie. Noël [Coward] – summing it up for most people – said: "England does not wish for a Queen Cutie."'

Baldwin asked Attlee, Sinclair and Churchill: if the King insisted on marrying Mrs Simpson would they come down on the government side against the marriage or would they form a government if summoned by the King? 'The first two pledged their absolute loyalty to Mr Baldwin by saying they would not form an alternative government. Mr Churchill said although his outlook was a little different, he would certainly support the Government.' Baldwin, now authorized to do so by the King, put to the Dominion governments specifically the idea of a morganatic marriage and asked for their views. The telegrams conveying this request were, many historians now believe, couched in such a way that a negative response was inevitable. It was pointed out at the Cabinet, as the Marquess of Zetland, Secretary of State for India, told Lord Linlithgow, the Viceroy, in 'the most secret letter I have ever written', that if the King persisted in his intention of marriage and the Government resigned this 'would give rise to a constitutional issue of the first magnitude viz the King v the Government. It seems that the K has been encouraged to believe that Churchill would in these circumstances be prepared to form an alternative Government ... this clearly would be fraught with danger of the most formidable kind.' In reality, however, the idea of a King's party was faint; supporters were a miscellaneous collection who could never have commanded a majority in Parliament. The Australian Prime Minister, Joseph Lyons, cabled that in his country there would be outspoken hostility to His Majesty's proposed wife becoming queen while any suggestion that she should become consort and not queen 'would not be approved by my Government'. He went further and indicated that abdication might be the best solution in any event as the Crown had already suffered so grievously. South Africa considered that abdication was the lesser of two evils, as marriage would prove a permanent wound.

The Irish Free State, then still a member of the Commonwealth, was a cause of serious concern for Baldwin. Prime Minister Eamon de Valera had already alarmed Sir Harry Batterbee, Assistant Under-Secretary at the Dominions Office, by saying in November that 'it was politically impossible for him at the present time to ask the Dail to do anything regarding the succession to the Crown or to declare their consent to the UK Parliament legislating'. Malcolm MacDonald, then Dominions Secretary, tried warning de Valera that if the Free State failed to pass legislation approving the abdication and the succession of George VI, Edward would remain king of Ireland and Mrs Simpson, once they married, would be queen of Ireland. De Valera may not have welcomed that scenario but, always nudging his country towards independence, used the crisis to bring in legislation which removed from the British monarch the formal functions which still remained to him in the Free State. The British, relieved at having resolved the crisis with relative speed and ease, hardly objected as long as Ireland was prepared to legislate. But it was a step along the road towards weakening the constitutional ties with Ireland, so crucial in the coming war when the British were constantly fearful of the Axis powers taking advantage of Irish neutrality.

New Zealand believed that a morganatic marriage might be possible but agreed to be guided by the 'Home' government, while Canada, where Edward was still warmly remembered and had a ranch home, showed a more nuanced view. Mackenzie King, admitting that Canadians would prefer abdication to Wallis becoming queen consort, warned Baldwin that he did not want it put about that Canadian opinion had been a determining factor in the situation. In his diaries Mackenzie King makes clear his personal sympathy as well as his belief that voluntary abdication was the only honourable course if the King were to retain both his own self-respect and respect in the eyes of his people and other nations.

These were enormous issues of international importance with much to play for at any time, but as 1936 drew to a close it is impossible to exaggerate their significance. Wallis, in the eye of this hurricane, was seriously unwell by the end of November. She was also terrified. She told Ernest how loathsome she found most of her so-called friends for accepting money in return for revealing stories about her. 'Herman was offered ten thousand dollars for a snapshot of me in his garden! [he refused] – however a few gentlemen still seem to be alive.' And she confided to him something of her deepest feelings in a letter full of self-pity but also revealing how much she despised herself:

Such awful things have happened to me inside during the past month that I have a new girl to know and she's not very nice ... I've been pretty flattened out by the world in general and have certainly had the full crack of everything from the beginning – used by politicians, hated by jealous women, accused of everything and, though I have no resilientse [sic] at the moment, I trust I'll be able to lift my weary body up from under the load some day and laugh and play once more. The other side of the story, if written in my life time, will be the answer to them all.

By the time she came to attempt writing her own answer in 1956, the belief that she had been ill used had hardened: 'As a woman in love I was prepared to go through rivers of woe, seas of despair and oceans of agony for him.' The hyperbole may seem excessive, but Wallis genuinely saw herself as suffering.

The King had done his best to shelter her by giving her his chauffeur George Ladbroke and the royal housekeeper Mrs Mason, and sending red roses daily at £5 a bunch from Constance Spry. But none of that could allay her palpable and not unreasonable fear of violent attacks. In addition to receiving poison-pen letters written with an increasingly menacing tone, there were stones thrown at her windows in Regent's Park. She could no longer make her regular visits to hair and beauty salons such as Elizabeth Arden or even go shopping without risk of being accosted. Baldwin himself thought 'that some woman might shoot her', and an American news agency reported an attempted bomb plot. When the police advised that they could no longer guarantee her safety, the King had Wallis moved down to the Fort.

And on the last day of November, Crystal Palace burned down. The destruction of this magnificent symbol of Victorian confidence and splendour was, as Winston Churchill was only too aware, the end of an age. But that catastrophe was not on Wallis's mind when she wrote to Sibyl Colefax, Foxy Gwynne and Ernest. She told her former husband what she had not yet told the King:

> . . . I shan't be able to see you after all for which I'm very sorry for I've decided to [go] away some time this week. The US press has done such harm here and worked people up to such an extent that I get the most alarming letters threatening my life unless I leave. Naturally I am upset over it all. I cannot tell HM I am going because I know what would happen – so I am really simply telling him the old search for hats story – I shall stay safely away until after the coronation, or perhaps for ever, one cannot tell. But I can never forgive my own country for what they have done to the King and to myself . . .

And in the midst of all her woes she voiced two other concerns: 'the expense of it all has been appalling and the money which I spent on the decoration, which I've never been able to enjoy as being in the place makes one nervous as I am threatened with bombs etc. I haven't told Aunt B the danger side, simply that my very presence here was hurting the K.' Aunt Bessie, she explained, was going to remain at the house for a while as she did not want to give the waiting journalists and voyeurs the idea that she was not returning.

Finally, she could not resist telling Ernest of her fury with Mary, the woman he was about to marry, whom she accused of having 'thrived on the publicity she has got through me and never refuses any of it. I know what I am writing. Anyway you are no longer in a position to say I am trying to upset your and Mary's social career in London … well, my dear, I hope you have a happy life – if I am put on the spot, Ipswich etc will have been a great waste of time, as far as I am concerned, won't it?'

To Sibyl too she wrote that she was planning to go away, alone for a while:

> I think everybody here would like that – except one person perhaps – but I am constructing a clever means of escape – after a while my name will be forgotten by the people and only two people will suffer instead of a mass of people who aren't interested any way in individual feeling but only the workings of a system. I have decided to risk the result of leaving because it is an uncomfortable feeling to remain stopping in a house when the hostess has tired of me as a guest. I shall see you before I fold my tent.

But she did not. Overtaken by events, she had to leave before she was ready. Wallis often wrote about herself being neither good nor nice but never about being weak. Nonetheless, in those final few days in England while she desperately tried to formulate a plan, she lacked both physical courage and emotional strength to leave. For years, she lived in fear of violence, and photographers would recount her fright whenever a flashbulb exploded. Once she was away in the South of France, she admitted her failure to Sibyl:

> Brain is so very tired from the struggle of the past two weeks – the screaming of a thousand plans to London, the pleading to <u>leave</u> him, not <u>force</u> him, I know him so well. I wanted them to take my advice but no, driving on they went, headed for this tragedy … If only they had said 'let's drop the idea now and in the Autumn we'll discuss it again' – and Sibyl darling, in the Autumn I would have been so very far away I [would] have already escaped.
>
> Some day if we ever meet I shall tell you all. The little faith I have tried to cling on to has been taken from me when I saw England turn on a man that couldn't defend himself and had never been anything but straight with his country.

9
Wallis on the Run

'Concentrate on the legal side now'

O n a cold and foggy afternoon in early December 1936 the King told Wallis that it was no longer safe for her to stay at the Fort. She must leave the country as soon as could be arranged. He had telephoned Perry Brownlow, a personal friend and lord in waiting, that morning and asked him if he would be prepared to escort her abroad. Brownlow offered Wallis his own home, Belton House in Lincolnshire, as a safe refuge, but she declined, so he made preparations for the journey to France. He drove to Windsor where he found the King 'rather pathetic, tired, overwrought, and evidently dreading Wallis's departure, almost like a small boy being left behind at school for the first time'.

The dramatic change in the situation resulted from an outspoken speech delivered by the inadvertently historic figure Dr A. W. F. Blunt, Bishop of Bradford, to his Diocesan Conference on Tuesday 1 December. Bishop Blunt preached on the King's need for divine grace in the months before the Coronation service, adding that 'it could be wished that he showed more awareness of this need'. The Bishop claimed he had written his speech six weeks earlier following a discussion with a businessman about the commercial versus religious aspects of the Coronation and had no intention of referring to current rumours about Mrs Simpson, only to the King's negligence in churchgoing.

The British press could restrain themselves no longer. All the newspapers now reported this attack on the Sovereign, which opened the floodgates of publicity. Suddenly pictures of Mrs Simpson appeared in British newspapers. For most readers these were the first images of the American woman who was said to be the King's 'close friend'. The Bishop's speech came to Mr Baldwin 'as did the ravens feeding Elijah in a predicament in the wilderness', in Nancy Dugdale's phrase, while her husband believed that Bishop Blunt's address 'could not have been brought about in a more desirable and less scandalous way . . . purely religious, non political, non sectarian – just SB's luck!'

In spite of widespread assumptions that either the Archbishop of Canterbury or Baldwin had written the speech, it came as a shock to both men to see the report in the press the following day. But while Baldwin might have been relieved, the Archbishop was aghast; if any clerics was to give the King advice, it should be him. Yet he was only too aware of how he had failed to give him any, confiding to his diary that 'I had reason to know that H.M. would not receive or listen to any advice (for which he did not himself ask) except from the Prime Minister, who had a constitutional right to advise him.' After lunching with the Crown Prince of Sweden, who told him that King Edward's affair was a matter affecting not just the British Empire but all countries where the monarchy survived, 'I issued a plea that on the following Sunday those who spoke from the pulpit or otherwise should refrain from speaking directly on the King's matter but that everywhere prayer should be offered for him and his ministers.'

Baldwin and Dugdale already had a secret appointment to meet the King set for 9 p.m. on 2 December – the secrecy at the King's behest – to report back on the morganatic marriage proposal. But, in the wake of the Blunt speech, this had taken on a desperate urgency. While Dugdale paced up and down the garden with detectives, Baldwin informed the King of the answer obtained from the Dominion prime ministers, from the British Cabinet, from the Leader of the Opposition, Mr Attlee, and from the leader of Liberals: they all said a morganatic marriage was impossible and were strongly opposed to it. 'The King was ill tempered and petulant at this meeting,' Nancy Dugdale recorded, 'and very angry about Bishop Blunt. Mr Baldwin had to calm him and generally treat this wrong headed little man like a doctor treats a case, never putting his back up, never giving in. The King suggested broadcasting, placing himself at the mercy of his people.' The audience lasted one hour and the King's attitude to the Dominions was 'there are only very few people in Canada, Australia and the colonies . . . meaning that the question of colonial responsibility did not count for a great deal'.

According to Nancy Dugdale, at the end of the meeting Baldwin said to the King – 'and it won over his complete confidence – "well, sir, whatever happens I hope you will be happy."'[13] Subsequently the King alluded many times to this phrase saying: 'Not even my so called friends who are on my side have ever wished me happiness.'

The two men left the Palace feeling 'sad at heart for the little man, despising him, loving him, and pitying him all at the same time and hating the woman who goaded him on to fight until the struggle became one between the Prime Minister and Mrs Simpson through the person of the King'. Dugdale, quoting Flaubert, believed that the King was that day 'Vaincu enfin par la terrible force de la douleur'.

The King drove down to the Fort and immediately reported the latest events to Wallis, telling her she must now leave. He had heard that *The Times*, the newspaper he feared most, was preparing to run a fierce attack on her the next day and, although he had asked Baldwin to stop it, his request had been refused. This was not within the Prime Minister's power, even had he wished to stop such an article. In any case, the *Times* editor, Geoffrey Dawson, was a staunch supporter of the government, unlike Beaverbrook or Harmsworth.

The final evening for Wallis at the Fort was painful. Brownlow asked the King if he intended to abdicate. '"Oh no," he replied. He had just told me the first and last important lie of our friendship.' Brownlow believed that Wallis 'had taught him to lie'. In fact there was an element of truth in the King's reply as he had it in mind to go to Switzerland and then see if he was called back with Mrs Simpson at his side. As they departed the King 'leant across to her to get one last touch of her hand – there were tears in his eyes and on his cheeks, and his voice was shaking – wherever you reach tonight, no matter what time, telephone me. Bless you, my darling.'

---

13 Nancy Dugdale later added that Baldwin, on reading this diary in February 1939, maintained that the exchange had occurred at Fort Belvedere on the occasion of his last meeting with the King. 'TLD [Tommy Dugdale] says he is quite certain SB is mistaken and that the exchange is rightly placed in this interview at Buckingham Palace (Nancy Dugdale diary).

Others remember the departure more prosaically. Mrs Simpson left by walking through the King's bedroom on to the lawn without saying goodbye to any of the staff, with whom her relationship had never been easy.

'Well, that's the end of that,' said one of the footmen to the butler, Osborne, who had always believed Wallis 'had got her knife into them'.

'Don't be too sure,' Osborne replied.

'We'll keep our fingers crossed.'

Since Wallis would not fly, driving to the Herman Rogers villa, Lou Viei, near Cannes, was seized on as the only option. Wallis talked almost incessantly on the journey but it was only as they crossed to Dieppe that Brownlow discovered to his horror that he was also responsible for Wallis's jewels, which she had brought with her, 'presents from the King worth at least £100,000 – to carry them savoured a little of the deportee or exile', he felt. Though they were travelling under the pseudonyms of Mr and Mrs Harris, the King's Buick was quickly recognized and they were followed for much of the journey, forcing the King's chauffeur to take sudden side-turnings in towns he did not know in the hope of throwing off their pursuers. They arrived at the Grand Hôtel de la Poste in Rouen at 5.15 a.m., spoke to the King for fifteen minutes and finally got to bed around six o'clock for a few hours' sleep. After two days on the road, they arrived at Lou Viei – a twelfth-century converted monastery, which Brownlow rather uncharitably described as 'small and dark ... unsuited to winter conditions' – with Wallis humiliatingly crouched in the back of the car, covered by a blanket. She felt every inch the hunted animal. The journey was an agonizing experience and 'the feeling of desperation that was my invisible and relentless companion during the entire trip is not difficult to recapture'. Still manipulating the agency wires where he could, Bernard Rickatson-Hatt loyally delayed announcing Mrs Simpson's destination until she had reached Cannes.

'Tell the country,' she had scribbled in one final note to the King, referring to the very modern idea they had discussed before she left, that he should broadcast an appeal directly to the country to be allowed to marry and remain king. Television broadcasts were completely new and untried and even Christmas radio broadcasts by the monarch had been used only since 1932. But Wallis, admitting that a radio broadcast was her idea, said she had in mind the 'extraordinary impact on public opinion of President Roosevelt's "fireside chats"'. Back at the Fort, without Wallis, the King's confidence quickly drained. He no longer believed he could have both Wallis and the throne, in spite of Churchill urging that he should not be rushed and that, with time, something could be done short of abdication – an unpopular line which even his wife Clementine disagreed with. Churchill in 1936 was viewed as a man of flawed political judgement, yet his opinions were coloured not just by romance. His own mother was American and had been vilified for her love life. However, by the time he rose to speak in the House of Commons on Monday 7 December the mood had changed and he was shouted down on all sides. Baldwin gave thanks for the power of a weekend.

The King now abandoned the idea of using a broadcast as an appeal remain as King and marry Wallis. Nonetheless, emboldened by what he perceived as the successful South Wales tour, he still wanted to speak directly to the nation before departing. This was a misreading of the situation, however, as there were many Nonconformists in South Wales who were extremely critical of Edward's behaviour. Likewise in England, as Mrs Hannah Summerscales asserted when she wrote to the King's Proctor: 'Even though the King thinks that working people are with him, I know that they are not. I was born a working woman and I know that working people want the moral cleanliness of their homes and moral cleanliness of the crown and throne . . .' But it was also deeply unconstitutional for the King to go above the heads of his government and the notion had a whiff of dictatorship about it at a time when any threat to democracy was a very serious matter. Baldwin pragmatically explained to the King that if he made such a broadcast 'he would be telling millions of people throughout the world, including a vast number of women, that he wanted to marry a married woman', and had his Home Secretary, Sir John Simon – not known as Sir John Snake for nothing – swiftly draft a paper to show that constitutionally a king can broadcast only on the advice of his ministers. Aware of the stark choice, the King now prepared himself for abdication.

Sir Edward Peacock, the King's Canadian-born principal financial adviser who was very close to him at this time, stated that the wavering in the final days was 'as I know, upon the insistence over the phone of the lady that he should fight for his rights. She kept up that line until near the end, maintaining that he was the King, and his popularity would carry everything. With him this lasted only a very short time then he recognized the falsity of the position and put it definitely aside ... the lady persisted in her advice until she saw that that tack was hopeless.'

The long-distance telephone calls between the pair, on a crackly and faint line, which punctuated the next few days were something none of the participants ever forgot. The King was always distraught waiting for Wallis to call but wrung dry after she had. They were in daily contact – not easy in 1936, even for a king – and the lines had to be kept free for at least two hours for her exclusive use. William Bateman, the King's private telephone operator at the Palace, had been instructed to give priority to all calls and messages from her. But it was difficult to hear clearly, so Wallis shouted, and the King found these conversations emotionally draining as all his negotiating power was evaporating in the face of his one remaining desire: to marry Wallis. He often had Ulick Alexander, Keeper of the Privy Purse, or his solicitor, George Allen, by his side to prompt him while speaking to Wallis and at a critical moment in one conversation he covered the phone with one hand and asked Allen what he should say to summarize the situation to her. Allen wrote, and the King relayed, 'The only conditions on which I can stay here are if I renounce you for all time.' She knew he was never going to do that.

He had hoped to secure the right to a substantial pension, the right to return to the Fort as his home in due course, the right of his future wife to share his royal title and, most urgently, an Act of Parliament making Wallis's divorce absolute immediately to ensure that they could be married. Monckton, managing astutely to remain the King's adviser while retaining the trust of the politicians, took up the latter issue urgently on the King's behalf. He was genuinely alarmed by the cruel possibility awaiting the King if he abdicated and then found that Wallis was not free after all. He suggested the idea of a special Bill to free her immediately at the same time as the abdication, an obvious way of tidying things, pointing out that divorces by Bill were once the only way of getting a divorce. But, although in those fraught final days Baldwin was prepared to consider this, ultimately he had to remind the King that 'even his wishes were not above the inexorable fulfilment of the law and he was afraid he could not interfere'. However, it was more complicated than that because any such action might have been misinterpreted as a government ploy to persuade the King to abdicate, which it could not be seen to do. In the event, the King in his all-consuming desire to have Wallis, played into the government's hands and failed to secure any of these rights before he too left.

Within hours of her arrival in Cannes, a confused and exhausted Wallis tried to persuade the King to stay on the throne. She issued a statement claiming that she was anxious to avoid damaging His Majesty or the Throne and stating her readiness 'if such action would solve the problem to withdraw forthwith from a situation that has been rendered both unhappy and untenable'. Hardinge, not surprisingly, insisted that she was not sincere in this and was merely posturing, knowing what the King's response would be. Nancy Dugdale described the statement as 'undisguised humbug. After having done her utmost to split the country from Land's End to John O'Groats she now played the part of the gilded angel who, having failed to accomplish this, only wanted to act for the best.'

As Zetland pointed out: 'She did *NOT* say she was ready to withdraw her petition for divorce.' But she did send the King a long and rambling letter urging him not to abdicate. 'Don't be silenced and leave under a cloud, I beseech you and in abdication no matter in what form unless you can let the public know that the Cabinet has virtually kicked you out ... I must have any action of yours understood by the world [or] we would have no happiness and I think the world would turn against me.'

Reading this, along with her earlier note to Sibyl Colefax, it is clear she was finally trying to extricate herself, painfully aware now how history would view her as the woman who forced a man to give up his throne. Wallis was utterly genuine in her desire to disappear from the King's life, if only to preserve her own sanity rather than from motives of altruism or to protect the King let alone the institution of monarchy. She, not the King, retained a keen awareness of the world beyond. But she also knew better than anyone, other than Monckton perhaps, how difficult it was going to be to leave him. 'With the King's straightness and directness,' he wrote, 'there went a remarkable determination and courage and confidence in his own opinions and decisions. Once his mind was made up one felt that he was like the deaf adder that stoppeth his ears ... for myself ... I thought that if and when the stark choice faced them between their love and his obligations as King Emperor they would in the end make the sacrifice, devastating though it would be.' Nancy Dugdale was perhaps right in claiming that Wallis's renunciation statement 'came many, many weeks if not years too late and was despised by everyone except the vacuous women of society whom she had vamped and who were touched by her magnanimous gesture', but wrong in failing to recognize how sincerely Wallis wanted to get out of a predicament she now loathed, even without any clear plans as to how she would fend for herself if she had to.

Theodore Goddard also understood, through awkward conversations on 'a very bad phone line with much shouting and confusion', that his client was completely 'ready to do anything that would ease the situation but that the other end of the wicket was determined'. Since Wallis, not the King, was his client, Goddard faced another problem. He had information which made him seriously concerned that, following the Francis Stephenson intervention with the King's Proctor, the divorce might not be granted after all. This potentially disastrous situation made it imperative for him to meet with his client for her sake, even though the King, a semi-prisoner himself at the Fort, was strongly opposed to his going or to any action which might put pressure on Wallis to withdraw. Nonetheless, Goddard ignored royal opposition and bravely flew, for the first time in his life, in a small government plane to the South of France. It was a terrifying flight as one of engines broke down, forcing him to land at Marseilles, and he eventually arrived at two o'clock on the morning of Tuesday 8 December. Also in the party was a doctor – Goddard had a weak heart. But since Dr Kirkwood was a gynaecologist, rumours immediately spread that Wallis was pregnant. Brownlow was infuriated by this further annoyance and had to issue a statement that Dr Kirkwood was there only as Goddard's personal physician.

At nine the next morning Goddard had a long talk with Wallis 'and asked if she was sure that what she was doing was wise? Two things stand out,' Goddard stated later. 'She was definitely prepared to give up the King and he was definitely not prepared to give her up … he intended to abdicate and eventually marry her.' Nonetheless, after increasingly tense phone calls between Cannes and Fort Belvedere, Wallis signed a further, much stronger statement which, according to Goddard, the King agreed to only in order to protect her from criticism. Goddard returned, by train this time, with a document in which Mrs Simpson unambiguously expressed her readiness to withdraw from her entanglement. But nothing was done with this statement: 'It was not available until the afternoon of Wednesday the 9th and, as you know,' the Downing Street adviser Sir Horace Wilson explained to Monckton, 'you and others had been at the Fort the previous evening on what proved to be the final attempt. During Wednesday morning's cabinet, decisions were taken which with Tuesday's proceedings made it clear that nothing would come of the statement nor of Goddard's efforts. I see that after hearing his account on Wednesday afternoon I noted that I did not think that G's client had fully taken him into her confidence!' There also exists in the Bodleian Library in Oxford what Alan Lascelles in depositing it there called 'a curious little document', found among Baldwin's political papers. It was a half-sheet of grey notepaper bearing the heading 'Lou Viei, Cannes' but with no date. On it is written in pencil, in what is believed to be Brownlow's handwriting, 'With the deepest personal sorrow, Mrs Simpson wishes to announce that she has abandoned any intention of marrying his Majesty.' It is signed (in ink) 'Wallis Simpson'. This statement is unequivocal.

But it, too, presumably also arrived among Baldwin's papers via Goddard and never saw the light of day. For, as Goddard relayed to Dugdale, he had found his client 'in a most terrified state of nerves, complete capitulation and willingness to do anything'. The atmosphere at the Rogers villa was appallingly tense for all. The King had given orders that Wallis should have police protection, but Inspector

Evans and his colleague begged to be allowed to return to England, complaining in particular of Brownlow and his high-handed ways. They particularly resented being told to take their hands out of their pockets when speaking to him. Goddard believed Wallis's desire to disappear from Europe was genuine – she had contemplated going to the Far East – but by 9 December neither plans nor statements were of any use, as Wallis probably feared all along. Although the King now was resolute in his decision to abdicate, with Wallis gone he had no friends with whom to discuss the matter. Churchill, out of sympathy and pragmatism, continued to beg him not to rush. He even wrote to Baldwin saying how cruel and wrong it would be to extort a decision from the man in his present state. He had visited the King and believed that he should see a doctor as 'the personal strain he had been so long under and which was not at its climax had exhausted him to a most painful degree'.

But none of this washed with the House of Commons and by Tuesday 8 December Baldwin, who paid his last visit to the Fort that day, knew it was all over. There were still many unresolved questions about the King's future status and finances but nothing could persuade him to remain. American newspapers were already reporting the abdication. Baldwin had found all his conversations with the King difficult, partly because it was:

> like talking to a child of 10 years old. He did not seem to grasp the issues at stake, he seems <u>bewitched</u> ... He has no religious sense. I have never in my life met anyone so completely lacking in any sense of the – the – what is <u>beyond</u> ... And he kept on repeating over and over again: 'I can't do my job without her ... I am going to marry her, and I will <u>go</u>' ... There simply was no moral struggle and it appalled me.

Even when the Prime Minister warned the King that he risked the destruction of the monarchy he 'would keep on throwing his arms out with a curious gesture repeating: "SHE is beside me ... the most wonderful woman in the world."' But on the night of the 8th the King was in 'what I can only describe as a perfectly exalted condition. He would spend nearly the whole day telephoning to that woman and would come in from the telephone box with the most beautiful look I have ever seen on his face, like a young knight who has just seen the Holy Grail and say: "I've just been talking to Her: talking to the most wonderful woman in the world." It was hopeless to reason with him.'

Baldwin told his Cabinet that he had then, as a last resort, said to the King: 'Suppose if an archangel asked you to give up Mrs Simpson would it have any effect?' 'Not the least,' replied the King. And the Prime Minister told his wife on his return home that he felt 'as though he had been in Bedlam'. Dugdale asked the Duke of Kent at this time, 'Do you think the King will be happy?' and received the reply: 'Happy? Good heavens no, not with That Woman.'

The King, as he tried in those vital last hours to negotiate his future, was desperately alone. He had abandoned the support of his family months previously and now, at his lowest point, was almost without advisers he trusted. 'He was', as his biographer Philip Ziegler acknowledged, 'agonised by the fear that he would let Wallis down, secure for her less than she deserved, earn her contempt.' At the final dinner before the abdication, where the King spoke to each of his brothers in turn and tried to explain, there was yet another telephone conversation with Wallis in Cannes, partially overheard by Dugdale, in which the King 'was heard to tell her he would get less than he hoped for, which caused a harsh voiced twang of rich American invective from Cannes'. Under such pressure he clutched at any straw which he thought might help him improve his bargaining position. But then, as Ziegler puts it, 'he told for reasons of self-interest, a foolish and suicidal lie . . . He was to suffer the consequences until the day he died.'

The precise size of Edward VIII's fortune before abdicating is a matter of historical debate. Sir Edward Peacock, a man of immense experience as a former governor of the Bank of England as well as adviser to George V and Edward when Prince of Wales, later put it at around £1.1 million, excluding his Canadian ranch. A year before he became king, the Prince had asked Peacock to put his money in securities outside England, setting up a trust with provision for Mrs Simpson. When Peacock warned the Prince that if this became known it would reflect badly on him the Prince insisted he still wanted it done. 'Peacock told me this to show that Wales had in mind to get

Three generations of royalty: the Duke (*far right*) with his father George V and grandfather Edward VII (*seated*) on board the royal yacht in 1910 shortly before the latter's death later that year.

The handsome Prince of Wales, as he embarked on a world tour in 1920. He became a pin-up for millions of young girls around the world, the cigarette between his teeth only adding to his appeal.

Mr and Mrs Ernest Simpson
presented at court in June 1931.
Wallis borrowed her formal clothes
from friends but could not resist
additional jewels. Ernest wore his
uniform of the Coldstream Guards.

Wallis, still married to Ernest,
cruising along the Dalmatian
coast on the *Nahlin* yacht with
the new King. This picture,
with Wallis's restraining hand
on the King's arm, was widely
published abroad before most
people in England had any idea
who Wallis Simpson was.

The bracelet of crosses, each separately inscribed, which Wallis wore on many occasions before her relationship with the Prince of Wales was public, gave rise to intense speculation as to their meaning.

Wallis in 1936 with plenty to look pensive about. She is wearing the enormous Cartier platinum and emerald engagement ring that Edward had given her following her decree nisi while awaiting the decree absolute.

Married at last: the new Duke and Duchess of Windsor posing for photographs by Cecil Beaton at the Chateau de Candé in France, 3 June 1937. Wallis wore a figure-hugging Mainbocher gown in a shade of blue henceforth known as 'Wallis blue'.

The fatal smile. Wallis, Duchess of Windsor, shakes hands with the Nazi leader Adolf Hitler, while the Duke looks on during their 1937 visit to Germany.

Mary Kirk, Wallis's longest-standing school friend, married Ernest Simpson in Connecticut on 19 November 1937, six months after Ernest's divorce from Wallis.

23 September 1939. The Duke and Duchess of Windsor with Major Fruity Metcalfe at his home in Sussex where they are his guests just after the outbreak of war.

The Duchess of Windsor at a Paris depot in December 1939, still wearing her jewelled bracelet, helps to make up packages for the troops at the front.

The Duke and Duchess on their way to the Bahamas. Wallis is wearing the spectacular diamond, emerald, ruby, citrine and sapphire flamingo brooch just made by Cartier in Paris in 1940.

Wallis in Nassau wearing her uniform of the Bahamas Central Branch of the British Red Cross of which she was President.

America's First Lady, Eleanor Roosevelt, meets the Duchess of Windsor in Washington, October 1941. Later that day the Windsors were entertained to lunch at the White House.

The Duke with his mother, Queen Mary, at Marlborough House, October 1945.

The new Mr and Mrs Ernest Simpson returning to London onboard HMS Queen Mary after their wedding in Connecticut, 1937. Ernest and Mary had one child together in 1939, before Mary died of cancer in 1941.

One of Ernest's personal favourites – a picture of him shortly after his marriage to Mary Kirk Raffray.

In 1952 the Windsors were offered the use of a magnificent house by the Paris municipal authorities, 4 Route du Champ d'Entraînement in the Bois-de-Boulogne.

out of England long before the abdication,' Joseph Kennedy, the US Ambassador, wrote in his diary following a lunch with Peacock. 'This was all invested and very wisely,' Kennedy continued; 'with cash and other interests he had about £1,000,000. This figure confirmed later by Sir Horace Wilson ...' Nevertheless when the King met his family for the last time at the Fort he 'distinctly told his brother [the Duke of York] that ... he did not think he had £5,000 a year' and made an impassioned speech about how badly off he was, citing his father's will, which still rankled, giving him a life interest in Sandringham and Balmoral. He told Churchill a similar sob story about how poor he was and about his need for a subsidy if he was going to survive in a suitable manner for an ex-king of Britain. In the abdication settlement there was a proposal for a grant from the government of approximately £25,000 a year free of tax. But Baldwin was worried that, if debated in Parliament, this would lead to a heated discussion. Nancy Dugdale was probably correct in her belief that most people think 'public money should not be voted for the ex King in the Civil List ... the Royal family, who all inherited the late King's private fortune, should give their brother enough to live on'. She also reported hearing 'considerable public annoyance because the King has given Mrs Simpson Queen Alexandra's jewels ... Lawyers have discovered that they were left to King Edward as head of House of Windsor ... a position he subsequently relinquished therefore the jewels go to his successor. The King has given Mrs Simpson vast sums of money placed in banks all over world.' The legend of Queen Alexandra's emeralds, said for years to have been spirited away by the King and given to Mrs Simpson, persisted throughout their lives in spite of vehement denunciations from their lawyers and by Wallis herself as Duchess of Windsor. In reality, the likely sources of the jewels the Duke gave to Wallis, both loose and set, were his private family heirlooms, therefore genuinely personal property, as well as gifts given to him while he was travelling the Empire as Prince of Wales, especially during his tour of India in 1921 and 1922.

But in order to avoid an unpopular public discussion about how much the ex-King would need, the future King agreed to underwrite this amount to his brother out of the Privy Purse. According to

Ambassador Kennedy: 'Peacock advised Edward that he thought Baldwin had done the best he could and agreed with Baldwin that it should be given up in Parliament.' When King George VI later learned the truth about his exiled brother's sizeable fortune he wrote to him in subdued shock to say 'that I was completely misled'.

Until that time he – if not Wallis – had retained the underlying affection of his sister-in-law the Duchess of York, who wrote one of the most moving letters of the whole drama just before the abdication, begging her brother-in-law to be kind to Bertie, who finds it 'awfully difficult to say what he thinks, you know how shy he is – so do help him'. She went on: 'I wish that you could realize how hard it has been for him lately. I *know* that he is fonder of you than anybody else and as his wife I must write to tell you this. I am terrified for him – so DO help him, and *for God's sake* don't tell him that I have written.'

On 10 December, less than six weeks after Wallis Simpson had appeared at Ipswich assizes pleading for a divorce, the King signed the Instrument of Abdication at Fort Belvedere with his three brothers present. Once Parliament had endorsed this, he would become a private individual and his most pressing obligation was to speak directly to the nation and earn Wallis's respect by making plain to posterity how hard she had tried to dissuade him from abdicating. He had been working on such a speech for days but felt goaded into action by what he perceived as Baldwin's unforgivable failure when speaking to the House of Commons about these events to explain the nobility of Wallis's behaviour. Most people in Britain had first learned of the drama and heard mention of the American woman he loved only in the previous few days. 'We Londoners, with our insatiable thirst for scandalous gossip,' wrote Lieutenant Colonel Tweed to the former Prime Minister David Lloyd George, 'tended to assume that everybody knew all about Mrs Simpson and I was rather staggered on visiting Birmingham and Manchester a week prior to the crisis breaking to find that not a single soul I talked to had even heard of Mrs Simpson.'

The abdication speech, with its expression of heartfelt longing for a woman and desperation to appear courageous in her eyes, was essentially Edward's own creation, with some Churchillian improvements and flourishes. After a final lunch at Fort Belvedere, Churchill bade his own emotional farewell to the man who had ceased to be king while they were lunching; with tears in his eyes he began to recite two lines of poetry, tapping his stick the while: 'He nothing common did or mean / Upon that memorable scene,' words written by Andrew Marvell on the execution of King Charles I. Churchill was not alone in making the comparison with Charles I. The writer Virginia Woolf and the society hostess Lady Ottoline Morrell, transfixed like most of the country by the dramatic events, had gone to the House of Commons to be as close as possible to unfolding history. Woolf wrote in her diary of how, as the women walked along Whitehall, Ottoline, pointing to the great lit-up windows of the Banqueting House in their frame of white stone, remarked: 'That's the window out of which Charles the First stepped when he had his head cut off.' Woolf said she felt she was 'walking in the seventeenth century with one of the courtiers; and she was lamenting not the abdication of Edward, but the execution of Charles. "It's dreadful, dreadful," she kept saying. Poor silly little boy. No one could ever tell him a thing he disliked.'

Today, the abdication speech has achieved iconic status and become shorthand for those who wish to make clear what is meant by a sacrifice for love. It was also a big nod to the modernity for which he had hoped to be remembered, given that broadcasting, especially royal broadcasting, was in its infancy. The ex-King sat in front of a single microphone in the tower room of Windsor Castle, set up as a temporary studio, introduced by the Director General of the BBC, Sir John Reith, and started by declaring his allegiance to the new King, his brother. After a reminder of his twenty-five years of service to the country, he explained:

> ... I have found it impossible to carry the heavy burden of responsibility and to discharge my duties as King as I would wish to do without the help and support of the woman I love.
>
> And I want you to know that the decision I have made has been mine and mine alone. This was a thing I had to judge entirely for myself. The other person most nearly concerned has tried up to the last to persuade me to take a different course.
>
> I have made this, the most serious decision of my life, only upon

the single thought of what would, in the end, be best for all.

This decision has been made less difficult to me by the sure knowledge that my brother, with his long training in the public affairs of this country and with his fine qualities, will be able to take my place forthwith without interruption or injury to the life and progress of the empire. And he has one matchless blessing, enjoyed by so many of you, and not bestowed on me – a happy home with his wife and children.

I now quit altogether public affairs and I lay down my burden. It may be some time before I return to my native land, but I shall always follow the fortunes of the British race and empire with profound interest, and if at any time in the future I can be found of service to his majesty in a private station, I shall not fail.

Wallis listened to the broadcast on a crackly radio at Lou Viei with Perry Brownlow, she lying on the sofa, Herman and Katherine Rogers and all the domestic staff gathered around to hear. 'David's voice came out of the loudspeaker calmly, movingly … After he finished, the others quietly went away and left me alone. I lay there a long time before I could control myself enough to walk through the house and go upstairs to my room,' she wrote dramatically. She explained that she listened with her hands over her eyes 'trying to hide my tears'. They were tears of rage, pity, fear and bafflement.

Queen Mary flinched when her son, now known as the Duke of Windsor, said he had been 'denied' the happiness of his brother in having a wife and children, 'as if he might not at any time have honestly possessed this happiness if he had chosen', while Nancy Dugdale found the conclusion 'God bless you all' rather jarring 'as everyone knows his belief in God is rather a faint reality'.

Monckton drove the new Duke to Portsmouth and then tactfully – if not entirely accurately – wrote to Queen Mary that:

during the journey he talked quietly of old times and places well remembered by us both but above all he talked of you, how grand you were and how sweet to him especially at the last. I left him on the destroyer. He was still full of the same gay courage and spirit which has amazed us all this week. There is and always will be a greatness and glory about him. Given his faults and his follies [in an unsent draft the word 'madness' is here crossed out] are great ... I will go on trying to help him when he needs.

Ulick Alexander and Piers (Joey) Legh, whose birthday it was, agreed to accompany their former sovereign in the early hours of that foggy December morning as they left England on HMS *Fury*. The captain, having been given his sailing orders at the very last minute, was obliged to borrow from the royal yacht some bed linen, crockery and glass as well as an experienced steward who knew the ex-King and would serve him during the crossing. For one of the most tragic aspects of the departure was the decision of his staff, including his valet Crisp, not to accompany their royal master into exile. The Duke carried his small Cairn bitch up the gangway himself and the dog later disgraced herself in the private quarters of the Captain, Cecil Howe. As Legh's stepson Freddy Shaughnessy was to recount:

> The exiled king was, not surprisingly, in a state of high nervous tension and restlessness that night. He sat up in the wardroom until four in the morning drinking brandy and going over the events of the last few weeks. Legh and Alexander, already exhausted by the strain of the whole abdication trauma ... longed for HRH to retire to his cabin so they themselves could turn in.

Duty was the watchword of the moment or, as the Duke said in the television account of his departure, *A King's Story*, created more than thirty years later, by which time his American accent was even more pronounced: 'The path of dooty was clear.' Others saw his duty very differently. Lucy Baldwin wrote: 'But in the background there is that ache of which I spoke, the ache for the man who took the wrong path and chose inclination and desire instead of duty and responsibility. One just aches for his future, regrets his want of background and anchorage and prays for him with all one's heart.'

And the former Duchess of York, now Queen of England, who had been in bed with a high temperature on the day of the abdication, decided that the first letter of her new reign should be to her friend, the Archbishop of Canterbury, assuring him not just of how deeply she and the new King felt their responsibilities and duty at this difficult time, but of how miserable they were, 'as you know, over his change of heart and character during the last few years and it is alarming how little in touch he was with ordinary human feeling – Alas! He had lost the "common touch", she wrote and signed her letter for the first time 'Elizabeth R'.

Queen Mary, in a post-abdication letter largely written for her by Lang and published in the next day's newspapers, also spoke of 'the distress in a mother's heart' when she contemplated how 'my dear son has deemed it his duty to lay down his charge'. But she begged the British people, 'realizing what it has cost him to come to this decision, and remembering the years in which he tried so eagerly to serve, [to] keep a grateful remembrance of him in your hearts'. Lang himself observed that when he went to see Queen Mary 'she was much moved and distressed but wonderfully self controlled'.

Did Wallis want to be queen of England? Some of those who witnessed her confidently greeting her sister-in-law, the Duchess of York, at Balmoral on the ill-fated night of 26 September believed that there was the evidence that she did, that it was 'a deliberate and calculated display of power'. But that makes no allowance for her natural American brashness, which for example allowed her to comment on that same visit, when taken to see the beach at Loch Muick by the King, 'Just like Dubrovnik' – a comparison, according to Helen Hardinge, 'which did not go down any better than the casual careless way of referring to a voyage [on the *Nahlin*] which had not been popular in many respects'. Nor did it make any allowance for her state of mind at the time. Chips Channon among others had consistently reported her as 'looking unhappy' (7 July) or 'worn out and on a fish diet' (27 July) and, by the end of November, he recorded 'that she had had a sort of breakdown and must be kept quite quiet and away from visitors' (29 November).

Perhaps the realization that she was now desperately trapped was most clearly visible in her unvarnished letters to Ernest and in her increasingly evident physical fear. Ernest's attempts to visit Baldwin, telling him he could help with 'the psychological aspect of the matter' were based on the probably correct belief that he understood his wife;

he did not, however, have the same understanding of the King. But his message to the Prime Minister, explaining that he was convinced she was not as much in love with the King as the King was with her and therefore, if she was seen by 'somebody in authority', might be persuaded to leave him, was not followed up. According to Wigram, Ernest was even prepared in early December to turn King's evidence and 'come forward and say that the divorce was entirely a collusion between HM, himself and Mrs S'. Not only would this have prevented the divorce going through, it would have been hugely embarrassing. As Cecil Beaton recognised, 'she loves him, though I fear she is not in love with him . . .'. Ministers were advised not to meet Ernest.

Today it seems clear that becoming queen was far from what she wanted. 'I who had sought no place in history would now be assured of one – an appalling one, carved out by blind prejudice,' she wrote in *The Heart Has its Reasons*. The self-pity may grate. But while it is easy with hindsight to see why 'Queen Wallis' would never have been acceptable as consort to a monarch of the British Empire, it is also important to remember that when Edward VIII came to the throne in 1936 he was hailed as the most widely travelled man of his time, with so much excitement and hope based on his perceived glamour and youthful charm, his daredevil smile, his apparent ability to connect with ordinary people, that anyone not familiar with Britain might easily have assumed he would win through. Lloyd George had declared in 1922 after his 41,000-mile tour as Prince of Wales: 'Whatever the Empire owed him before, it owes to him a debt which it can never repay today.' Wallis may not have known the speech but she was aware of the sentiment. She had grown up with it. What she totally failed to understand, as she frankly admitted later, was the King's true position in the constitutional system. For not only had she lived in Washington and London circles where divorce was acceptable at the highest echelons, she had never thought her relationship with Edward would last longer than a few years. When it did, and she suddenly found herself the King's adored favourite, she believed that:

the apparent deference to his every wish, the adulation of the populace, the universal desire even of the most exalted of his subjects to be accorded marks of his esteem – all this had persuaded me to take literally the maxim that 'the King can do no wrong'. Nothing that I had seen had made me appreciate how vulnerable the King really was, how little his wishes really counted for against those of his ministers and parliament.

And the British constitution is, after all, famously unwritten.

By December 1936, when she realized that the King was going to forfeit the throne in order to possess her – the only British monarch to have voluntarily renounced the throne since the Anglo-Saxon period[14] – she knew that the cost for her was the total destruction of her reputation. Hardly comparable sacrifices, some might think. But Wallis, who owned little, did make that comparison and made sure the ex-King did too. She remained convinced that she had been used by the politicians. As she wrote to one of her closest London friends two weeks after the abdication: 'The pitiful tragedy of it all is that England still remains in the hands of the men that caused the tragedy – using a woman as their means.' She was not alone in such views. Lloyd George, away in Jamaica throughout the crisis writing his memoirs, was furious at the way Baldwin and his allies had 'got rid of a king who was making himself obnoxious by calling attention to conditions which it was to their interest to cover up. Baldwin has succeeded by methods which time and again take in the gullible British public. He has taken the high line in order to achieve the lowest of aims.' Lloyd George did not hold 'the woman Simpson' personally in high regard, considering that she 'is not worth the price the poor infatuated King was prepared to pay'. Nor was he without bitter personal prejudice against the Conservative leader. But he had a natural sympathy with a man whose love life was unorthodox, believing 'all the same if he wished to marry her it could have been arranged, quietly, after the coronation ... if the King wants to marry his American friend – Why not? I cannot help thinking the Govt. would not have dealt so brusquely with him had it not been for his

14 At least two kings in the eighth century, Ine and Ceolwulf, gave up their thrones voluntarily and embraced religion.

popular sympathies. The Tories never really cared for the little man.'

If there is a sense in which, as Wallis persuaded herself, the abdication crisis appears as a government plot to be rid of a difficult king, it is sharpened by the speed with which events unfurled after 27 October, at a time when communications were normally difficult and slow. As early as 1927, Lascelles had remarked in desperation to Baldwin: 'You know, sometimes when I am waiting to get the result of some point-to-point in which he is riding, I can't help thinking that the best thing that could happen to him, and to the country, would be for him to break his neck.' 'God forgive me,' said Baldwin, 'I have often thought the same.'

However, at the beginning of 1936 Baldwin and his ministers, and experienced courtiers such as Hardinge, Wigram and Lascelles, who all knew each other and understood each other well, were neither plotting nor acting in unison. They all wanted to retain the King, but on their own terms. And they wanted to do this not for themselves but as a matter of duty to the public interest. By November that year, however, they saw that the problem was not simply that the new King might be difficult or interfering; that could be managed. What made Edward VIII worryingly unsafe was his total lack of a sense of public duty, without which a workable relationship seemed impossible. These men and their wives all had a high moral agenda. Wallis Simpson clashed irredeemably with that and in doing so played a valuable role in focusing them on what sort of monarchy Britons wanted and needed to face the looming European crisis.

One other reason should not be overlooked in explaining why the drama played out so swiftly. Edward VIII was at the top of a hereditary system, yet what greater failure could be imagined than the failure to provide an heir? If he believed he was sterile, or if he knew that Wallis was infertile, abdicating could be seen as a welcome release for him. Giving up was something he had contemplated before, as his father recognized when he said to Ulick Alexander: 'My eldest son will never succeed me. He will abdicate.'

Having failed to detach herself from the King and realizing that she was doomed to a life of exile as despised consort to an ex-king, Wallis now fought for every penny she could, an overwhelming recurrence of her childhood insecurity. As well as being overheard, her telephone was being tapped (by the Metropolitan Police), which she appears not to have known, and her conversation with the Duke at midnight on 14–15 December – two days after he had undergone the massive emotion of abdication – was recorded.

Mrs S: If they don't get you this thing [presumably money] I will return to England and fight it out to the bitter end. The coronation will be a flop compared with the story that I shall tell the British press. I shall publish it in every paper in the world so that the whole world shall know my story. Your mother is even persecuting me now. Look in all the Sunday papers, you will see what she has done. On the front page of every paper is a black bordered notice stating that she has never seen or spoken to me during the past 12 months. I know it is true but she need not persecute me. She could have helped you so much, you the only son that matters. Did you get a good picking from Ulick? After all I am a British subject and entitled to protection from Scotland Yard. You must change one of these men not the new one he is an honest type of fellow but the other one is not loyal and is anxious to get back . . .

Concentrate on the legal side now. That is the side that counts. We must have that fixed up because of April. Harmsworth has been so helpful and promises to do all he can. He has a villa in Cannes and was here during the few vital days.

'I told him I didn't want to be Queen,' Ralph Martin, one of her earliest biographers, quotes her as telling him in an interview. 'All that formality and responsibility . . . I told him it was too heavy a load for me to carry. I told him the British people were absolutely right about not wanting a divorced woman for a Queen.' The version may have been polished with the years but the truth was, as she understood, 'that if he abdicated every woman in the world would hate me and everybody in Great Britain would feel he had deserted them . . . we had terrible arguments about it. But he was a mule. He didn't want to be King without me . . . if I left him he would follow me wherever I went.'

Had the crisis not arisen in December, with Christmas looming,

Wallis might, perhaps, have won more time and been able to escape her fate. But Baldwin always maintained that it would be impossible for politicians to go away for Christmas without a settlement. Far from wanting to be queen, she had a vaguely sketched plan to escape, but it was too late. Blinded by fear, she was also aware of the King's fragile state of mind and health, aggravated by lack of sleep and fitful or non-existent meals. In addition to the concern shown by Churchill, Piers Legh was so worried about him that he insisted that the Surgeon Commander for the royal yacht should travel with them on the *Fury* in case he needed medical attention while at sea.

From pity, Francis Stephenson, the clerk, withdrew his intervention with the King's Proctor after hearing the broadcast. Monckton went back to Fort Belvedere, now abandoned, to clear up and in the room used by Wallis found a biography of George IV's mistress, Mrs Fitzherbert.

But, as 1936 drew to a close, Wallis was still writing to Ernest and, even more extraordinary, Ernest was writing to the King. 'My heart is too full for utterance tonight,' he insisted on the eve of the King's abdication. 'What the ordeal of the past weeks has meant to you I well know, and I want you to know that my deepest and most loyal feelings have been with you throughout!'

From Lou Viei Wallis wrote five days after the abdication:

> Ernest – none of this mess ... is of my own making – it is the new Peter Pan plan. I miss you and worry about you – in spite of the fact that due to the letters [the hate mail] I shan't live very long and in fact am a prisoner. Four detectives. Oh dear, wasn't life lovely, sweet and simple.
> Wallis
> Isn't everything awful including the pen?

Finally she apologized to her second husband: 'I have nothing for you for Christmas because I can't move on account of threats so sit all day.' It was in Wallis's interest to tell the world that she had not wanted a divorce until Ernest's adultery with her best friend forced her hand, a story that was both true and untrue. What was true is that she had not wanted to divorce Ernest. And Ernest, although grateful for Mary's loving support and comfort, never really fell out of love with Wallis.

'I know that somewhere in your heart there is a small flame burning for me. Guard it carefully, my darling, and don't let it go out,' he wrote to her in October after leaving Bryanston Court for the last time, 'if only in memory of the sacred lovely things that have been.'

If the King acted greedily, was it fair to blame Wallis? 'Money was an obsession,' wrote Alastair Forbes of the Duke, an obsession that grew worse with the years, 'and he was obsessively mean about it. To the last this was a "royal" who counted his royalties.' When Sir John Wheeler-Bennett wrote his official life of George V he told the author and diplomat Sir Robert Bruce Lockhart that a key concern was that 'he would have to put in writing how greedy for money the Duke of Windsor had been and what demands he made on King George VI, who had generously responded at considerable sacrifice to himself'.

If the King lied, was it fair to blame Wallis for teaching him? How truthful had he ever been in his relationships with previous women? Yet the establishment and most of the royal family did blame her; whatever failings the King had, he was one of theirs and, just as at Ipswich, essentially beyond reproach. It was she and she alone who was responsible for the near-disastrous opprobrium heaped on the British throne in the last months. The true feelings of the royal family – and especially those of the new Queen Elizabeth about the woman shortly to become her sister-in-law – is revealed in a letter sent from Windsor Castle to the Dominions Secretary, Lord Lloyd, in 1940 and only recently released with the agreement of the Royal Archives and after the Queen Mother's death in March 2002.

The views expressed in this sternly worded memorandum sent from the Queen via Alec Hardinge, who was 'sure you shared H.M.'s sentiments as most of us do', include the assertion that a woman such as Wallis with 'three husbands alive' could never 'lead or set an example' and therefore represented an inevitable lowering of standards since 'the people in our lands are used to looking up to their King's representatives'. Wallis, according to this letter, is 'looked down upon as the lowest of the low'. This attitude bedevilled all future relationships between the British Court and the departed uncrowned King.

10

Wallis in Exile

'Mummy dear, isn't it nice to have a Royal Family again'

In a controversial broadcast the day after the abdication Archbishop Lang denounced the sovereign for giving in to 'a craving for private happiness':

> From God he had received a high and sacred trust. Yet by his own will he has abdicated – he has surrendered the trust.
>
> Even more strange and sad it is that he should have sought his happiness in a manner inconsistent with the Christian principles of marriage and within a social circle whose standards and ways of life are alien to all the best instincts and traditions of his people.
>
> Let those who belong to this circle know that today they stand rebuked by the judgement of the nation which had loved King Edward.

Although Baldwin insisted that the broadcast was 'the voice of Christian England', and the BBC's Sir John Reith wrote, 'Few more momentous or impressive messages have ever been delivered . . . we are honoured to have been the medium,' the speech was generally considered a disaster, appearing as 'clerical vindictiveness towards a beaten and pathetic figure'. Lambeth Palace was deluged with more vituperative letters than the staff had ever known. Gerald Bullett, the popular novelist, wrote a widely circulated poem:

> *My Lord Archbishop, what a scold you are*
> *And when your man is down how bold you are*
> *In Christian charity how scant you are*
> *Oh Auld Lang Swine how full of Cantuar*

A strong letter to the *New Statesman* from the drama critic Ivor

Brown helped explain why such a lack of compassion was causing nervousness on all sides:

> The departure into exile of Mrs Simpson and the Duke of Windsor is a smashing clerical victory and the cock-a-hoop tone of the bishops last Sunday, led by the primate, seems to me thoroughly sinister. You may say that Parliament won – so did the prudes and the Pharisees; a dangerous victory ... no doubt according to their principles the Churchmen had to fight the proposed marriage ... we may be sure that clericalism will now fight harder than ever to hold all its forts of intolerance and obscurantism.

Lang had truly believed for months that the ex-King had 'a pathological obsession which completely unbalanced his mind'. He and his Chaplain Alex Sergeant seriously considered that Edward was 'definitely abnormal psychologically if not mentally or physically. Drink or drugs may have contributed to the result which is that he became a sort of <u>slave</u> to this woman and cannot do without her. It is not a case of normal love.' Because of Edward's 'disastrous liking for vulgar society and infatuation for this Mrs Simpson', the Archbishop had been dreading the Coronation 'as a sort of nightmare'. He was now confident in the new King and Queen's regard for traditional morality and 'sure that to the solemn words of the Coronation there would be a sincere response', and his broadcast left no one, least of all Wallis, in any doubt of that.

The Archbishop's personal sense of relief that he could now proceed with a meaningful Coronation was surpassed by an even greater sense of relief within the royal family at how smooth the transition to the new King and Queen had been and how readily the nation took to the new family with their photogenic young daughters. The country rejoiced that such an unpleasant episode was now behind it, a delight expressed clearly by a seven-year-old Welsh girl: 'Mummy dear, isn't it nice to have a Royal Family again.'

But such relief did not signal a general relaxation in attitudes to the exiled former King, sympathy for whom was considered highly dangerous politically in case he proved more popular than the socially awkward, less glamorous George VI. It was generally agreed that should the Duke return to London his presence would be an embarrassment both to the government and to the royal family. But he was well within his rights to return had he wished. As the Attorney General had told the House of Commons on 11 December 1936, a king who voluntarily abdicated was not compelled to leave the country. The new Queen was concerned about further stress for her husband, who had not been brought up to be the centre of attention and whose stammer was a serious problem when it came to public speaking; she was concerned too for their young daughters, whom she wanted shielded from comment and scrutiny. But others worried about more sinister elements who might look to exploit the situation. On the eve of the abdication the British Union of Fascists had made an abortive attempt to rally popular support for King Edward VIII, their leader Sir Oswald Mosley always claiming that he was in direct communication with the King hoping to be asked to form a government. However unlikely this scenario, since Mosley was not then in the House of Commons, the Fascists, while outwardly proclaiming loyalty to King George VI, made no real secret of their support for the Duke of Windsor and for any move for him to return to this country and if possible the throne. Since the Fascists looked forward to any visit with enthusiasm and were certain to arrange some sort of welcome, the Metropolitan Police feared a situation which might serve Communist purposes, as the Communists would be watching and, if there was support for their opponents, would immediately attack both Fascists and the Duke.[15]

Virginia Woolf understood the volatility of human emotions, noting in her diary the views of her grocer's young female assistant, 'We can't have a woman Simpson for Queen ... She's no more royal than you or me,' before commenting,

---

15 The only organization working openly for the Duke's return was an obscure group called the Society of Octavians, membership of which was never more than a few hundreds, the majority of whom were Fascists. According to the police, 'no person of any prominence has so far identified with them other than [the novelist] Compton Mackenzie, who is a member ... generally speaking they are innocuous' (HO 144/22448, Special Branch, 5 Jan. 1939, Note to Commissioner marked 'secret', NA PRO).

But today we have developed a strong sense of human sympathy: we are saying Hang it all – the age of Victoria is over. Let him marry whom he likes. Harold [Nicolson] is glum as an undertaker and so are the other nobs. They say Royalty is in Peril. The Empire is Divided ... never has there been such a crisis ... The different interests are queueing up behind Baldwin or Churchill. Mosley is taking advantage of the crisis for his own ends ...

In this febrile time of swift realignments, the writer Osbert Sitwell cleverly captured the mood in his cruel satirical poem 'Rat Week', which was not printed at the time for fear of being found libellous. Was the ex-King 'quite sane', he asked or merely weak and obstinate and vain? Was Lady Colefax 'in her iron cage of curls' one of the rats to desert the sinking ship? Copies were circulating privately and Attlee typed up on his own typewriter all eight verses.

> *Where are the friends of yesterday*
> *That fawned on Him*
> *And flattered Her*
> *Where are the friends of yesterday*
> *Submitting to His every whim*
> *Offering praise of Her as Myrrh*
> *To him?*

> *What do they say, that jolly crew?*
> *Oh ... her they hardly knew,*
> *They never found her really nice*
> *(And here the sickened cock crew thrice) ...*

The apprehension of the new Court, and antipathy towards anyone thought to have been part of the ex-King's circle, was made painfully clear to Perry Brownlow when he returned from France at the end of the month and found his services no longer required. He complained at being 'hurt and humiliated more than I have ever known before ... I am afraid that when I came back last week I did not realise the depth of personal feeling against myself in certain circles: perhaps you should have told me more frankly or maybe I should have understood your hint in the "formula of resignation" shown to me,' he wrote to the Lord Chamberlain, the Earl of Cromer. 'My resignation from His Majesty's household was both obvious and desirable,' he agreed, but was it necessary to be demanded 'in such a premature and unhappy manner'? Lord Cromer tried to reassure Brownlow that the request was not personal as the new King was very grateful for his loyal service in escorting Wallis abroad. But the reality was that he was criticized severely for helping her and remaining friendly to the Duke, who was after all godfather to his young son. Baldwin at least accepted that Brownlow 'had a difficult row to hoe', and Wallis, who understood that any intervention from her would only make matters worse, wrote: 'You know my dear that if there was anything I could do about it I would have done it long ago.' Spurned by the new Court, Brownlow offered to visit the Duke, brooding at a castle in Austria, Schloss Enzesfeld.

'The strain here [at Enzesfeld] is pretty great, as you can imagine, and the Archbishop's outburst hasn't helped,' wrote Piers Legh, who, firmly out of sympathy with the Duke and Mrs Simpson and not able to speak German, was hoping to be relieved as soon as possible. Brownlow put it more strongly to Alan Don after visiting the Duke in Austria. He thought the Duke was 'a pathological case. If Mrs Simpson now lets him down anything might happen.' But, as the Duke saw it, the only people letting him down were those in England, mainly his own family. When Dudley Forwood replaced Legh to become sole equerry he described the Duke as 'a broken man, a shell, yet he still expected a full service, a monarch's service'. If Forwood forgot to bow on arriving in the Duke's bedroom in the morning to announce the day's business, he would receive a reprimand.

Schloss Enzesfeld, owned by Baron Eugène de Rothschild, had been chosen in hasty desperation in December as it was clear the Duke could not be in the same country as Wallis. At least it had a golf course, skiing was near by and he could get around by speaking German. His grandfather, King Edward VII, had stayed there on a visit to the Baron's father. The introduction now came thanks to the Baroness, Kitty de Rothschild, a thrice-married friend of Wallis. According to a newspaper cutting sent to Archbishop Lang, heavily underscored and with exclamation marks in the margins, Kitty (née Wolf) had left Bavaria as a child and emigrated to America with her parents. An uncle educated her and at twenty she married for the first time a Mr Spotswood, a Philadelphia dentist. She divorced him, went to Paris in 1910 and became a Catholic in order to marry Count Erwin Schönborn-Buchheim, a wealthy diplomat. Later she divorced Schönborn and in 1924 'accepted the Jewish faith' in order to marry Baron Eugène de Rothschild. What really irked courtiers who knew the Duke well was hearing how enthusiastically he read the lesson at a Vienna church on Christmas Day when they recalled how resistant he had always been to going to church when it was required of him. Wallis spent Christmas Day at Somerset Maugham's Villa Mauresque at Cap Ferrat, with Sybil Colefax attempting to cheer her up.

Bored and unable to amuse themselves – knitting was only so much fun – both Wallis and the Duke were finding fault with those who were trying their best to entertain them. Boredom at least gave Wallis time to read the first of many books published about her. By December 1936 the New York publishers E. P. Dutton had managed to release a biography of her by one Edwina H. Wilson. This superficial and rather breathless account of Mrs Simpson's furs, nail varnish, jewellery and accomplishments was hugely successful and went into three printings in a fortnight. 'She can complete a jigsaw puzzle in half the time the average person takes,' readers were informed. They were then told not to despair, as 'those who envy Wallis Simpson her success' could be given hints to guide them, for example on how to emulate her: 'A wise hostess never entertains at the same time her bridge-playing friends and those who shun the game.' Wallis, who read it immediately, was furious to find the amount of inside knowledge it contained and concluded that Mary had had a heavy hand in it.

'Have you read Mary's effort at literature called "Her Name was Wallis Warfield"? . . . It is written by Mary and one other bitch,' she wrote furiously to Ernest. 'Charming to make money out of one's friends besides sleeping with their husband. Everyone in London says the amount of stuff she has sold is the top . . . I warned you of this ages ago but you wouldn't believe me. I am very sad.' Even more upsetting was the appalling waxwork effigy of her in Madame Tussaud's, where she was grouped not with the royals but with Voltaire, Marie Antoinette and Joan of Arc. She begged Walter Monckton to do something about it. 'It really is too indecent and so awful to be there anyway.' But he was powerless.

Walter Monckton, ever the emollient diplomat, was trying to keep the peace on all sides and generally advising patience and turning the other cheek, his tact and usefulness evidenced by the fact that he was the first knight of the new reign, dubbed KCVO by George VI on 1 January 1937. Sir Walter, as he now was, had to fly to Austria, which he found extremely frightening in a small plane in horrible weather, to appease the Duke, who was bombarding his brother, the new King, with what he thought was advice as well as demands for future status and income. Numerous stories did the rounds about how Wallis would telephone from France berating and shouting at the Duke, mostly about money but also about position. And she was once, apparently, heard to accuse the Duke over the phone of having an affair with his hostess, Kitty, even though she had written to her friend in advance imploring her to 'be kind to him. He is honest and good and really worthy of affection. They simply haven't understood.' Now she remarked: 'It is odd, the hostess remaining on. Must be that fatal charm!' She told him she had heard terrible rumours, but 'I can only pray to God that in your loneliness you haven't flirted with her (I suspect that).' As the atmosphere at Enzesfeld deteriorated dramatically, Kitty left the castle in early February, appalled at the cost of the long phone calls – £800 after three months – which the Rothschilds were expected to pay. The Duke failed to say goodbye to her. Most nights as he sat down for dinner with whomever was staying, he would hold forth to a baffled audience about what a wonderful woman Wallis was.

She was certainly a jealous and frightened woman, convinced that she was more than ever a target for royalist fanatics. In her memoirs she admits that even in her most depressed moments she had never anticipated the enormity of the hatred she would arouse 'and the distorted image of me that seemed to be forming in minds every-where ... there can be few expletives applicable to my sex that were missing from my morning tray', she explained. There had been 'a spot of bother' with Lord Brownlow and the two police officers assigned to her in Cannes even before the abdication, and in a memorandum of 10 December 1936 it was stated that the Commissioner of the Metropolitan Police, Sir Philip Game, had instructed the unhappy officers to stand by pending further orders. 'The senior officer then said, what was understood from guarded language to be, that Mrs Simpson intended to "flit" to Germany. [This is underlined in pencil and marked with three vertical lines and a cross.]' According to the memorandum, the Prime Minister informed Sir Horace Wilson of this at once and confirmed with the Commissioner 'That there is no question of the officers moving without further orders'. The two detectives were therefore asked to stay on, more now as informers than to offer protection, 'though it's a most unusual measure to be kept as quiet as possible there or questions would be asked in Parliament. The new King suggested today that he should pay.'

But although Wallis's phone calls were bugged there is no other evidence that Germany was her intended destination. She simply wanted to escape her predicament and, no doubt recognizing that she would be something of a prize in Germany, was also playing with ideas of where else she might go if the English courts set aside the decree nisi and so obliged her to seek a valid divorce in another jurisdiction. In fact, as the letters to Sibyl Colefax indicate, China – 'the only other distant country that I knew . . . seemed the best choice'. She still had friends there who she believed would 'take her in'. However, as Stephen Cretney points out, she was probably unaware that 'at that time a married woman's domicile was dependent on her husband and so long as Mr Simpson remained domiciled in England a divorce obtained by her elsewhere would have been ineffective in English law'. When it was too late to escape anywhere for good, all she could contemplate were shopping trips to Paris couturiers for her wedding gown and trousseau, and for her hair, face and nails. Intense anxiety always led to dieting for Wallis, and Aunt Bessie, who had been to stay, thought she was 'too thin and should put on six pounds'. Thinner than ever, she at least enjoyed buying eighteen pieces from Elsa Schiaparelli's summer collection that year and several from Molyneaux, who showed in Cannes. Nonetheless she was writing to the Duke about how much weight she had gained and how heavy she now was. But in early 1937 having a wedding of any kind was still not a certainty for them.

In February she wrote to Ernest, a letter expressing some of her deepest fears and regrets and for once acknowledging how much flak he too was facing as the authorities examined whether or not he had been paid to keep quiet, an accusation he decided to fight vigorously as contrary to all notions of gentlemanly behaviour. His solicitors argued that such allegations had damaged his standing in the City. He could not avoid being aware of 'current luncheon table gossip . . . and widespread rumours that I was paid handsomely (some reports put the figure as high as £200,000!) to allow myself to be divorced. Needless to say none of my friends believe it and I have scores of people batting for me,' he reassured his elderly mother in New York. But when he discovered that Mrs Arthur Sutherland, a woman he did not know, had made an offensive comment – 'she's the only one I have been able to catch red handed since she made the remark at a luncheon in front of Maud, not knowing that M. was my sister. It is villainous, malicious slander and must be stopped' – he decided he had to sue her.

'Ernest dear,' Wallis wrote, sending 'my dearest love to you':

I am really so sorry about all the unjust criticism you have had. I feel your suit will change things. I am sorry you have Patrick H. [Sir Patrick Hastings KC] against you – he's so clever & v lucky besides – however I have perfect faith in your abilities as a witness.

I'm in a fog about the US bank account . . . Life here is one colossal bore. I don't go places as I think it more dignified to be quiet. One hopes to keep the name from the papers but even doing nothing is no protection against their intentions.

In a remarkably frank account of her own emotions Wallis admitted to Ernest, 'It never should have been like it is now.' She went on:

. . . I am so illogical and so groomed by my pride that – when that is touched nothing will stop what I'm capable of doing and this situation shows the truth of that remark because if I had told you

I would go to such lengths you wouldn't have believed it humanly possible, and of course you had every right to have a flirtation. So really you see what a queer girl I am.

I think Peter Pan should have written you too, but then you see he doesn't understand ...

Write me sometime please & above all make your life again <u>with care</u>. You are so good and sweet. The IOU's are in a tin box at Windsor but you can consider them torn up.

And she was desperate to leave Cannes, as she confided to Ernest: 'I am going to move from here – nobody knows it – so please don't tell ... I'm going to a house belonging to some friends of the Rogers near Tours, a change from their climate is also needed. You can imagine how much I want to kill Katherine by now ... !'

Although most courtiers agreed that for the King's Proctor now to disallow the divorce would be unnecessarily cruel, no one could say with certainty, least of all Wallis, that he would not be obliged to do so as the angry letters continued to pour in. Mary and Ernest were worried too. Mary wrote to her sister that 'E was such an angel – if only that damn King's Proctor doesn't upset the divorce. We are staying very quiet on purpose ... I have been mentioned many times as having been the corespondent [sic] in the Simpson divorce case which is unpleasant ... and no one would have wanted to take a chance on being nice to me if they [the Windsors] hadn't left the country, which is a great break for me ... but I love my life and E and I am happy.' She told her sister that she dreaded the idea that she might ever again meet Wallis in case she should have to curtsey to her. 'But as bitterly as I feel towards her for what she did to me, I do not envy her her life with that nervous difficult little man. They say he doesn't realize at all that he is no longer King.' And she believed the rampant rumours that Wallis had somehow made off with Queen Alexandra's emeralds, jewels apparently bequeathed to the Duke by his grandmother but in fact spread among various female members of the royal family. The gossip about Wallis's jewellery was a hot issue. The former Constance Coolidge, Comtesse de Jumilhac, who stayed with Wallis immediately before her wedding, wrote to a mutual friend:

About those emeralds . . . Queen Alexandra never left any emeralds. The only emeralds in the royal family all belong to Queen Mary, who bought them or acquired them from the Tzarina. She still has them. The Duke never had any jewels at all. He even had to buy his own silver when he went to Belvedere. The jewels that Wallis has are all new jewels he has bought for her here in Paris – some at Cartier's and mostly at Van Cleef and Arpels. She has lovely jewels but no great stones except her emerald engagement ring which I find a little dark. I like her sapphire one better and also the diamond. The ruby is small. She has several sets of jewels but they are all modern. After all she would have told me if they had come from the royal family. I asked her and she said no – none of them, that the Duke had not been left any jewels at all.

In her determination to quash rumours, Wallis exaggerated. Of course the Duke had some family pieces but whatever Wallis wore was newly set or new stones entirely.

Some courtiers felt a nagging doubt that Wallis might not actually go through with a wedding. On 5 March Lascelles spotted an announcement in the evening newspaper about the activities of the King's Proctor and the Simpson divorce which disturbed him. 'But I tracked Walter Monckton down in the Savoy and he reassured me as to its being only formal routine,' he told his wife. 'Just when I finished talking to him HM sent for me to know what it was all about and I was able to reassure him in turn.'

So, when Sir Thomas Barnes eventually announced the results of his enquiries on 18 March and ruled that in spite of gossip and hearsay he had not been presented with any actual evidence to indicate why the decree absolute should not go ahead, there was huge relief. He was criticized for not having interviewed the one servant who could possibly give more information – Wallis's maid, Mary Burke. But as he explained in his instructions to counsel: 'By reason of the fact that she is still in the employ of petitioner it is impossible to interview her . . . it is not the practice of the King's Proctor to endeavour to get information from such servants.'

But had Barnes chosen deliberately not to pursue information which would have shown the ex-King to be involved in a collusive divorce? There were those who offered him evidence of the King's adultery but only if he paid for it. For example, when Wallis and the then Prince had stayed in Budapest in 1935, returning from their skiing holiday, hotel staff as well as detectives on duty observed their behaviour and (according to an unsigned three-page memorandum in the King's Proctor files at the National Archives) 'there appears to be no doubt that the evidence which is being sought exists ... even a cursory enquiry showed that evidence going to the root of matters does in fact exist.'

'Whilst there is a possibility of obtaining confidential and oral information from them – none of them would take the risk of making a statement in writing or of giving evidence before a commissioner of court' for fear of losing their jobs, unless they were offered compensation. Barnes decided not to proceed with seeking their story on the grounds that 'it would not be proper to pay witnesses to give evidence.' Not only that, unless they had actually been in the room, what evidence could they give beyond stating that Wallis and the Prince had shared a room?

In early March Wallis had left for the Château de Candé in the Loire Valley with loyal Mary Burke and twenty-seven pieces of luggage. Thanks to an introduction from Katherine Rogers, with whom she was now fed up, she went to stay with Charles Bedaux, the French-born American industrial millionaire, and his second wife Fern, who had offered their castle as a wedding venue, thrilled by the publicity that such an illustrious guest would bring them. Charles Bedaux was a mysterious self-made entrepreneur who, after a spell in the Foreign Legion, had made his money by inventing a labour management efficiency system for industry. Not surprisingly this earned him the hostility of organized labour, but it held great appeal for the Nazi German leadership and he was under surveillance from the British and French security services, both of which were aware of his German contacts. The only condition insisted upon by M. and Mme Bedaux was that they be given full publicity as hosts for the royal couple. 'For I am a hard working businessman and in these critical times if the erroneous thought were to penetrate the public that we rented Candé for the purpose intended, it would be sure to have a disastrous effect on my business career.' Charles and Fern Bedaux, who had bought the castle and surrounding estate ten years previously and had lavishly modernized it, were to prove dubious hosts for the Windsor wedding. When allegations of collaboration were made against Charles in 1941, it was Fern's old friend Katherine who supplied the Americans with evidence. Facing a trial for treason, he committed suicide.[16] But for the moment Wallis was enamoured with Fern's hostessing skills and her attention to detail as well as with the up-to-date American plumbing and central-heating system. A bathtub that could be filled and emptied in less than a minute and a telephone, which at the time was almost unheard of in a French residence (it was directly connected to the exchange in Tours, and therefore required an operator to be present in the castle), were luxuries that mattered more than Charles Bedaux's politics. Fern even had her own gymnasium with all the latest exercise equipment at the castle.

There was another month to wait before the news that a decree absolute would be granted, but the day that the announcement was made – 3 May – the Duke immediately left Austria, where he felt he had been imprisoned, to be with Wallis, similarly fractious even in her luxurious confinement at the château. It was no coincidence that the announcement was made a week before the Coronation, the date of which – 12 May – had been chosen months previously when it was assumed that it was Edward VIII who would be crowned (with Wallis by his side, Edward himself had once hoped). The new King and Queen agreed to do what King Edward had refused – to attend a great Empire Service in St Paul's after the Coronation.

Ernest and Mary watched the Coronation from a first-floor balcony at 49 Pall Mall, 'one of the best places in London to see the show', which had been quietly arranged for them by well-connected friends. Mary was enthralled by the pageantry and sent her family

---

16 After the war, the new French government investigated Bedaux's wartime activities and, on evidence that he had in fact sabotaged German factory production and protected Jewish property, awarded him a posthumous knighthood of the Légion d'Honneur. Fern lived on at Candé until 1974.

detailed accounts of the uniforms, carriages and costumes:

> But finally came the gold coach drawn by the eight white horses
> called the Windsor Greys ... and the King and Queen looking so
> young and pale and grave, unsmiling and not bowing ... looking
> as if they were taking on their responsibilities with the greatest
> seriousness.
>
> Ernest said to me, once we were listening to the service in the
> Abbey, when the Queen was crowned: 'I couldn't have taken it if it
> had been Wallis' [a rare insight into the man's otherwise stoic
> performance]. But that is of course not for publication. We all had
> a terribly good time. Marvellous food sent up from Fortnums.

That same day, making no reference to activities in London, Wallis was
writing to Ernest from the Château de Candé: 'I have taken back the
name of Warfield as I really felt I had done the name of Simpson
enough harm. Now the target can be Warfield as I don't expect the
world will let up on its cruelty to me for some time ... It's impossible
to have anyone here & also impossible to move – literally surrounded
by press and photographers etc ... The publicity has practically killed
me.'

And when the Duke eventually sent out a paltry handful of
wedding invitations he announced his bride imaginatively as Mrs
Warfield, which she never was. Those who received one felt as if they
had been sent a poisoned chalice, whether the bride was Mrs Simpson
or Mrs Warfield. Godfrey Thomas, declining the invitation, wrote of
how terribly sorry he was that, 'largely owing to this damned press,
things have developed in this way', while John Aird, who had written
to accept, hurriedly recalled his letter when he realized the consequences, admitting in his diary: 'Feel a slight shit at leaving HRH
to be married with only the Metcalfes [Edward 'Fruity' Metcalfe, the
Duke's close friend and former equerry, and his wife Lady Alexandra
'Baba' Metcalfe] and Walter Monckton at the ceremony.' As Philip
Ziegler observes: 'No one emerges with great credit from this episode
except for Hugh Lloyd Thomas, who made it clear he would attend
the ceremony whether given permission or not, and the Duke, who
met these humiliating rebuffs with stoical dignity.'

The Duke had filled much of his time in Austria trying to organize his financial affairs, his wedding and a royal title for Wallis. He insisted that the desire for a religious service was mutual. But what Wallis wanted was not so much the religion *per se* as an occasion that would be spoken of as a rival coronation, a notion she revealed in letters to the Duke. It was he, rather than Wallis, who was adamant that, after all he had given up, he was not prepared to make do with some hole-in-the-wall ceremony solely at a French registry office. While various friends and members of his circle had been deputed to sound out the likely response from the new King, Walter Monckton went directly to Lambeth Palace to see Alan Don to find out the best arrangements that could be made. He told the Archbishop's chaplain that the Duke was very obstinate and determined to satisfy his bride with the dignified ceremony he thought she deserved, conducted by a royal chaplain. But Don pointed out that all four Houses of Convocation had lately passed resolutions deprecating the use of the marriage service where groom or bride had a former partner still living. At one stage it had seemed possible that Canon Leonard Andrews, a rector in the diocese of Truro, and therefore having an official connection with the Duchy of Cornwall, might be willing to go to France and officiate. However, as Wigram reportedly told Monckton when the latter tried in early April to organize some sort of religious service, he would 'hound Andrews out of the College of Chaplains for suggesting such a thing'. Not surprisingly, the rector withdrew.

Monckton also pressed for another of the Duke's wishes to be met: that some of the royal family might be present at the wedding. Wigram responded by telling him, as he reported to Archbishop Lang:

that if any of the King's family were present with the approval of HM this would be a firm nail in the coffin of monarchy. I have told the King that he can shelter himself behind Baldwin and the Dominion Prime Ministers and I am sure they would never advise HM to allow any of his family to be present at such a mock ceremony. Fortunately Alec [Hardinge] and I are hand in glove and he says he wants me to continue to deal with this. Excuse this outburst but my religious feelings are really hurt by such monstrous suggestions.

The new King, by retaining the services of both Hardinge and Lascelles, could not have been surprised to be given the sort of advice he was. But the Duke felt that his brother's weakness was being exploited by men who were his old enemies and were still kicking him because they disapproved of Wallis. This was a close-knit group of friends many of whom had been to Harrow and, as Monckton pointed out, Baldwin and Churchill were Old Harrovians too. Edward wrote to his brother begging him to help give him and Wallis a 'dignified background' for their marriage. 'Of course a great deal of the bunk is levelled at Wallis and I can't take it because you must always think of Wallis and myself as one from henceforth ... and anything said or aimed against her hits me a thousand times harder.' Nonetheless King George VI steeled himself to what he perceived his duty, insisting that this was not simply a private family matter and writing to tell his elder brother that none of the family could come out to his wedding: this was something 'I loathe having to do ... but you will appreciate the fact that I cannot do anything else'.

As the Duke searched in vain for a royal chaplain, one man now bravely offered himself for the job: the eccentric vicar of St Paul's, Darlington, the Reverend R. Anderson Jardine. Jardine had been apprenticed to an architect when, aged nineteen, he had experienced a sudden conversion and became a street preacher. After he had taken charge of a chapel in a Yorkshire mining village, his father apparently disinherited him and attempts were made on his life. But he persevered in his chosen calling and, in 1923, was ordained into the Church of England and four years later appointed to the living of St Paul's with a parish of 13,000 souls. But he was a controversial preacher and sometimes described himself now as a faith healer. Jardine explained that when he read in a newspaper that the ex-King could have no religious blessing on his marriage he was so shocked that he could not even finish his breakfast. He went immediately to the bottom of his garden and prayed in an old army tent he kept there. He said he heard a voice telling him he must go to France and offer his services. He wrote to Herman Rogers and learned that the Duke was overjoyed at the prospect of being married by an English clergyman according to the Book of Common Prayer, even if it would not be the full church wedding he might at one time have wished for.

Jardine had already crossed paths with his bishop, Dr Herbert Hensley Henson, Bishop of Durham, and one of the most notable intellectuals of his day. Henson, by deliberately remaining silent when Lang uttered his post-abdication broadside, had earned the respect of the new King and Queen, who did not wish to be seen as part of an establishment attack on their own family. Whatever they thought privately about Lang's comments, they recognized that the speech had not been well received in the nation at large, and Henson was invited to stay at Windsor Castle. Henson himself, although far from being an admirer of the Duke of Windsor, was equally no bigot and in fact was a supporter of A. P. Herbert's divorce Bill. Nonetheless, he declared that 'if any clergyman of his diocese were to marry the Duke he, Henson, as Bishop, would inhibit the man at the doors of his Parish Church' – a threat that in the end he failed to enact.

Henson explained to a small group of influential politicians 'in the quietest and most friendly manner in the world … that in the eyes of the church the Reno divorce of Mrs Simpson (for incompatibility of temper) is not recognised as a divorce by the Church of England [for which adultery was still the only grounds for divorce] and that a marriage with the Duke of Windsor will therefore be doubly bigamous'. Churchill, one of those present, was deeply perturbed 'and said plaintively "but why were we not told this before?"' Aside from the fact that her divorce was granted in Warrenton, Virginia, not Reno, Nevada, and was on the grounds of Win Spencer's (alleged) desertion, the conversation illustrates further the depth of misunderstanding about Wallis. In secular American society her divorce from Spencer was legally valid and she had every reason to believe that it entitled her to marry Ernest Simpson. But the Church was another matter and the King's Proctor had been sent a cutting from the *Washington Herald* dated 7 December 1936 which asserted that, in the eyes of the US Protestant Episcopal Church, Wallis was still the wife of Commander Spencer. 'We neither recognize her divorce from him nor her subsequent marriage and divorce from Ernest Simpson … Regardless of what the English authorities may hold in this diocese she must remain Mrs Spencer until divorced from Commander Spencer under the canons of the church or separated from him by death.'

The violent reaction in the British establishment was provoked by Wallis herself, not merely because she was either American or a double divorcée but because she was also brash. The constant rebuffs made her even less guarded. She wrote to the Duke: 'I blame it all on the wife [Queen Elizabeth] – who hates us both.' But she had little sympathy for the brother either. 'Well who cares, let him be pushed off the throne.' She did not trouble, at the various dinner parties to which she was invited, to hide her views, views which made their way to London where it was noted that she never referred to her future sister-in-law as the new Queen but always as the Duchess of York or by a variety of unflattering nicknames to do with her dress sense or figure. The fact that it had long been recognized, even at the Palace in George V's day, that Americans had different rules for divorce and sometimes 'the ladies being American seems to be sufficient justification for exceptional treatment' was conveniently ignored where Wallis was concerned. She knew of other twice-divorced women – an old friend, Dottie Sands, was one – who were married in church. 'So what?' was her reaction. In a letter addressing the former King as 'Dearest Lightning Brain' because he never seemed to appreciate what the Palace was doing to him she asked: 'Why you have been singled out to be crucified I can't see.'

Nonetheless Henson, however much he may have wanted to take a tough line with Jardine, could actually do little. He issued a statement saying: 'The Rev R. A. Jardine has no authority to officiate outside his parish and diocese. If the Duke's marriage were to take place within the diocese of Durham, the Bishop would inhibit him but the Bishop has no jurisdiction [elsewhere] …' So Jardine made his way to Tours. Also on the road to Candé was the photographer Cecil Beaton, the Duke's lawyers, George Allen and Walter Monckton, and the society florist Constance Spry, a woman who, partly because of her own irregular romantic entanglements and a failed marriage, was a long-standing and sympathetic ally of the Duke and Duchess in their plight and was determined to do all she could to make the day special. Spry had been one of the first to know of the Prince's relationship with Mrs Simpson as they were two of her best customers, and she had firmly insisted to her staff that they must be 'absolutely silent and loyal'.

Immediately after the abdication, Spry's close association with the former King meant that she missed out on the prestigious – and lucrative – Coronation work. Nonetheless, when she received an invitation at very short notice from Wallis to do the floral display for her wedding at the Château de Candé on 3 June she did not hesitate, even though she knew that this would result in further years of lost commissions from the royal family. She went with her assistant Val Pirie to the Paris flower markets and ordered dozens of Madonna lilies and peonies and then went to Val's family home near Tours and picked enough to cram the car with wild flowers, roses and more peonies. Cecil Beaton described the two women as 'laden Ganymedes' who decorated the whole castle with 'magnificent mountains' of flowers. 'The flowers were out of all proportion to the scale of the house and the small numbers of people who would see them,' he recalled. For although the whole place was under siege from a motley crew of well-wishers, reporters, dogs and delivery vans, there were embarrassingly few friends.

Brownlow, believing until a few weeks before the wedding that the Duke might ask him to be his best man, had been helping to advise Wallis with press arrangements for the wedding, suggesting that the journalist Frederick Lonsdale would be the man to come out to the château with him because he is 'as you know a gentleman' who could be relied upon to write the account 'in good style and good taste'. But then he started to receive letters, including one from the Lincolnshire MP Harry Crookshank and one from the Bishop of Lincoln, suggesting that if he or Lady Brownlow attended the wedding 'the Lincolnshire side of your life would become very difficult'. Brownlow was lord lieutenant of the county, a post undertaken by his family for eight generations and one which he valued highly. At the end of the month the Brownlows received their invitation to the wedding as well as a suggestion that they should come out early. Before accepting, Brownlow decided that it would be courteous to obtain the King's consent. But two days later, having learned that the invitation had been refused by courtiers on his behalf, he told Hardinge that he was no longer asking His Majesty for a ruling and had decided to decline the invitation. He always insisted his decision had nothing to do with fears of losing the lord lieutenancy.

Spry did not let the small number of guests dictate how she would decorate the castle and her magnificent floral displays took two days of preparations. She could not help noticing that the ex-King spent hours on his knees pathetically reading old and damp copies of *The Times*, which she had spread out underneath her arrangements.

The wedding day itself dawned warm and sunny. At noon everything stopped while Charles and Fern Bedaux and Herman and Katherine Rogers went out for lunch, braving the waiting crowd at the gates. Among the hundreds of jostling international journalists, two, Randolph Churchill and Charles Murphy of Reuters, were invited in after the ceremony. The small bridal party remained in the castle to eat, with Wallis trying to inject some jollity into the occasion by recounting the story of her maid, who thought that all the palaver was enough to put anyone off getting married. 'I couldn't let the poor girl be put off matrimony for life. I felt it my bounden duty to say: "Oh it's not always as bad as this, but it just happens to be if you're marrying the ex-King of England."' An embarrassed silence met this remark – the irony of a woman embarking on her third marriage explaining why hope continued to triumph over experience presumably was not lost on the assembled diners.

Jardine, 'a comic little man with a red bun face, protruding teeth and a broad grin', according to Beaton, arrived on the morning of 3 June and was immediately introduced to the bridegroom. As they shook hands the ex-King said: 'Thank God you've come thank God you've come. Pardon my language, Jardine, but you are the only one who had the guts to do this for me.' There followed a small crisis over the makeshift altar – an oak chest ('bogus renaissance', according to Cecil Beaton) with carved fat female figures, dragged from the hall into the music room. Wallis shrieked that 'the row of extra women' must be covered up and suggested a tea cloth they had bought as a souvenir in Budapest. There was a further crisis as Jardine refused to have a crucifix on the chest, but no one could immediately produce a plain cross. Then someone remembered the nearby Protestant chapel which obligingly offered theirs. After that was found there appeared to be no more hurdles and the service could get under way.

Wallis's tight pale-blue crepe dress and small matching jacket with a halo-style hat by Reboux has become a defining image of the twentieth century. The colour was chosen by Mainbocher to match her eyes in a shade henceforth called 'Wallis blue', while the style was designed to make her look impossibly thin. At her neck she wore an Art Deco clip of sapphires over a fan of baguette diamonds made for her earlier that year by Van Cleef and Arpels. Such clips became part of Wallis's personal style, copied by others. But in fact Beaton had taken some photographs the day before, mostly outside, as the green walls and pink upholstery did little to set off the pale-blue dress. The most vivid account of the day itself came from Lady Alexandra Metcalfe, daughter of Lord Curzon and wife of the Duke's best man, Fruity Metcalfe, who stepped in belatedly to perform that task when the royal brothers could not attend as supporters. In her unpublished diaries Baba Metcalfe admitted frankly that she was dreading the day and would have 'given a fortune for the train not to stop'. She arrived the night before the wedding and on greeting Wallis noted that she 'had forgotten how unattractive is her voice and manner of speaking'. The Duke, she thought, looked well and in high spirits, but he 'sees through Wallis's eyes, hears through her ears and speaks through her mouth'. Although sad that his staff were unable to come, he 'took badly Perry Brownlow backing out. Wallis not being HRH was the worst blow.'

For weeks both Wallis and the Duke had feared this final rebuff, the likelihood of which was being openly discussed in England. Mary Raffray, still awaiting her own divorce, was following her old schoolfriend's difficulties closely. 'Much as I loathe Wallis, I can't help feeling half pleased half sorry for the slap in the face she's had not being Royal Highness and to me much worse, none of their friends or sycophants going to the wedding. The Brownlows felt it bad for home work and so did most people and I think she was too proud to ask her American friends.'

But the Duke had not been told formally that Wallis was to be refused the status of HRH until Walter Monckton arrived with a letter from the King. In it he tried to explain that, far from taking anything away, the Duke – not being in the line of succession – was not automatically HRH, and he (the King) had actually given him a title by issuing Letters Patent even though the honour was specifically limited to him alone. This formula was contrived by Sir John Simon after an appeal from Wigram, as 'HM hopes you will find some way to avoid this title being conferred'. King George had admitted to Baldwin that he and his family 'all feel that it would be a great mistake to acknowledge Mrs Simpson as a suitable person to become Royal'.

'This is a nice wedding present,' the Duke said when he read the letter. Baba Metcalfe saw the bitterness in both of them. 'He had an outburst to Fruity while dressing for dinner,' she recorded. 'He is through with the family. He will be loyal to the crown but not to the man, his brother. He blames him for weakness in everything.' It was in this mood that a wedding present from the Kents, a Fabergé box, was returned with anguish and disappointment. The Duke felt betrayed by his entire family and had no interest in accepting objects such as this when the one thing he craved, recognition of his wife, was not forthcoming.

The Duke's initial reaction had been to give up his own HRH, but Monckton, who insisted he had always been in favour of granting the honour to the Duchess, together with Wallis, dissuaded him from doing that on the grounds that it would achieve nothing except arouse further satisfaction in London. Eventually they agreed that they would fight the decision, and thereafter the Duke referred to Wallis as Her Royal Highness; household staff were told to address her thus and to curtsey. This confusion created awkwardness for everyone, and the orders were occasionally ignored.

'Wallis has lots to say about the behaviour of friends and family and realises there is no insult they have not heaped on her,' observed Baba. The Metcalfes alone among their friends were always stalwart allies. Wallis kept repeating to Baba her effusive thanks for being there. And there were some who, while critical of the Duke, nonetheless opposed such implied punishment. As Sir Maurice Gwyer,

First Parliamentary Counsel and the ultimate authority on constitutional matters, told Wigram: 'I should have thought myself that an attempt to deprive the Duke's wife of the title of HRH would have the most disastrous results.'

Although most lawyers pointed out then and subsequently that the announcement of Letters Patent was based on fallacious premises and a royal title for the Duchess should have followed automatically from marriage – had it not, then Wallis would after all be marrying the Duke morganatically, which had been ruled out as an impossibility months before – the Duke obviously guessed that there would be strong opposition from his family and therefore had written to his brother in mid-April asking him to announce the Duchess's HRH formally. The request resulted in a flurry of activity, with some courtiers so convinced that the marriage would not last that they feared there would eventually be a number of ex-wives parading as HRH. One can only speculate about what might have happened had the Duke not persisted in asking. However, without such a title they would never live in England and in this way they were effectively kept as exiles.

Baba Metcalfe wrote that, although the wedding was a never-to-be-forgotten occasion, 'perhaps more than the actual ceremony was the rehearsal in the small green drawing room with the organist trying out the music next door. Fruity walks in with HRH and stands on the right of the altar. Wallis on Herman's arm comes in under the tutelage of Jardine . . . they go over the service, Walter, Allen and I watched with such a mixture of feelings. The tune played for "O Perfect Love" was not the proper one so I sang it to the organist and he wrote it down . . . seven English people present at the wedding of the man who, six months ago, was king of England.' The total wedding party comprised Metcalfe and his wife, Charles and Fern Bedaux, Herman and Katherine Rogers, Walter Monckton, Aunt Bessie Merryman, Lady Selby (her husband, Walford Selby, had been advised not to go), Dudley Forwood and George Allen. Just before the ceremony began, a bouquet of red, white and blue flowers tied with a tricolour ribbon, the gift of the French Prime Minister Léon Blum, was delivered, further underlining that there was no official British presence.

Once home, Jardine was offered large sums for the inside story of the wedding. Although he declined and had committed no illegality in giving a religious blessing to a couple who had minutes earlier in the same room been legally married by a French mayor, he found himself ostracized in his parish and repudiated by his Church; within a month he had left England to live in America. Walter Monckton, who would spend many more hours trying to sort out the financial arrangements between the brothers, had a great sense of foreboding that day. He had constantly advised the Duke to be cautious and not inflame matters, but, as he wrote later, he had always been in favour of granting Wallis a title because he foresaw the bitterness that would fester as a result. Once again the Dominions, especially Australia and Canada, were blamed for being immutably opposed to an honour, or rather a style, for someone who had nearly destroyed the Empire. And Wallis well knew how she was loathed in the Empire. Among the piles of hate mail she received, 'the most abusive, oddly enough, came from Canadians, from English people residing in the United States and from Americans of British birth or connections', she noted in her memoirs.

It was a scene of enormous loneliness, hardly the alternative coronation Wallis might have wished for, and both the rivalry and the sense of abandonment were to be played out for another four decades. A telegram from Elizabeth and Bertie insisting 'We are thinking of you with great affection on this your wedding day and send you every wish for future happiness much love' rang eerily hollow.

'It was hard not to cry. In fact I did,' wrote Baba; 'afterwards we shook hands in the salon. I knew I should have kissed her but I just couldn't. In fact I was bad all day: my effort to be charming and to like her broke down. I don't remember wishing her happiness or good luck as though she loved him. One would warm towards her but her attitude is so correct and hard. The effect is of an older woman unmoved by the infatuated love of a younger man.'

'I explained to her after the wedding', wrote Walter Monckton, 'that she was disliked because she had been the cause of the Duke giving up the throne but that if she made him happy that would change. If she made him unhappy nothing would be too bad for her. She took it very simply and kindly just saying: "Walter, don't you think I have thought of all that? I think I can make him happy."'

Wallis at War

*'And with all her charity, she had not a word
to say for "That Woman"'*

Having failed to make Wallis his queen or even win her a royal title, having failed to give her a dignified wedding blessed by a royal chaplain, having failed to convince the world, let alone his own family, what a uniquely wonderful woman Wallis was and how worthy of all those things, having instead forced her to hide under car seats and to be abused, threatened or insulted, the Duke of Windsor's natural tendency towards self-abasement and flagellation was now redoubled. A feeling that he had somehow let Wallis down, although Wallis herself had been clear-eyed about the royal family's disinclination to welcome her, set the ground rules for their marriage. He had believed right to the last that his brothers would attend his wedding. When they did not, this most bitter blow on top of all the others made him feel that he could never do enough to make up to Wallis for all, as he perceived it, that she had been forced to endure, and because he felt so blessed by having her as his wife. In the short term this meant fighting for money he believed due to him, especially 'considering the position I shall have to maintain and what I have given up'. When she was ill or in pain from neuralgia he rushed her to the best doctors and dentists, while praying that the pain would disappear 'as I can't bear to see her suffering'. And she, in turn, determined to give the Duke whatever she could to make up for what he had abandoned, especially where a display of material possessions was concerned.

Dudley Forwood recalled one evening when the Duchess appeared 'beautifully dressed as always but blazing with rings, earrings, brooches, bracelets and necklaces and almost stooping under their weight. I said "Ma'am I wonder if you aren't wearing a few too many jewels?" She said "You forget that I am the Duchess of Windsor. I shall never let the Duke down."'

The honeymoon was spent largely at Schloss Wasserleonburg, a secluded castle in the Carinthian mountains belonging to a cousin of their friend Lord Dudley. En route they stopped in Venice, where Mussolini's Fascist government had arranged an impressive array of gondolas and flowers to meet the newlyweds. And then, at last, they were left in peace.

In her memoirs Wallis wrote disingenuously that she 'recognised with incredulity' a note awaiting her on the morning tray sent by Ernest about ten days after the abdication. But she had no reason to be surprised since she had been writing to him from the moment when she first felt so alone facing the crowd of reporters in Ipswich. More surprising than Ernest writing to her – 'you may rest assured that no one has felt more deeply for you than I have' – is that she continued to write to her second husband even while on her honeymoon with her third. She told him: 'I think of us so much, though I try not to.' She craved news about him: 'I wonder so often how you are? How the business is getting on etc. I thought I'd write a few lines to say I'd love to hear from you if you feel like telling me a bit.' She admitted she was at least peaceful in the mountains and trying 'to recover from these terrible months that we all went through before starting out in the future. I have gathered up courage for that,' she wrote from Schloss Wasserleonburg.

But it was peace thanks to material comforts rather than peace from passionate love that she had found and she knew that Ernest understood that. 'The dual side of my nature will out and you filled my one side so utterly. If we could only have done these things. Anyway I shall always be struggling with myself to the grave and whereas other people will become happy I shall never be able to answer either of my sides satisfactorily. If only one of me was stronger than the other,' she wrote with remarkably Freudian insight into her own personality. 'I am so glad you won your suit. I knew you would,' she concluded. In fact the case against Mrs Sutherland had been settled out of court and Ernest contented himself with costs.

From Wasserleonburg, as she told Ernest, she and the Duke were travelling around Europe to Budapest and Vienna, 'as well as to Czechoslovia [sic] (wrong I'm sure) for more shooting ... Then a city for a dentist'. In the years to come, Wallis was often in need of dental treatment. They returned to Venice for an occasional day and even managed a visit to Salzburg, a surprising outing given the Duke's dislike of opera. By the end of September they had done enough travelling and finished up in Paris, staying mostly at the Hôtel Meurice, while they looked for a house, the Duke all the while wondering how soon he could return to England. They did not find anything suitable until February 1938, when they rented a house at Versailles, but later that year they moved again to a more solid and substantial mansion on the Boulevard Suchet, which offered possibilities for entertaining on a regal scale. Mary Kirk, who became Ernest Simpson's third wife in November 1937, heard about the house from a mutual friend and wrote in her diary: 'it was deeply interesting what he told me about being there ... going over the house from top to bottom there was not ONE single book in it'.

Wallis was unsettled. Although they had visitors there was an awkwardness of which she was only too aware:

> As for all one's 'friends', I think they find it very difficult to know anybody but the new regime though I must say they all put in unexpected appearances in Paris. But then even a title of peculiar origin and a slight idea that the Duke may be heard from in the future is enough to bring that type of English to one's side ... It is horrid having no home & living like snails yet how difficult to decide where to live with every country quivering.

'I don't agree it was fate,' she insisted to Ernest, but 'a woman's ambition which has left a wound that will never heal and a woman's pride were the causes. I curse the latter because it made me lose control. The former was Mary's way to be satisfied, the latter pushed me over the cliff. Anyway I shall write about it again. It is very painful and it is too late. Wherever you are you can be sure that never a day goes by without some hours thought of you & for you & again in my eanum prayers at night. With love, Wallis.' Her use of the word 'eanum' in a letter to her ex-husband reveals a surprising assumption of his familiarity with what had been part of the lovers' private language.

From now on there is an appalling sense of aimlessness to the Duke and Duchess's lives compounded by abandonment by their friends. Above all they were cut off from sources of good advice, which left them alarmingly vulnerable. Walter Monckton and Winston Churchill both retained a strong sense of obligation towards a former monarch, the latter from a more romantic standpoint but at some cost to his own reputation, the former constantly counselling patience while hoping to counteract what he called 'influences working the other way', that is Wallis. Another source of advice was Bernard Rickatson-Hatt, Ernest's old friend, still editor in chief at Reuters, who played something of a double game in the post-abdication years, offering the Duke occasional advice on public relations and Ernest and Mary occasional press seats for events as well as titbits about the lives of the royal exiles. The Duke asked Rickatson-Hatt, whenever there was negative publicity about Wallis, to contradict the statements or give 'the lie to false rumours . . . What is vitally important to us . . . is that any renewal of newspaper interest in us should be met with good publicity.' So, for example, when they were invited for dinner by the British Ambassador in Paris, Rickatson-Hatt was asked to ensure that the occasion was given what would now be called a favourable spin. The Duke was grateful and told Rickatson-Hatt, who sent on some clippings, how pleased he was 'that your friends co-operated so willingly . . . Wallis and I have been greatly amused over the Buck House attitude: not the King's of course, but that of the same old Palace enemies.'

But where once he had been surrounded by counsellors, now there were none. In this abyss it is easy to see how alluring was the advice of his host at Tours, Charles Bedaux. Bedaux had substantial business interests in Germany and was keen to use the Duke to further these. The idea of the Duke and Duchess making a trip to Nazi Germany had been in his mind from the first and he broached it with the Duke even before the wedding. The Duke needed little persuasion that such a visit would be a good way to cement ties between the two royal families, broken after the First World War, and thus promote peace. The trip genuinely appealed to his belief that, if he could study the housing and working conditions of the German labour force, there might come a time when such knowledge would be useful, and an announcement in August that the Duke wished to make a study of working conditions in various countries was read with alarm in London to mean that he was doing so with a view to returning to England at a later date as a champion of the working classes.

In fact there was another, more pressing reason why the idea so appealed. A visit to Germany afforded a real opportunity for Wallis to sample a state visit, a chance for her to experience something of what it was like to be the wife of someone who commanded the respect of a major power; most Germans had a high regard for the Duke, with his often stated love of Germany. At Oxford his German tutor had been the influential Professor Hermann Fiedler, a man who in May 1937 wrote to *The Times* that he was 'appalled' that Oxford had refused to send an official representative to celebrate the 150th anniversary of Göttingen University, by then purged of Jews. Yet even Mensdorff, the Austro-Hungarian diplomat, was surprised at the strength of his pro-German feelings. Recording a talk he had had with the Prince in 1933, he declared that, having been summoned to see him at 5 p.m. the previous day, 'I am still under his charm.' He went on:

> It is remarkable how he expressed his sympathies for the Nazis in Germany. 'Of course it is the only thing to do, we will have to come to it, as we are in great danger from the Communists here, too.' He naturally condemns the peace Treaty [Versailles, 1919]. 'I hope and believe we shall never fight a war again,' he commented. 'But if so we must be on the winning side and that will be the German, not the French' ... I asked him how he imagined that one got out of the National Socialist dictatorship ... He seemed not to have thought very much about these questions. It is, however, interesting and significant that he shows so much sympathy for Germany and the Nazis.

Dudley Forwood believed that the most compelling motive for the visit was to give Wallis a taste of being queen, 'and when the Foreign

Office and George VI asked him not to go, he felt … they'd been bloody to me why the hell should I do what they want? They denied my wife her right. It showed his great respect for the throne that even on this most vexed question he would never in public question his brother the King but in private … it hurt him a lot.' Relations with his family were now strained almost to breaking point. As the Duke told Walter Monckton, he embarked on the trip in the wake of 'a series of rather tricky letters I have had to write to bring home to my mother and the King how sore I feel from their humiliating treatment of me ever since I left England in December.'

The Windsors went by train from Paris to Berlin in early October and there to greet them on the Friedrichstrasse station platform were a number of Nazi leaders, including Dr Robert Ley, the boorish, alcoholic leader of the Nazi National Labour Front, but from the British Embassy there was only a junior member of staff. That night Ley gave a magnificent banquet in their honour at which several of the most senior German leaders were present, among them Goebbels, Himmler, Hess and Ribbentrop – the latter, according to the British Ambassador Sir Eric Phipps, pronounced himself delighted by the trip, declaring that 'HRH will some day have a great influence over the British working man'. They were taken to visit various housing projects, hospitals and youth camps in Dresden, Nuremberg, Stuttgart and Munich by Ley in his enormous and powerful Mercedes, and local authorities were instructed always to refer to Wallis as Her Royal Highness – and they did not disobey. The visit was well covered in British newspapers which showed the Duke, relishing an opportunity to speak German, clearly enjoying himself even when visiting a beer hall in Munich. They went by train to see a major German coalmine, deep in the Ruhr at Kamp-Lintfort, 'because it was known how pro-German he was', according to a woman, whose father accompanied the Duke on that occasion. 'There was jubilation at the Kamp to have a former King visit. He was totally enraptured by the technical innovations of the German mining industry,' she recalled.

Wallis, uninterested in the politics, could not resist writing naively to Ernest about the tour: 'This is a most interesting trip, though very strenuous, starting at 8 am each morning and ending at 5. Tomorrow, to vary the tour a bit, we take the train at 7.15 am. Peter Pan is determined to help working conditions. He really likes those people much better than any of us – and I'm sure they are much nicer.'

But she did not write to him about the climax of the trip, a meeting with the Führer himself at his mountain home, the Berghof, just outside Salzburg. Since it came three days after the pro-appeasement British Foreign Secretary, Lord Halifax, had called on Hitler hoping to come to some permanent agreement with Germany over its expansionist aims, the Duke's visit had the effect of encouraging Hitler further in his belief, however erroneous, that when the time came to install a puppet government in England the Duke would be willing to be restored to the British throne with Wallis as queen. There are several photos recording the historic meeting but none more evocative than that showing the Duchess smiling broadly and enjoying the pomp and pageantry as the Führer leans over to kiss her hand while the Duke looks on proudly.

After the war the Duke wrote: '[The] Führer struck me as a somewhat ridiculous figure, with his theatrical posturings and his bombastic pretensions.' But Dudley Forwood, also a German-speaker, who was present at the hour-long meeting, gave a different account: 'My Master said to Hitler the Germans and the British races are one, they should always be one. They are of Hun origin.' Wallis was not included in the private interview. She was offered tea by the fireplace with Rudolf Hess instead. Later she insisted that when she asked the Duke afterwards what he had discussed he told her, 'I'd never allow myself to get into a political discussion with him!'

'His tour was ill-timed and ill-advised but not a crime,' is Philip Ziegler's sober assessment. Since the Duke had agreed to make no formal speeches while in Germany there are at least no words to be quoted back at him. But the grainy newspaper images showing a smiling Wallis and Edward meeting uniformed Nazi leaders against a vivid backdrop of swastikas, flags and jackboots have become indelibly imprinted in the public imagination. By not condemning any aspect of the German social experiment, the Duke was tacitly condoning it and thus allowing himself to be used by the Germans. For Queen Mary there was a still greater crime, and one that solidified with time: forsaking his sacred duty as king of a glorious empire. She was not afraid to make her views known to her son.

Meanwhile Charles Bedaux was busy organizing another, rather grander tour for the Duke and Duchess, a visit to the United States, which Wallis had told Ernest would last a month and feature more visits to factories in an attempt to examine working conditions in America. But, in the wake of the German trip, it was clear that a visit to America would prove disastrous on several counts, principally because the American labour unions hated Bedaux for what they saw as his brutal ideas about workers' efficiency. According to Dudley Forwood, 'they could not even vouch for his security'.

And it was the projected American trip that caused so much ill-feeling in London.

The fear at Court – the King and Queen advised by Hardinge and Lascelles – was that the Duke, behaving abominably, was trying to stage a come-back. Coincidentally, the British Ambassador in Washington, Sir Ronald Lindsay, was on home leave while the trip was being discussed and he argued that if the Duke went ahead with the visit he should be accorded the full courtesies of the Embassy. Lindsay could feel the King's continued sense of vulnerability vis-à-vis his brother, 'and up to a certain point he is like the medieval monarch who has a hated rival claimant living in exile'. Lindsay recognized that there were many grounds for objecting to this trip, but recorded that Queen Elizabeth's view was that:

> while the men spoke in terms of indignation she spoke in terms of acute pain and distress, ingenuously expressed and deeply felt. She, too, is not a great intellect but she has any amount of *intelligence du coeur* ... In all she said there was far more grief than indignation and it was all tempered by affection for 'David'. He's so changed now and he used to be so kind to us. She was backing up everything the men said but protesting against anything that seemed vindictive ... and with all her charity she had not a word to say for 'That Woman'.

The new King and Queen were not yet ready to make any state visits themselves and their first was not to be until 1938 when they went to

Paris. Queen Elizabeth was acutely sensitive to the damage being inflicted on her husband by living out this unexpected public duty and laid the blame squarely at Wallis's feet. In response to a remark just after the Paris trip that the Duchess of Windsor had 'done much for the Duke – stopped him drinking – no more pouches under his eyes', she retorted, 'Yes, who has the lines under his eyes now?'

So although the suggestion that they should visit North America, combining a tour of Canada with a trip to the United States, had already been mooted as early as 1937 when the Canadian Prime Minister, William Mackenzie King, came to London for the Coronation, such a tour needed careful planning. It was felt that, once people had had an opportunity to see the new King and Queen in person, the wounds from the abdication and the loss of such a popular monarch as Edward VIII would be finally healed. And President Roosevelt was also keen for such a visit but, by the time all the arrangements had been made, it did not actually take place until May 1939, making it a deeply significant trip given the worsening situation in Europe. The idea of the Duke and Duchess of Windsor making a tour of North America in 1937, advised by such dubious friends as Charles Bedaux and in advance of the new King and Queen, could only be interpreted as a blatant attempt to upstage the British sovereign.

When Wallis wrote to Ernest, who was in New York, on 30 October, just a year after her divorce, she knew the US trip was hopeless: 'Ernest dear, What can I say when I am standing beside the grave of everything that was us and <u>our</u> laughter rings in my ears over "letter from New York". My opinion is the same only more strong than that because the events in London more than proved what we were laughing about. Only oh my very dear, dear Ernest I can only cry as I say farewell and press your hand very tightly and pray to God. Wallis.' In fact, the Duke did not call off the trip until 6 November when he made a statement in *The Times* denying that he was 'allied to any industrial system ... or for or against any particular political or racial doctrine'. From now on a sense of despair inflamed his already raw bitterness against his family, especially his mother and sister-in-law whom he blamed for the situation.

Whether the Windsors would return to Britain was a constant source of gossip, and Mary Simpson's diary reflects this at a personal level. 'Life in London would be unbearable for us if they lived here too,' she wrote on a November day in 1938 reflecting on a meeting between the Windsors and the Duke and Duchess of Gloucester who happened to be in Paris. Prince Henry, who had married Lady Alice Montagu Douglas Scott three years before, had never been especially close to Edward. But as Mary perceived:

> This really makes them respectable. It's funny when I think of all the things we did together at school, how we fought, how we hated and loved each other, how jealous we were until we both married, then it was so different ... however, memories aside, if she comes back to England ... I won't let it disturb me ... I feel that I'm lucky now not to feel more bitterness. But if they lived here I believe it would poison my life ... everyone would want to curry favour in the higher sphere and I think she'd see to it that life was difficult on that score for us.

Walter Monckton, the skilful go-between, was well aware that the Queen and Queen Mary remained implacably opposed to the Windsors' return, whether for a brief visit or for a prolonged stay. As long as Wallis was denied her royal appellation and the dignity of being received, it was unlikely she would return, which was what both Queens wanted. 'He couldn't come back. You can't have two kings,' was Elizabeth's view. Her mother-in-law agreed and, while feeling sorry for her son, genuinely believed 'of course we know she is at the back of it'. But in February 1939 Monckton tried to move things forward and asked to see Queen Mary to enquire whether she would receive the Duke and Duchess if they came to London. When she sent a message to say she would not, Monckton asked King George to give the Duke some hope that he and the Duchess would eventually be received. 'To put the matter at its lowest, I find it increasingly difficult to keep him quiet ... I should hate to see any open controversy about it.'

The refusal to meet Monckton, as well as an argument with his family over the dedication to his father George V's tomb, was the catalyst for an eruption from the Duke, who finally wrote to his mother accusing her of destroying any remaining feelings he had for his family and adding that 'You … & BERTIE, BY HIS IGNO-MINIOUS CAPITULATION TO THE WILES OF HIS AMBI-TIOUS WIFE, have made further normal correspondence between us impossible.'

Throughout all of this Winston Churchill remained doggedly loyal to his former sovereign. Having argued in 1936 that the King should not be hurried into abdicating, he now wrote supportively to the Duke after the German tour, informed by his son Randolph who had been reporting it. 'I was rather afraid beforehand that your tour in Germany would offend the great numbers of anti-Nazis in this country, many of whom are your friends and admirers, but I must admit that it does not seem to have had that effect and I am so glad it all passed off with so much distinction and success.' He also did his best to ensure a suitable financial settlement for the Duke and Duchess. As he confided to his wife: 'HMG are preparing a dossier about the DOW's finances, debts and spendings on acct. of Cutie wh I fear they mean to use to his detriment when the Civil List is considered.'

Churchill was well aware that the King had informally promised, at Fort Belvedere at the time of the abdication, to ensure that his brother received £25,000 a year, if necessary paid for by himself, as a pension. But all discussions about money had been poisoned by revelations that the Duke was in fact far better off than he had led his brother to believe. The Duke defended his position by arguing that he was badly off and that his personal fortune – according to George Allen he had deposited £800,000 abroad, with a large part of it under the control of Mrs Simpson – was irrelevant to the £25,000 which he looked upon in the light of rent for Sandringham and Balmoral, both left to him in his father's will. As it soon became clear that the House of Commons was in no mood to vote the Duke money from the Civil List and no one wanted an acrimonious parliamentary debate on the matter, the haggling dragged on unpleasantly for months and the size and nature of the Duke's pension was not finally settled until 1938. Churchill did all he could to avoid a discussion in the Civil List Committee, arguing that for the maintenance of the honour and dignity of the Crown, the Duke should be dealt with as one of the King's sons, not as an outcast.

Churchill, whatever his private thoughts about 'Cutie', made a point of visiting the Windsors in the South of France, where they now rented a magnificent villa in Cap d'Antibes called the Château de la Croë, hidden behind high walls on a twelve-acre estate over-looking the Mediterranean. Wallis tried as best she could, with the help of interior designers such as Elsie Mendl, to recreate here the palatial and royal residence she believed her husband deserved. They had liveried servants, who were never quite paid the going rate but were asked to refer to the Duchess within the household as Her Royal Highness, and there were reminders everywhere of a past regal life. Pride of place in the drawing room was given to the imposing desk at which the ex-King had sat to sign the Instrument of Abdication; it was a piece of furniture that they tried to ensure followed them to every house in which they lived. The dogs, too, followed them everywhere – three spoiled Cairn terriers called Pookie, Detto and Prisie who were often literally spoon-fed from silver bowls by the Duke or Duchess meals that had been especially prepared for them. The Windsors' dogs increasingly were the children they never had but were indulged as no royal nanny would ever allow royal children to be indulged. Churchill explained to his hostess, Maxine Elliott, at the end of 1937: 'There is just one uncertainty that faces me on 5th [January 1938]: the Duke is leaving on 6th and I have to go and see him on 5th ... whatever he suggests I shall have to do as I have not seen him since that dark day when he left our country and, as you know, I am a devoted servant.'

Clemmie, harsher than her husband in her judgements on the Windsors, was less devoted and Winston even had to coax her into writing a thank-you to the Duke, who had sent them a Christmas card. 'You can refer to her as the Duchess, thus avoiding the awkward point,' he advised. In fact, both Clemmie and Winston were scru-pulous over the years in unfailingly bowing or curtseying to the Duchess. When they finally met for dinner at Maxine's villa early in 1938, the house that the Windsors had so nearly rented the previous year instead of the *Nahlin*, he reported back: 'The W's are very pathetic, but also very happy. She made an excellent impression on me and it looks as if it would be a most happy marriage ...' Harold Nicolson, who met them at the same dinner party, was also struck by their dilemma. As an excuse for the couple's late arrival the Duke said: 'Her Royal Highness couldn't drag herself away. He had said it. The three words fell into the circle like three words into a pool. Her (gasp) Royal (shudder) Highness (and not one eye dared to meet another).' Later in the evening Nicolson had a chance to talk to the Duchess and she left him in no doubt that living in England again was what they both wanted; 'after all', she told him, 'I don't want to spend all my life in exile'. Matters cooled slightly thanks to Colin Davidson, a young equerry, who warned the Duke that 'every time they heard in England that he was doing it [referring to his wife as HRH] the reconciliation and the arrangements for his return were probably retarded'. Bravely, to set an example, Davidson refused to bow to the Duchess himself.

And so the Windsors remained, perching in France, constantly hoping to be given word that a return to Britain was in order. In the Duke's mind, a visit in spring 1939 seemed possible – that was already a delay from a suggested November visit – and Monckton too thought that the new King's position was firmly enough established that a short private visit then would cause no embarrassment and break the ice. As the Duke's friends (and lawyers) continued to point out, permanent exile had never been intended in 1936. Allowing the situation to fester was insulting. When the Duke sought legal advice he was told by counsel that nothing short of an Act of Parliament could rob a British subject of his right to return to the UK. As Churchill wrote to his wife two years after the abdication, 'They do not want him to come, but they have no power to stop him.' The power was vested in the refusal to grant Wallis a royal appendage.

Walter Monckton became their only channel of official communication, and Wallis was frank with him. 'This is just a reminder', she wrote in February, should he feel inclined to speak to Neville Chamberlain, who had been prime minister since 1937, 'about the rather difficult position the British Embassy has put the Duke of

Windsor in as regards the reaction of the French themselves and their Embassies here. After all we live in foreign countries to please England therefore why must England make this more unpleasant? The ambassador here did <u>not</u> answer HRH's letter and as I said we are never asked there. It is a small thing but an unnecessary insult to the brother of the King.' Colin Davidson reinforced the same message in letters to Monckton:

> The public must soon realise that she is making him very happy and that she must have some reward. And that the only way to manage him is to refrain from what he thinks is insulting him. If only his family would sink their own personal disinclinations to treat her as his wife, I feel they would be doing a National Service. She may be a little common and twice divorced but nevertheless she is the legal wife of the ex-King of England and after all he did abdicate. He was not kicked out.

A Gallup poll conducted in 1939 concluded that 61 per cent of the British public wanted the Windsors to return to England, with only 16 per cent opposed.

But there were constant delays, deliberate or not, caused by indecision over where they would stay, who would meet them on arrival and where, and the form of words to be issued in pre-visit statements to clarify who had instigated the meeting. Because of the importance of this 'greater question', Wallis exercised enormous self-restraint in reacting to the press and turned away myriad requests for interviews. She hated the relentless media intrusion which had destroyed her peace of mind. Nonetheless, she did not object to being named in 1938 one of the ten best-dressed women in the world, an accolade she was careful to retain for the next four decades. But she did relent in the spring of 1939, telling Alice Henning of the London *Sunday Dispatch* that she and the Duke 'in many ways live more quietly than the average married couple ... I expect to take my husband's name and rank, that is all. And I expect ordinary human graciousness in human relationships.' She went on to discuss the dresses I wear 'and all that ... Those are not the real things of life. I hope as I grow older I realise it.'

Then two months later in May, just as the King and Queen finally sailed to the United States, the Duke was invited by Fred Bate, head of British and European operations at the National Broadcasting Company of America and an old friend of the Windsors, to make a speech on the world situation pleading for peace. The Duke wrote the broadcast himself without advice, and at some point it was decided that it would have greater impact if he made it from Verdun after a visit to the battlefield. Following a genuinely heartfelt appeal for peace, he concluded: 'I personally deplore for example the use of such terms as "encirclement" and "aggression". They can only arouse just those dangerous political passions that it should be the aim of us all to subdue.' Although some, especially Americans, wrote to praise the Duke, the BBC decided not to carry the broadcast; 'aggression' was precisely the word to describe Hitler's activities in Austria and Czechoslovakia and there was a feeling that having abdicated the Duke had no right to step so clearly into the political arena. Mary Simpson, knowing Fred Bate, concluded that the notion they just happened to be at Verdun was 'blatant hypocrisy . . . eyewash' and wondered 'how people could be such fools and rogues' to believe it. The broadcast did nothing to advance the Duke's case and so the months passed without agreement on a return, the Duke now urging an autumn 1939 visit rather than an August one, when he feared his friends would be away.

But by August 1939 war was imminent and the issue of his return became acute. Monckton was now fielding pressing requests from the Duke to do appropriate war work while insisting on suitable arrangements being made for his return journey to England. Could the French government help him with the removal and storage of his effects in France, he asked, evidently feeling himself entitled to such assistance, which Monckton felt, in the current chaos and panic, he was not. As other British subjects were fleeing as fast as they could from France, the Duke and Duchess would have to make the best arrangements they could by themselves, he believed. Then, at the end of August, the Duke sent a telegram to Hitler pleading for peace. 'Remembering your courtesy and our meeting two years ago I address to you my entirely personal simple though earnest appeal for your utmost influence towards the peaceful solution of the present problem.' Hitler replied on 2 September, the day after Germany had invaded Poland, assuring the Duke 'that my attitude towards England remains the same'. The next day England was at war with Germany, and suddenly the question of how to get the Windsors home became urgent.

Lady Alexandra Metcalfe was incensed by the way the Windsors were treated at this time. Writing a full account in her diary she said that once it had been decided that they had to return to England 'they were offered no accommodation anywhere so I invited them to stay at South Hartfield [the Metcalfe home in Sussex] ... not only were no rooms offered to the Windsors during their visit but no car was made available to meet them. Walter asked the Palace but was told nothing was going to be done from that quarter so they were our guests.' Walter Monckton recorded later, in a succinct account of the arrangements to bring the Duke and Duchess back to England, that he had offered on the eve of war to send the King's personal plane to Antibes but that the Duke wired the night before refusing to make the journey unless promised accommodation at Windsor. 'I was therefore compelled to cancel the flight and war was declared with the Duke and Duchess still at Antibes.'

But the reality of events in those tense days of early September was far more dramatic. Wallis was terrified of flying, especially in such a small plane, a fear that was aggravated by the Duke's anger at the way his family was treating them. Fruity Metcalfe, deeply upset by the Duke's refusal of the King's plane, fed Monckton a vivid account of the overwrought atmosphere. 'The lady here is in a panic, the worst fear I've ever seen or heard of – all on account of the aeroplane journey, talks of jumping out, etc.'

So when Monckton told the Duke on 2 September that he was coming in the morning with a pilot and should be at Cannes by 10 a.m. and that he hoped they would be ready, the Duke responded by asking how many people the plane could carry. When told just four he asked Monckton why it was necessary for him [Monckton] to come too as he would take up valuable space on the return journey which he wanted for luggage. Monckton said he had been told to fly out in the hope that he could help. The Duke then asked what was to be their destination in the UK, and insisted that unless his brother was ready to have him and his wife to stay in one of their houses, they would not return to England. Nevertheless, he said, he still wanted the plane to take Metcalfe and a secretary back home. Monckton reported this conversation to Hardinge, who decided that the flight would not take place at all under the circumstances. The next day, 3 September, there was further communication between the Duke and the British Embassy in Paris, with the Duke telling the Ambassador that the plane would have to make two journeys, because in addition to himself and the Duchess there was also Metcalfe, a secretary, a maid and luggage as 'they could not be expected to arrive in England for a war with only a grip'. He thought a destroyer in one or two days' time would definitely be a better plan. Metcalfe, appalled by this behaviour, did not shirk from telling them that in his view they had 'behaved as two spoiled children ... women and children are being bombed and killed while YOU talk of your PRIDE'. Monckton did indeed fly out to the Windsors in the first week of September in an attempt to explain in person how things stood. In the event, Churchill, who was now First Lord of the Admiralty, organized a destroyer, as the Duke had wanted all along. HMS *Kelly*, commanded by Lord Louis 'Dickie' Mountbatten, sailed to Cherbourg to bring home the former monarch and his wife. They were met on 12 September at Portsmouth by Alexandra Metcalfe and Walter Monckton. There were no members of the royal family.

'We arrived at about 6.30 p.m. and went to the Queen's Hotel,' wrote Baba Metcalfe in her diary.

We booked a ghastly red plush double room for Wallis and HRH. Luckily the C-in-C of Portsmouth played up well and said he would put them up ... At 8.30 p.m. a message came to say the Destroyer Kelly with the Windsors on board would be in at about 9.30 p.m. We went down to the Dock (the same one from which Walter saw HRH off after the abdication). A Guard of Honour of one hundred men, wearing tin hats and gas masks, was drawn up and a strip of red carpet was laid to the gangway ... This part of the show was done bang up, all due to Winston, who had given orders for the Windsors to be received with all due ceremony ... Walter and I went first, followed by the Admiral. After a lot of handshaking and guard reviewing, we went down and had dinner in Dickie's cabin. Fruity had made the whole trip with the Windsors by motor, from the South of France to Cherbourg, where Winston had sent Randolph to meet them ... Later we all went to Admiralty House [in Portsmouth] and left the Windsors there for the night. Fruity and I, Walter and Randolph went to the Queen's Hotel, where Fruity and I had the ghastly plush suite. Next morning, I went to fetch the Windsors in my car, while Fruity drove our van with their luggage ... The Duke never once gave the impression of feeling and sensing the sadness of his first return after the drama of his departure.

Apart from one sentimental visit to the overgrown Fort Belvedere, Wallis and Edward spent most days at the Metcalfes' London house, 16 Wilton Place. It was here with the furniture under dust sheets, that the Duke's business was transacted: clerks, secretaries, War Office officials, boot makers, tailors and hairdressers all streamed in and out, fed by sandwiches and tea from a Thermos flask. Two weeks later, reflecting on the visit, Baba wrote: 'There have been moments when the ice seemed dangerously thin and ominous cracks have been heard but night has brought a thickening up and we have skated on.'

Wallis did not cause a fuss over the way her husband's family ignored her; she almost accepted it and displayed some dignity in doing so. 'So far as David's family, or the court, were concerned, I simply did not exist,' she observed later. That was not quite true of course, but she did not exist as the Duchess of Windsor and, when not referred to as 'That Woman', she was still, after more than two years of marriage to the Duke, 'Mrs S'. When the Duke went to visit his brother to see what job he would be given, he went alone. It had been prearranged by Monckton and Hardinge that neither of the wives, Wallis nor Elizabeth, would be present. Baba admired Wallis for the way she was able to restrain the often irate Duke, who was always eager to fire off a letter or react to the insults. 'All things considered, they have been very grateful, sweet and completely simple,' she concluded. As the years went on it often fell to Wallis to persuade the Duke not to fight his family to obtain 'justice' for her.

At the end of September, the Duke returned to France to take up his new job outside Paris assigned to the British Military Mission, with Fruity Metcalfe appointed his ADC. According to Wallis, this was not the job he wanted and he would have preferred to stay in Britain in a civil defence post that had first been offered. Nonetheless they went, travelling back again to Cherbourg in a destroyer, with Wallis crouching on the floor of the captain's cabin this time as the ship rolled around in rough seas, the Duke in shock at his isolation from his family. Baba noted: 'I see endless trouble ahead with the job in Paris . . . I do think the Family might have done something. Except for one visit to the King, the Duke might not exist. Wallis said they realised there was no place ever for him in this country and she saw no reason for him ever to return.'

With the Duke stationed at Vincennes, Wallis moved first into a hotel in Versailles from where she joined a French relief organization, the *Colis de Trianon*, but only after she had been rebuffed by the various British agencies. She poured out her heart to Walter Monckton, as she was often to do in the years ahead:

> I have in fact given both time and money to the French, having waited for some time to see what attitude would be taken by the numerous British organisations formed here for British troops. It soon became apparent that there was no use waiting to be of use to them. Had I had some backing from the Embassy or GHQ I think I could have been useful regarding the canteens in the station. The young British officers there were longing to have some helpers in the French canteens that knew and speak English.

So she decided to move back into their house on the Boulevard Suchet and took a job with the *Section Sanitaire Automobile* (SSA) of the French Red Cross, delivering plasma, bandages and cigarettes to the hospitals behind the Maginot Line in eastern France. 'I was busier and perhaps more useful than I had ever been in my life,' she admitted. Realizing that the British press would not write about her activities, the Duke urged Rickatson-Hatt to get his wife some publicity for her work visiting hospitals and the forward areas of the French army and carrying out other duties on behalf of the SSA. He sent Rickatson-Hatt a long account of how Wallis was billeted within the sound of gunfire and had much interesting information about the conditions in which French troops were living at the front. But British views of her remained unchanged by knowledge of such work, which in any case did not last long. While the Duke was stationed at Vincennes they saw each other rarely, but then, on 10 May 1940, Germany invaded the Netherlands, quickly broke through French defences and threatened Paris. It was time once again to flee.

Desperate families, loading all their possessions on to carts or car roofs, jammed the roads out of Paris. With the help of their chauffeur George Ladbroke, the Duke and Wallis (she never learned to drive) joined the jostling hordes on the road to Biarritz on the Spanish border. The Duke deposited Wallis there and then returned to his job in Paris. Two weeks later he was back, his need to be with his wife so over-powering that he now abandoned his oldest and most loyal friend, Fruity Metcalfe, without a word of warning, leaving him to make his own way back to England without any means of transport. Not surprisingly Metcalfe saw this as a callous disregard of twenty years of friendship and threatened never to forgive him. 'He deserted his job in 1936, well he's deserted his country now, at a time when every office boy and cripple is trying to do what he can. It is the end,' he told his wife. Philip Ziegler defends the Duke on the grounds that he probably left Paris with the approval – indeed to the relief – of the Military Mission. More significantly perhaps, the Duke also understood that at a time when everyone else seemed to be against the Duchess, he had to be with her to support and defend her. From Biarritz the pair went to their home at Château de la Croë and waited there for news of the German advance and French collapse. It was agreed with the British Embassy in Madrid that the Duke and Duchess were to get to Spain somehow ahead of the fleeing French government whose members it was expected the Germans would try to bomb once they arrived at Perpignan. In mid-June they set off in convoy with the Duke's equerry, Major Gray Phillips, driving through the night, camping where they could, intending to get to officially neutral Spain. But the Spanish Fascist leader, General Franco, was far from a reliable friend of Britain and it was clear that this was only a temporary post and they would have to be moved on as quickly as possible.

On 22 June 1940, the day the new French leader, Marshal Pétain, signed an armistice with Hitler, it became known to the British government that the Windsors had arrived in Barcelona. The Foreign Office telegraphed to the Madrid Embassy: 'Please invite their Royal Highnesses to proceed to Lisbon.' As Michael Bloch points out, this was the most critical moment of the war, the French defeat having left Britain dangerously alone now to fight the Germans. 'Yet Hardinge, the King's secretary, could find time to write to the FO reprimanding the official who had used the forbidden words "Their Royal Highnesses" and expressing the King's desire that steps be taken to ensure that such an error never occur again.'

There followed one of the most bizarre episodes in the entire history of the Duke and Duchess's lives. Churchill had now taken over from Chamberlain as British prime minister, yet even at this low point in the war he made it his concern to instruct the Ambassador in Spain to establish contact with the Windsors and ensure they were looked after. They were soon installed in comfort at the Ritz Hotel in Madrid. Churchill wanted the Duke to go immediately to Lisbon and then fly home to England. But a difficulty arose because his brother the Duke of Kent was about to visit Portugal to celebrate the 800th anniversary of Portuguese independence and no one wanted the two Dukes there together. So matters were delayed before they moved on to stay at the mansion home of an eminent Lisbon banker, Dr Ricardo de Espírito Santo Silva. But the Duke still insisted on certain conditions before he would agree to return. Above all he wanted an assurance that his wife would be given the same status as other members of his family. He made it clear that this meant he and the Duchess should be received at Buckingham Palace if he returned and, in addition, if his return involved them in additional taxation due to their loss of non-resident status, then this should be made good from the Civil List or other public funds.

*

The Duke's stubborn and self-centred behaviour at this most critical juncture in British history, when the country of which he had once been king was fighting an existential battle and he was telling diplomats privately 'that the most important thing to be done was to end the war before thousands more were killed or maimed to save the faces of a few politicians', has not endeared him or the Duchess to posterity. Churchill now finally lost patience with the man he had defended for so long and at the end of June reprimanded him for failing to obey military authority; though not actually accusing him of desertion, he believed the Duke had left Paris in May in doubtful circumstances and ordered him home. Wallis may have shared his views on conflict in Europe, but they were unquestionably his, long held and deeply felt – as were his views on his wife's dignity and status. It suited the Germans to keep the Windsors on the Continent. Entire books have been written about plans to kidnap the Duke and use him as a pawn, plans that were known to Churchill thanks to British intelligence intercepting coded messages. Would the defeatist Duke have agreed to become a puppet king if Hitler had invaded and occupied Britain? It is of course unknowable, and Philip Ziegler has argued that he was too much of a patriot ever to have been part of such a scheme. But he had only himself to blame that people should believe such a ruse possible. Wallis was not only *not* part of this, she desperately wanted to return to England. As long as they remained in France she felt they were 'like rats in a trap until the end of the war'. She had chosen to live there more than ten years before and now more than ever believed that, if she returned there, the difficulties with her husband's family might be ironed out. In vain, she urged her husband to return and not quibble in advance about terms.

'What followed now seems fantastic and perhaps even a little silly,' Wallis wrote later reflecting on events.

But David's pride was engaged and he was deadly serious. When after some time he felt it necessary to tell me what was going on he put the situation in approximately these terms: 'I won't have them push us into a bottom drawer. It must be the two of us together – man and wife with the same position. Now, I am only too well aware of the risk of my being misunderstood in pressing for this at such a time. Some people will probably say that with a war on these trifles should be forgotten. But they are not trifles to me. Whatever I am to be I must be with you; any position I am called upon to fill, I can only fill with you.'

In mid-July the Windsors were informed that the King was pleased to appoint his brother the Duke governor of the Bahamas. The Duke, who had offered to serve anywhere in the Empire, accepted, but then threatened 'to reconsider my position' if the travel arrangements he had made for himself and Wallis were not acceded to. Churchill would not change his position and Alan Lascelles and Walter Monck-ton advised that the Duke be treated 'as a petulant baby'. The couple finally sailed from Lisbon on 1 August 1940, in the first available ship, the *Excalibur*, crowded with desperate refugees.

12

Wallis Grits her Teeth

'"Les Anglais" are very strange people, I find'

The twenty-nine islands known collectively as the Bahamas were, even in total, half the size of Wales. Most of the 70,000 inhabitants – 60,000 of whom were black or of mixed race – lived in Nassau, the capital, on New Providence Island, a town which boasted three historic buildings, high unemployment and a heavy dependence on rich American tourists. The Bahamas were well known as the British Empire's most backward-looking colony and the Duke and Duchess, as they viewed one of these buildings, the semi-derelict Government House built in 1801 and designated as their new home, can have had no doubt that they were being fobbed off with one of the least important positions available for such a high-ranking former soldier and member of the royal family and one that would keep them out of Europe for as long as possible. Michael Bloch describes it as 'a kind of punishment station in the Colonial Service, combining a minimum of importance with a maximum of frustration'.

The climate was unbearably hot and humid in summer, often reaching 100 degrees Fahrenheit (38 degrees Centigrade), and the Duke, as Wallis wrote vividly in her memoirs, was sweating so profusely in his thick khaki uniform on the day they arrived in mid-August 1940 that there were several black patches of wet to be seen on his tunic as he dripped his way down the receiving line. The rest of the year was mild, dry and pleasantly temperate, in fact perfect weather for the Duke to enjoy the local golf course. But for Wallis neither the golf course nor the Bay Street shops held much appeal, and almost the only attraction of the post was its proximity to Miami, where she had to make an emergency visit in December for treatment on an impacted wisdom tooth. Never one to miss an opportunity for a wisecrack, she told one reporter: 'all my life I've disliked hot weather and coming to Nassau has been like taking a permanent slimming cure'. What they called 'the Nassau Drip' soon became something of a mantra for them both; the one thing they both liked about the post was that it was 'certainly good for the figure'. Publicly she did not complain, and many remember her working hard and efficiently in a variety of capacities as the Governor's wife, for the Red Cross, of which she was automatically local president, and for the local branch of the Daughters of the British Empire. But she was, in many ways, far from her natural comfort zone.

Frank Giles, later editor of the *Sunday Times* but then working as ADC to the Governor of Bermuda, Sir Denis Bernard, encountered the couple during their week-long stopover en route to Nassau and was struck by how 'extraordinarily nice Wallis was to people as she went around inspecting homes and crèches, and always had the right word for everyone, always able to make whomever she was talking to feel they were the person she'd been waiting all her life to meet, which was very flattering'. As Giles observed at the time, this was not something she had learned from experience: she was naturally very good at it. 'Now this is a trick, obviously, but it's a very flattering trick when it happens to you.'

And this was in spite of the cable sent by Lord Lloyd to Sir Denis with instructions, noted Giles, that 'the Duke should receive a half curtsey and the Duchess none at all and to be addressed as "Your Grace" not "Your Royal Highness". This made him angrier than ever and he said he'd never heard of a half curtsey and as for addressing her as "Your Grace" only servants did that, whereupon he turned on his heel and strode off in a passion.' Wallis was, as Giles and others noticed gratefully, very good at calming the Duke or 'nannying' him. On this occasion, for example, she reminded him that he must go and work on the speech he was to make on arrival at Nassau, but she nonetheless wrote to Monckton herself later. 'Also the title, or lack of one, is an issue and Lloyd took pains to issue a telegram to Bermudans and here to say how I was to be treated thus stressing for all concerned the whole sorry story. I doubt if he would wish his own wife to have been the subject of such orders.'

After less than a week in Nassau it was clear when a chunk of ceiling fell to the floor in a room where Wallis was sitting that Government House was in need of urgent reconstruction and that the Windsors would have to move out while this happened. It was not simply a question of the decor being a little shabby or the cracked swimming pool being filled with debris, the house was structurally unsound and infested with termites. This involved further difficult negotiation, through Lord Lloyd, with a government in London that had rather more critical concerns on its mind. And so although the local legislature eventually voted – grudgingly, according to Philip Ziegler – about £4,000 for essential repairs, the Windsors paid for most of the internal redecoration themselves.

Wallis instinctively understood, over and above any need for her own comfort, that if her husband was to be successful in his job – and he did make a spirited attempt to build up the economy of the islands so that they were not exclusively reliant on American tourism – they would need to entertain the few extremely wealthy white traders, such as Harold Christie and the Canadian goldmining millionaire Sir Harry Oakes, lavishly and with style. She knew she needed to develop friendships with the merchants' wives, cemented over the dinner table. While the extensive repairs and refurbishments were being carried out the Duke had suggested to London that he and Wallis might stay at his ranch in Canada for three months. They were also worried about La Croë, their abandoned home in France, which housed everything they had taken from the Fort. Like thousands of others in wartime they had no idea what would become of their possessions, but, not surprisingly, the proposal that they take temporary leave of absence was met with horror. Both the royal family and the government professed shock and outrage that no sooner had they arrived than, once again, they were abandoning their post.

It was this perceived dereliction of duty that marked a serious shift in Churchill's attitude to the former King. He was, Monckton told the Duke, '"very grieved" to hear that you were entertaining such an idea when the people of Britain were suffering so much and at the very least had thought you would be willing to put up with the discomfort and remain at your post until weather conditions made things less unpleasant'. In a lengthy letter, which also tried to address some of the Duke's pressing concerns about money and the tax status of the Duchess as an American citizen married to an Englishman, Monckton reminded them that now, while the rest of Europe was grappling with the devastating privations of war, was scarcely a propitious moment to urge such a request.

And so the gulf in understanding was only to widen. Wallis, finding herself with no other channel, took to writing long and heartfelt letters to Monckton. He may have dreaded the sight of her large round handwriting on the familiar blue paper telling him 'this hot little hell is so far from the war and how one misses Europe's air raids and all we have known for the past months', but he continued to do his best for them. Those who knew her at this time admired the element of Southern nobility in the way she was standing by her man and getting on with the job in hand, however distasteful to her. She tried to explain matters from their point of view:

> The place is too small for the Duke. I do not mean that in any other way but that a man who has been Prince of Wales and King of England cannot be governor of a tiny place. It is not fair to the people here or to him. The spotlight is on an island that cannot itself take it and the appointment is doomed to fail for both concerned. One can put up with anything in wartime in the way of discomforts, even if one knows one is not contributing to the war effort, as we cannot from here, but it is really impossible to live in a house that has been so neglected for years that insects are eating it away . . . I do wish we were not so far away from you, dear Walter.

In the event the Windsors remained in Nassau, staying in one of Sir Harry Oakes's homes until the refurbished Government House and gardens were ready. Wallis, using bright chintzes, imported French wallpapers and a pale-green carpet, managed to fill the old, dark rooms with a feeling of light. Her own portrait, painted by Gerald Brockhurst, took pride of place above the drawing-room fireplace. But she was not able to put all her redecoration schemes into practice. Before their arrival a portrait of Queen Elizabeth had been ordered for the Red Cross headquarters and the Duchess, as president, made a convincing acceptance speech stating what a great honour it was for the office to have a portrait of Her Majesty Queen Elizabeth.

They both believed that the blocking of their travel plans was further evidence of continuing ill-usage. 'I am amazed', Wallis told Monckton in October 1940, 'that in the middle of a life and death struggle the government still has time to continue its persecution of us. These actions do not increase the prestige of the royal family in the US and this I have straight from American journalists, of which we have seen any number.' A few weeks later she wrote to him again:

> There is no doubt that England carries on propaganda against us in the States in a sort of whispering campaign of the most outrageous lies about us – such as the hairdresser [it was rumoured that she had one regularly flown in from New York] – and as Government House was uninhabitable it had to be repainted not decorated. There are many ways to twist things ... There will always be the court and the courtiers engaged in fifth column activities against us ... it makes tears come to my eyes to see the Duke doing this ridiculous job and making good speeches as though he were talking to the labouring classes of England and inspiring them on to work ... better to be in a shelter or called anything than buried alive here. Do write, Walter, and, if I have any friends, remember me to them.

Privately, no one was in any doubt that she viewed what was to be a five-year stay on this 'charming little isle' as her banishment to Elba where torrid summers were followed by vile hurricane warnings and the Duke had 'a worrying little job with no future'. She asked her aunt Bessie 'where did you stay when you came to this dump and why did you come here? I hate this place more each day ... we both hate it, and the locals are petty-minded, the visitors common and uninteresting.' At least in 1940 and 1941, while the United States was still not at war, there were visitors and tourists. Wallis was to hate it even more once that changed.

In 1941 the Duke and Duchess made two separate visits to North America. The first, in April, was a brief, unofficial visit to Miami where the Duke consulted with Sir Edward Peacock and Wallis socialized at Palm Beach. The new British Ambassador in Washington, Lord Halifax, who had replaced Lord Lothian after the latter's premature death in December 1940, had warned the Foreign Office in London that to refuse them permission for this might encourage meddlesome elements in the US press to write articles depicting the Windsors as martyrs. Nonetheless Churchill deeply disapproved of the visit and plainly told the Duke so, advice which was ignored.

'I note what you say, Walter my dear,' wrote Wallis, 'about Your Man over here, but I can't feel that any Englishman understands, or shall we say wants to understand, my husband because if they did "something would be done" and "difficulties" and "position" would be solved.' But they continued to press for a much longer and more controversial tour which, they hoped, would include a visit to Washington and a planned lunch with the President and Mrs Roosevelt. In those fateful months of 1941, before America entered the war, what the Windsors did or did not say was critical. Wallis was sharp enough to know that she was being exploited: 'The feelings of Americans are very intense at the moment and everything that gives the "stay out of war" groups a chance for a crack at the whip ... is used by them and so I have become an American who was badly treated by England and am used by them as such.' But equally she was so frustrated that she had only Walter to whom she could explode. She sent him copies of American articles that were complimentary about the Duke, and more especially about her:

> because I know that no English person in the US would send on anything along these lines to London because it isn't in line with British policy. However, the fact is there is none of this sort of idea among the people in America ... Winston, Duff [Cooper, now Minister of Information], Halifax go on with their wishful thinking and the trash of the US articles are allowed to be published in your daily papers, which to me is proof of London wanting BAD publicity for us and which Winston <u>did not deny</u> in the last flurry of cables with the Duke.

Wallis believed fiercely that powerful voices in London were actively campaigning against them and that Winston and his colleagues were frightened of allowing them near official America from a belief that they were not reliable, 'and the last exchange of cables has surpassed those of Lisbon – which raises the standard quite high as you know'. On the subject of whether or not America would enter the war, Wallis made her position clear: 'I think it's all hideous and if one's in it one must pull for it. I am in complete disagreement, however, with the idea that if you mention peace you are pro-Nazi and there is no relation between the two that I can conjure up. And when free speech is taken from us it is alarming.'

Churchill was deeply concerned about this sort of attitude, which smacked of defeatism to him and thousands of others, and he well understood the dangers of the Windsors' comments being misused at such a critical time. In a letter marked 'secret', he wrote to the Colonial Secretary on 11 June 1941 about the urgent need to find the Duke a press secretary before he went to America as 'I hear from various quarters of very unhelpful opinions being expressed both by Duke and Duchess.' Monckton sympathized; the Duke had been writing to him in appallingly gloomy terms about the catastrophic losses in Europe[17] that rivalled blunders made in the First World War and blaming the strategists. Churchill proposed 'a competent American publicist who'd come down from time to time to Nassau and try to instill sound ideas into that circle. It doesn't matter if there is a row. We want someone of sufficient character and standing to say "this sort of stuff you put out in your interview has done a great deal of harm. I can only tell you the opinion in the US. It will affect your influence there, or again, language of this kind would cut you off from the great mass of the American people" ... the less there is on paper the better.'

As it happened Wallis, in defiant mood, was also in favour of a press secretary. 'Every prominent American be they politicians, café society, movie stars or just <u>too</u> rich men – employ what is called in the US a public relations man,' she explained to Walter. 'He keeps

---

17 By early June 1941 most of the Balkans had fallen into Axis hands, culminating in the capture of Crete by German and Italian forces on 1 June 1941.

unpleasant items out of the press and for those who want it (as we do) the minimum of publicity.' The problem was the enormous salary paid to such people. According to Wallis, Viscount Astor paid a hefty $25,000 a year:

> So you see we simply could not afford one. What we had in mind was that publicity regarding us would be handled in the same manner that England has conducted publicity regarding its royal family for many years and has been most successful – because any of those members would have a difficult job with the US press were they left on their own, as we have been for four years. The real truth, Walter, is that the government simply do not care what sort of stuff is printed and hide behind or blame us by saying 'what a pity such things are written' . . . it really is a waste of your time to beat around the bush with the idea of anything being done to help us because we realise it won't be. Anyway such requests are like a thermometer of the powers that be's policy regarding us. It's always the same and will never change. However if we didn't have to work for them it wouldn't be so difficult. Alas we shall have to carry on I suppose for the duration but with victory won, we're off!! Best of luck, Walter dear, and what a <u>shame</u> Duff was <u>only</u> ill two weeks.

The man they found to coach the Duke before and during his American trip was René MacColl from the British Embassy in Washington. 'MacColl arrives next Friday,' Wallis told Walter. 'I understand he's very nervous over it all. I believe he thinks HRH is for "appeasement", "negotiated peace" and all the rest of the lies pinned on the Duke.' Monckton, tactful as ever, replied with the suggestion that they should go to the theatre to see Coward's *Blithe Spirit* while they were in New York – such a refreshing antidote to war, he told them.

As the time approached for departure Wallis told Walter that she was beginning to feel like the Monk of Siberia, 'who with a hell of a yell burst from his cell'.

In the event the lunch at the White House had to be cancelled at the last minute when Mrs Roosevelt's brother fell ill. But they were nonetheless delighted by the warm welcome from large crowds in Washington, New York, Chicago and Baltimore. For the local girl made good, Baltimore was unquestionably the high spot. Here she was heartened to find that she had brought out crowds estimated by some at 200,000, waving Union Jacks and American flags and cheering. As they rode in an open-topped car with Mayor Howard W. Jackson they experienced a welcome neither of them was used to. Jackson told them to regard Baltimore as a second home 'where you will always find peace and happiness'. They also spent time with some Warfield relations in the countryside outside Baltimore where Wallis had passed so many childhood holidays. Some of these relations she had not seen for years and she was as keen for them to meet the Duke as he was to show her his ranch – the EP Ranch as it was known, in the hills of Alberta, near the town of High River. In 1919 he had told his beloved Freda Dudley Ward that if only she would live with him there 'I'd never want to return to England; I've got thoroughly bitten with Canada and its possibilities. It's the place for a man, particularly after the Great War, and if I wasn't P. of W. well I guess I'd stay here quite a while!!!'

It was there in October 1941 that Wallis heard the news that Mary Simpson, her once best and oldest friend from Baltimore, had died after a two-year fight with an aggressive and intensely painful cancer. Like Wallis, she was just forty-five. Mary had been ill on and off since the birth of her son, Ernest Henry Child Simpson, in September 1939 and within months had had a radical mastectomy and been told that her chances of survival were slim. Having qualified as a St John Ambulance first-aid worker at London's Lancaster Road Baths, she continued her volunteering work as long as she could, telling friends that, in spite of her illness, 'life is pretty good after all when one has an Ernest like mine'. In addition to the cancer, the Simpsons had recently lost most of their possessions in a fire at the warehouse where they had been stored while they looked for a house. Ernest's lifelong collection of antiquarian books was destroyed as well as the furniture from Bryanston Court, chosen by Wallis, 'which we are not crying over'.

Mary, bravely facing up to the knowledge she did not have long to live, desperately wanted to be reunited with her baby son, who had been evacuated to friends in North America at the start of the war, and to bring him back to England where his father could take care of him. But a return flight across the Atlantic in the middle of war was an impossibility, they found. As they made enquiries the Prime Minister came to their rescue. 'Winston Churchill, recognising what a gentleman Ernest had been in 1937 and how smoothly the divorce had gone through thanks to him when he might have put all sorts of information and obstacles in the way', managed to arrange a government plane for Mary, who was so fragile she had to be carried on a stretcher and driven to and from the plane by ambulance. 'The family always knew this was Churchill's recognition of Ernest's good behaviour. But the gesture could never be made public.' Just before she died, Mary wrote pathetically in her diary, 'Ernest still thinks the Windsors are perfect.' After Mary's death Wallis wrote to Ernest from the ranch telling him, 'God is difficult to understand at times for you deserved a well earned happiness. If ever I can soften the blow that fate has dealt you, the Duke and myself are ready to help in anyway you may ask. Dear Ernest, I who know you very well and all your honest and beautiful qualities, I know the depth of your sufferings – your son will be a stronghold for the future.'[18]

In early November, the Windsors returned to Nassau having avoided the worst of the heat but not the opprobrium heaped on them, as expected, for escaping. Even MacColl had not been able to prevent that. He wrote in his memoirs not merely of how Wallis

18 Henry was for a second time bundled off to America and did not see his father again until he was eight, by which time Ernest had married for the fourth time, a deeply happy marriage at last to the widowed Avril Leveson-Gower. Henry was sent to Harrow, an unhappy experience where he was teased for being the son of Ernest Simpson. Shortly after he left school Ernest also died. Henry was never really to know his father. In what he perceived to be a final act of vindictiveness against her younger brother, knowing how hard Ernest had tried to conceal it, Maud decided after Ernest's death to share some family secrets with Henry, principally that his grandfather was born Jewish and had changed his name from Solomon(s). This knowledge persuaded Henry to change his own name by deed poll to Aaron (or Aharon) Solomons in 1962 and emigrate to Israel, where he lived for many years, brought up a family and served in the Israeli army.

dominated the Duke – 'I have rarely seen an ascendancy established over one partner in a marriage to quite so remarkable a degree' – but of the intense pleasure he derived whenever he won her approval. MacColl noticed how once during the trip an American journalist had asked him to make the Churchillian V-sign. He had started to lift his hand when the Duchess shot him a look. 'She shook her head. The Duke dropped his arm.'

There were criticisms of the amount of luggage they had taken with them – according to some estimates, eighty cases. The *Washington Star*'s Henry McLemore commented: 'you almost have to question the sanity of a man or a woman who would start on a short trip with 58 bags and trunks full of clothing'. The accusations of extravagance could not be easily brushed aside when it was made known that Wallis had set up an appointment with her favourite couturier, Mainbocher, while she was in New York. Much to her annoyance the 'spoiled Mainbocher, who simply attends to those on the spot' and had declined to come to Nassau to see Wallis, could not resist talking about his famous client to the newspapers, which gave lurid accounts of Wallis's improvidence in wartime. She transferred her patronage for a while to Valentina but could not resist returning to Mainbocher soon afterwards. According to one report she had bought thirty-four hats. She retaliated in the press by correcting the number to five and saying that since she had not been shopping since May 1940, more than a year before, 'I don't think anyone could consider this outrageous.' But of course that is precisely what many people in the American, as well as the British, press did consider it: 'an ostentatious display of jewellery and finery at a period when the people of this country are strictly rationed'.

But on 7 December 1941, after the Japanese had attacked Pearl Harbor and the US entered the war, life changed dramatically for the islanders of the Bahamas and Wallis's relief work now took on urgent meaning. She spent every morning at the Red Cross HQ and every afternoon at the canteen she had set up in a former gambling casino to feed the thousands of British RAF officers now stationed on the island in connection with the Coastal Command training programme, as well as members of the US Army Air Force detachment based there.

'Wallis is very busy fixing up the RAF canteen,' wrote Rosa Wood, her friend and assistant. 'It will be rather a canteen de luxe when it is furnished. It wanted quite a lot doing to it. I really admire the way Wallis has thrown herself into all her various jobs. She really is wonderful and does work hard. I do hope that people <u>everywhere</u> are realising all the good she is doing. I think she has such charm and is always amusing to be with I really don't know what I would do without her.' Wallis changed the name of the Bahamian Club to the United Services Canteen Nassau and herself paid to have some USCN badges made for its workers so that they looked smart and had a sense of identity. She was the guest of honour at bazaars and at garden and cocktail parties, although 'we have made a rule that we never attend a party that isn't for charity', she told Monckton. 'I have even learned to make short and trembling speeches,' she added, 'in the most drab and pathetic surroundings.' In a turnaround that would have surprised Lucy Baldwin, she also founded a clinic for the care of expectant mothers and young children which involved a considerable commitment of time and money, usually working with the native Bahamian population. But, for servicemen, it was the numerous plates of bacon and eggs, personally served by the Duchess of Windsor at the canteen, that they remembered for years afterwards.

Wallis herself, writing to her New York friend Edith Lindsay, admitted: 'We are as busy as bees with the canteen for the troops plus the outfitting of survivors and it is so much better having personal work to do rather than sweating over taxes being sent off to England.' But she missed society and wrote constantly to her New York friends, as well as to Herman and Katherine Rogers in Washington, begging them to come and visit and relieve the Nassau tedium or 'Nassau disease', which she described as 'the normal desire of any excuse to stay away as long as possible, which if I didn't always want to be with HRH, I would be looking for excuses too. We were offered Bermuda while in NY but the Duke refused, which did not make me sorry as I don't believe in letting islands become a habit ... How I long for the sight and sound of human beings – my mentality is getting very dire after over two years here and only two months leave,' she complained. When she heard there were to be visitors she wrote that not only was she absolutely thrilled, 'in fact the whole island is in an uproar at the thought of "new faces". We had just decided to send for masks as we all felt we could not look at each other any more.' Even the knowledge that all her letters were read by an official censor, and that in Europe an existential war was being waged, did little to make her tone down her desperation. It was not simply that the endless bridge, golf and fishing did not amuse her. Her frustration was rooted in the anger that, since they had been deliberately placed in a backwater away from the war, there was little they could do to help.

Two events caused deep concern during their five years in the Bahamas. The first was the death in a plane crash in August 1942 of the Duke's younger brother, Prince George, who along with his wife Marina had always shown sympathy and understanding for the Windsors. This was a bitter personal blow. It did nothing to promote a rapprochement with his remaining family even though Queen Mary wrote to the Duke: 'Please give a kind message to your wife, she will help you to bear your sorrow,' a message which represented a distinct softening of attitudes. Some historians have suggested that, had the Duke been prepared to build on this without constantly pressing for his wife to be called HRH, there might have been further reconciliation. The message had resulted from an initiative taken by Wallis to write to her mother-in-law politely proposing that she might wish to meet the retiring Bishop of Nassau, John Dauglish, who had connections to the royal family and was returning to England and who could pass on details of her son's life in the Bahamas. Queen Mary did indeed summon the Bishop, who reported back to Wallis that although the Queen listened with interest to matters concerning her son, when he began to talk enthusiastically about the Duchess there appeared 'a stone wall of disinterest'.

The second event was the brutal murder of Sir Harry Oakes in July 1943. Oakes was found battered to death and partly burned, with feathers strewn over the corpse. The Duke made a number of blunders in his treatment of the case from the moment he summoned the

Miami police force to investigate rather than the local detectives and without consulting Scotland Yard first. He clearly believed that Oakes's son-in-law, Alfred de Marigny, a man he personally disliked, was guilty of the killing. In the event de Marigny was found not guilty at his trial and the police were accused of manufacturing evidence. De Marigny was ordered to be deported, a hazardous procedure in wartime. The crime remains unsolved today, although it has been the subject of several books and a film. Theories abound, the most likely of which, according to the late Diana Mosley, is that his business associate Harold Christie hired an assassin for the job.

The Duke may have shown poor judgement, at the very least, in the way he dealt with the case, but Wallis was circumspect in anything she said then or later. Two weeks after the murder, she wrote to Edith Lindsay: 'You can imagine what the rumour clinic is doing to the sad Oakes case. It really is all too tragic.' But she gave nothing else away other than her boredom. July was especially painful because of the fierce heat, which meant, she added, that 'There is really no one here as with the loosening of the exchange control everybody has fled to the cool breezes ... Everything is really so <u>intensely dull</u> here and I long for news of the big world no matter how trivial the news. I miss you very much and would like to go shopping with you this minute.' But leaving the island was now impossible and in any case 'each time I find it harder to return! So think I better not tempt myself with all your bright lights and attractive people.'

To what extent is it fair to see the grumblings of the Duke and Duchess as undermining morale and the war effort and, in addition, to describe them as pro-Hitler or Nazi puppets in waiting? 'I suppose,' Wallis herself explained frankly on the eve of their autumn 1941 visit to America,

> even though everybody wants the sufferings of so many to end, one's own personal feelings can't help but creep in and I do most devoutly pray for the end of the war so that the Duke may be released from the difficult situation of being in a firm whose head is an arch enemy. Everything so far has gone well with the Embassy in Washington regarding us ... Canada is another thing; the family

element again and we have had the usual snub from 'The Great Dominion'. Strange that an Englishman is treated with politeness in a foreign country like the US but Canada, his own land, is rude. So you see what I mean when I pray for the day when the Duke is free once more.

These feelings, his as much as hers, were not to change throughout their time in Nassau and, in the current atmosphere in Britain, were inevitably seen as defeatist. But then, as she confessed to her principal New York correspondent Edith Lindsay, '"Les Anglais" are very strange people, I find.' The tone of her letters, even those to officials, was defiant, never deferential. As she wrote to her aunt in July 1940:

We refused to return to England except under our own terms as the Duke is quite useless to the country if he was to receive the same treatment as when he returned in September ... one humiliation after another ... Can you fancy a family continuing a feud when the very Empire is threatened and not putting every available man in a spot where he would be most useful? Could anything be so small and hideous? What will happen to a country which allows such behaviour?

Shortly after Wallis wrote that letter, the Duke foolishly gave an interview to the American novelist Fulton Oursler, which was published in *Liberty* magazine in March 1941. Appearing at this critical moment in the battle to persuade America to join the Allies, the article could scarcely have been worse timed. Discussing whether an outright victory was ever possible in modern warfare, Oursler opined: 'I am inclined to doubt it ... The Germans might say there will always be a Germany so long as one German remains alive.' The Duke responded rhetorically: 'And you can't execute the death sentence on 80,000,000 people?'

However much the Duke insisted that he had been fed the answers, the interview greatly angered Churchill. It coloured all their subsequent wartime exchanges. Churchill told the Duke that the article:

gives the impression and can indeed only bear the interpretation of contemplating a negotiated peace with Hitler. That is not the policy of the Government and vast majority of the people of the United States ... later on, when the atmosphere is less electric, when the issues are more clear cut and when perhaps Your Royal Highness's public utterances ... are more in harmony with the dominant tides of British and American feeling, I think that an agreeable visit [to the US] for you might be arranged.

This exchange deteriorated when the Duke pointed out that a recent American edition of *Life* had carried an article in which his sister-in-law, the Queen, referred to the Duchess as 'that woman'. But eventually, after a three-month silence, the Duke ate humble pie and wrote to Churchill assuring him that as long as he held an official position, 'I play the game of the Government that appointed me.' Six months after the disastrous article in *Liberty*, 'chaperoned' by MacColl, the Duke and Duchess were allowed to make their first official visit to the American mainland.

Yet the Duke never gave up bombarding Churchill with requests for Wallis to have minor medical treatment in the US or about staffing arrangements at Government House, as well as reverting to the one major request that was consuming them both: her royal status, or lack of it. In an eight-page letter to Churchill in November 1942 he not only reminded the British Prime Minister that 'I asked you to bear me in mind should another suitable appointment fall vacant'. He also urged that 'after five and a half years, the question of restoring to the Duchess her royal status should be clarified'. He went on to explain that he had been officially requested by the Secretary of State for the Colonies to submit the names of local candidates for the New Year honours list. 'I am now asking you, as Prime Minister, to submit to the King that he restores the Duchess' royal rank at the coming New Year not only as an act of justice and courtesy to his sister in law but also as a gesture in recognition of her two years of public service in the Bahamas. The occasion would seem opportune from all angles for correcting an unwarranted step.'

The King replied to Churchill on 9 December that he was 'sure it would be a mistake to reopen this matter ... I am quite ready to leave the question in abeyance for the time being but I must tell you quite honestly that I do not trust the Duchess's loyalty.' There was a part of Wallis which also longed for the whole issue to be dropped or just kept in abeyance. It was tiring to go on and on fighting. As she wrote to Edith Lindsay in 1943: 'I can't see why they just don't forget all about the Windsors and let us be where we want to be in obscurity . . .'

But as the King expanded his views in a separate memorandum, addressed to the Prime Minister and marked 'private and confidential', there was 'no question of the title being "restored" to the Duchess because she never had it. I am sure there are still large numbers of people in this country and in the Empire to whom it would be most distasteful to have to do honour to the Duchess as a member of our family . . . I have consulted my family, who share these views.'

While it may be open to debate whether the royal family seriously questioned her loyalty to Britain or whether this was a convenient umbrella, several British politicians before the abdication believed, as Sir Horace Wilson stated, that Wallis Simpson was a woman of 'limitless ambition' with a desire to 'interfere in politics' and who was in touch with the Nazi movement. In 1940 Churchill, in writing to Roosevelt, had said of the Duke, 'though his loyalties are unimpeachable there is always a backlash of Nazi intrigue that seeks to make trouble about him now that the greater part of the continent is in enemy hands'.

The Duke's close involvement with Axel Wenner-Gren, the Swedish millionaire owner of Electrolux, was part of this backlash. Wenner-Gren, a suave white-haired businessman, part-educated in Germany, had made his money through patenting a type of vacuum cleaner and a refrigerator. Having built his fortune in the early part of the century it suited him now to preach a doctrine of peace in order to protect his worldwide interests and to continue dealing with Nazi Germany as well as Britain and the United States. A friend of Charles Bedaux and Hermann Göring, he also had an interest in the German arms manufacturer Krupp, and manufactured munitions for the Germans through another Swedish company, Bofors, which was protected by Swedish neutrality. Before the war he bought one of the world's largest and most lavishly appointed yachts, the *Southern Cross*, once owned by Howard Hughes, and set sail for the Bahamas with his American wife and children in 1939. There he took up residence in an impressive mansion, which he named Shangri-La, founded the Bank of the Bahamas and used the island as a base from which to continue his business activities.

Wenner-Gren was tipped off in a cryptic message in 1940 that the new family arriving in Nassau would be of interest to him and his friends. This message, intercepted by Washington, was assumed to mean that Wenner-Gren was a German sympathizer and would quickly recruit the Duke and Duchess to his cause. British and American diplomats were from the first deeply worried about this connection as the Duke, pleased to find a man who was not only cultured but offered a chance to build up investment on the island, did indeed nurture the friendship. Wenner-Gren – a boastful man – would often brag about having friendships with other unsavoury political figures, such as Mussolini and Mexico's pro-Fascist General Maximino Camacho, and in fact may not have been as important as he made out. The American government was so concerned it placed Wenner-Gren on the black list of those to be treated as enemy aliens, which effectively put a stop to his friendship with the Windsors. The Duke's biographer, Philip Ziegler, commented that 'it is not hard to feel that in this case he – as well as the unfortunate Swede – was misused. On other points he is less easily defended.' And his friendship with Charles Bedaux was equally dubious. For the Duke and Duchess to befriend such questionable characters at this dangerous time was ill advised at the very least.

Throughout the war, the US Federal Bureau of Investigation kept a sizeable file on the couple, now largely declassified but with names redacted, mostly comprising unsubstantiated denunciations from outside sources explaining why they believed the loyalty of either the Duke or Duchess, or both, was suspect – beliefs based on little more than gossip or hearsay. There are many notes in the file insisting on a pre-war affair or relationship between Wallis and Ribbentrop and on the Windsors' pro-German tendencies. Others express apprehension about the couple's friendship with Wenner-Gren or even suggest that, as the Duchess sent her clothes for dry cleaning in New York, she doubtless used this as a method of sending secret messages.

Later in the war, in August 1944, when there was a revival of interest in the Duchess, the FBI undertook a survey of opinion in the literary and publishing world to ascertain the attitude of publishers and others in the US media to the Windsors. They concluded 'that the Dutchess [sic] was of extreme news interest and that she was exceedingly unpopular in certain political circles of the US and England because of her social contacts prior to her marriage ... however no sources could give evidence of a concerted effort to campaign against her'. Moreover, an influential New York advertising executive stated that 'she and her husband are considered a pathetic couple by the leading publishers and editors'. The couple were well aware they were being watched – when they travelled to the United States they were accompanied not only by bodyguards but by FBI special agents 'to exercise discreet observations', but they believed they were being spied on in Nassau as well. At a formal dinner in Government House, after the Duke and Duchess had been piped in, 'the Duchess made some remark to a dinner guest and then turned to the piper and said: "you can also report that to Downing Street", an indication to everyone present that they thought the piper was some kind of spy for England'. They were 'forever making remarks like that which were out of place'.

Once America entered the war, the Windsors took a more positive view of the likely outcome. Yet, throughout the years she was in Nassau, Wallis never stopped worrying about whether she would have enough money once the war was over, only now 'enough money' was a rather different proposition as she needed enough to live in the style to which a king and his consort were accustomed. She admitted to Monckton her anxieties about 'money in the years ahead'. She asked him what would happen if 'the Windsor holdings are perhaps lost in the shuffle'. She reminded him of 'the need to keep our heads above water in the long pull ahead ... unless we take a job in the U.S. There seem to plenty of those dangling in front of the Duke's eyes.' But by the end of the war, with doubts about his loyalty circulating freely, jobs in the US for the Duke were no longer being dangled.

There was some discussion about finding him 'a high level job' at the Washington Embassy. But it was hard to specify precisely what task he was best fitted for other than a vague desire to further Anglo-American relations, and the proposal was apparently abandoned because Clement Attlee, who became Prime Minister in July 1945, and his Foreign Secretary Ernest Bevin were adamant that it was not a good idea. Churchill continued to hope that there might be an ambassadorial job available for the ex-King and insisted that he was 'very sorry about this foolish obstruction by Bevin and Attlee and I wish I had it in my power to overcome it' – a comment which, the Duke told Monckton, 'has amused us a good deal for, after all, he wasn't all that cooperative himself during his five year residence at Number 10'.

The Windsors left Nassau on 3 May 1945 ahead of another sweltering summer, and went first to America with no clear idea of where they would settle or what they would do. Relations with Churchill were from now on edgy, although he remained always respectful towards his former monarch, and in 1948 he and Clemmie spent their wedding anniversary staying with the Windsors at La Croë. But there are known to be letters, kept secret at the request of the royal family, which reveal his anger and frustration with the Duke, exacerbated by the ex-King offering unsolicited advice about the prosecution of the war. Churchill did not flinch from telling him he could not accept advice from someone who 'had given up the greatest throne in world history'.

Best-Dressed Wallis

'The Windsors' prestige is not what it used to be'

After six years of uncertainty following the end of the war, Wallis still felt rootless and 'homeless on the face of the earth'. The Windsors rented and borrowed houses until there could be no possible doubt that returning to England was out of the question. It was Wallis who finally recognized that there would never be meaningful work offered to the Duke anywhere in the world and that they would never be able to make their home in England. She had summoned up the necessary courage to face the future life of which she had been the cause. She had always shown remarkable self-awareness of her own shortcomings, even if she was unable to change them, and now she tried to give the Duke some of the courage she was scraping together as he, often depressed or ill, faced a still-hostile family and an ever colder world. She was now determined to create in France, where they felt welcome, an environment fit for a former monarch and attended to the Duke's emotional and physical needs in minute detail. All their guests and visitors attested to her extraordinary resolve to make wherever they lived as regal as possible. But how, as well as where, to fill their remaining days was the immediate postwar priority.

Their first trip to England together in the autumn of 1946 was a disaster. They stayed with their friends the Earl and Countess of Dudley at Ednam Lodge near Sunningdale, hurt that the Fort was clearly not available[19] and that no other royal residence was on offer.

---

19 The Fort was eventually leased to the Hon. Gerald Lascelles, a nephew of the Duke, who had been imprisoned in Colditz and was a distant relation of his former Private Secretary.

On 16 October a burglar broke into the house, apparently through an open window, and stole more than £25,000 worth of Wallis's jewellery, which she had decided to bring with her in a small trunk-like jewel case and had left unsecured when they went out for the evening. Wallis was distraught; the jewellery had defined her romance with the then Prince and given her security. An exotic bird of paradise brooch, with a cabochon sapphire breast and a plumage of diamonds, had just been made for her by Cartier that year. She never saw it, or any of the other stolen pieces, again.

The household was in turmoil, as police taking fingerprints jostled with reporters seeking interviews. The quiet visit with a minimum of publicity that they had promised an 'unrelenting royal family' was now splashed all over the British newspapers. In a country hard hit by post-war austerity, discussion of such a fabulous haul of jewellery (estimated by the Windsors to be worth $80,000) elicited little sympathy. According to Lady Dudley, Wallis in the hours after the robbery showed 'an unpleasant and to me unexpected side of her character … She wanted all the servants put through a kind of third degree. But I would have none of this, all of them except for one kitchen maid being old and devoted staff of long standing … the Duke was both demented with worry and near to tears.'

The next day there was another drama. Before going out for a stroll Wallis, according to Laura Dudley, who told the story in her memoirs, asked the Duke to put away a small brooch of sapphires and rubies with their entwined initials and an inscription 'God Bless WE Wallis', which had been an early gift in 1935 and had eluded the burglars only because she had been wearing it. When they returned from the walk he could not remember where he had put it. 'We stayed up most of the night; he obviously feared to go to bed empty-handed. At about 5 a.m. by some miracle we found it, under a china ornament. Never have I seen a man so relieved.'

Lady Dudley, indignant at the way Wallis had behaved, wrote later that the haul had included 'a great many uncut emeralds which I believe belonged to Queen Alexandra', a comment that caused, yet again, an enormous brouhaha over why the Duchess had had these in the first place. Most likely she did not, but the rumours were reignited and the friendship with the Dudleys came under severe strain.

Ten days later, Kathleen (Kick) Kennedy, daughter of the American Ambassador and now the widowed Lady Hartington, who met the Windsors at that time, wrote: 'The Duchess continues to talk of nothing but her robbery [the words 'and is really nothing but a bore' are crossed out but remain visible] and how she has nothing left – so far I haven't seen her with the same jewel. He seems so pathetic but full of charm ... Really no one here takes any notice of them and the extraordinary thing is that I actually feel that she is jealous of what I, an American, have got out of England[20] and which has always been denied to her.'

The Duke never gave up trying to rectify that which had been denied his wife. Insurance money helped him to start a new collection of jewellery for her and in April 1949 he again consulted Viscount Jowitt for a legal opinion on the question of her title. In 1937 the then Sir William Jowitt had based his opinion on the view that 'he became "His Royal Highness" not by virtue of any Letters Patent, but for the simple reason that he was the son of his father who was the Sovereign of this country'. He went on to declare 'that the Duchess of Windsor is, by virtue of her membership of the Royal family, entitled in the same way as other royal duchesses, to be known by the style and title of "Her Royal Highness"'. This time, while not wavering from that opinion, he concluded in a clever note for the record, 'that the marks of respect which the subject pays to Royal personages are, as I said, in no source a legal obligation. They are rather a matter of good manners.' Yet while insisting that it was simply a matter of good manners he nonetheless pointed out that the present situation, however erroneous, could be formally and effectively reversed only by fresh Letters Patent and since these would not be issued by the King save on the advice of his ministers it was unlikely they would be issued at all. This meant, effectively, that the Duke and Duchess

---

20 Kathleen Kennedy married William 'Billy' Cavendish, Marquess of Hartington, in May 1944. He was killed in combat three months later. Although widowed, she was at the heart of British society.

were permanent, half-royal exiles – arguably the desired effect. Notwithstanding this, their staff in France, thirty in all spread between two houses, learned to refer to her as 'Son Altesse Royale' (perhaps SAR sounded less threatening than HRH and certainly fell into the category of 'good manners'), footmen wore royal livery and Wallis's notepaper had a small crown above a 'W'.

And the British royal family could not prevent the Duke buying Wallis gifts of jewellery fit for a royal highness. The Duke had visited Cartier in Paris just before the fall of France with pocketsful of stones, some of Wallis's bracelets and a necklace, together with instructions to make up at least one piece, a remarkable indication of his obsession with pleasing one woman above all the terror, privation and dislocation surrounding him in France. He was apparently oblivious to the notion that his requirements for the production of such a jewel in wartime might strike some as insensitive. The bold diamond flamingo clip, with startling tail feathers of rubies, sapphires and emeralds, was made in Paris in 1940 according to his instructions that the brooch should have retractable legs so that Wallis could wear it centrally without a leg digging into her chest if she bent down. Wearing this magnificent three-dimensional flamingo with its brilliant plumage would have been audacious at any time. Wallis, who used jewellery not simply as a display of wealth but to express her bold style and above all her personality, wore it as she set off on her controversial October 1941 visit to the United States with the Duke. Where clothes or jewels were concerned, she was never fearful. She had some magnificent jewelled powder compacts 'and was always making up at table, which of course is very sexy', according to the high-society interior designer Nicholas Haslam. The Duke's habit of providing the stones by breaking up existing pieces in order to create an original object in a modern setting resumed as soon as the war was over in 1945. Together he and the Duchess became major jewellery buyers and connoisseurs. Wallis loved daring colour combinations and original designs, such as the two so-called gem-set bib necklaces made by Cartier, one in 1945 with rubies and emeralds, the other in 1947 with amethyst and turquoise, both large, strikingly modern pieces and stunning pieces of jewellery at any time. In those post-war years, when many in Europe were concentrating on basic necessities such as food and homes, they were especially remarkable. Although Wallis patronized different jewellers, she was lucky to find in Jeanne Toussaint, Louis Cartier's intimate companion, a woman who understood her position as an outsider and with whom she developed a strong personal and professional relationship. Toussaint and the Duke collaborated on many jewellery projects for the Duchess, and her post-war 'Great Cat' jewels were the inspiration of Toussaint, herself known as La Panthère, and Cartier designer Peter Lemarchand. One of the most striking of these brooches features a sapphire and diamond panther astride an enormous Kashmir sapphire; bought and made in 1949 'for stock' but with the Duchess in mind. Wallis chose to wear on her coat this beautiful, strong panther sitting proudly on top of the world when she attended the 1967 unveiling in London by Queen Elizabeth II of a memorial plaque to Queen Mary at Marlborough House in Pall Mall.

In the photographs taken at this event Wallis appears soignée with her bouffant hairstyle and well-cut coat, although a fur wrap around her neck is a somewhat odd choice for June. But, perhaps not surprisingly, she looks worried and drawn. She seemed to be in good health but by this time had had at least two serious internal operations and long-standing problems, apparently from an ulcer. Philip Ziegler writes of stomach cancer in 1944 followed by cancer of the womb in 1951. Charles Higham specifies cancer of the ovaries in 1951. Others commented on the Duchess being hospitalized for a major internal operation, the nature of which was never disclosed. Without access to hospital records, which have never been made available, all that can be stated for certain is that Wallis had serious problems which necessitated internal surgery. Quite possibly she was suffering from a complication arising from an internal abnormality which had been treated earlier and now flared up again but which it was imperative to keep secret. But the idea of her having a cancer as life threatening as ovarian cancer in 1951 and surviving into her ninetieth year is insupportable. Without the chemotherapy regime available today, women diagnosed with ovarian, stomach or womb cancer rarely lived ten years and most managed only five. Whatever the problem, she made a good recovery.

There is another interpretation of her frequent operations. It is not uncommon, according to clinical psychiatrist Dr Iain Oswald, 'for a patient who is preoccupied with her body to undergo a series of investigations and even operations in an attempt to attend to these feelings. This can be seen as a form of displacement where attention is shifted from one part of her body felt to be defective (for instance where she is unable to have a child) to a hyper-attention to correct another part of her body. This, of course, could include cosmetic surgery as well as other forms of surgery.'

At all events by 1952 the Windsors had reached a decision about where they should base themselves: France. They would live informally at the Mill, a house they bought at Gif-sur-Yvette, forty-five minutes outside Paris to the south of Versailles and the only house after the war that they owned, and in formal splendour in Paris itself at a house in the Bois de Boulogne, 4 Route du 'Champ d'En-traînement, loaned to them for a peppercorn rent by the City of Paris. It was Wallis who arranged the decor of both, making sure the town house appeared as imposing a mansion as possible for a build-ing that was not an actual palace. In the drawing room hung a full-length portrait of Queen Mary, the mother-in-law who would never agree to meet her daughter-in-law, as well as one of the Duke, equally resplendent in Garter robes. His red and gold silk banner, with coat of arms, hung over the galleried marble entrance hall where other royal memorabilia were also displayed.

Just as the Windsors were deeply involved in expensively refur-bishing both houses, the Duke's brother, George VI, died, aged just fifty-six, in February 1952. A heavy smoker, he had been suffering from lung cancer. But the perception now hardened that somehow the premature death had been Wallis's fault as the burdens of state, for which unlike his elder brother he had not been groomed, had hastened his death. The Duke went to London alone for his brother's funeral. The accession of the Duke's twenty-five-year-old niece, Queen Elizabeth II, was to make little difference to the Windsors' standing in the eyes of the remaining royal family, even though

Elizabeth had been a child at the time of the abdication, because both her grandmother, Queen Mary, and her mother, Queen Elizabeth, now known as the Queen Mother, were still alive. But with the King's death went the personal allowance from him agreed at the time of the abdication. 'They are beasts to continue to treat you the way they do ... I am afraid Mrs Temple Sr. [the Queen Mother, whose elder daughter they had nicknamed Shirley Temple] will never give in,' Wallis wrote to the Duke who, in reply, told her that while some Court officials were friendly and correct on the surface there was 'only granite below'.

Wherever the Windsors lived – and they also retained Suite 28A in New York's Waldorf Towers, part of the Waldorf Astoria hotel – they were both locked in stasis. There were a few new friends providing an occasional shot of circulating blood. But most of their visitors wanted to talk about the past. Every day from now on was lived in the shadow of 1936, with no possibility of moving forward as money worries, the inevitable illnesses of old age and bitterness against the British royal family all jostled for attention.

Such new activity as they embarked on inevitably evolved around reliving the old. The Duke was, almost as soon as peace descended in Europe, approached to write his memoirs. He started by writing a series of articles for *Life*, helped by the former Reuters journalist Charles Murphy, now a staff writer on the magazine. The collaboration was stormy almost from the outset because Wallis disliked Murphy. But the money was useful and the Duke described Murphy as 'a good egg and quite brilliant journalist'. *Life* was pleased with the finished work, which led to a lucrative book and, a decade later, to the documentary film, both called *A King's Story*; it also led to Wallis herself writing her own volume of memoirs, *The Heart Has its Reasons*. Wallis may not have been familiar with the source of this famous quotation, taken from the work of the French mathematician and physicist Blaise Pascal. And those who knew her well may have queried its suitability. But she liked what it implied. She told Ernest when writing to ask for his co-operation with the book that she had not intended to write her memoirs but had 'been forced into this uncomfortable position by no less a person than solicitor Sir G.

Allen. He feels that with all that has been written, a bit of truth should be forced to the top.'

In spite of their earlier differences, she too tried to work with Murphy as her ghostwriter. When that arrangement broke down in disagreement, she hired the American author Cleveland Amory, but he likewise did not prove as pliable as she wished. When he withdrew in 1955 she decided to complete the manuscript herself. But she needed time on her own for this, undistracted by the Duke's undiminished and constant need for her. She went off to the Mill, alone, to put the finishing touches to the manuscript, and the book was published in 1956 by Houghton Mifflin in New York. In spite of much that was obscured or omitted, many people were surprised by how much of Wallis's personality it revealed. The following year, to celebrate their twentieth wedding anniversary, the Duke gave Wallis a diamond-encrusted, heart-shaped brooch with 'W' and 'E' in entwined emeralds and – determined that she should have her emblem – a ruby and gold crown perched on top of the heart.

The American author Maxine Sandberg read *The Heart Has its Reasons* while recuperating from depression and told the Duchess it gave her strength to overcome her illness. For years following the publication of the book Sandberg kept up a virtual bombardment of the Duchess, hoping to be granted access and permission to write the first authorized biography. She sent presents of slippers and bed covers and flowers, as well as letters in which she recounted in detail the history of her stays in various hospitals. The Duchess's secretary wrote polite letters to thank her for all the presents and insisting that 'Her Royal Highness' had been most interested to read about her attempts to write about her experiences in hospitals. In due course, Sandberg was invited to meet the Duchess, with a view to exploring the possibility of collaboration. But after the meeting, according to Sandberg, the Duchess changed her mind and said she thought it would be unwise to ask friends to give interviews. Sandberg none-theless continued with the writing but promised not to publish in Wallis's lifetime, then, in 1965, she made a renewed attempt to work with the Duchess. But eventually the project petered out.

Walter Monckton, as official gatekeeper, still played a part in their lives and occasionally came to stay in Paris with his wife. He had negotiated the deal for them on their townhouse in the Bois de Boulogne, but the friendship cooled somewhat after he was created a viscount in 1957 and she accused him of managing to get a title for himself 'but you didn't get *me* one'. And he was only moderately successful in keeping at bay the hordes who wished to write about them, as the Sandberg story indicates. Linda Mortimer, daughter of Fruity and Alexandra Metcalfe, and therefore an acceptable insider, was brought in to help with the film of *A King's Story*. With such direct connections to the *dramatis personae*, she was able to smooth a variety of bumpy paths and ruffled feathers, but she remarked that 'One never forgot who one was with the Duke and Duchess. One was always very conscious of who they were.' She not only admired but loved the couple, insisting that Wallis was one of the kindest and most thoughtful people she knew. Few who worked for or came across the Windsors in other circumstances felt the same warmth from now on. Wallis's one source of unconditional love, Aunt Bessie, who had supported her niece regardless, lived on until she was a hundred, dying shortly after her birthday in 1964. Wallis was desolate at being unable to attend her funeral: she was in hospital following an operation on her foot and the doctors refused to release her.

Charles Pick, the publisher who oversaw publication of *The Heart Has its Reasons*, had several meetings with the Duchess, whom he 'certainly did not find witty or endearing in any way, but a rather brittle hard and vain person'. Having been warned in advance by the Foreign Office that he was not to refer to her erroneously as Her Royal Highness, he was on his guard when they first met. She was, he recalled, lying full length on a chaise longue, with a large round box of Charbonnel et Walker chocolates within reach, but probably untouched. 'As she rose to greet me her opening remark was: "Can you tell me who Marilyn Monroe's publicity agent is? I have all the newspapers each day and I was generally on the front page. But now I see that Marilyn Monroe is . . . Well, somebody has pushed me off."' Pick, recognizing that he was in for a difficult time, had to explain that he was not able to help her in displacing Monroe from the headlines.

Elsa Maxwell, the gossip columnist and professional party hostess who got to know Wallis after the war, had a very public falling out with her partly in connection with jealousy over Marilyn Monroe stealing headlines. There was eventually something of a reconciliation but, in an article previewing *The Heart Has its Reasons*, Maxwell wasted few opportunities to attack her former friend. She pointed out that as the Duchess 'seeks to compensate for all she hoped for and lost with an almost feverish pursuit of pleasure ... many of the things she has done in this search, largely because of the high-handed selfish way in which she has done them, have contributed to her final frustration – the fact that the Windsors' prestige is not what it used to be and the Windsors' romantic aura is sadly diminished'. She went on:

> When you see the Duchess today it is difficult to picture her as the heroine of one of the greatest love stories of all time. She's so brittle, hard and determined. Her hands, which were always large, never compliant or feminine, are less attractive than ever ... one incident, which stands out unpleasantly in my memory, is the Duchess' reaction to the death of Iles Brody shortly after he authored his unflattering book *Gone with the Windsors*.[21] 'See,' she said snapping her fingers, 'see what happens to them when they go against me!'

Maxwell had seen at first hand how much time and effort the Duchess devoted to planning menus and consulting with markets and cooks about what was fresh and available. 'One of her favourite dishes, I remember, was bacon cooked in molasses ... a reflection of the Duchess' southern background ... Only a woman with a will of iron could resist the food she serves. But she does. I doubt she will tell you [in her memoirs] about the Spartan diet she follows for the sake of her appearance.' This, coming from Maxwell, was rich but true: neither she, nor the Duke, ever let up on their strict dieting.

In March 1953, the Duke's mother, Queen Mary, died, little more than a year after the death of her second son, George VI. Again the

---

21 *Gone with the Windsors* was such a good title that it was used again in 2005 by Laurie Graham for a work of fiction about the couple.

Duke went, alone, to England for the funeral, bitterly aware of all the pain that his mother's refusal ever to accept Wallis as her daughter-in-law had caused and desolate that the acceptance he craved for his decision to marry Wallis had been withheld until the end. 'My sadness was mixed with incredulity', he famously wrote to Wallis, 'that any mother could have been so hard and cruel towards her eldest son for so many years ... I'm afraid the fluids in her veins have always been as icy cold as they are now in death.' Wallis wrote to him while he was away like a fussing mother: 'Please eat and take care of yourself ... don't fetch and carry for everyone including servants.' But she also begged him to 'Work [for the restoration of the allowance] on Cookie [the Queen Mother] and Shirley [Temple, that is the new Queen].'

With or without the allowance, Wallis and her team of interior decorators went ahead with plans to make 4 Route du Champ d'En-traînement as palatial as possible. Yet, in spite of the Windsors' beautifully appointed home and fine cuisine, the number of import-ant and interesting people who sought them out rapidly diminished. Wallis did little to conceal her fury and frustration that the brilliant Court of statesmen and artists – glimpsed for just a few tantalizing months in 1936 – had evaporated. The Mill, in contrast, was neither magnificent nor particularly elegant. Diana Mosley (née Mitford), wife of the British Fascist leader Sir Oswald, who became a close friend in the 1950s, was critical of the rather garish interior decor. 'It was very bright with patterned carpets, lots of apricot and really more Palm Beach than English or French.' Cecil Beaton called the Mill 'overdone and chichi ... Medallions on the walls, gimmicky pouffs, bamboo chairs. Simply not good enough.' And the American decorator Billy Baldwin was even more dismissive: 'Most of the Mill was awfully tacky but that's what Wallis had – tacky southern taste, much too overdone, much too elaborate and no real charm.' Both the Windsors were keen collectors of a variety of objects, and where Wallis's taste was left unfettered by decorators, this often resulted in a kind of cluttered vulgarity at the Mill. But, as most of their enter-taining was done in the city, only their closest friends saw this. Wallis always preferred town life, while the Duke was happier at the Mill than anywhere else and once again took up the gardening activities which had given him so much pleasure at the Fort.

Susan Mary Patten, wife of an American diplomat who became an acquaintance at this time, described the problem:

> I never saw a man so bored: He said to me 'you know what my day was today? ... I got up late and then I went with the Duchess and watched her buy a hat and then on the way home I had the car drop me off in the Bois to watch some of your American soldiers playing football and then I had planned to take a walk but it was so cold that I could hardly bear it. In fact I was afraid that I would be struck with cold in the way people are struck with heat so I came straight home ... when I got home the Duchess was having her French lesson so I had no one to talk to ...'

Harold Nicolson was similarly embarrassed when asked to give some editorial help on an article the Duke was writing. According to Nicolson's biographer, James Lees-Milne, there was much in the article he thought best left unsaid, but, more troubling than that, 'Harold was ever more distressed by the fading charm of the Duke and the aimlessness of his life in exile.'

By the mid-1950s the Windsors had established a routine. In addition to their two French homes, they would spend three months of the year in America and summer holidays staying with friends or going somewhere warm such as Biarritz, which became a favourite destination for a while, or Spain. But whether in Paris or New York, their life varied little, consisting of shopping, formal dinners and answering occasional demands to be patron of a charity. What jewels she was buying or had been given, what clothes she wore, how her hair was coiffed or her make-up applied was still a regular source of newspaper interest, which pleased her as she tried to regain some control of her circumstances and environment. This was the only way she knew to keep her many fears and phobias at bay and neither a hair on her head nor a cushion on her sofa was allowed to be out of place. Her sheets were ironed every night and the water in her vases was always crystal clear. The one exception in this highly regulated universe was the freedom allowed their scarcely house-trained pug dogs – Trooper, Disraeli and Diamond were the favourites – who ate their dinner from solid silver bowls on the lawn, had attention constantly lavished on them and were rarely reprimanded whatever they did inside or out. These were their substitute children, discussed and addressed in the special invented baby language of the Duke and Duchess. In 1936 the then King even referred to the dogs as 'the babies' who 'send you eanum flowers'. At home they had pug statues, pug sculptures and paintings of pugs and in 1952 Cartier created for the Duchess a gold and enamel pug-dog brooch with sad, citrine eyes.

Wallis sometimes wore a tiny gold notebook on a chain around her wrist and would use it to write down instructions. According to some stories, she would dab face powder on the walls of her home and demand of the decorators that they match the colour. Her rules for living were widely quoted – 'If you can afford it, then there is no pleasure in buying it,' or 'You cannot be too rich or too thin' – apocryphal, perhaps, but it was how she talked. Those who admired her, such as the interior decorator Nicholas Haslam, found her quick wit refreshing. He recounted how in 1960, when the engagement of Princess Margaret Rose to Anthony Armstrong Jones was announced, the Duchess quipped that these days: 'She's dropped the Rose and picked up the pansy.'

Her desire to be thin took on a new urgency once the eyes of the media began watching to see how she fared in the harsh light of the post-war world. If one day she weighed a pound more, she would starve that day. According to a journalist who knew her well, she weighed ninety-seven pounds (approximately seven stone) as she left the Bahamas and looked thinner than when she had arrived. But such weight loss resulted in 'her jaw becoming squarer ... her smile more downward and her eyebrows more satirical in their upward rise'. From now on breakfast for both of them was grapefruit juice and black tea, and lunch perhaps one egg or, for the Duke, one piece of fruit. She gave her chef written instructions about the weight of her portion of grilled meat: 190–200 grams, no more. And it was quickly noted by hostesses that she ate hardly anything and that even tiny portions were mostly just pushed around her plate while she talked. She understood the need to be in command of her image and generally had a surer touch with the style of her clothes than with her decor. She had a front-row seat at most of the Paris haute-couture shows with Dior, Balenciaga, Givenchy and Schiaparelli, as well as Mainbocher and Vionnet, among her favourites. Nonetheless, her craving to be first with the latest fashion led to one or two ghastly *faux pas* such as sequinned hot pants on one occasion and a Paco Rabanne ultra-modern spacesuit on another, and her muscular shoulders were less than ideal when it came to strapless evening dresses. But mostly she was impeccably chic and meticulously groomed, choosing plain clothes better to show off her enormous jewels, and (relatively) short skirts to show off her good legs. She was one of the first to make knee-length evening dresses acceptable for this reason. Whenever she was in New York she shopped at Bergdorf Goodman, ate at the Colony Club on the Upper East Side with her few women friends, and called at Elizabeth Arden's salon for beauty treatments and massages. Stories of how her multiple facelifts had left her with an immobile face and eyes that could never close even when she was asleep did the rounds.

When Wallis attended a Pillsbury Grand National bake-off competition in December 1950, held in the Waldorf where they were living at the time, she apparently wrote her own speech and the one quote that was remembered was 'there is one thing we all have in common ... we've all cooked a meal for the man we love'. It was a very American type of event in which the unsung heroine – the home-maker – was honoured for her kitchen skills. At the time it was a new and rather special event organized by the Pillsbury foodstuffs company and important for Wallis because she was hardly considered a home-maker – more a home-breaker – and she struck just the right note. During the war she had produced a cookbook of her favourite Southern recipes with royalties going to the Red Cross and now she became an adviser to a dress-pattern company. But it was still hard to convince the British public that this was a woman interested in domesticity of any kind.

Frank Giles, who had seen the couple in Bermuda, met them again in the 1950s when he was the *Times* correspondent in Paris and was invited to dinner. 'It was a large dinner party, rather unsavoury characters ... sort of blue rinse American widows and jet setting Europeans and hangers on. I thought the atmosphere was not very nice. But a very good dinner.' Giles recalled the Duke discussing Prime Minister Anthony Eden as 'a bad man, a hopeless man ... he helped precipitate the war through his treatment of Mussolini ... that's what he did, he helped to bring on the war ... pause ... and of course Roosevelt and the Jews ... When he was not making remarks about the Jews he could be charming. My opinion of her was that she had become rather coarse and raucous with a twanging yankee voice. Her opinions and her sort of cackling laughter were very unattractive – she had become, I thought, far less admirable if admirable at all.'

Her wit, sharpened by the bitterness of exile, was rarely appreciated by visiting Britons, and Giles was not alone in his views. The diplomat Jock Balfour once sat next to her at a dinner in Biarritz. When she dropped her handbag he bent down to pick it up – a gentlemanly gesture which elicited the sharp response: 'I like to see the British grovelling to me.' He may not have been amused, but she had a circle of American friends who relished her company.

From time to time, though, Wallis went too far, behaving disgracefully to the Duke in public. Many of their friends, even as the relationship began, observed her occasionally cruel verbal abuse, which the Duke had always appeared to need and respond to, presumably because the moment of forgiveness was sublime. Those who saw them now, in the last phase of their lives, remarked on the Duke's total devotion, the way his eyes would follow her around a room and take on a deep sadness when she was not there. Kenneth de Courcy, one-time confidant of Cabinet ministers and a controversial dining companion of the Duke of Windsor who had favoured appeasement, recalled a typical occasion shortly after the war:

I was staying near La Croë and the prefect of the Haute Maritime laid on a dinner for us ... [Wallis] was sitting down the table, quite a long way down, and he was sitting almost opposite me, next to the wife of the British Consul in Cannes. The municipality was building a new golf course in Cannes and the Duke of Windsor started talking to this woman about the new golf course. Perfectly harmless conversation but he played golf. Suddenly, in front of forty people, the Duchess yelled across the table: 'Oh do stop talking nonsense, David, you know nothing whatever about golf courses, do stop lecturing that woman.'

I lost my cool and said 'If I may say so, His Royal Highness presided over one of the greatest real estate concerns in the world, the Duchy of Cornwall, and knows all about golf courses and property.' She piped down at once.

Much more shocking was Wallis's flirtation with the millionaire homosexual playboy Jimmy Donahue. The Windsors first met the outrageous Donahue, heir to the Woolworth fortune, in 1947, and Wallis, always restless and often bored, was intrigued by his salacious conversation and often sordid actions. The Windsors and Donahue became a well-known threesome for a while, even though many in society were scandalized by their friendship with such a character. Wallis may have initially responded to Donahue out of jealousy, seeing a mutual attraction between the two men, and then deliberately set about making the Duke jealous in turn by embarking on some sort of a relationship with Donahue herself which excluded the Duke. Many concluded that she had acted out of boredom. Nicholas Haslam's view was that 'Donahue had originally caught the eye of the Duke and a sisterly rivalry developed with Wallis ... having known Jimmy later and spent weekends at his country house Broad-hollow (known as Boyhollow) on Long Island, I can't think he could ever have touched any woman let alone one as rigidly un-undressable as Wallis.' But as Michael Bloch recognized: 'There can be no doubt of the Duchess's preference for gay men: her favourite people included Cecil Beaton, Chips Channon, Somerset Maugham and indeed Coward himself ... many of her favourite moments were spent in the largely homosexual world of the great decorators and couturiers.'

Whatever went on between them, the Duke was publicly humiliated and privately hurt and the relationship ended suddenly. According to some this was because the Duke demanded it and Wallis obeyed; others claim that Donahue was eating so much garlic that his breath became offensive to the Duke and Duchess. 'Quite apart from other differences,' Wallis wrote in her memoirs, 'women seem to me to be divided into two groups: those who reason and those who are for ever casting about for reasons for their own lack of reason. While I might wish it to the contrary, the record of my life, now that I have for the first time attempted to see it whole, clearly places me with the second group. Women, by and large, I have concluded were never meant for plans and planning.'

Charles Pick, who published these memoirs, understood as well as anyone why Wallis concluded that planning was futile. Her own determination to lead a life of financial security had brought her neither great happiness nor satisfaction. Some years after publication of that book Pick and his wife were returning from New York on the *Queen Mary* when he heard that the Duke and Duchess were also on board, and were due to disembark at Cherbourg.

I spoke to the captain to ask if perhaps the Duke would like to meet. He explained that the Duchess was ill and that he had been given strict instructions that neither the Duke nor the Duchess were going to come out of their state room. All their meals were to be sent up and they didn't want to meet anybody.

When we arrived at Cherbourg at about 6 o'clock in the morning I was up and looking over the rails at the few passengers who disembarked. One was the Duke of Windsor, carrying a plastic carrier bag full of dirty laundry, and as he waited at the quayside various other items bought in America were unloaded and piled up beside him. He looked such a sad figure and I thought how pathetic that this once King of England should be taking his own laundry off the Queen Mary.

At the Mill, 'our only real home', as Wallis insisted, the Duchess had a mural painted on the main wall of the upstairs reception room showing a stone watermill wheel entwined with the words 'I'm not the miller's daughter but I've been through the mill.' The Duke enjoyed showing visitors a map displayed in his room with small lights which lit up to illustrate the places where he had travelled as Prince of Wales. But what he really treasured, on the opposite wall, was a framed collection of the regimental buttons of every British unit which fought in the trenches in the 1914–18 war, a further indication of his abiding sense of guilt at not being allowed to stay longer at the front and do more himself. His punishing physical regime and profound need for Wallis's harsh words make sense in this context. Nothing else in his life gave him any sense of achievement other than his marriage to Wallis. For him it was enough, almost. Wallis provided him with a mother's love and a mother's chiding. He genuinely saw no other way to continue his life and adored her to the end. It was an obsession. For her, the slavish devotion was at times claustrophobic and she was not afraid to show it. But love is famously impossible to define and in their case especially so. Few who knew them well described what they shared as love.

The Duke died, on 28 May 1972, after six months of acute pain from throat cancer, Wallis, as ever, his only solace. She was summoned to his bedroom at 2 a.m., took his hand and kissed his forehead, whispering 'My David'. He was seventy-five and, like his brother, had been a heavy smoker all his life. Just ten days earlier he had had a meeting with his niece, Queen Elizabeth II, who was then making a state visit to Paris. The Duchess received the royal party graciously, took tea with them, and then left the desperately ill Duke to meet the Queen of England alone, upstairs. The two women met again in England for the Duke's funeral on 5 June.

The Duke, like all old people, had worried about arrangements for his funeral. But in his case it was imperative to have a watertight agreement for himself as well as for Wallis, and he was relieved two years before he died to learn that permission had been granted by Queen Elizabeth for both his and Wallis's remains to be buried in the royal burial ground of Frogmore, the secluded Georgian house in the grounds of Windsor Castle where many of the British royal family had been buried since 1928. The Duchess, having long since conquered her fear of flying, flew over on 2 June 1972, accompanied by her French maid, American doctor and Grace, Lady Dudley, the

3rd Earl of Dudley's third wife, now one of her most loyal friends and a widow herself. She spent three nights as a guest of the Queen at Buckingham Palace and later told friends that although everything was correct she found the attitude of the royal family cold. Little had changed, even now.

At almost seventy-six, Wallis looked as elegant as ever in her mourning clothes, a plain black Givenchy coat with matching dress and waist-length chiffon veil, made in twenty-four hours especially for this occasion. She could not resist remarking to friends later how amusing she found her sister-in-law's outfit, especially the hat which she described as looking as if a white plastic arrow had been shot through it. In the morning at St George's Chapel, Windsor, she looked bewildered but showed dignity and composure, just as she did after lunch as she watched the Duke's coffin being lowered into the burial plot at Frogmore. Once again all those who saw her either face to face at the small private ceremony before lunch or in the televised proceedings of the afternoon could not escape their thoughts dwelling on 1936.

Over lunch itself, as Wallis told friends later, both Prince Philip and Lord Mountbatten, seated on either side of her, wasted no time in asking her what she intended to do with the Duke's possessions and papers and where she proposed to live. 'Don't worry. I shan't be coming back here,' she retorted, sharp as ever. She knew that wherever she lived it would be a kind of hell. She had long been terrified of a life alone and revealed in those frightening days in London that she had always hoped she would die first. Any thoughts she might have entertained about being brought back into the royal fold now that the Duke had gone were dashed when it became clear that no member of the royal family was prepared to accompany her to the airport, behaviour which the British press was not slow to pass comment on. The enduring image of Wallis alone, still in her elegant Givenchy silk mourning outfit, walking across the tarmac to the plane that would take her back to Paris, was for many in Britain the last they saw of her.

Wallis Alone

'All the wicked things she's done in her life'

I n one of her last diary entries the former Mary Kirk wrote:

> If I believed in that sort of thing, I might say that my getting
> cancer again was a judgement on me because I once wished that
> when Wallis came to die she'd be fully conscious and know it
> because she is the most arrant coward I ever knew and terrified of
> dying. I had hoped she knows it is to pay her back for all the wicked
> things she's done in her life – for I think of her as people think of
> Hitler, an evil force, for force she is in her way, not really intelligent
> or clever because there is no intellect, but full of animal cunning –
> how she would panic if forced to live now in England. I can just
> imagine what her terror of bombing would be. So now it is me
> that has to face dying . . . and although up to now I am not in the
> least afraid of dying I do want awfully to live.

Mary's anguished pencilled words, written in 1941, forty years or so
before Wallis's eventual death, are one of the most tragic and chilling
indictments imaginable – no less for the hate and pain embedded in
them than for the accurate prophecy they contain. Mary knew and
understood Wallis better than anyone and her closeness arguably
skewed her final verdict. 'If anyone could have damaged another
person she damaged me. I who had never done an unkind act or
treacherous thing to her in the many years we had been friends.'

There are many accounts of Wallis's long, lingering death, fed by
tubes as she lay on her narrow iron hospital bed, with her few
remaining friends such as Linda Mortimer, Grace Dudley, Aline,
Countess of Romanones and Diana Mosley prevented from seeing
her. One of those who did described her as turning wizened and

black, 'like a little monkey'. The British diplomat Walter Lees, who retained a fondness for the Duchess, was distressed when his glimpse of her lying in bed revealed a lifeless form with a tube in her nose.

Wallis, by then too ill to show fear, had lost any vestige of the control over her life which she so craved. Maître Suzanne Blum, an elderly French lawyer, who through her first husband had had a connection with the Duke's legal advisers at Allen and Overy and in her own right had successfully prosecuted a number of high-profile and celebrity cases in the late 1950s and 1960s, assumed total control of Wallis's life in her final decade. Wallis's friends blamed Maître Blum for refusing them entry. How did this happen?

Wallis returned to France after the Duke's funeral with all the ancient insecurities revived. She was terrified that she might now be bankrupt, that the French would terminate the arrangement on the house and that she would be thrown out on to the streets in poverty. In spite of an emotional attachment to the Mill – several of her pug dogs were buried under its trees – she quickly sold it for nearly £400,000, dispensed with a number of staff and then discussed her financial situation with Lord Mountbatten. He reassured her that as the Duke had left her everything – a fortune of around £3 million – and there was also a small discretionary allowance from the Queen, she would have plenty to live on. But she was not reassured, and when Mountbatten continued to pay her visits, urging her to make out a new will in favour of the Duke's family, it increased her anger and her neuroses. She told her friends that Mountbatten would sweep through the villa, picking up this and that, and exclaiming, 'Ah this belongs to the Royal Collection,' behaviour which made her adamant that it did not.

In 1973 Wallis visited England for the last time. She laid flowers on her husband's grave at Frogmore, took tea with the Queen at Windsor Castle and immediately returned to an empty life in Paris, frail and alone. With no family of her own in Europe, she was keenly aware of her continued exclusion from her late husband's family and of a lack of advisers to help her. Charles, Prince of Wales, wrote her a warm letter of condolence praising his great-uncle, and for a short time Wallis found this a comforting sign that relations might improve.

She even considered leaving some of her jewellery to Prince Charles, hoping that his future wife might wear it. But her enthusiasm for this act of generosity petered out in the face of Mountbatten's aggressive campaign to get as much as he could returned to England.

For a while she had the services of the distinguished lawyer Sir Godfrey Morley, of Allen and Overy, with whom she was on good terms, as well as her private secretary, John Utter, with whom she was not. There was also a personal secretary, the multilingual Johanna Schutz. Wallis dined out occasionally at Maxim's and received friends at home. Symbolically, she no longer wore her big, bouffant hair created by her trusted coiffeur, Alexandre, but reverted to the flatter style, with a middle parting, of her younger days. She ate less and drank more, often on an empty stomach. Alcohol had become her closest friend long before the Duke's death, and the writer Lesley Blanch had memorably described the Windsors as 'tiny twins with large bottles of drink'.

Within a year of the Duke's death, Wallis was in hospital with a broken hip. But, just as this was mending, she fell again while in hospital, apparently demonstrating the Charleston to a bemused nurse. A few months after she was finally discharged she fell once more, this time against a bath, and cracked several ribs. The nurses now found her confused and senile, asking the same questions dozens of times. Friends noticed that she would speak of the past as if the Duke were still present, even begging him not to abdicate. When she was discharged after this accident her doctor, Dr Jean Thin, advised that all alcohol be removed. But it was too late. At the end of 1975 she was back in the American hospital with either a perforated ulcer or Crohn's disease, or possibly both, seriously debilitated and ill. She recovered enough to be released the following year to a house where most of the staff had now been dismissed, only to be readmitted in February 1976 – this time diagnosed with a near-total physical collapse, according to some reports, following a massive intestinal haemorrhage.

It is impossible not to imagine that she wanted to die, that she was now terrified of living. Yet, according to a young doctor who attended her at the hospital at this time, although she was confused she still looked immaculate, her hair coiffed and raven black and her lips reddened, thanks to the ministrations of a hairdresser and beautician. In the autumn of that year, the Queen Mother was in Paris on a state visit and proposed a meeting with Wallis, by then slightly recovered but still in a weak and fragile state. Dr Thin and Maître Blum decided that after all these years of silence this was not the moment. Instead, the Queen Mother sent a bouquet of two dozen red and white roses with a card signed, 'In Friendship, Elizabeth'. Although according to the author, Hugo Vickers, the visit was never going to happen but was merely 'a sop to the press'.

The formidable Maître Blum now became the Duchess's spokesman and declared herself the Duchess's friend as well. Blum, born into a provincial French Jewish family as Suzanne Blumel, had survived the war by fleeing with her then husband to the US, where she studied law at Columbia University. She was tough and now saw her role as not only to protect the Duchess's material interests by preventing the British royals from acquiring the Duke's possessions, but also to defend the Windsors' reputation, which she felt had been unjustly maligned. Another responsibility was keeping the Duchess alive as long as possible, which proved an expensive business over more than a decade and, to the horror of friends, necessitated selling off some of the Windsor trinkets. Those who crossed Blum in an attempt to get directly to the Duchess often ridiculed her, but they did not win. For another decade the Duchess lived on, with only occasional moments of semi-lucidity, scarcely able to do anything for herself. Initially she was lifted into a wheelchair for much of the day, bathed and spoon-fed mouthfuls of food. Cruelly, even the weighing continued, although no longer as part of the attempt to shed pounds. Her personal maid, Señora Martin, who had been with the Windsors since 1964, recounted how, just before the final collapse, she would lift the Duchess into her arms like a limp rag-doll and then stand on the scales with her. Señora Martin's weight would then be deducted from the total in order to assess the dwindling weight of the Duchess. But the decline was steep and soon her long hair was allowed to grow white; she was almost totally blind and paralysed so severely that she could neither speak nor swallow. Still, she was not in a coma and her eyes were said occasionally to flicker into life. Could she have been aware of her suffering and abandonment?

Wallis Warfield, so full of fun and life as a child, had outlived three husbands and most of her women friends. Now she lay in a darkened room, hallucinating, desperately emaciated and bedridden. The house was almost as dilapidated as its former owner with a leaking roof and rising damp. It would be hard to imagine a more desperate, lingering death than hers, just as her erstwhile friend Mary had once imagined for her. She died finally, aged ninety, on 24 April 1986. There was no autopsy.

The Lord Chamberlain, Lord Airlie, flew to Paris to escort the body back to an England which had refused to welcome her when she was alive. Nearly 200 people attended her funeral service in St George's Chapel, Windsor. The Duchess of Marlborough, a friend although no longer a close one, observed: 'I went to look at the flowers … It was tragic. They were all from dressmakers, jewellers, Dior, Van Cleef, Alexandre. Those people were her life.' After the funeral a small party, including the Queen and the Queen Mother, who went on to live for another eighteen years, saw Wallis to her final resting place. A hedge, which had bothered Wallis when she spotted it at the Duke's funeral, had now been removed so that Wallis's earthly remains could be placed next to the Duke's at Frogmore and not far from those of Queen Victoria and her beloved husband, Prince Albert, for whom the mausoleum at Frogmore had been built.

The transformation from flesh-and-blood character to imagined myth had begun long before her death, while she was still a ghostly presence often referred to in hushed whispers or angry asides as 'That Woman'. With no new photographic images, the headlines in the fashion pages of newspapers abruptly ceased just as the mystery increased. The reclusive widow in a darkened room frozen in time has echoes of Miss Havisham in Dickens's *Great Expectations*. Yet Wallis, far from being jilted, had found herself obliged to go ahead with a wedding she had not wanted. And the abdication, not in itself a crisis but a solution to a crisis, was a drama not unlike a wedding that failed to go ahead. After reigning for 325 days, it was Edward VIII who jilted his country on the eve of his own Coronation. This was too big a drama not to be immortalized on stage and in film, as indeed it has been many times. *Crown Matrimonial*, a 1972 play by the English writer Royce Ryton, broke new ground for being the first time a living member of the royal family was portrayed on stage. The play, while emphasizing the virtues of duty and responsibility, nonetheless laid the groundwork for what was described as the greatest love story of the century but a love story where the heroine was a one-dimensional, grasping adventuress with an unhealthy knowledge of bizarre sexual practices. Writers and artists, aware of how the establishment wanted her to be seen, remain attracted by the need to get beyond this and strip away the myth. Nonetheless, the perceptions have been exceedingly slow to shift and – to date – most writers and artists have created unflattering portraits.

The publicity surrounding the first sale of the Duchess of Windsor's jewellery, held by Sotheby's in Geneva within a year of her death – selling it in London was considered offensive to the royal family – played heavily on the romance. Although both Duke and Duchess had apparently agreed that no other woman was to wear the jewellery, which they wanted broken up and reset, they did not leave written instructions for this. Extracts from the love letters were included in the catalogue, which portrayed the Duke as a man who spoke with authority about style while the lady for whom the jewels were destined was 'elegance personified'. The sale raised a phenomenal $50,281,887, approximately seven times the estimate. The diamond and platinum brooch in the shape of the Prince of Wales feathers, an item Prince Charles had contemplated buying, was bought by the actress Elizabeth Taylor for $567,000. Even the house where Wallis had died became caught up not in fire but in myth. After the Duchess's death it returned to state ownership and was immediately leased by Harrods owner Mohamed al-Fayed and expensively restored over several years, as a fitting tribute to what he described as 'the couple's romantic legacy'. It was the last place to which Dodi Fayed, his son, took another royal outsider, Princess Diana, hours before her tragic death in Paris in the early hours of 31 August 1997.

The American social-realist painter Jack Levine was one of the first to give artistic expression to Wallis. He found the Duke and Duchess rewarding subjects for his Hogarthian, expressionist-style paintings, and *Reception in Miami* (1948) cleverly satirized the Windsors' recent visit to Florida as well as recalling the 1937 moment when the Duchess smiled and curtseyed to Hitler. Levine said at the time he had been inspired by the way 'our co-nationals began to scrape and bow' as they greeted the honoured guests. He felt 'it was a kind of violation of everything that the Declaration of Independence and Constitution stand for'.

Fiction, too, often exaggerates the unbelievable in order to help us understand whatever appears strange in a life and in literature. Any mention of 'Mrs Simpson', as she was henceforth generally known to history, soon became shorthand for a certain type of woman. As early as 1960 Anthony Powell in *Casanova's Chinese Restaurant*, the fifth in his twelve-volume *Dance to the Music of Time*, found her compelling as a minor character off. For the awkward, faintly ludicrous Kenneth Widmerpool, a meeting with Mrs Simpson in the 1930s supplies him with lustre; he can talk of nothing else and sees himself as a result as a man of the world. It is perhaps easier for novelists than playwrights to look at the mismatch between public glamour and private anguish by exploring the dark heart of what it was like to be Wallis Simpson. Actors including Faye Dunaway, Nichola McAuliffe, Joely Richardson and Andrea Riseborough have all found Wallis a most challenging and satisfying role, and there is no shortage of those who want to interpret That Woman. But, as theatre critic Dominic Maxwell, reviewing one of the latest attempts to put Wallis on stage, noted, however full of humour and panache, any play on the subject risks suffering from a necessary frenzy of facts when what is wanted is feelings.

The 'facts' were soon supplied by the official histories and biographies. Frances Donaldson started work on her official biography of Edward VIII as early as 1969, when many of the main protagonists, as well as her subject, were still alive, with obvious advantages and disadvantages. Her account, published in 1974 two years after the Duke's death, was justly praised and provided the basis for the 1978 British television series *Edward and Mrs Simpson*, to which Maître

Blum strongly objected – in vain. Mary Kirk's sister Buckie belatedly wrote to Lady Donaldson wishing to discuss what she believed were important areas 'upon which I could throw a little more light'. Her twenty-four-page account was never used, but Buckie's insight has informed my understanding of the role the Kirk sisters played in Wallis's life.

Sharply aware of the limitations of authorized works, the British essayist and novelist William Boyd wrote a 'fictional autobiography' *Any Human Heart* (2002), in which Logan Mountstuart journeys through the entire twentieth century. Boyd devotes a considerable part of his story to the latter's meetings with, and ultimate betrayal by, the Duke and Duchess of Windsor. Boyd is intrigued not only by the dark heart of Wallis herself but by the darkness surrounding her. He not only recognizes the Windsors' selfishness and obliviousness of those around them but sees how, in marrying the Duke, the Duchess swallowed a form of poison which slowly corroded both their lives. Boyd is especially interested in what he perceives as the Duke's duplicitous role when, as governor of the Bahamas in 1943, he colluded with corrupt detectives in order to 'solve' the Oakes murder case, thereby perverting the course of justice and risking the death of an innocent man. To what extent was his conscience troubled and, if not troubled unduly, what sort of woman can devote her life to such a man, he asks? Although the novel was published in 2002, long after his protagonists were dead, Boyd has written both fiction and non-fiction about the Duke and Duchess, undertaking, as any historian must, months of research 'poring over photographs and memoirs and generally trying to get inside their heads ... to imagine them into life'. Yet he believes there is a greater truth available to the novelist who tells his story well. His is a damning portrait which does little to rehabilitate the pair.

Other novelists of various nationalities have been attracted not merely by the vivid personalities of the Duke and Duchess but by the dramatic history swirling around them in the 1930s. Timothey Findley, the Canadian author of *Famous Last Words* (1981), wrote of the Duke and Duchess prepared during the war to sell their souls to the devil. In Findley's hands Wallis, learning that the Duke had abdicated, reacts with hatred. 'I hate him,' she says repeatedly. 'I do, I hate him.' Of course the hatred was necessary for the novelist's plot, which sees the Windsors conspire with Ribbentrop to overthrow Hitler, assume control of the Nazi Party and plan a takeover of Europe. And indeed there were, in real time, moments when something very close to hatred came perilously close to the surface. Perry Brownlow, who knew both the Duke and Duchess well, suspected that living with Wallis taught the Duke to lie. But as a young man the Duke had insisted to Freda Dudley Ward: 'I feel more and more strongly that it's absolutely legitimate to lie and that we are more than within our rights to do so when it concerns our own private affairs, angel.' Perhaps living with Wallis strengthened the toxic mix. More recently the Spanish novelist Javier Marías, in the first part of his trilogy *Your Face Tomorrow*, tells the story of the glamorous naval intelligence officer Sir Peter Russell, thinly disguised as Sir Peter Wheeler, who acted as custodian, companion, escort and even sword of Damocles to the Duke and Duchess, 'that frivolous pair ... not prepared to go into exile ... without her wardrobe, her table linen, her royal bed linen, her silver and her porcelain dinner service'. Wheeler in the story insists that the Duchess 'wasn't that ugly ... well she was, but there was something troubling about her too'. In order to ensure that his charges arrived safely in the Bahamas in 1940 Wheeler was issued with a revolver not simply for use against the Germans. 'No, we understood that we should use those pistols against the Duke and Duchess. Better dead than in Hitler's hands.'

It is this tantalizing version of counterfactual history – what if Hitler had won the war? – that has led not only conspiracy theorists but serious historians as well as novelists to give Wallis Warfield of Baltimore a deeply significant role in world history. Merely by marrying the ineffectual King she did not only England but the world a favour. His removal from the throne ensured that his own patriotism was never tested nor was the nation ruled, in the midst of an existential struggle against Nazi Germany, by a man whose intimates at times questioned his very sanity. And one does not have to believe the extreme versions of some conspiracy theorists to see the merit of such an argument. It leads to another thought about her significance. Every generation throws up an ordinary person who, through luck or circumstance or the infinitely variable nature of the human condition, diverts the course of history in unpredictable ways. In the 1930s Wallis was certainly That Woman.

The Duke and Duchess of Windsor Society, an international affinity group dedicated to disseminating information about the historical importance of the lives of the Duke and Duchess through its quarterly journal and website, lists on its home page at least twenty books of fiction which use Wallis as a protagonist. The list is growing and there are dozens more books of non-fiction, some dealing with particular episodes in their lives, as well as films and plays awaiting viewing. Opinions are slowly changing. Rose Tremain, in her 2006 novella *The Darkness of Wallis Simpson*, imagines the pain of Wallis as an octogenarian whose thoughts were all twisted up, who could no longer walk unaided to the door, begging to be allowed to forget, to be allowed to die. Tremain compounds the already cruel fate of the elderly Wallis by making her character able to remember only her painful early life, while 'the little man', the husband who made her notorious, she cannot remember at all. It's a sympathetic portrayal, and as such may be part of an ongoing reassessment of Wallis.

Wallis saw herself as an ordinary woman, born with none of the privileges that money or good looks can bring, but possessed of insatiable ambition. So she determined to make the best of what she had and focused determinedly on a goal to enhance that. 'I really had no idea of exactly what I intended to make of my life, but I was determined to make it a success within my capacities,' she wrote. 'It was not quite enough for me to be, or at least to try to be, the life of the party or to spend my existence merely taking part in good conversation. I wanted something more out of life.'

In fashioning something more of and for herself she collided brutally with others; Win Spencer, Ernest Simpson, Mary Kirk, Audrey Dechert, Foxy Gwynne, Bernard Rickatson-Hatt and Nancy Dugdale, to take a handful, found that their lives were skewed, sometimes painfully, through contact with Wallis.

Decades after her death, Wallis continues to exercise a stronger magnetism for writers than almost any other royal personality, film star or historical character. Why would a novelist, in the folds of whose rich imagination any invented character in any situation at any time in history can lurk and take shape, choose to limit his or her focus to a character, however enigmatic, who is already known? Perhaps the explanation for our fascination lies partly in the fact that she remains elusive. She is not and cannot ever be completely known. Her personality offered both light and shade, good and evil, darkness underneath the gloss. Her life was full of adventure and travel, escape and deception – ingredients a novelist devours – and it followed a natural narrative arc, ending, in one sense, in 1936. Wallis in her lifetime defied her critics and yielded few secrets about what it was about her that forced a man to renounce everything he had been born to enjoy and to give up one of the most illustrious thrones in the world. Because we cannot, by any rational means, explain why a middle-aged, married woman with large hands and a mole on her chin convinced a troubled, boyish prince to believe that his life could have no meaning unless lived alongside her, novelists and playwrights, actors and historians need to dig into their imagination in order to explain it.

Wallis's life, unbelievable in so many ways, demands both imagination and factual accuracy if any sense is to be made of it. For her appeal is not simply that a lot happened to her. Above all of this, what has made her irresistible to a wide swathe of writers and artists is her personal sparkle – the echo of her magnificent jewellery – as well as her wit, her charisma and, in the end, her courage and grace that enabled her to endure a predicament she had created for herself and live with a man she privately ridiculed. She may have been terrified of dying, but in a very real way she lives on, preserved for posterity as others saw her.

Notes

Abbreviations

AB: Aunt Bessie
Baldwin Papers: Philip Williamson and Edward Baldwin (eds), *The Baldwin Papers: A Conservative Statesman 1908–47*
Bodl. Lib.: Bodleian Library, Oxford
EP: Prince Edward
EAS: Ernest Simpson
DoW: Duke of Windsor
FDW: Freda Dudley Ward
HHR: Wallis Windsor, *The Heart Has its Reasons*
LAM: Lady Alexandra Metcalfe
LFP: Rupert Godfrey (ed.), *Letters from a Prince*
MHS: Maryland Historical Society, Baltimore
MKR: Mary Kirk Raffray
NA PRO: The National Archives, Public Record Office, Kew
NLD: Notes for Lady Donaldson
TLS: *Times Literary Supplement*
TOMS: Anne Kirk Cooke and Elizabeth Lightfoot, *The Other Mrs Simpson*
W: Wallis
WM: Walter Monckton
WSC: Winston S. Churchill

Chapter 1: *Becoming Wallis*

4 entered a room: Nicholas Haslam, *Redeeming Features*, Jonathan Cape 2010, pp. 191–6

6 'church in Baltimore': Wallis Windsor, *The Heart Has its Reasons*, Michael Joseph 1956 (hereafter *HHR*), p. 20

6 'of several friends': Nellie W. Jones, *A School for Bishops: A History of the Church of Baltimore*, City Publications 1952, p. 37

6 'alone the clock': *HHR* p. 130

7 'above two others': Alastair Forbes, *Times Literary Supplement* (hereafter *TLS*), 1 Nov. 1974

9 'be like you': *HHR* p. 19

10 'to the moon': ibid., p. 24

10 'touch the chair': ibid., p. 22

10 '"just a minute?"': ibid., p. 23

11 'cover the rent': ibid., p. 28

11 'thrown much together': ibid., p. 25

11 'and disturbing barrier': ibid., p. 27

12 'give me things': WW to Aunt Bessie (hereafter AB), 18 Nov. 1935, Michael Bloch (ed.), *Wallis and Edward: Letters 1931–1937: The Intimate Correspondence of the Duke and Duchess of Windsor*, Weidenfeld & Nicolson 1986, p. 143

12 'my Baltimore obscurity': quoted in Jehanne Wake, *Sisters of Fortune*, Chatto & Windus 2010, p. 51

13 'in every setting': *HHR* p. 35

14 'for being forbidden': Ralph Martin, *The Woman He Loved*, W. H. Allen 1974, p. 29

15 'of the kimonos': Mary McPherson, *A History of Oldfields 1867–1989: A Feeling of Family*, privately printed n.d., p. 45

15 under a pseudonym: Edwina Wilson, *Her Name was Wallis Warfield*, New York, E. P. Dutton 1957, p. 5

16 'those days) cowardice': Anne Kirk Cooke and Elizabeth Lightfoot, *The Other Mrs Simpson: Postscript to the Love Story of the Century*, New York, Vantage Press 1976 (hereafter *TOMS*), p. 10

16 'made it entertaining': unpublished memo by E. B. Kirk, Notes for Lady Donaldson (hereafter NLD), 1979

16 'boys in droves': NLD

17 'of our parents': *TOMS*, p. 8

17 'anyone except YOU!': ibid.

17 'Oldfields went to college': *HHR* p. 50

18 'did indeed continue': ibid., p. 48

18 'did not say': NLD

19 'my heart broke': *HHR* p. 47

19 'outside of Maryland': Martin, *The Woman He Loved*, p. 11

21 'most fascinating aviator': *HHR* p. 59

21 'struck me instantly': ibid., p. 61

21 'in a tight place': ibid.

22 'waiting too long': *HHR* p. 65

23 'cause of the nation': *Chicago Tribune*, 20 Aug. 1917

23 'assemblage of guests': *Baltimore Sun*, 9 Nov. 1916

24 'wife of Major General Barnett USMC': ibid.

24 'or his hand': *HHR* p. 74

Chapter 2: *Understanding Wallis*

26 'opposite was true': *HHR* p. 20

26 'was safely past': ibid., p. 76

27 'out of curiosity': ibid., p. 64

27 globally per annum: 2006 Survey by the Scottish Audit of Genital Anomalies

28 'use the word': Dr Jonathan Hutchinson, *Archives of Surgery*, 1896, pp. 64–6

29 'woman at all': Michael Bloch, *The Duchess of Windsor*, Weidenfeld & Nicolson 1996, p. 11

30 'cold, overbearing, vain': Nancy Dugdale, wife of Thomas Dugdale MP, PPS to Prime Minister Stanley Baldwin, unpublished diary of the constitutional crisis occasioned by the Abdication of the King, Crathorne Papers

30 'all of a piece': Christopher Inglefield FRCS, Conversation with author, 14 Jan. 2010

31 'changed her appearance': ibid.

32 'of my own': *HHR* p. 367

33 'a special gift': Dr Domenico di Ceglie, Conversation with author, 24 Feb. 2010

33 'opposite was true': *HHR* p. 20

33 their parents indicate: *Duke and Duchess of Windsor Historical Society* quarterly issue 409, p. 21

34 'take his place': *Chicago Tribune*, 30 Jan. 1918

34 brutal, a cad: Kirk Hollingsworth, Conversation with author, 1 Nov. 2009

34 'at a party': *HHR* p. 83

34 'the same interests,' ibid., p. 84

35 'I certainly did': ibid., p. 83

35 'personal Mason–Dixon line': Donald Spoto, *Dynasty: The Turbulent Saga of the Royal Family from Victoria to Diana*, Simon & Schuster 1995, p. 223

36 'received by the Prince . . .': *Baltimore Sun*, 12 Nov. 1936

36 'presented to her': *Baltimore News-Post*, July 1953

36 'at Del Monte': all the above quoted by Professor Benjamin Sacks, *Journal of San Diego History*, 1988, vol. 34, no. 1, www.sandiegohistory.org/journal/88winter/duchess.htm

36 'with ball and mallet': ibid.

37 'near unto cwying': Prince Edward (hereafter E) to Freda Dudley Ward (hereafter FDW), 8 April 1920, Rupert Godfrey (ed.), *Letters from a Prince, March 1918–January 1921*, Warner Books 1998 (hereafter *LFP*), p. 334

37 'deal of unhappiness': Ethel Spencer, *Chicago Tribune*, 4 Dec. 1936

37 'like a tonic': Mrs E. Clarence Moore, charity ball souvenir programme, quoted by Professor Sacks in *Journal of San Diego History*, 1988, vol. 34, no. 1

38 'took to the bottle': *HHR* p. 87

38 'mixed-up neurotic': ibid.

38 'myself in check': ibid.

39 'disgrace upon us': ibid., p. 91

Chapter 3: *Wallis in Wonderland*

40 'and my emotions': *HHR* p. 94

42 'all its aspects': ibid., p. 97

42 'bubbled like champagne': Martin, *The Woman He Loved*, p. 70

44 'of a plane': *HHR* p. 106

45 one biographer claims: Greg King, *The Duchess of Windsor: The Uncommon Life of Wallis Simpson*, Aurum Press 1999, p. 61

45 'over the girls': *HHR* p. 107

45 'her lotus year': ibid., p. 112

49 guise of relief: FO 148, marked 'Secret evidence of Bolshevik activity in the Far East', National Archives, Public Record Office (hereafter NA PRO)

49 'as pornographic material': Harriet Sergeant, *Shanghai*, Jonathan Cape 1991, p. 340

50 'him as "Robbie"': *HHR* p. 108

50 'even more pleasant': ibid.

50 'then predominantly British': ibid.

51 'of quasi-independence': ibid., p. 109

52 'responsible for me': ibid., p. 110

53 'of an athlete': ibid., p. 112

53 'stay with them': ibid., p. 113

53 'expect to know': ibid., p. 114

53 'whole long roll': NLD

53 'in her heart': *HHR* p. 115

54 'have different meanings': Martin, *The Woman He Loved*, p. 79

55 'of her forehead': Alberto Da Zara, *Pelle d'Ammiraglio*, Milan, Mondadori 1948, p. 183

55 'among adoring males': Diana Hutchins Angulo, *Peking Sun, Shanghai Moon: A China Memoir*, ed. Tess Johnston, Hong Kong, Old China Hand Press 2008, p. 27

55 'complimentary than women': Diana Hutchins Angulo, Correspondence with author, July 2010

55 inscribed 'To you': Angulo, *Peking Sun, Shanghai Moon*, p. 27

55 'old aristocratic families': Diana Hutchins Angulo, Correspondence with author, July 2010

55 'very taken by her': ibid.

56 and botched abortion: Charles Higham, *Mrs Simpson: Secret Lives of the Duchess of Windsor*, Sidgwick & Jackson 1998, p. 50, quoting Mrs Miles. See also Ray Moseley, *Mussolini's Shadow: The Double*

Life of Count Galeazzo Ciano, New Haven, Yale University Press 2000, pp. 9–10

Chapter 4: *Wallis on the Lookout*

57 'a strange city': *HHR* p. 121

58 'her last lap': Martin, *The Woman He Loved*, p. 85

58 'with equal satisfaction': ibid., p. 124

58 'call inferior decorating': ibid., p. 122

60 'and not remarry': *Baltimore News*, 28 Oct. 1927

60 sister Buckie, furious: NLD

61 by Jacques' syphilis: Kirk Hollingsworth, Conversation with author, 1 Nov. 2009

61 'marry for money': NLD

61 'provided with money': NLD

62 'a man's world': *HHR* p. 128

62 'finally, to everything': Cleveland Amory, *Who Killed Society?*, New York, Harper & Brothers 1960, p. 238

63 his own expense: Bernard Susser, *The Jews of South-West England: The Rise and Decline of their Medieval and Modern Communities*, University of Exeter Press 1993

66 'looking after me': Bloch, *The Duchess of Windsor*, 15 July 1928, p. 27

67 'in a flash': *HHR* p. 139

67 'seem so important': Bloch, *Letters*, p. 11

67 'at Victoria Station': *HHR* p. 139

67 'since early childhood': ibid.

67 'to the core': Brendon Papers, Bren 2/2/1, Churchill Archives

68 'the human spirit': *HHR* p. 146

68 'a second sex': ibid., p. 143

68 'vacantly before me': ibid., p. 144

69 'in England live': Mary Kirk Raffray (hereafter MKR), *TOMS*, p. 5

70 'and many pillows': MKR to Mrs Henry Child Kirk, 2 June 1931, *TOMS*, p. 1

70 'her feminine interests' *HHR* p. 159

70 'right through one': ibid., p. 149

72 'and dinner parties': ibid., p. 160

72 'widely appreciated knack': ibid., p. 161

72 'wants to leave': MKR to her mother, 7 June 1931, *TOMS*, p. 15

72 'bathroom with her': NLD

Chapter 5: *Wallis on the Sidelines*

73 'mind made up': W to AB, 13 Jan. 1931, Bloch, *Letter*s, p. 24

73 'his cultural horizons': Philip Ziegler, *King Edward VIII: The Official Biography*, Collins 1990, p. 41

74 'his own thoughts': ibid.

74 'a brute to his children': James Lees-Milne, *Harold Nicolson*, vol. II: *1930–1968*, Chatto & Windus 1981, pp. 230 and 235

74 'allowed to fight!!': Ziegler, *King Edward VIII*, p. 57

75 'of his inadequacy': ibid., p. 58

75 and exercise less: see *LFP*, p. xvii

75 'am guilty of': EP to King George V, 5 Sept. 1920, Royal Archives, quoted in Ziegler, *King Edward VIII*, p. 109

75 'unfair on Papa': ibid., p. 75

76 'killed or wounded': Alan Clark (ed.), *A Good Innings: The Private Papers of Viscount Lee of Fareham*, John Murray 1974, pp. 138–9

76 'long to angel!!': EP to FDW, 26 March 1918, *LFP* p. 10

77 'fed up they are': EP to FDW, 22 Dec. 1918, *LFP* p. 147

77 'a national disaster': EP to FDW, 26 Oct. 1919, *LFP* p. 267

78 'and sounds Bolshevik': EP to FDW, *LFP* pp. 346–7; *Daily Telegraph*, 6 June 2001

78 'can't live together': EP to FDW, 7 Nov. 1919, *LFP* p. 276

78 'feel like "resigning"!!': EP to FDW, 24 Oct. 1919, *LFP* p. 266

78 'work for him': EP to FDW, 18 Oct. 1921, *LFP* p. 262

78 'beloved little mummie!!' EP to FDW, 14 Oct. 1919, *LFP* p. 259

79 'ancestry as poor Edward P': Alan Lascelles to Nigel Nicolson, 5 Sept. 1965, Lascelles Papers, Lasl 8/8 Churchill Archives

79 'get away with it"': ibid.

79 '"lock him up"': ibid.

80 'once a week': ibid.

80 'the next morning': interview with Sarah Bradford, Brendon Papers, Bren 2/2/1, Churchill Archives

80 'for his role': Duff Hart-Davis (ed.), Introduction to *In Royal Service: The Letters and Journals of Sir Alan Lascelles 1920–1936*, Hamish Hamilton 1989, p. xi

81 'conventions of polite society': Hector Bolitho, *King Edward VIII: His Life and Reign*, Eyre & Spottiswoode 1937, p. 75

82 'of one's employer': Ziegler, *King Edward VIII*, p. 110

82 'the couple concerned': EP to Queen Mary, quoted in ibid., p. 171

82 'a flirtatious nature': Wake, *Sisters of Fortune*, p. 208

82 'cos it'll destroy me': Ziegler, *King Edward VIII*, p. 173, 20 Feb. 1924, Broadlands Papers S 395

83 'mostly about trivialities': King, *The Duchess of Windsor*, p. 96

83 'for this drama': Sir Henry Channon, *Chips: The Diaries of Sir Henry Channon*, ed. Robert Rhodes James, Penguin 1967, p. 66; Ziegler, *King Edward VIII*, p. 223 for supplying the name

83 'coloured symphony toy': Lady Diana Cooper, *The Light of Common Day*, Rupert Hart-Davis 1959, p. 162

84 'weekends, I suppose': HRH The Duke of Windsor (hereafter DoW), *A King's Story*, Cassell 1951, p. 237

84 'voyage would end': Gloria Vanderbilt and Thelma, Lady Furness, *Double Exposure: A Twin Autobiography*, New York, David McKay 1958, p. 266

85 'frighteningly high': *HHR* p. 171

85 'and utter naturalness': ibid., p. 169

85 'but bad manners': Vanderbilt and Furness, *Double Exposure*, p. 275

85 'I am right': *HHR* p. 165

86 'an informal way': W to AB, 13 Jan. 1931, Bloch, *Letters*, p. 24

86 'of them again': W to AB, 5 Feb. 1931, Bloch, *Letters*, p. 28

86 'frowzy dressed town': W to AB, 24 Jan. 1932, Bloch, *Letters*, p. 48

86 'without the cold': W to AB, 16 April 1932, Bloch, *Letters*, p. 32

87 'talked until 2 o'clock': MKR to Mrs H. C. Kirk, 2 June 1931, *TOMS*, p. 4

88 'for it anyway': ibid.

88 'such an extravagance': *HHR* p. 174
88 'imitations but effective': W to AB, n.d., Bloch, *Letters*, p. 35
88 'the women look ghastly': *HHR* p. 175
89 'can never marry her': MKR diary, private archive
89 'can't help me': W to AB, 16 April 1931, Bloch, *Letters*, p. 31
89 '"out of danger, Buckie"': NLD

Chapter 6: *Wallis in Control*

91 'went very well': *HHR* p. 190
91 'an unsavoury nature': Nancy Dugdale diary
92 'billhook and whistling': *HHR* p. 201
92 'ping pong balls': ibid., p. 183
92 'to say what': W to AB, 4 Feb. 1932, Bloch, *Letters*, p. 50
93 'could not resist': W to AB, 26 Feb. 1932, Bloch, *Letters*, p. 60
93 'next six months': W to AB, 11 Dec. 1932, Bloch, *Letters*, p. 62
93 'to a friendship': *HHR* p. 191
94 'Thelma handed me': NLD
94 'you need me': W to AB, 17 May 1933, Bloch, *Letters*, p. 68
95 'to my figure': ibid.
95 'Princess of Wales': W to AB, 30 May 1933, Bloch, *Letters*, p. 70
95 'have refused her': ibid.
95 'selfish old pig': W to AB, 29 Oct. 1933, Bloch, *Letters*, p. 76
96 'look after him?': *HHR* p. 192
96 'to be lonely': Vanderbilt and Furness, *Double Exposure*, p. 291
96 'cheer him up': W to AB, 26 Jan. 1934, Bloch, *Letters*, p. 84
96 'am the latest': W to AB, 12 Feb. 1934, Bloch, *Letters*, p. 87
96 'with his papers': *HHR* p. 193
96 'man is exhausting': W to AB, 12 Feb. 1934, Bloch, *Letters*, p. 87
96 'during the dancing': *HHR* p. 193
96 'all is safe': W to AB, 18 Feb. 1934, Bloch, *Letters*, p. 89
97 'with him *alone*': (Wallis italics) W to AB, 25 April 1934, Bloch, *Letters*, p. 93
97 'swansong before 40': ibid.
97 'loved it all?': W to AB, postmarked 21 April 1934, Bloch, *Letters*, p. 93

97 'time will show': W to AB, 18 Nov. 1935, Bloch, *Letters*, p. 143

97 'all the time': W to AB, 27 Oct. 1934, Bloch, *Letters*, p. 101

98 'as a Mason': JCCD/d Feb. 1936, JCCD Papers 26, The Parliamentary Archive, House of Lords Record Office

98 'into sponsoring him': Thomas Papers, quoted in Ziegler, *King Edward VIII*, p. 278

98 'from him again': Sarah Bradford, *Sunday Times* cutting 1998 n.d., private archive

99 'him exceedingly well': Vanderbilt and Furness, *Double Exposure*, p. 298

99 '"is definitely no"': *HHR* p. 194

100 'them more often': Ziegler, *King Edward VIII*, p. 229

100 'not the second': Aird Papers quoted in ibid.

100 'join the party': *HHR* p. 195

100 'coward at heart': Aird Papers quoted in Ziegler, *King Edward VIII*, p. 230

100 'cash in best': ibid.

100 'like a dog': ibid.

101 'friendship and love': *HHR* p. 197

101 'keep them both': W to AB, 5 Nov. 1934, Bloch, *Letters*, p. 101

102 'my own house!': Ziegler, *King Edward VIII*, p. 231; Kenneth Rose, *King George V*, Weidenfeld & Nicolson 1983, p. 392

102 enclosure at Ascot: Ziegler, *King Edward VIII*, p. 231, citing memo from Wigram, 12 April 1935, KEVIII Ab, box 4, Royal Archives

102 'of meaningless pleasantries': *HHR* p. 205

102 'in the world': HRH Prince Christopher of Greece, *Memoirs of HRH Prince Christopher of Greece*, Hurst & Blackett 1938, p. 62

102 'and especially me': W to AB, 30 Dec. 1934, Bloch, *Letters*, p. 105

103 'awfully nice stones': W to AB, 29 April 1935, Bloch, *Letters*, p. 117

103 'jewels and clothes': Channon, *Diaries*, 7 Oct. 1935, p. 43

103 'the New Year': Marie Belloc Lowndes, *Diaries and Letters of Marie Belloc Lowndes*, ed. Susan Lowndes, Chatto & Windus 1971, pp. 145–6

103 'doing splendidly, Wallis?': *Daily Telegraph* obituary of Dudley Forwood, 27 Jan. 2001

104 'at the end': W to E, n.d., Bloch, *Letters*, p. 118

104 'easier for me?': ibid.

104 'from your youthfulness': ibid.

104 £6,000 per annum: Ziegler, *King Edward VIII*, p. 238

105 'Prince of Wales': Channon, *Diaries*, p. 41

105 'her company, ourselves': Helen Hardinge, *Loyal to Three Kings*, William Kimber 1967, p. 55

106 'to find it': ibid., p. 54

106 'enter Royal society': ibid.

106 'half an hour': Channon, *Diaries*, p. 47

106 'charming, cultivated woman': Ziegler, *King Edward VIII*, p. 232

107 'has admitted this': 25 June 1935, marked 'Secret', MEPO 10/35, NA PRO

107 'is not clear': S. M. Cretney, 'The Divorce Law and the 1936 Abdication Crisis: A Supplemental Note', *Law Quarterly Review*, 2004, pp. 163–71

107 'trouble with POW': MEPO 10/35, NA PRO

107 when in drink': 25 June 1935, signed Superintendent, marked 'Secret', MEPO 10/35, NA PRO

108 'but not Wallie': Amanda Smith (ed.), *Hostage to Fortune: The Letters of Joseph P. Kennedy*, Viking 2001, p. 263

108 'lived with her': Ziegler, *King Edward VIII*, p. 233

108 'and no mistake': ibid.

108 'married except David': Rose, *King George V*, p. 390

108 'and the throne': Mabell, Countess of Airlie, *Thatched with Gold*, Hutchinson 1962, p. 197

109 'of her friends': Hardinge, *Loyal to Three Kings*, p. 57

109 'such as me': *HHR* p. 216

109 'Silly Jubilee': W to AB, 9 April 1935, Bloch, *Letters*, p. 115

109 'from royal lips': Diary of Rev. Alan Don, ms 2863, Lambeth Palace Archives [herafter Don diary]

110 'significance had increased': Philip Williamson, 'The Monarchy and Public Values, 1910–1953', in Andrzej Olechnowicz (ed.), *The Monarchy and the British Nation, 1780 to the Present*, Cambridge, Cambridge University Press 2007, p. 223

110 'the upper classes': Frank Prochaska, *Republic of Britain*, Penguin Books 2000, pp. 207–9

110 'the younger generation': ibid.

110 'air about it': ibid.

111 'of my dreams': W to AB, 31 July 1935, Bloch, *Letters*, p. 130

111 'angelic Ernest again': W to AB, 14 Oct. 1935, Bloch, *Letters*, p. 141

111 'this eanum body': EP to W, n.d., Bloch, *Letters*, p. 139

Chapter 7: *Wallis Out of Control*

112 'feel like a cigar': Dr Catherine Blackledge, *The Story of V: Opening Pandora's Box*, Weidenfeld & Nicolson, p. 182

112 'delay the genitals': Higham, *Mrs Simpson*, p. 40

114 'your hair etc': Diana Cooper diary, DUFC 2/17, Churchill Archives

115 '"care of that, Sir"': Alfred Shaughnessy, *Both Ends of the Candle: An Autobiography*, Peter Owen 1976, p. 44

115 'reduced to tears': Ziegler, *King Edward VIII*, p. 237, quoting Alfred Amos

115 'the offending nail': Cooper, *The Light of Common Day*, p. 163

116 'possible, even likely': Ziegler, *King Edward VIII*, p. 236

116 '"likes of me"': W to AB, 30 Jan. 1936, Bloch, *Letters*, p. 158

116 returning for more: I am grateful to Dr Domenico di Ceglie, Child and Adolescent Psychiatrist at the London Tavistock Centre, for explaining to me how this theory would fit the known characteristics of Wallis's behaviour and personality. For further clarification of this personality type see Domenico di Ceglie and David Freedman, *A Stranger in my Own Body: Atypical Gender Identity Development and Mental Health*, Karnac Books 1998

117 'than marrying her': 2nd Earl of Birkenhead, *Walter Monckton: The Life of Viscount Monckton of Brenchley*, Weidenfeld & Nicolson 1969, p. 126

117 'and harassed soul': Martin Gilbert, *Winston S. Churchill*, vol. 5: *The Prophet of Truth 1922–1939*, Minerva 1990, p. 810

117 'of divorcing another': marked 'personal and very secret', October 1936–December 1937, Char 2/264, Churchill Archives

118 'marriage was impossible': letter to Princess Royal, quoted in

Francis Watson, *Dawson of Penn*, Chatto & Windus 1950, p. 296

118 'in twelve months': Keith Middlemas and John Barnes, *Baldwin: A Biography*, Weidenfeld & Nicolson 1969, p. 976

118 'other so tight': Ziegler, *King Edward VIII*, p. 240

118 'have been weak': W to EP, early Feb., Bloch, *Letters*, p. 156

118 'you have passed': Ernest Simpson (hereafter EAS) to EP, 21 Jan. 1936, Bloch, *Letters*, p. 156

118 'silly little affairs': Watson, *Dawson of Penn*, p. 285

119 'whence she came': Channon, *Diaries*, p. 71

119 'without an e!!': W to AB, 1 Feb. 1936, Bloch, *Letters*, p. 159

119 '1066 families here': ibid.

120 'difficult to imagine': Papers of Sir Edward Spears 6/4, Churchill Archives

120 'I don't mind': ibid.

120 'leave this about!': Alan Lascelles to Joan Lascelles, Lascelles Paper, Lasl 11/01/15, Churchill Archives

120 'very clever woman': ibid.

121 'who reads Balzac': Brian Masters, *Great Hostesses*, Constable 1982, p. 140

121 'she has done': Queen Mary to Prince Paul, quoted in Forbes, *TLS*, 4 Jan. 1980

121 '*and* Mrs Simpson': Masters, *Great Hostesses*, p. 141

121 'at the Palace': W to AB, 9 Feb. 1936, Bloch, *Letters*, p. 159

122 'up the Can Can': Channon, *Diaries*, p. 76

122 'but not profound': ibid.

122 'a dangerous attribute': Philip Ziegler, Conversation with author, 19 Jan. 2010

122 '"it quite soon"': Philip Ziegler, *Diana Cooper*, Collins 1987, p. 176

123 'none at all': Philip Williamson and Edward Baldwin (eds), *The Baldwin Papers: A Conservative Statesman 1908–47*, Cambridge, Cambridge University Press 2004 (hereafter *Baldwin Papers*), Monica Baldwin, Conversation with Uncle, p. 419

123 'is still there': Michael Thornton, *Royal Feud: The Queen Mother and the Duchess of Windsor*, Michael Joseph 1985, p. 99, quoting James Lees-Milne's biography of Harold Nicolson

123 'Ernest and H.M.': Wallis to AB, 4 May 1936, Bloch, *Letters*, p. 173

123 'violent infatuation': Airlie, *Thatched with Gold*, p. 198

124 great war in Europe: FO 371/19892, NA PRO, quoting Baldwin

124 'for doing so': Memorandum of the Foreign Secretary, Anthony Eden, 8 March 1936, quoted in W. N. Medlicott, Douglas Dakin and M. E. Lambert (eds), *Documents on British Foreign Policy, 1919–1939*, vol. XVI: *The Rhineland Crisis and the Ending of Sanctions March–July 1936*, HMSO 1977, pp. 60–6

125 look after Wallis: all the above from Birkenhead, *Walter Monckton*, pp. 128 and 157

125 'and Cabinet papers!!!!!': JCCD/d Feb. 1936, JCCD Papers 26, The Parliamentary Archive, House of Lords Record Office

126 'an extravagant basis': Birkenhead, *Walter Monckton*, p. 128

126 'the Duchess's loyalty': George VI to Winston Churchill (hereafter WSC), 9 Dec. 1942, Churchill War Papers 20/52

126 'without appearing discourteous': Sir Roderick Jones to G. W. D. Tennant, 15 June 1933, Thomson Reuters Archive

126 'genial and friendly': Don diary, 5 June 1935

126 'most glorious flowers': E. B. Kirk, NLD

127 'for Nazi Germans': 26 Nov. 1936, the Hon. Lady Murray Papers

127 'state of collapse': W to AB, 14 April 1936, Bloch, *Letters*, p. 171

127 'old nervous indigestion': W to AB, 4 May 1936, Bloch, *Letters*, p. 174

127 'by this prospect': *HHR* p. 222

128 'get a divorce': MKR diary, private archive

128 'the previous year': NLD

128 'to by everyone': MKR to Anne Kirk, 23 April 1936, *TOMS*, p. 22

128 'Wallis' life forever': NLD

129 'ventured nothing gained': W to AB, 16 March 1936, Bloch, *Letters*, p. 169

129 'slightly second rate': Harold Nicolson, *Diaries and Letters 1930–39*, ed. Nigel Nicolson, Athenaeum 1966, p. 255

129 '"Master of the Mistress"': Duchess of Devonshire to Lady Airlie, 25 Feb. 1936, British Library Add. Mss 82766

130 '"my future wife"': *HHR* p. 225

130 'without its good side': Middlemas and Barnes, *Stanley Baldwin*, p. 981

130 'sad beyond calculation': Lord Reith, *The Reith Diaries*, ed. Charles Stuart, Collins 1975, p. 188

131 'much, Mr Rubinstein': Masters, *Great Hostesses*, pp. 182–4

132 'heard of Mrs Simpson?': 30 April 1936, Lascelles Papers, Lasl 11/01/15, Churchill Archives

132 'judge public opinion': Conclusions of meetings of the Cabinet, 28 October–16 December 1936, CAB 23/86, Addendum to Cabinet Conclusions, NA PRO

132 'was highly evident': *HHR* p. 225

132 'other American interest': ibid.

132 'account for much': Lady Mosley to Duchess of Devonshire, 5 June 1972, in Charlotte Mosley (ed.), *The Mitfords: Letters between Six Sisters*, Fourth Estate 2007, p. 582

133 'became her implacable enemy': Thornton, *Royal Feud*, p. 75, citing private information, letters to author, 30 May, 12 June 1983

133 'more and more': EP to W, n.d., Sotheby's *The Jewels* 1987 catalogue, pp. 86–7

133 'he won't move': EP to W, 5 June 1936, Bloch, *Letters*, p. 180

133 'starting divorce proceedings': *HHR* p. 226

134 'pain for a month': W to AB, 22 June 1936, Bloch, *Letters*, p. 182

134 'here with me': TS 22/1/2, NA PRO

134 'this stupid manner': Ziegler, *King Edward VIII*, p. 282

134 'amount to £100': ibid.

135 with other men's wives: ibid.

135 'nicest man here': 4 Sept. 1936, Lascelles Papers, Lasl 11/001/016, Churchill Archives

135 'yak milk diet': DUFC 2/17, Churchill Archives

136 'on her wrist': ibid.

136 'as a King': Ziegler, *King Edward VIII*, p. 284

136 'were looking for': Diana Cooper, DUFC 2/17, Churchill Archives

137 *'folie à deux'*: Forbes, *TLS*, 1 Nov. 1974, quoting Frances Donaldson biography of Edward VIII

137 'be dropped all night': DUFC 2/17, Churchill Archives

137 'in old days': Alan Lascelles to Joan Lascelles, 30 August 1936, Lascelles Papers, Lasl 11/01/15, Churchill Archives

Chapter 8: *Wallis in the Witness Box*

138 'they loathe adultery': Lees-Milne, *Harold Nicolson*, vol. II, pp. 77–8

138 'the British public': Dugdale diary

139 'with unremitting enjoyment': A. G. Gardiner, *Certain People of Importance*, J. M. Dent 1929, pp. 107–8

140 'of social tyranny': DoW, *A King's Story*, p. 258

141 'without reference [to him]': Memo, 9 Oct. 1936, Press Association/Thomson Reuters Archive

141 'create disaster together': W to E, 16 Sept. 1936, Bloch, *Letters*, p. 94

141 take his life: William Shawcross, *Queen Elizabeth The Queen Mother: The Official Biography*, Macmillan 2009, p. 366; Ziegler, *King Edward VIII*, p. 287

142 'cannot live with': EAS to Mrs E. L. Simpson, 17 March 1937, private archive

142 'out at once': *Baldwin Papers*, Monica Baldwin, p. 423

142 'along so well': W to EAS, 16 Feb. 1937, private archive

143 'performance as Sovereign': Helen Hardinge diary, pp. 101–3, Hon. Lady Murray Papers, quoted in Shawcross, *Queen Elizabeth The Queen Mother*, p. 365

143 'myself against her': 'secret' memo by WSC, Char 2/300, Churchill Archives

144 'from the throne': J. G. Lockhart, *Cosmo Gordon Lang*, Hodder & Stoughton 1949, p. 397

144 'with the King': Thornton, *Royal Feud*, p. 393, citing private information

144 'woman he loved': Ziegler, *King Edward VIII*, p. 172

145 'about it sometimes': Duchess of York to Queen Mary, 11 Oct. 1936, Royal Archives QM/PRIV/CC12/34A, quoted in Shawcross, *Queen Elizabeth The Queen Mother*, p. 368

145 'with the American harlot': TS 22, NA PRO

145 'never forgive him': Channon, *Diaries*, 11 Nov. 1936, p. 101

146 'I am so lonely': W to EAS, 25 Oct. 1936, private archive

146 'education and maintenance': TS 221/2, NA PRO

147 'Prince of Wales': *Time*, 26 Oct. 1936

148 'Queen Mary's place': Nancy Dugdale diary

148 'but no heart': Stanley Baldwin quoted in *Baldwin Papers*, p. 423

148 'hard bitten bitch': Walter Monckton (hereafter WM) quoted in Tom Jones diary, November 1936, *Baldwin Papers*, p. 388

149 'the public view': Duff Cooper diary, Jan. 1936, *Baldwin Papers*, p. 387; Ziegler, *King Edward VIII*, p. 248

149 'hated the idea': Lucy Baldwin, 17 Nov. 1936, *Baldwin Papers*, p. 390, SB additional papers

149 'courteous and nicest': ibid.

149 'was a lie': Stanley Bruce to Stanley Baldwin, 16 Nov. 1936, series M104, Australian Archives

149 'it all intensely': Lucy Baldwin, *Baldwin Papers*, p. 390

149 'to marry her': Monica Baldwin account of conversation, *Baldwin Papers*, p. 421

150 cloth to advocate: 1 Nov. 1936, Lang Papers, vol. 318, Ziegler, *King Edward VIII*, p. 293

150 'short of life': Violet Bonham-Carter to WSC, Char 2 264, Churchill Archives

151 their final decree: I am most grateful to Dr Stephen Cretney for supplying me with this information from *the Civil Judicial Statistics 1935–8*

151 'its highest standards': *New York World Telegram*, 21 Nov. 1936

152 'been indirectly involved': TS 22 1/1, NA PRO

152 'marriage was intended': diary of Hilda Runciman, Nov. 1936, Newcastle Library Ref. WR ADD. A/11. By kind permission of the librarian, Robinson Library

153 'his responsibility acutely': Don diary, 16 Nov. 1936

153 'and Wallis Simpson': Thursday 19 Nov. 1936, Runicman Papers, Newcastle Library Ref. WR 282/8

153 'to do so': Lockhart, *Cosmo Gordon Lang*, pp. 395–8

153 'he quite normal?': Don diary, 28 Oct. 1936

154 'could be certified': Ziegler, *King Edward VIII*, p. 275, citing memo by Wigram, 15 Feb. 1936, KEVIII Ab. Box 4, Royal Archives

154 'happy Prince Charming': Channon, *Diaries*, 3 Nov. 1936, p. 96

154 'upon your deliberoitions': Harold Nicolson diary, quoted in Ziegler, *King Edward VIII*, p. 265

154 'of the divorce': Don diary, 4 Nov. 1936

154 '"Yes – Mrs Simpson"': Channon, *Diaries*, 10 Nov. 1936, p. 100

154 Queen Mary acknowledged: Sir Robert Bruce Lockhart, *The Diaries of Robert Bruce Lockhart 1915–38*, ed. Kenneth Young, Macmillan 1973, 13 Nov. 1936, p. 357

154 'and complete person': Herman Rogers to W, 28 Oct. 1936, Bloch, *Letters*, p. 209

155 'has become irretrievable': Hardinge, *Loyal to Three Kings*, p. 133

155 'him to Gallipoli?': 27 Nov. 1936, Statement at Cabinet Meeting, *Baldwin Papers*, p. 394

156 'an alternative government': Bruce to Baldwin, 16 Nov. 1936, series M104 item 4, Australian Archives

156 'marry Mrs Simpson': Lucy Baldwin diary, *Baldwin Papers*, p. 390

156 'he said good-bye': ibid., p. 391

156 '"kettle of fish!"': Monica Baldwin, *Baldwin Papers*, p. 425

157 'of all concerned': E to Queen Mary, 20 Nov. 1936, quoted in Shawcross, *Queen Elizabeth The Queen Mother*, p. 373

157 'was so divergent': Nancy Dugdale diary

157 'temporarily gone into': W to Sybil Colefax, n.d., Colefax Papers, Ms eng c 3272 ff. 1–15, Bodleian Library (hereafter Bodl. Lib.)

158 'getting it now': Nicolson, *Diaries and Letters*, 18 Nov. 1936, p. 279

158 'man she loves': *HHR* p. 247

158 'catastrophe for me': ibid., p. 246

159 'disgustingly conceited fellow': Ziegler, *King Edward VIII*, p. 303

159 '"a Queen Cutie"': Cole Lesley, *The Life of Noël Coward*, Jonathan Cape 1976, p. 187

159 'support the Government': Nancy Dugdale diary

160 'most formidable kind': 27 Nov. 1936, Zetland Papers, Mss Eur D 609/7

160 'by my Government': Ziegler, *King Edward VIII*, p. 306

160 'UK Parliament legislating': Documents on Irish Foreign Policy, 1932–36, National Archives of Ireland

161 and other nations: 28 Nov. 1936, http://www.collections
canada.gc.ca/databases/king/index-e.html

161 'seem to be alive': W to EAS, 11 Jan. 1937, private archive

161 'to them all': ibid.

161 'agony for him': *HHR* p. 247

162 'might shoot her': *Baldwin Papers*, p. 423

162 'and to myself': W to EAS, n.d. but postmarked 30 Nov. 1936,
private archive

162 'was hurting the K': ibid.

163 'concerned, won't it?': ibid.

163 'I fold my tent': W to Sybil Colefax, n.d., Monday, Colefax Papers,
Ms eng c 3272 ff. 1–15, Bodl. Lib.

163 'straight with his country': W to Sybil Colefax, 18 Dec. 1936,
Colefax Papers, Ms eng c 3272 ff. 1–15, Bodl. Lib.

Chapter 9: *Wallis on the Run*

164 'for the first time': Brownlow diary, Brownlow Papers, BNLW
4/4/9, Lincolnshire Archives

164 'of this need': Lang Papers 1936, Lambeth Palace Archives

165 'in the wilderness': Nancy Dugdale diary

165 'just SB's luck!': ibid.

165 'to advise him': 4 Dec. 1936, Lang Papers, Lambeth Palace Archives

165 'and his ministers': ibid.

166 'a great deal': Nancy Dugdale diary

166 '"will be happy"': ibid.

166 'wished me happiness': ibid.

166 'de la douleur': ibid.

166 'you, my darling': Brownlow diary

167 'knife into them': Shawcross, *Queen Elizabeth The Queen Mother*,
p. 364

167 'our fingers crossed': Ziegler, *King Edward VIII*, p. 310

167 'deportee or exile': Brownlow diary

167 'to winter conditions': ibid.

167 'difficult to recapture': *HHR* p. 265

167 she had reached Cannes: Thomson Reuters Archive

167 'Tell the country': W to EP, n.d., Bloch, *Letters*, p. 216

168 'Roosevelt's "fireside chats"': *HHR* p. 253

168 'crown and throne': TS 221, NA PRO

168 'a married woman': *Baldwin Papers*, p. 402

169 'tack was hopeless': Sir Edward Peacock notes, Dep. Monckton Trustees 22, fol. 277, Bodl. Lib.

169 'for all time': Humphrey Keenlyside, *Allen & Overy: The Firm*, vol. I: *1930–1998*, Allen & Overy 1999

170 'could not interfere': Nancy Dugdale diary

170 'unhappy and untenable': *HHR* p. 273

170 'for the best': ibid.

170 'petition for divorce': Zetland Papers, Mss Eur D 609/7

170 'turn against me': Susan Williams, *The People's King: The True Story of the Abdication*, Penguin Books 2003, p. 191

171 'it would be', 'WM typed account of events October to Dec 1936 with postscripts and additional comments from others', Dep. Monckton Trustees 22, fols. 1–103, Bodl. Lib.

171 'her magnanimous gesture': Nancy Dugdale diary

171 'wicket was determined': Sir Horace Wilson to WM, 5 Feb. 1949, Dep. Monckton Trustees 20, fol. 37, Bodl. Lib.

172 'eventually marry her': 13 Aug. 1949, Dep. Monckton Trustees 20, fol. 74 TG statement, Bodl. Lib.

172 'into her confidence!': Sir Horace Wilson to WM, 5 Feb. 1949, Dep. Monckton Trustees 20, fol. 37, Bodl. Lib.

172 'curious little document': Lascelles to WM on Buckingham Palace notepaper, 6 Jan. 1949, Dep. Monckton Trustees 22, fol. 30, Bodl. Lib.

172 'to do anything': Ziegler, *King Edward VIII*, p. 313, citing Thomas Dugdale diary, 9 Dec. 1936, Crathorne Papers

173 speaking to him: 10 Dec. 1936, MEPO, NA PRO

173 'most painful degree': Gilbert, *Winston S. Churchill*, vol. V, pp. 814–17

173 'it appalled me': Monica Baldwin, *Baldwin Papers*, p. 422

173 '"in the world"': ibid.

174 'reason with him': ibid.

174 not the least: Conclusions of Meetings of the Cabinet 28 Oct.–16 Dec. 1936, vol. LIII, CAB 23/86, NA PRO

174 'been in Bedlam': *Baldwin Papers*, p. 411

174 'with That Woman': Thomas Dugdale diary, 8 Dec. 1936, Cranthorne Papers

174 'earn her contempt': Ziegler, *Edward VIII*, p. 327

174 'invective from Cannes': Thomas Dugdale diary, 8 Dec. 1936, Cranthorne Papers

174 'day he died': Ziegler, *Edward VIII*, p. 327

175 'Sir Horace Wilson . . .': 13 June 1938, Smith, *Hostage to Fortune: The Letters of Joseph P. Kennedy*, p. 262

175 '£5,000 a year': Ziegler, *Edward VIII*, p. 326

175 'all over world': Nancy Dugdale diary

176 'up in Parliament': Smith, *Hostage to Fortune: The Letters of Joseph P. Kennedy*, p. 262

176 'I was completely misled': Ziegler, *Edward VIII*, p. 327

176 'I have written': ibid., p. 324

176 'of Mrs Simpson': Lt Col Tweed to Lloyd George, 15 Dec. 1936, J. G. Jones, 'Lloyd George and the Abdication of Edward VIII', *National Library of Wales Journal*, vol. 30, 1997, pp. 89–105

177 King Charles I: DoW, *A King's Story*, p. 409

177 'thing he disliked': Virginia Woolf, *Selected Diaries*, ed. Anne Olivier Bell, Vintage 2008, 10 Dec. 1936, p. 401

178 'hide my tears': *HHR* p. 278

178 'he had chosen': Lang Papers, Lambeth Palace Archives

178 'a faint reality': Nancy Dugdale diary

179 'when he needs': draft letter to Queen Mary, Dep. Monckton Trustees 14, fols. 64–65, Bodl. Lib.

179 'could turn in': Shaughnessy, *Both Ends of the Candle*, p. 45

179 'all one's heart': Lucy Baldwin to Nancy Dugdale, reproduced in Nancy Dugdale diary

180 'Elizabeth R': Don diary, 12 Dec. 1936

180 'wonderfully self controlled': 10 Dec. 1936, Lang Papers, Lambeth Palace Archives

180 'display of power': Thornton, *Royal Feud*, p. 112, citing private information

180 'in many respects': Hardinge, *Loyal to Three Kings*, p. 114

180 'away from visitors': Channon, *Diaries*, 29 Nov. 1936, p. 111

180 'somebody in authority': Memorandum by Sir Thomas Barnes, 22 Feb. 1937, TS 22/1/4, NA PRO

181 'and Mrs S': Ziegler, *Edward VIII*, p. 330, citing Memorandum by Wigram, 7 Dec. 1936, KEVIII Ab. box 4, Royal Archives

181 'love with him': Cecil Beaton, *Self-Portrait with Friends: The Selected Diaries of Cecil Beaton 1926–74*, Weidenfeld & Nicolson 1979, p. 305

181 'to meet Ernest': Baldwin Papers, p. 410

181 'by blind prejudice': *HHR* p. 276

181 'never repay today': quoted in Jones, 'Lloyd George and the Abdication of Edward VIII', p. 92

182 'ministers and parliament': *HHR* p. 247

182 'as their means': Nancy Dugdale diary, citing 'letter that came into my hands' from W to Mrs George (Kitty) Hunter, postmarked 3 January 1937

182 'was prepared to pay': 'Lloyd George and the Abdication of Edward VIII', *National Library of Wales Journal*, vol. 30, 1997, p. 95

183 'the little man': Lloyd George to Megan Lloyd George, 9 Dec. 1936, MS 20 475C no. 3150, National Library of Wales

183 'thought the same': Duff Hart-Davis (ed.), *The King's Counsellor: Abdication and War – The Diaries of 'Tommy' Lascelles*, Weidenfeld & Nicolson 2006, p. 50

183 'He will abdicate': Ziegler, *Edward VIII*, p. 199

184 'few vital days': MEPO 10/35, NA PRO

185 'wherever I went': Martin, *The Woman He Loved*, p. 12

185 Mrs Fitzherbert: Beaverbrook Papers, series G 25, memo of 9 Sept. 1949

185 'with you throughout!': Ziegler, *Edward VIII*, p. 330, citing Royal Archives DW 3059

185 'so sit all day': W to EAS, postmarked 22 Dec. 1936, private archive

185 'that have been': EAS to W, Oct. 1936, letter sold at auction widely quoted in UK press and Vickers, p. 417

186 'counted his royalties': Forbes, *TLS*, 1 Nov. 1974

186 'sacrifice to himself': Sarah Bradford to Piers Brendon, Brendon Papers 2/2/1, Churchill Archives

186 'lowest of the low': letter to Lord Lloyd, 6 July 1940, marked 'Windsor Castle copy', Papers of Lord Lloyd of Dolobran, GLLD 21/7, Churchill Archives

Chapter 10: *Wallis in Exile*

187 'loved King Edward': speech widely reported – this version *Daily Telegraph*, Monday 14 Dec. 1936, Amel 1/5/25, Churchill Archives

187 'been the medium': Reith to Lang, 14 Dec. 1936, Lang Papers, 192 FO 380

187 'and pathetic figure': Rev. Dr A. C. Bouquet, quoted in G. Machin, 'Marriage and the Churches in the 1930s', *Journal of Ecclesiastical History*, vol. 42, 1991, 68–81

188 'intolerance and obscurantism': *New Statesman*, 19 Dec. 1936

188 'of normal love': Lang Papers, vol. 318, Lambeth Palace Archives

188 'a sincere response': 21 Dec. 1936, Lang Papers, Notes on the Abdication, Lambeth Palace Archives

188 'Royal Family again': quoted in letter from 'A Scout' to A. J. Sylvester, 5 Jan. 1936 [*recte* 1937], Jones, 'Lloyd George and the Abdication of Edward VIII', p. 104

189 leave the country: Hansard, House of Commons, vol. 318, col. 2216

189 form a government: Francis Beckett, *The Rebel Who Lost his Cause: The Tragedy of John Beckett MP*, Allison & Busby 2000, p. 141

190 'his own ends': Woolf, *Selected Diaries*, 7 Dec. 1936, p. 400

190 'cock crew thrice': quoted in Masters, *Great Hostesses*, p. 186

191 'shown to me': Brownlow to Cromer, 23 Dec. 1936, Brownlow Papers, BNLW 4/4/9/6/11, Lincolnshire Archives

191 'row to hoe': Baldwin to Brownlow, 12 Jan. 1937, Brownlow Papers, BNLW 4/4/9/5/7/a, Lincolnshire Archives

191 'it long ago': W to Brownlow, 'Friday 19th' [either Feb. or March 1937], Brownlow Papers, BNLW 4/4/9/5/9, Lincolnshire Archives

191 soon as possible: 15 Dec. 1936, Legh to Thomas, quoted in Ziegler, *King Edward VIII*, p. 339

191 'anything might happen': Don diary

191 'a monarch's service': *Daily Telegraph* obituary of Dudley Forwood, 27 Jan. 2001

192 'shun the game': Wilson, *Her Name was Wallis Warfield*, Dec. 1936

192 'am very sad': W to EAS, n.d., private archive

193 'be there anyway': 22 Dec. 1936, Dep. Monckton Trustees 14, fol. 77, Bodl. Lib.

193 'simply haven't understood': W to Kitty Rothschild, 18 Dec. 1936, Bloch, *Letters*, p. 235

193 'that fatal charm!': W to EP, n.d., Bloch, *Letters*, p. 253

193 '(I suspect that)': ibid.; also quoted in Williams, *The People's King*, p. 268

194 'my morning tray': *HHR* p. 280

194 'he should pay': all the above from CAB 21/4100/2 index to secret file, NA PRO

194 'take her in': *HHR* p. 277

194 'in English law': Stephen Cretney, 'The King and the King's Proctor', *Law Quarterly Review*, vol. 16, 2000, 583–620

194 'on six pounds': Higham, *Mrs Simpson*, p. 210

195 'must be stopped': EAS to Mrs E. L. Simpson, 1 Jan. 1937, private archive

195 'against their intentions': W to EAS, 16 Feb. 1937, private archive

195 'it is now': ibid.

196 'them torn up': W to E, 16 Feb. 1937, private archive

196 'Katherine by now ... !': ibid.

196 'is no longer King': MKR to Annie Kirk, 7 Jan. 1937, *TOMS*, p. 50

197 'jewels at all': Constance Coolidge Atherton, Comtesse de Jumilhac, to 'Crownie', 28 May 1937, Maryland Historical Society (hereafter MHS) MS 1772 Windsor Collection

197 'only formal routine': Alan Lascelles to Joan Lascelles, 5 March 1937, Lascelles Papers, Lasl 11/001/16a, Churchill Archives

197 'him in turn': ibid.

197 'from such servants': TS 22/1/A, NA PRO

198 'does in fact exist': ibid.

198 to give evidence: ibid.

199 'my business career': Ziegler, *King Edward VIII*, p. 363

200 'up from Fortnums': MKR to Jacques Raffray, 18 May 1937, *TOMS*, pp. 53–5

200 'practically killed me': W to EAS, 12 May 1937, private archive

200 'in this way': Ziegler, *King Edward VIII*, p. 356

200 'at the ceremony': ibid.

200 'with stoical dignity': ibid.

201 to the Duke: Sarah Bradford, Brendon Papers, Bren 2/2/1, Churchill Archives

201 'such a thing': Alec Sergeant's notes marked 'Private and Confidential', Lang Papers, Lambeth Palace Archives

202 'such monstrous suggestions': Wigram to Lang, 5 April 1937, Lang Papers, vol. 318, Lambeth Palace Archives

202 'thousand times harder': Ziegler, *King Edward VIII*, p. 348

202 'do anything else': ibid., p. 355

202 finish his breakfast: Owen Chadwick, *Hensley Henson*, Oxford University Press 1983, p. 232

203 'his Parish Church': 5 May 1937, Crawford Papers, John Vincent (ed.), *The Journals of David Lindsay, 27th Earl of Crawford and 10th Earl of Balcarres 1871–1940*, Manchester University Press 1984, p. 579

203 'be doubly bigamous': ibid.

203 '"told this before?"': ibid.

204 'him by death': cutting in TS 221/8, NA PRO

204 'hates us both': W to DoW, 7 Feb. 1937, Bloch, *Letters*, p. 258

204 'off the throne': Higham, *Mrs Simpson*, p. 220

204 'for exceptional treatment': Stamfordham to Davidson, 29 July 1922, Archbishop Davidson Papers, 6/76

204 'I can't see': W to DoW, 6 Feb. 1937, Bloch, *Letters*, p. 256

204 'has no jurisdiction': Chadwick, *Hensley Henson*, p. 231

205 'silent and loyal': Sue Shephard, *The Surprising Life of Constance Spry*, Macmillan 2010, p. 204

205 'would see them': ibid., p. 207

205 'and good taste': Brownlow to W, 26 April 1937, Brownlow Papers, BNLW 4/4/9/5/17, Lincolnshire Archives

205 'become very difficult': Nugent Hicks to Brownlow, 18 May 1937,

Brownlow Papers, BNLW 4/4/9/5/21, Lincolnshire Archives

206 '"ex-King of England"': Shephard, *The Surprising Life of Constance Spry*, p. 207

206 'a broad grin': ibid., p. 205

206 'this for me': Chadwick, *Hensley Henson*, p. 232

207 'the worst blow': private diaries of Lady Alexandra Metcalfe (hereafter LAM), with thanks to David Metcalfe for permission to quote from them

207 'her American friends': MKR to Buckie Kirk, 30 May 1937, Radcliffe/Schlesinger collection

208 'title being conferred': Ziegler, *King Edward VIII*, p. 358

208 'to become Royal': ibid., p. 359

208 'a nice wedding present': ibid., p. 360

208 'weakness in everything': LAM diary

208 'heaped on her': ibid.

209 'most disastrous results': Ziegler, *King Edward VIII*, p. 358

209 'king of England': LAM diary

210 'birth or connections': *HHR* p. 280

210 'happiness much love': Dep. Monckton Trustees 15, fol. 176, Bodl. Lib.

210 'a younger man': LAM diary

210 '"make him happy"': Birkenhead, *Walter Monckton*, p. 362

Chapter 11: *Wallis at War*

211 'have given up': Ziegler, *King Edward VIII*, p. 351

211 'see her suffering': DoW to WM, 31 Oct. 1938, Dep. Monckton Trustees 16, fol. 176, Bodl. Lib.

212 '"the Duke down"': *Daily Telegraph* obituary of Dudley Forwood, 27 Jan. 2001

212 'recognised with incredulity': *HHR* p. 282

212 'try not to': W to EAS, Monday 30 Aug. 1937, private archive

212 'courage for that': ibid.

212 'knew you would': ibid.

213 'for a dentist': ibid.

213 'book in it': Mary Simpson diary, 1938, private archive

213 'With love, Wallis': W to EAS, n.d., private archive

214 'the other way': WM to Tommy Dugdale, 23 Dec. 1936, Dep. Monckton Trustees 14, Bodl. Lib.

214 'with good publicity': DoW to Bernard Rickatson-Hatt, 18 May 1938, Thomson Reuters Archive

214 'old Palace enemies': ibid.

215 'and the Nazis': quoted in Rose, *King George V,* citing Mensdorff Papers, 11 Nov. 1933, State Archives, Vienna

216 'him a lot': Brendon Papers, Bren 2/2/7, Churchill Archives

216 'England in December': DoW to WM, 16 July 1937, Dep. Monckton Trustees 15, fol. 237, Bodl. Lib.

216 'British working man': Ziegler, *King Edward VIII,* p. 390, quoting Phipps

216 'German mining industry': Brendon Papers, Bren 2/2/6, Churchill Archives

216 'are much nicer': W to EAS, n.d., private archive

217 'his bombastic pretensions': DoW, *A King's Story,* p. 277

217 'of Hun origin': Higham, *Mrs Simpson,* p. 259

217 'discussion with him!': *HHR* p. 308

217 'not a crime': Ziegler, *King Edward VIII,* p. 386

218 'for his security': Brendon Papers, Bren 2/2/7, Churchill Archives

218 'for "That Woman"': Crawford Papers, Vincent, *Journals of David Lindsay,* pp. 616–21

219 'his eyes now?': Sir Robert Bruce Lockhart, *The Diaries of Robert Bruce Lockhart 1915–38,* ed. Kenneth Young, Macmillan 1973, 10 Dec. 1938, p. 413

219 'pray to God. Wallis': W to EAS, Saturday 30 October 1937, private archive

219 'or racial doctrine': Ziegler, *King Edward VIII,* p. 396

220 'score for us': Mary Simpson diary, private archive

220 'back of it': Shawcross, *Queen Elizabeth The Queen Mother,* pp. 423–4

220 'controversy about it': ibid., p. 446

221 'between us impossible': ibid.

221 'distinction and success': Ziegler, *King Edward VIII,* p. 393

221 'List is considered': WSC to Clementine Churchill, 7 Jan. 1937, Mary Soames (ed.), *Speaking for Themselves: The Personal Letters of Winston and Clementine Churchill*, Doubleday 1998, pp. 422–3

222 'a devoted servant': WSC to Maxine Elliott, 30 Dec. 1937, Char 1/300/86, Churchill Archives

222 'most happy marriage': WSC to Clementine Churchill, 10 Jan. 1938, Soames, *Speaking for Themselves*, p. 433

223 'life in exile': Nicolson, *Diaries and Letters 1930–39*, p. 351

223 'were probably retarded': Colin Davidson to WM, 5 Sept. 1938, Dep. Monckton Trustees 16, fol. 134, Bodl. Lib.

223 'to stop him': WSC to Clementine Churchill, 18 Jan. 1939, Soames, *Speaking for Themselves*, p. 449

223 'just a reminder': W to WM, 2 Feb. 1938, Dep. Monckton Trustees 16, fols. 31–32, Bodl. Lib.

224 'brother of the King': ibid.

224 'not kicked out': Colin Davidson to WM, 5 Sept. 1938, Dep. Monckton Trustees 16, fol. 134, Bodl. Lib.

224 'older I realise it': *Sunday Dispatch*, 12 March 1939

225 'all to subdue': Ziegler, *King Edward VIII*, p. 399

225 'fools and rogues': Mary Simpson diary, private archive

226 'remains the same': copies of both telegrams, 27 Aug. 1939, Dep. Monckton Trustees 17, fol. 93, Bodl. Lib.

226 'were our guests': LAM diary

226 'still at Antibes': Dep. Monckton Trustees 22, fols. 1–103, WM typed account of events October to December 1936 with postscript, Bodl. Lib.

226 'jumping out, etc': Ziegler, *King Edward VIII*, p. 403

227 'only a grip': DoW to British Ambassador in Paris, 3 Sept. 1939, relayed to WM, Dep. Monckton Trustees 17, fol. 122, Bodl. Lib.

227 'of your PRIDE': Ziegler, *King Edward VIII*, p. 403, quoting Metcalfe Papers

228 'of his departure': LAM diary

228 'have skated on': ibid.

228 'did not exist': *HHR* p. 324

228 'and completely simple': LAM diary

229 'ever to return': ibid.

229 'and speak English': W to WM, 2 Jan. 1940, Dep. Monckton Trustees 18, fols. 13v–14, Bodl. Lib.

229 'in my life': *HHR* p. 328

230 'is the end': Ziegler, *King Edward VIII*, p. 417

231 'never occur again': FO 800/326 f. 195, NA PRO

232 'a few politicians': Ziegler, *King Edward VIII*, p. 421

232 ordered him home: Char 20/9A/11–12, Churchill Archives

232 'end of the war': W to WM, 2 Jan. 1940, Dep. Monckton Trustees 18, fol. 12, Bodl. Lib.

232 'a little silly': *HHR* p. 41

233 'fill with you': ibid.

233 'reconsider my position': 18 July 1940, Char 20 9A/76, Churchill Archives

233 'a petulant baby': 20 July 1940, Char 20 9A/76, Churchill Archives

Chapter 12: *Wallis Grits her Teeth*

234 'maximum of frustration': Michael Bloch, *The Duke of Windsor's War*, Weidenfeld & Nicolson 1982, p. 96

235 'permanent slimming cure': King, *The Duchess of Windsor*, p. 356

235 'for the figure': DoW to WM, 27 Sept. 1940, Dep. Monckton Trustees 18, fol. 108, Bodl. Lib.

235 'happens to you': Brendon Papers, Bren 2/2/7, Churchill Archives

235 'off in a passion': ibid.

235 'of such orders': W to WM, 16 Sept. 1940, Dep. Monckton Trustees 18, fols. 100–101, Bodl. Lib.

237 'things less unpleasant': WM to DoW, 26 Aug. 1940, Dep. Monckton Trustees 18, fol. 90, Bodl. Lib.

237 'the past months': W to WM, 16 Sept. 1940, Dep. Monckton Trustees 18, fol. 99, Bodl. Lib.

237 'you, dear Walter': ibid.

238 'seen any number': W to WM, 2 Oct. 1940, Dep. Monckton Trustees 18, fols. 113v–114, Bodl. Lib.

238 'me to them': W to WM, 23 Oct. 1940, Dep. Monckton Trustees 18, fols. 125–129, Bodl. Lib.

238 'with no future': W to Edith Lindsay, 30 Aug. 1942, MHS

238 'common and uninteresting': Michael Bloch, *The Secret File of the Duke of Windsor*, Transworld 1988, p. 175

239 'would be solved': W to WM, 5 March 1941, Dep. Monckton Trustees 19, fol. 22, Bodl. Lib.

239 'them as such': W to WM, 16 May 1941, Dep. Monckton Trustees 19, fols. 81–82, Bodl. Lib.

239 'with the Duke': ibid.

240 'as you know': W to WM, 30 April 1941, Dep. Monckton Trustees 19, fols. 43–44, Bodl. Lib.

240 'it is alarming': ibid.

240 'paper the better': WSC to WM, 11 June 1941, Dep. Monckton Trustees 19, fol. 97, Bodl. Lib.

241 'only ill two weeks': W to WM, 17 June 1941, Dep. Monckton Trustees 19, fols. 103–106, Bodl. Lib.

241 'pinned on the Duke': W to WM, Sept. 1941, Dep. Monckton Trustees 19, fols. 197–201, Bodl. Lib.

241 'burst from his cell': ibid.

242 'peace and happiness': King, *The Duchess of Windsor*, p. 364

242 'quite a while!!!': EP to FDW, 7 Sept. 1919, *LFP* p. 228

242 'Ernest like mine': Mary Simpson diary, April 1940, private archive

242 'not crying over': Mary Simpson to Anne Kirk, 24 Oct. 1939, *TOMS*, p. 128

243 'be made public': Kirk Hollingsworth, Conversation with author, 1 Nov. 2009

243 'Windsors are perfect': Mary Simpson diary, 1 Dec. 1940, private archive

243 'for the future': W to EAS, 3 Oct. 1941, private archive

244 'remarkable a degree': René MacColl, *Deadline and Dateline*, Oldbourne Press 1956, pp. 124–5

244 'dropped his arm': ibid.

244 'full of clothing': Ziegler, *King Edward VIII*, p. 467

244 'those on the spot': W to Edith Lindsay, April 1943, 'On board the boat and rocky', MHS, MS 1772, Windsor Collection

244 'consider this outrageous': King, *The Duchess of Windsor*, p. 364

244 'are strictly rationed': *Washington Star*, 29 Oct. 1941

245 'do without her': Rosa Wood to Edith Lindsay, 25 Oct. 1942, MHS

245 'isn't for charity': W to WM, 5 March 1941, Dep. Monckton Trustees 19, fols. 197–201, Bodl. Lib.

245 'and pathetic surroundings': ibid.

245 'off to England': W to Edith Lindsay, 28 March 1942, MHS, MS 1772, Windsor Collection

246 'two months leave': W to Edith Lindsay, 30 Aug. 1942, MHS, MS 1772, Windsor Collection

246 'other any more': W to Edith Lindsay, 5 Feb. 1943, MHS, MS 1772, Windsor Collection

246 been further reconciliation: Ziegler, *King Edward VIII*, p. 484

246 'wall of disinterest': Bloch, *The Secret File of the Duke of Windsor*, p. 202

247 'all too tragic': W to Edith Lindsay, 23 July 1943, MHS, MS 1772, Windsor Collection

247 'you this minute': ibid.

247 'and attractive people': W to Edith Lindsay, Sept. 1943, MHS, MS 1772, Windsor Collection

248 'free once more': W to WM, Sept. 1941, Dep. Monckton Trustees 19, fols. 197–201, Bodl. Lib.

248 'people, I find': W to Edith Lindsay, Sept. 1943, MHS, MS 1772, Windsor Collection

248 'allows such behaviour?': W to AB, 15 July 1940, Bloch, *The Secret File of the Duke of Windsor*, p. 163

248 'on 80,000,000 people?': *Liberty*, March 1941, quoted in Bloch, *The Secret File of the Duke of Windsor*, p. 187

249 'might be arranged': Bloch, *The Secret File of the Duke of Windsor*, p. 188

249 'that appointed me': ibid., p. 189

249 'an unwarranted step': DoW to WSC, 10 Nov. 1942, Churchill Papers 20/63, Chartwell Trust

250 'the Duchess's loyalty': King George VI to WSC, 9 Dec. 1942, Churchill Papers 20/52, Chartwell Trust

250 'be in obscurity': Wallis to Edith Lindsay, 23 April 1943, MHS, MS 1772, Windsor Collection

250 'share these views': King George VI to WSC, 8 Dec. 1942, Churchill Papers 20/52, Chartwell Trust

250 'interfere in politics': Horace Wilson to Chancellor of Exchequer, 10 Dec. 1936, PREM 1/453, NA PRO

250 'in enemy hands': FO 371/24249 f. 155, NA PRO

251 'less easily defended': Ziegler, *King Edward VIII*, p. 458

252 'campaign against her': Unsigned confidential memorandum, New York, 1 Aug. 1944, FBI Papers, US Department of Justice

252 'publishers and editors': ibid.

252 'exercise discreet observations': Department of State to Attorney General, 18 April 1941, FBI Papers, US Department of Justice

252 'out of place': Memorandum for the Director, 21 April 1941, FBI Papers, US Department of Justice

252 'the Duke's eyes': W to WM, 30 April 1941, Dep. Monckton Trustees 19, fol. 41, Bodl. Lib.

253 'at Number 10': DoW to WM, 1946, Dep. Monckton Trustees 20, fol. 24, Bodl. Lib.

253 'in world history': *Sunday Telegraph*, 21 Oct. 2001.

Chapter 13: *Best-Dressed Wallis*

254 'of the earth': Bloch, *Duchess of Windsor*, p. 184

255 'unrelenting royal family': *Time*, 28 Oct. 1946

255 'near to tears': Laura, Duchess of Marlborough, *Laughter from a Cloud*, pp. 104–5

255 'man so relieved': ibid.

255 'to Queen Alexandra': ibid.

256 'denied to her': Kathleen Kennedy Hartington, 27 Oct. 1946, Smith, *Hostage to Fortune: The Letters of Joseph P. Kennedy*, p. 632

256 'Sovereign of this country': *The Duke's Consultations of Jowitt on the Question of the Duchess's Title*, cited in Bloch, *The Secret File of the Duke of Windsor*, p. 311

256 '"Her Royal Highness"': ibid., p. 310

256 'of good manners': ibid., p. 312

257 'is very sexy': Suzy Menkes, *The Windsor Style*, Grafton Books 1987, p. 191

259 'forms of surgery': consultant psychiatrist Dr Iain Oswald, Conversation with author, 13 Feb. 2011

260 'only granite below': Bloch, *The Duchess of Windsor*, p. 195

260 'and quite brilliant journalist': DoW to WM, 8 Dec. 1948, Dep. Monckton Trustees 20, fol. 24, Bodl. Lib.

261 'to the top': W to EAS, 13 July 1955, private archive

262 'get *me* one': J. Bryan III and Charles J. V. Murphy, *The Windsor Story*, Granada 1979, p. 519

262 'who they were': Linda Mortimer, Conversations with author, New York, 2 Nov. 2009

262 '"pushed me off"': Charles Pick, unpublished memoir courtesy of Martin Pick, n.d.

263 'is sadly diminished': Elsa Maxwell, *American Weekly*, 18 Dec. 1955

263 '"go against me!"': ibid.

263 'of her appearance': Elsa Maxwell, *American Weekly*, 11 Dec. 1955

264 'now in death': Ziegler, *King Edward VIII*, p. 538

264 'Cookie and Shirley': 7 March 1953, Bloch, *The Secret File of the Duke of Windsor*, p. 273

264 'English or French': quoted in Menkes, *The Windsor Style*, p. 62

264 'not good enough': ibid., p. 63

264 'no real charm': ibid.

265 '"to talk to"': Susan Mary Alsop, *To Marietta from Paris 1945–1960*, Weidenfeld & Nicolson 1976, p. 54

265 'life in exile': Lees-Milne, *Harold Nicolson*, vol. II, p. 269

266 'you eanum flowers': Menkes, *The Windsor Style*, p. 17

266 'up the pansy', Haslam, *Redeeming Features*, p. 193

266 'their upward rise': Helen Worden, *American Mercury*, June 1944

268 'admirable at all': interview with Frank Giles, Brendon Papers, Bren 2/2/7, Churchill Archives

268 'grovelling to me': John Balfour, *Not Too Correct an Aureole*, John Russell 1983, p. 64

269 'down at once': interview with Kenneth de Courcy, Brendon Papers, Bren 2/2/5, Churchill Archives

269 'un-undressable as Wallis': Haslam, *Redeeming Features*, p. 194

269 'decorators and couturiers': Bloch, *The Duchess of Windsor*, p. 191

269 Duke and Duchess: Higham, *Mrs Simpson*, p. 455

270 'plans and planning': *HHR* p. 365

270 'the Queen Mary': Charles Pick, unpublished memoir courtesy of Martin Pick, n.d.

272 'coming back here': Bloch, *The Duchess of Windsor*, p. 216

Chapter 14: *Wallis Alone*

273 'awfully to live': Mary Simpson diary, private archive

273 'had been friends': ibid.

274 a small monkey: Haslam, *Redeeming Features*, p. 195

274 in her nose: Caroline Blackwood, *The Last of the Duchess*, Macmillan 1995, p. 14

274 from the Queen: Ziegler, *King Edward VIII*, p. 555

274 it did not: King, *The Duchess of Windsor*, p. 489

275 'bottles of drink': Anne Boston, *Lesley Blanch: Inner Landscapes, Wilder Shores*, John Murray 2010, p. 226, citing Maureen Cleave interview in *Daily Telegraph*, 1987

276 'to the press': Hugo Vickers, *Behind Closed Doors*, Hutchinson 2011, p. 127

276 of the Duchess: Nichola McAuliffe, *Daily Mail*, 14 Feb. 2009

277 'were her life': Menkes, *The Windsor Style*, p. 139

278 'couple's romantic legacy': www.alfayed.com

279 'Constitution stand for': Kenneth W. Prescott and Emma-Stina Prescott, *The Complete Graphic Works of Jack Levine*, New York, Dover Publications 1984, p. 48

280 'little more light': E. B. Kirk to Lady Donaldson, May 1979, Kirk Family Archive

280 'them into life': William Boyd, *Bamboo*, Hamish Hamilton 2005, p. 573

281 'private affairs, angel': EP to FDW, 21 Sept. 1919, *LFP* p. 240

281 'porcelain dinner service': Javier Marías, *Your Face Tomorrow*, New Directions 2005, pp. 460–3

281 'in Hitler's hands': ibid.

282 'within my capacities': *HHR* p. 97

282 'out of life': ibid.

Select Bibliography

Place of publication is London unless otherwise stated.

Airlie, Mabell, Countess of, *Thatched with Gold*, Hutchinson 1962

Alsop, Susan Mary, *To Marietta from Paris 1945–60*, Weidenfeld & Nicolson 1976

Amory, Cleveland, *Who Killed Society*, New York, Harper & Brothers 1960

Angulo, Diana Hutchins, *Peking Sun, Shanghai Moon: A China Memoir*, ed. Tess Johnston, Hong Kong, Old China Hand Press 2008

Attlee, Clement R., *As It Happened*, New York, Viking 1954

Balfour, John, *Not Too Correct an Aureole*, John Russell 1983

Beaton, Cecil, *The Wandering Years*, Boston, Little Brown 1961

Beaton, Cecil, *Self-Portrait with Friends: The Selected Diaries of Cecil Beaton 1926–74*, Weidenfeld & Nicolson 1979

Beaton, Cecil, *The Unexpurgated Diaries*, Weidenfeld & Nicolson 2002

Beckett, Francis, *The Rebel Who Lost his Cause: The Tragedy of John Beckett MP*, Allison & Busby 2000

Berger, Arthur, *The Art of the Seductress: Techniques of the Great Seductresses from Biblical Times to the Postmodern Era*, Lincoln, iUniverse 2002

Billinghurst, Jane, *Temptress: From the Original Bad Girls to Women on Top*, Greystone Books 2004

Birkenhead, 2nd Earl of, *Walter Monckton: The Life of Viscount Monckton of Brenchley*, Weidenfeld & Nicolson 1969

Blackledge, Dr Catherine, *The Story of V: Opening Pandora's Box*, Weidenfeld & Nicolson 2003

Blackwood, Caroline, *The Last of the Duchess*, New York, Pantheon 1995

Bloch, Michael, *The Duke of Windsor's War*, Weidenfeld & Nicolson 1982

Bloch, Michael (ed.), *Wallis and Edward: Letters 1931–1937: The Intimate Correspondence of the Duke and Duchess of Windsor*, Weidenfeld & Nicolson 1986

Bloch, Michael, *The Secret File of the Duke of Windsor*, Transworld 1988

Bloch, Michael, *Ribbentrop*, New York, Crown 1992

Bloch, Michael, *The Duchess of Windsor*, Weidenfeld & Nicolson 1996

Bocca, Geoffrey, *The Woman Who Would be Queen*, New York, Rinehart 1954

Bolitho, Hector, *King Edward VIII: His Life and Reign*, Eyre & Spottiswoode 1937

Bonham-Carter, Violet, *Champion Redoubtable: Diaries and Letters of Violet Bonham Carter 1914–45*, ed. Mark Pottle, Weidenfeld & Nicolson 1999

Boston, Anne, *Lesley Blanch: Inner Landscapes, Wilder Shores*, John Murray 2010

Boyd, William, *Any Human Heart*, Hamish Hamilton 2002

Boyd, William, *Bamboo*, Hamish Hamilton 2005

Brendon, Piers and Whitehead, Philip, *The Windsors: A Dynasty Revealed*, Hodder & Stoughton 1994

Brody, Iles, *Gone with the Windsors*, Philadelphia, Winston 1953

Bryan III, J. and Murphy, Charles J. V., *The Windsor Story*, Granada 1979

Chadwick, Owen, *Hensley Henson*, Oxford University Press 1983

Channon, Sir Henry, *Chips: The Diaries of Sir Henry Channon*, ed. Robert Rhodes James, Penguin 1967

Charmley, John, *Lord Lloyd and the Decline of the British Empire*, Weidenfeld & Nicolson 1987

Christopher of Greece, HRH Prince, *Memoirs of HRH Prince Christopher of Greece*, Hurst & Blackett 1938

Clark, Alan (ed.), *A Good Innings: The Private Papers of Viscount Lee of Fareham*, John Murray 1974

Cooke, Anne Kirk and Lightfoot, Elizabeth, *The Other Mrs Simpson: Postscript to the Love Story of the Century*, New York, Vantage Press 1976

Cooper, Lady Diana, *The Light of Common Day*, Rupert Hart-Davis 1959

Cretney, Stephen, *Law, Law Reform and the Family*, Oxford University Press 1998

Cumpston, I. M., *Lord Bruce of Melbourne*, Melbourne, Longman Cheshire 1989

Davidson, J. C. C., *Memoirs of a Conservative*, ed. R. V. R. James, Weidenfeld & Nicolson 1969

Da Zara, Alberto, *Pelle d'Ammiraglio*, Milan, Mondadori 1948

di Ceglie, Domenico and Freedman, David, *A Stranger in my Own Body: Atypical Gender Identity Development and Mental Health*, Karnac Books 1998

Donaldson, Frances, *Edward* VIII, Weidenfeld & Nicolson 1974

Gardiner, A. G., *Certain People of Importance*, J. M. Dent 1929

Gardiner, Juliet, *The Thirties: An Intimate History*, Harper Press 2010

Gilbert, M., *Winston S. Churchill*, vol. 5: *The Prophet of Truth, 1922–1939*, Minerva 1990

Glass, Charles, *Americans in Paris: Life and Death under Nazi Occupation*, New York, Penguin Press 2010

Godfrey, Rupert (ed.), *Letters from a Prince, March 1918–January 1921*, Warner Books 1998

Goodman, Jean, *Edward Seago: The Other Side of the Canvas*, Collins 1978

Hardinge, Helen, *Loyal to Three Kings*, William Kimber 1967

Hart-Davis, Duff (ed.), *In Royal Service: The Letters and Journals of Sir Alan Lascelles 1920–1936*, Hamish Hamilton 1989

Hart-Davis, Duff (ed.), *The King's Counsellor: Abdication and War – The Diaries of 'Tommy' Lascelles*, Weidenfeld & Nicolson 2006

Haslam, Nicholas, *Redeeming Features: A Memoir*, Jonathan Cape 2010

Herbert, A. P., *Holy Deadlock*, Methuen 1934

Higham, Charles, *Mrs Simpson: Secret Lives of the Duchess of Windsor*, Sidgwick & Jackson 1998

Johnston, Tess and Erh, Deke, *A Last Look: Western Architecture in Old Shanghai*, Hong Kong, Old China Hand Press 1992

Jones, Nellie W., *A School for Bishops: A History of the Church of St Michael and All Angels Baltimore*, City Publications 1952

Keenlyside, Humphry, *Allen & Overy: The Firm*, vol. I: *1930–1998*, Allen & Overy 1999

King, Greg, *The Duchess of Windsor: The Uncommon Life of Wallis Simpson*, Aurum Press 1999

Lees-Milne, James, *Harold Nicolson*, vol. I: *1886–1929*, Chatto & Windus 1980

Lees-Milne, James, *Harold Nicolson*, vol. II: *1930–1968*, Chatto & Windus 1981

Lesley, Cole, *The Life of Noël Coward*, Jonathan Cape 1976

Lockhart, J. G., *Cosmo Gordon Lang*, Hodder & Stoughton 1949

Lockhart, Sir Robert Bruce, *The Diaries of Robert Bruce Lockhart 1915–38*, ed. Kenneth Young, Macmillan 1973

Lowndes, Marie Belloc, *Diaries and Letters of Marie Belloc Lowndes 1911–1947*, ed. Susan Lowndes, Chatto & Windus 1971

MacColl, René, *Deadline and Dateline*, Oldbourne Press 1956

Machin, G., 'Marriage and the Churches in the 1930s', *Journal of Ecclesiastical History*, vol. 42, 1991, 68–81

Machin, G. I. T., *The Churches and Social Issues in Twentieth-Century Britain*, Oxford University Press 1998

McKibben, Ross, *Classes and Cultures England 1918–51*, Oxford University Press 1998

McPherson, Mary, *A History of Oldfields 1867–1989: A Feeling of Family*, privately printed 1989

Marías, Javier, *Your Face Tomorrow*, New Directions 2005

Marlborough, Laura, Duchess of, *Laughter from a Cloud*, Weidenfeld & Nicolson 1980

Martin, Ralph G., *The Woman He Loved*, W. H. Allen 1974

Marquis, John, *Blood and Fire: The Duke of Windsor and the Strange Murder of Sir Harry Oakes*, LMH Publishers 2005

Masters, Brian, *Great Hostesses*, Constable 1982

Medlicott, W. N., Dakin, Douglas and Lambert, M. E. (eds), *Documents on British Foreign Policy, 1919–1939*, vol. XVI: *The Rhineland Crisis and the Ending of Sanctions March–July 1936*, HMSO 1977

Menkes, Suzy, *The Windsor Style*, Grafton Books 1987

Middlemas, Keith and Barnes, John, *Baldwin: A Biography*, Weidenfeld & Nicolson 1969

Moseley, Ray, *Mussolini's Shadow: The Double Life of Count Galeazzo Ciano*, New Haven, Yale University Press 2000

Mosley, Charlotte (ed.), *The Mitfords: Letters between Six Sisters*, Fourth Estate 2007

Mosley, Diana, *The Duchess of Windsor*, Sidgwick & Jackson 1980

Nicolson, Harold, *King George V*, Constable 1952

Nicolson, Harold, *Diaries and Letters 1930–39*, ed. Nigel Nicolson, Athenaeum 1966

Olivier, Edith, *From her Journals 1924–48*, ed. Penelope Middleboe, Weidenfeld & Nicolson 1989

Pan, Lynn, *Shanghai: A Century of Change 1843–1949*, Hong Kong, Hai Feng Publishing 1993

Pope-Hennessy, James, *Queen Mary 1867–1953*, George Allen & Unwin 1959

Prescott, Kenneth W. and Prescott, Emma-Stina, *The Complete Graphic Works of Jack Levine*, New York, Dover Publications 1984

Prioleau, Elizabeth, *Seductress: Women Who Ravished the World and their Lost Art of Love*, Viking 2003

Prochaska, Frank, *The Republic of Britain*, Penguin Books 2000

Prochaska, Frank, *Christianity and Social Service in Modern Britain: The Disinherited Spirit*, Oxford University Press 2006

Reith, Lord, *The Reith Diaries*, ed. Charles Stuart, Collins 1975

Romanones, Aline, Countess of, *The Spy Went Dancing*, New York, Putnam 1990

Rose, Kenneth, *King George V*, Weidenfeld & Nicolson 1983

Sergeant, Harriet, *Shanghai*, Jonathan Cape 1991

Shaughnessy, Alfred, *Both Ends of the Candle: An Autobiography*, Peter Owen 1976

Shawcross, William, *Queen Elizabeth The Queen Mother: The Official Biography*, Macmillan 2009

Shephard, Sue, *The Surprising Life of Constance Spry*, Macmillan 2010

Silberman, Lauren R., *The Jewish Community of Baltimore*, Charleston SC, Arcadia Publishing 2008

Smith, Amanda (ed.), *Hostage to Fortune: The Letters of Joseph P. Kennedy*, Viking 2001

Soames, Mary, *Clementine Churchill*, Cassell 1979

Soames, Mary (ed.), *Speaking for Themselves: The Personal Letters of Winston and Clementine Churchill*, Doubleday 1998

Spoto, Donald, *Dynasty: The Turbulent Saga of the Royal Family from Victoria to Diana*, Simon & Schuster 1995

Stone, Lawrence, *Road to Divorce: England 1530–1987*, Oxford University Press 1990

Susser, Bernard, *The Jews of South-West England: The Rise and Decline of their Medieval and Modern Communities*, University of Exeter Press 1993

Thornton, Michael, *Royal Feud: The Queen Mother and the Duchess of Windsor*, Michael Joseph 1985

Tinniswood, Adrian, *Belton House*, National Trust Publications 1992

Tremain, Rose, *The Darkness of Wallis Simpson*, Vintage 2006

Vanderbilt, Gloria and Furness, Thelma, Lady, *Double Exposure: A Twin Autobiography*, New York, David McKay 1958

Vickers, Hugo, *Behind Closed Doors*, Hutchinson 2011

Vincent, John (ed.), *The Journals of David Lindsay, 27th Earl of Crawford and 10th Earl of Balcarres 1871–1940*, Manchester University Press 1984

Wake, Jehanne, *Sisters of Fortune*, Chatto & Windus 2010

Wasserstein, Bernard, *The Secret Lives of Trebitsch Lincoln*, New Haven, Yale University Press 1988

Wasserstein, Bernard, *Secret War in Shanghai: Treachery, Subversion and Collaboration in the Second World War*, Profile Books 1999

Watson, Francis, *Dawson of Penn*, Chatto & Windus 1950

Weiner, Deborah, *Voices of Lombard Street: A Century of Change in East Baltimore*, Jewish Museum of Maryland 2007

Wells Hood, Dina, *Working for the Windsors*, Allan Wingate 1957

Wheeler-Bennett, John W., *King George VI: His Life and Reign*, Macmillan 1958

Williams, Susan, *The People's King: The True Story of the Abdication*, Penguin Books 2003

Williamson, Philip, *Stanley Baldwin: Conservative Leadership and National Values*, Cambridge, Cambridge University Press 1999

Williamson, Philip, 'The Monarchy and Public Values, 1910–1953', in Andrzej Olechnowicz (ed.), *The Monarchy and the British Nation, 1780 to the Present*, Cambridge, Cambridge University Press 2007, 223–57

Williamson, Philip and Baldwin, Edward (eds), *The Baldwin Papers: A Conservative Statesman 1908–47*, Cambridge, Cambridge University Press 2004

Wilson, Edwina, *Her Name was Wallis Warfield*, New York, E. P. Dutton 1957

Windsor, HRH The Duke of, *A King's Story*, Cassell 1951

Windsor, Wallis, *Some Favourite Southern Recipes*, New York, Charles Scribner's Sons 1942

Windsor, Wallis, *The Heart Has its Reasons*, Michael Joseph 1956

Woolf, Virginia, *Selected Diaries*, ed. Anne Olivier Bell, Vintage 2008

Ziegler, Philip, *Diana Cooper*, Collins 1987

Ziegler, Philip, *King Edward VIII: The Official Biography*, Collins 1990

Index

1. Why has Wallis been demonized for so long?

2. What factors have contributed to a reassessment? Do you think revisionism is justified?

3. Why might Wallis have been seen as pro-Nazi?

4. To what extent was her Americanism part of the problem? Can you understand why, for some in America, Wallis has always been a heroine?

5. What characteristics of Wallis's personality are admirable?

6. How do you explain the attitude of the Queen Mother toward Wallis and toward Wallis and Edward?

7. Was the denial of royal honours for Wallis justified in the circumstances or vindictive?

8. Why has Edward VIII been so little criticized?

9. Why are duty and pluck no longer revered compared with today's goals such as ambition and personal fulfilment?

10. Has our attitude toward divorce changed for the better?

11. What about some of the other characters in the story: Why do you think Winston Churchill behaved as he did? Was Mary an admirable character?

12. What role do you think was played by the wives of politicians, such as Lucy Baldwin, Nancy Dugdale, Helen Hardinge, and Hilda Runciman, and why do you think their views have not been taken into account before?

13. Which of the characters do you feel most sympathy for: Mary, Ernest, Henry/Aharon, Aunt Bessie, or Alan "Tommy" Lascelles?

14. Which of the characters do you feel should have done more to understand or guide Edward earlier in his life? His parents, his private secretaries, the Archbishop of Canterbury and other church leaders, or his girlfriends?

15. Do you agree that Wallis performed a useful service by delivering a new monarch for such critical times?

16. How should she be remembered? As a style icon and, if so, why? Describe her style. Or as a victim and, if so, why?

17. Do you believe every generation has a different attitude toward key personalities according to historical context?

For more reading group suggestions,
visit www.readinggroupgold.com.